GAY
L.A.

GAY
L.A.

A History of Sexual Outlaws,
Power Politics, and
Lipstick Lesbians

LILLIAN FADERMAN
STUART TIMMONS

UNIVERSITY OF CALIFORNIA PRESS
Berkeley · Los Angeles · London

University of California Press, one of the most distinguished university presses in the United States, enriches lives around the world by advancing scholarship in the humanities, social sciences, and natural sciences. Its activities are supported by the UC Press Foundation and by philanthropic contributions from individuals and institutions. For more information, visit www.ucpress.edu.

University of California Press
Berkeley and Los Angeles, California

Previously published in 2006 by Basic Books, a member of the Perseus Books Group.

Library of Congress Cataloging-in-Publication Data

Faderman, Lillian.
   Gay L. A. : a history of sexual outlaws, power politics, and lipstick lesbians / Lillian Faderman, Stuart Timmons.
       p.   cm.
   Originally published: 2006.
   Includes bibliographical references and index.
   ISBN 978-0-520-26061-0 (pbk. : alk. paper)
       1. Homosexuality—California—Los Angeles—History.
2. Gays—California—Los Angeles—History.   3. Gay liberation movement—California—Los Angeles—History.   I. Timmons, Stuart, 1957–   II. Title.

HQ76.3.L7F33   2009
306.76'609794—dc22   2009015361

Manufactured in the United States of America

18   17   16   15   14   13   12   11   10   09
10   9   8   7   6   5   4   3   2   1

This book is printed on Cascades Enviro 100, a 100% post consumer waste, recycled, de-inked fiber. FSC recycled certified and processed chlorine free. It is acid free, Ecologo certified, and manufactured by BioGas energy.

For Phyllis—who makes everything possible
LF

For Jim Kepner, witness, activist, archivist, and friend
ST

And in memory of those Angelenos we have recently lost:
Betty Berzon
Vern Bullough
Frankie Hucklenbroich
Gavin Lambert
Brian Miller
William Moritz
Johnny Nojima
Jean O'Leary
Savina Teubal
Brenda Weathers

CONTENTS

ACKNOWLEDGMENTS

Our deep appreciation goes to all the Los Angeles gay men and lesbians who made the history we have written about in these pages. Hundreds of them opened their hearts and memories for this project. We are grateful to them for giving us hours of their time and so generously sharing their lives with us and our readers.

For their unfailing personal support, thanks to our families and friends, including Shirley Magidson, Trebor Healey, Bill Fishman, David Byrd, Joe Bessera, John Callahan, Cindy Friedman, Josy Cattogio, Phyllis Irwin, Beatrice Valenzuela, Steve Yarbrough, Cathy Conheim, and Donna Brooks. For Lillian's tireless work as editor, Stuart offers his lasting gratitude.

We thank those who kindly read all or parts of our manuscript and gave us their invaluable feedback, including Jehan Agrama, Malcolm Boyd, John Callahan, Jeanne Cordova, Terry DeCrescenzo, Bill Fishman, Linda Garber, Rich Jennings, Sharon A. Lilly, David Link, Ariana Manov, Mark Thompson, and Carolyn Weathers. We are grateful to those who hosted us during research trips, including Katherine Gabel and Connie Eddy, Robin Tyler and Diane Olson, Joey Cain, David Link, and Gay Timmons.

No history can be written without the help of archivists. Special thanks to Jay Johnson of the Los Angeles City Archives; Romaine Ahlstrom and the staff of the Huntington Library; Misha Schutt, David Moore, Joseph Hawkins, and Ashlie Mildfelt of the ONE National Gay and Lesbian Archives; Jo Duffy, Ann Giani, Marcia Schwemer, and Jeri Deitrick of the June Mazer Lesbian Archives; James Henley and Patricia

Johnson of the Sacramento Archives and Museum Collection Center; Lauren Buisson of the UCLA Arts Library Special Collections; Carolyn Coles and the many helpful professionals at the Los Angeles Public Library; John Cahoon of the Seaver Center; and the staff of the Southern California Library for Social Studies and Research, the Rosenbach Museum and Library, the Los Angeles Law Library, the Academy of Motion Picture Arts and Sciences, and the California State Archives.

For their invaluable help in providing materials or access to subjects, we thank Michael Marchand, Terry DeCrescenzo, Carolyn Weathers, Paul D. Cain, Donna Brooks, Jane Cantillon, Craig Collins, Rick Mechtley, Chuck Stallard, Tony Friedkin, Jim Weatherford, Ariana Manov, Ann Bradley, and Tony Barnard. Our gratitude goes to our agent Sandra Dijkstra. Lillian would like to thank the Historical Society of Southern California for a research grant that made her early work on this project possible. We are grateful for the research assistance provided by Phyllis Irwin, Kathy Hall, Jeanne Stanley, and Erin Cross.

The Doctor and Jonnie.
Author's collection.

An interracial "drag gay ball" at
the Club Alabam on Central
Avenue, L.A.'s "Harlem," 1945.
*Shades of L.A. Archives/courtesy
Los Angeles Public Library.*

Introduction

Los Angeles [was] a city of heretics, . . . a city of refugees from [the rest of] America. [Their] banishment was partly dreamed and partly real.

—Frank E. Fenton, *A Place in the Sun,* 1942[1]

YEARS BEFORE autobiographical novelist John Rechy presented gay Los Angeles as a "City of Night," he witnessed a small homosexual riot. It happened in the spring of 1959, at Cooper's Doughnuts, a downtown coffee shop on a seedy stretch of Main Street between two of L.A.'s older gay bars, the Waldorf and Harold's. Since their glamour days as early as the 1930s, both bars had grown shabby, but they offered refuge to the outcasts of that depressed enclave, who also made Cooper's Doughnuts their hangout. Cooper's was an all-night haunt, a place to get cheap coffee and doughnuts, a good place to camp or cruise or converse. Most patrons were queens, butch hustlers, their friends, and their customers. Many were Latino or black. The queens wore the half-drag of Capri pants and men's shirts, which, they hoped, would enable them to escape arrest for "masquerading" as women (though they knotted their shirts at the midriff in the feminine style of the day). Because the patrons were obvious or suspected homosexuals, Cooper's became a frequent target for the Los Angeles Police Department, which prided itself on being one of the most determined enemies of homosexuality in the nation.

That night in May, a patrol car circled the block a few times, parked, and two police officers entered Cooper's, demanding to see identification from those seated at the long rectangular counter. As usual, the police stated no reasons for their harassment. Pointing to Rechy and two others, they said, "You, you, and you—come with us," and ordered the men into their squad car. But just as would happen a decade later and a continent away at the Stonewall Inn, that night in Los Angeles the crowd rebelled. The arbitrary arm of the law had come down "one time too many," Rechy says:

> First people started throwing the doughnuts they were eating at the cops. Then paper cups started flying. . . . Then coffee-stirring sticks and other things started flying at them.

Under siege, the officers fled to their squad car without their prisoners, summoning backup. More squad cars arrived, sirens blaring. Rioters were arrested and jailed. Main Street was cordoned off and remained closed until the next day. Rechy and the other detainees were able to slip away, he says, smiling more than forty-five years later at the confusion that gave him freedom.[2] This was perhaps the first homosexual uprising in the world. But the historic moment went unreported and unrecorded.

That nearly-forgotten incident is emblematic of why we felt this book needed to exist, but there were myriad other reasons as well. We found traces of a thriving lesbian and gay life in Los Angeles in overlooked archival sources dating back to the nineteenth century. We found that there was much to say about the secret but lively community established in the 1920s and '30s by those who came to Hollywood to work in the movie industry. We were fascinated and disturbed by the stories gay men told us of how the L.A. vice squad sent officers who were handsome young males ("Hollywood rejects," they were called) into gay bars in the 1950s to serve as decoys to entrap homosexuals, and by the stories gay women told us of how they were hassled by the police simply because they walked down a Los Angeles street dressed in pants and a tailored jacket. We were moved by the stories of now-elderly women and men who told us how years ago they had lived and found love and companionship in the city. We discovered that, historically, more lesbian and gay institutions started in Los Angeles than anywhere else on the planet, and that L.A.'s multifaceted, multiracial, and multicultural lesbian and gay activism continues to have tremendous impact worldwide. These stories of Los Angeles lesbian and gay life and political achievements have never been sufficiently documented. As historians and lovers of that city, we wondered how such a history could have been discounted or left uncommemorated, and we grew determined to fill in what we considered a huge gap in the record of lesbian and gay America.

Together and separately, we sat in numerous archives, poring over old newspaper clippings, city council minutes, police ledgers, court transcripts, organizational papers, letters, pictures, and mementos. We interviewed approximately 300 people, aged from sixteen to eighty-something, mostly lesbians and gay men, of all races and ethnicities. We visited them in their mansions in the Hollywood Hills, tiny apartments in Compton, assisted-living facilities for the elderly, and group homes for troubled lesbian, gay, bisexual, and transgender teens.

The process of uncovering this history offered poignant moments. Lillian will always remember, for example, her interview with a stately seventy-three-year-old woman, a retired physician, who said that fifty years earlier she came to Los Angeles from Chile to study medicine, fell in love, and realized she could never again go home because she could not live in Santiago as she lived in L.A. She produced a picture of herself, a young woman in a dress and pumps, on the arm of a "handsome young man," Jonnie—who was in fact her now-deceased woman lover of forty years. Stuart will not forget the interview in which he asked a longtime Hollywood resident whether he happened to have any photographs relating to gay life, and the octogenarian obligingly pulled out an album of sepia snapshots pasted to tattered black pages that were dated "1937": The pictures were of film industry workers at a backyard party, lounging with movie stars whose faces are still familiar.

Though we have been fortunate in being able to uncover extraordinary material about lesbian and gay Los Angeles of earlier eras, our work has sometimes been frustrating because we know that much has been lost. For example, we found a tantalizing photograph at the Central branch of the Los Angeles Public Library, documenting a 1945 ball at the Club Alabam, which was in the heart of the black district, on 42nd Street and Central Avenue. Dexter Gordon and Charles Mingus played in the Club Alabam's house band, and Mae West, William Randolph Hearst, and Orson Wells listened to jazz there together with Duke Ellington, Jackie Robinson, and Joe Louis.[3] The 1945 photograph, however, shows two dozen young men, African American and white, wearing cocktail gowns, stoles, and Joan Crawford–style lipstick. The caption under the photo reads: "Crowds of people line up in front of the stage at the Club Alabam. Event was a 'drag' gay ball for the best dressed."[4] None of the individuals is identified, and their personal stories are lost to history.

In our quest for more information about such early drag balls, we discovered through a 1949 Halloween Bal Masque program that one particular drag ball had been staged annually for eighteen years, since 1931. We also discovered that various drag events were produced with regularity at half-a-dozen venues in South Central Los Angeles,[5] where the lively nightlife, dating back to at least the 1930s, had rivaled that of Harlem. But precise facts are sometimes murky. For example, several of our sources pointed us to Brothers, a South Central L.A. nightclub of the 1940s, which clearly had a speakeasy mystique and outlaw charm. It was located "off an alley or back of a place," and "you had to know somebody who knew somebody to take you there. That's the way it was."[6] Other details about Brothers, however, are contradictory. Some of our sources identified the eponymous "brothers" who owned the club as being two black lesbians.[7] Others, such as Clora Bryant, a woman trumpeter who was a habitué there, said that the name was "Brother's," not a plural but a possessive, and that "Brother," the owner, was a man, garbed in flowing robes.[8] Despite that contradiction, all sources do agree that Brothers was, as Bryant characterized it, "a hangout for guys who go for guys and whatever. [At Brothers] you could get whatever." Like at the Club Alabam, jazz musicians would drop in to Brothers after-hours, and movie stars would come to partake of the scene.[9] Such provocative traces of L.A.'s Harlemesque nightlife remain vivid, but the fine points—for instance, was Brothers run by two lesbians or by a man in flowing robes?—seem irrecoverable.

Such frustrations fueled our search. We wanted to locate the photographs, examine the written records, and talk with the people who knew about the hidden gay world of Los Angeles in bygone eras. We wanted to prevent fading memories from being snuffed out forever and more photos from becoming permanently obscure. We also wanted to capture more recent history, to find out how Angelenos were able to establish the biggest, wealthiest, longest-lived gay and lesbian international church, community center, and national magazine; how they became major players in city and state politics and in the movie industry that influences the world; how they entertain themselves in a city devoted to entertainment; how the steady stream of lesbian and gay immigrants that flock to L.A. for refuge have been able to make a life for themselves.

We opted to deal with both men and women in this book, even though, as we discovered, they often moved in separate circles and trod different paths around Los Angeles. Occasionally, they even waged internecine battles against one another. But, as we discovered too, they also saw each other as natural allies who shared common enemies. Through much of their history in L.A., both women and men had to hide who they were because of prejudice against homosexuality, and both suffered in their daily lives from the hostilities of a homophobic society. Although men were more likely to be prosecuted under the Los Angeles and California laws that targeted homosexuals, women too were threatened by many of those laws and even sent to jail under them. Realizing that they shared not only enemies but also ways of being that the rest of the world disdained, they banded together—"fronting" for each other, trusting one another with the secrets of their lives, sharing insider humor about, for instance, their challenges to "appropriate gender behavior." When external enemies attacked, they made common cause, and together they celebrated remarkable political victories. In the vastness that is Los Angeles, lesbians and gay men have formed multiple separate communities as well as a viable unified community.

We chose to call our book *Gay L.A.* because, as our older informants told us, "gay" in the 1930s, '40s, '50s, and '60s was the term that included homosexual men, lesbians, transgenders, and even bisexuals. Some of our younger informants call themselves "queer." Others prefer more specific designations that signify subtleties of sexual expression, or gender identification, or even racial variations on those phenomena, such as "boi," "MTF," or "stud." We have tried always to identify our narrators by the designation they prefer, but we have chosen "gay" as our umbrella term, just as it was the umbrella term historically for both men and women who loved their own sex, as well as those whose gender presentation or gender identification was unconventional.

We divided the research and composition tasks between us, but so that these pages would read smoothly, in one narrative voice, Lillian edited the writing. As coauthors, we are admittedly an odd couple. Lillian's experiences with gay L.A. began in 1956, in the seamy working-class gay girls bars on 8th and Vermont, where the butch and femme patrons could not escape the knowledge that they were outlaws; Stuart arrived in Los Angeles twenty years later to attend UCLA, and became active in a gay liberation movement and a gay world that celebrated its pride at huge sunlit parades. Stuart, a journalist and biographer, has been politically and culturally engaged in L.A. gay life for the last thirty years. Lillian has been an academic and a writer of lesbian histories for those same thirty years. We came to our partnership not only with our gender, generational, and past and present class differences but also with different worldviews, allegiances, and talents developed over the past decades. But our goal has been to uncover the histories of gay L.A.'s women and men of all ages, socioeconomic positions, ethnicities, and political affiliations; and we believe our own diversity has helped us to re-create those histories in all their fascinating complexity.

1: THE SILENT ERA

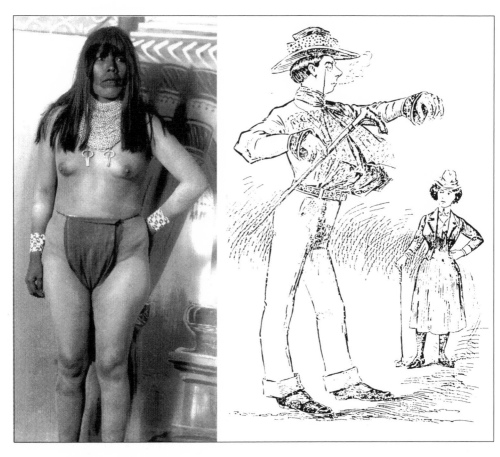

A female warrior of a southern California tribe, dressed in the traditional male garb of the breechcloth, circa 1890. *Autry National Center's Braun Research Library, Institute for the Study of the American West, Photo # 5506; "Wonders" of the new century as predicted by the* L.A. Times, *March 1900.*

CHAPTER 1

City of Angels and Devils

BEFORE THE CITY OF ANGELS

From the very beginning of the world it was meant that there should be homosexuals. . . .

— Naahwera, a Mohave traditional singer[1]

Under Spanish and Mexican influence, the Gabrielino Indian village of Yang-na was gradually transformed into the city of Los Angeles, and most of the Indians who had lived there were forcibly relocated or killed. Though in the early 1850s about half the population of Los Angeles was still Indian (4,000 whites and 3,700 Indians),[2] the new settlers knew little about the history of Native Americans and even less about their institutionalized gender and sexual practices. The white settlers' ignorance was perhaps fortunate for the Indians, who had already suffered greatly under the colonial Spaniards' imperative to impose on the Indians their Christian views of "sin." Captain Pedro Fages, who came in 1775 to the area that is now Santa Barbara, discovered to his horror that the men among the Chumash Indians were "addicted to the unspeakable vice of sinning against nature," and he dubbed their same-sex relations "excess so criminal that it seems even forbidden to speak its name."[3] The Spanish missionaries, who arrived in California soon after Fages, were also aghast at what they saw as "the sins of Sodom." "Horrible customs," Father Geronimo Boscana called the unconventional gender behavior and the homosexuality that often accompanied it when he observed the Indians around the Southern California mission of San Juan Capistrano.[4] Father Pedro Font's comment about these "nefarious practices" among the Indians of Northern California was chilling: "There will be much to do when the Holy Faith and Christian religion [take over]."[5] Although adultery and polygamy were deemed terrible sins by the padres, such sins paled compared to the sexual inversion they saw often among the local natives.[6]

The Spaniards had observed primarily male behavior. Typical of European men of the era, female same-sex relations, and even gender inversion, was the stuff of fantasy for them.[7] They were enamored of Garci Rodriguez de Montalvo's fifteenth-century protolesbian tale about a mythical island called "California," where Queen Califia lived with her beloved subjects, all of them masculine women. "And there were no males among them at all," Montalvo wrote. He described the women as having "energetic bodies and courageous, ardent hearts." Like the Amazons of Greek myth, they waged bloody war on other lands, killing most of the males but carrying away a few so that they might copulate with them for the sake of procreation. Female babies were kept among them; male babies were slaughtered.[8] In 1535, Hernan Cortes, sharing his era's enchantment with the story of these fierce, manless women, wrote the name "California" on a map of a strip of land on the west coast of North America. It has remained its name ever since—though the protolesbian source was long forgotten.

—

The missionaries did indeed find "much to do" in ridding the land of the gender and sexual behavior that shocked them, since Indians up and down California had always recognized that some males, as well as some females, were different from conventional men and women. The Indians had given those who were different an honorable place in their communities.[9] The Yurok called biological males who preferred to live and dress as women *wergern* and esteemed them as more spiritual than most people. The *wergern* were often made shamans. The Yuki called them *iwopnaiip* and permitted them to marry men. Among the Juaneño of the Southern California coast they were called *kwit,* and men considered them very desirable wives because they were robust workers in the household. Among the Yokuts, farther north and east, the cross-gendered males had honored spiritual roles, being charged with preparing corpses for burial or cremation.[10] Anthropologists generally used the French word *berdache* for Native American males as well as females who assumed gender and sex roles usually associated with the opposite sex; but more recent writers, pointing out that *berdache* means "kept boy" or "male prostitute," have rejected that term in favor of others such as "two-spirit people"[11]—an apt retort to the missionaries who dubbed sexual and gender behaviors they could not understand as bestial and godless.

The Native Americans, having had no notion in the eighteenth century that the Spanish padres would consider their culturally condoned practices to be bestial and godless, spoke freely to missionaries such as Father Boscana, who then wrote of his chagrin in discovering among the Southern California Gabrielino and Luiseno Indians that the male *berdache* were allowed to marry men, even tribal chiefs, and that the entire tribe approved of such marriages, even arranging "a grand feast" in celebration. Boscana was particularly horrified that certain boys were selected from an early age and instructed "in all the duties of the women—in their mode of dress—of walking, and dancing; so that in almost every particular, they resembled females." In his retrospective account, written in the 1820s, he noted with relief that this "detested race" (that is, the *berdache*) no longer existed in Southern California, thanks to the eradicating work of the padres.[12]

The missionaries did indeed make every effort to extirpate such behaviors out of the Native Americans, separating male same-sex couples by sending one member of the couple off to a distant mission and devising various cruel punishments for the recalcitrant. For example, Francisco Palou wrote that when the friars encountered a Santa Clara male Indian who wore women's clothes, they ordered the Spanish soldiers to strip him naked and force him to sweep the plaza in the nude for three days, to his intense shame. After his punishment, he was commanded to give up women's clothes forever. Palou observed that, rather than comply, the Indian fled his home and went elsewhere so that he might continue to live as a *berdache*.[13]

The Native Americans had surely learned by the nineteenth century that they must keep their gender and sexual preferences secret from the padres, so that it soon appeared to missionaries such as Boscana that the "detested race" had indeed been eliminated. But records published more than a hundred years after Boscana show that *berdache* customs and behaviors, among males as well as females, continued in Southern California tribes, including the Gabrielino, Luiseno,[14] and Chumash.[15] The Southern California Quechan Indians, who called *berdache* males *elxa',* continued to believe they had more power than the ordinary man and were a peaceful influence on the tribe.[16] Among the Quechan, divergent sexual behavior was not limited to the *elxa'*. Casual homosexuality among men and women was common and was not socially condemned.[17] Among the Mohave, *berdache* males, who were called *alyha,* continued to wear skirts and were initiated into their role through a testing ceremony in which the community would sing to the initiate; the true *alyha* would then publicly accept the role by dancing to the song "with much intensity."[18] Once initiated, *alyha* were believed to have been mystically transformed into their adopted sex. The Mohave thus created a social role that accommodated people that we could call "transgenders."

Biological females who desired to live as men also had institutionalized roles that continued in some tribes into the twentieth century.[19] The Southern California Kamia had traditionally honored such females by attributing the birth of agriculture to one of them, Warharmi, who was said to have been a "bearer of seeds of the cultivated plants" as well as an "introducer of Kamia culture."[20] Like the Kamia, the Mohave believed that these biological females, whom they called *hwame,* had existed ever since the world began and that they had always worn male garments and taken on male roles. The Mohave thought that whether a female would be a *hwame* or a male would be an *alyha* was determined in utero, through the pregnant mother's dreams. In puberty, the true *hwame* and *alyha* manifested their proclivities by preferring pursuits that were generally associated with the opposite sex. The *hwame* and *alyha* behaved much as did the "sexual inverts" described by European sexologists such as Richard von Krafft-Ebing and Havelock Ellis: For example, as an early-twentieth-century Mohave Indian told the anthropologist George Devereux, young *hwames* "like to chum with boys and adopt boys' ways." As he described them, "They throw away their dolls and metates, and refuse to shred bark or perform other feminine tasks. They turn away from the skirt and long for the breech-clout."[21]

Devereux's informant, speaking of his own era, the early twentieth century, when modern European concepts about gender and sexuality had taken a strong hold among Indians, said that Mohave families attempted to dissuade young people from becoming *hwame* or *alyha*. Nevertheless, he declared, when the families failed in their efforts, "they will realize that it cannot be helped." They then invited the community to a ceremony and bestowed upon the young person the status of "*hwame*" or "*alyha*." Another informant described such an initiation ceremony in which a girl became a *hwame*: "Proud of being stared at," he said, "she traipses and dances back and forth in a stooped posture over a flat stretch of damp land. That is how she acts if she is to be a true *hwame*."[22] The *hwame* then assumed a name that reflected masculine status and thereafter s/he was always referred to as "he."[23]

According to some twentieth-century sources, the *hwame* adult could assume almost all aspects of the masculine role among the Mohave, but she was not permitted to be a tribal leader—though in earlier eras and among other tribes such females could hold even that most honored position. For example, in pre-conquest days, Coronne, who appears to have been "*hwame*," was the chief of the Indians who inhabited the Southern California area that became San Juan Capistrano: According to Boscana's 1820s account, she was "of huge proportions, . . . very coarse . . . having no wish to marry [nor] feelings of love for any man." The area she ruled over was called Putuidem, which refers to an enlarged umbilicus that projects out—suggesting perhaps Coronne's pseudophallus.[24]

As in many of the Southern California tribes, the Mohave *hwame* could marry women and were considered "excellent providers." Because the Mohave believed that the paternity of a child would change if the pregnant woman had sexual relations with a new person, it was thought that a *hwame* could even become a father by having sex with her pregnant mate. The *hwame* and her partner sometimes formed a family not unlike the contemporary lesbian family, the *hwame* being acknowledged as a parent of the baby her partner bore. According to Devereux's informants, she would "take care of [the child] with pride, and love it very sincerely."[25]

Such community tolerance of same-sex marriage, cross-gendered behaviors, homosexual family life, and sexual fluidity had scarce parallel among the invading Euro Americans who, in the mid-nineteenth century, soon outnumbered the Indian population in Southern California.

"IN DRESS NOT BELONGING TO HIS OR HER OWN SEX"

The City of Los Angeles should change its name to that of Sodom or Gomorroh [sic].[26]

—"Los Angeles Disgraced," *California Argus,* 1896

Los Angeles in the 1840s was a Mexican town of ranchos and cattle, hundreds of miles from the center of the Gold Rush, but it grew rapidly as a result of the Rush. Money poured into L.A. not only from the sale of cows that were driven north to feed the gold miners but also from the gamblers and other lawless high-rollers who were driven south by the northern vigilante committees.[27] In 1850, California was admitted to the Union. Three years later, when Harris Newmark, a businessman, arrived in Los Angeles, he observed a town of "free-and-easy customs," in which people could "do practically as they pleased." There were no city ordinances against gambling, nor against drunkenness, drugs, prostitution, or high-noon showdowns in the middle of the street—all were common in neighborhoods such as Calle de los Negroes, also called "Nigger Alley" (the present-day Los Angeles Street), a district as wild as the wildest in the West.[28] By the mid-nineteenth century, Los Angeles' wild ways had earned it a nickname: "City of the Devils."[29]

Men far outnumbered women in Los Angeles, as they did everywhere in California according to the 1850 census, which recorded 12.2 males for every one female in the state.[30] Single Euro American females were slower to come to California since many of the get-rich-quick dreams and schemes that drew men west were closed to women—unless they came as "men," which some did, exchanging petticoats and tight bodices for men's garb. They escaped the restrictions of Victorian womanhood by passing as members of the putative stronger sex, and they claimed the right to men's adventures.[31] Other women did not try to pass, but they "butched it up," relying on their masculine demeanor to keep them safe in a man's world. Harris Newmark recalled fifty years later a "muscular-looking woman" he had met in Los Angeles in the 1860s. According to Newmark, she called herself "Captain Jinx," a revealing sobriquet she borrowed from a popular song about a cocky gentleman who proclaims:

> *I taught the ladies how to dance, how to dance, how to dance.*
> *I taught the ladies how to dance,*
> *For I'm a captain in the Army.*

Newmark's Victorian reticence did not permit him to speculate openly about Captain Jinx's sex life, but he seemed to be hinting at her inversion when he observed that she "half-strode, half jerked her way along the street. . . . She was very strong for women's rights, she said; and she certainly looked it."[32]

Frontier societies' willingness to tolerate such cross-gendered individuals was not ubiquitous. In Denver, for example, an 1875 ordinance concerning "Offenses Against Good Morals and Decency" made a man's or woman's appearance in public places "in dress not belonging to his or her own sex" a misdemeanor punishable by a fine of up to one hundred dollars.[33] Los Angeles in 1875 was still comparatively loose and lawless, and there were no such ordinances. But as L.A. grew from a Wild West town to a more staid city, the public became more ambivalent in its view of unconventional gender behavior. Near the end of the century, Los Angeles, too, adopted a law to force men to look like men and women to look like women. The law came as a result of an unrestrained yearly Saturnalia, All Fool's Night, that rivaled Mardi Gras in its sexual rowdiness and campy gender-play by both sexes.

All Fool's Night was the culminating event of La Fiesta, a weeklong ballyhoo of gaudy pageants and frolics dreamed up by the Los Angeles

Merchants Association in 1894 during a period of worrisome economic depression. Despite its trappings of "Old Spanish Days," La Fiesta followed the European tradition of Carnival, including a temporary suspension of city government, the election of a Fiesta Queen, and even the mock-jailing of the police. By 1895, La Fiesta and All Fool's Night were drawing a "merry, roistering crowd" of 100,000 to L.A.'s commercial area, to the great delight of businessmen.[34]

But the festivities also drew the ire of conservative Protestant groups that had been rapidly gaining power in Los Angeles. The religious Right of the era was shocked not only by the drunken revelries of All Fool's Night and what one newspaper account described as "a general male and female 'turn-loose'"[35] but also, and most especially, by the sight of men and women in drag. The religious Right could not decide which was the more reprehensible—men dressed as women or women dressed as men. In an article titled "Methodist Preachers Inveigh Against a Feature of the Fiesta," it was "the actions of young ladies dressed in men's clothes" that were particularly disturbing.[36] But what disturbed the author of "Hell Turned Loose on Los Angeles" the most was "the behavior of those [men] clad as women, [which] was disgusting in the extreme, and almost too vile to detail."[37] The newspapers granted that some of those crossdressers may merely have been "out for a frolic, with no further idea than 'a little fun' if such it may be called," but other cross-dressers "used the license of the occasion to [display] all their vicious and evil propensities."[38]

The threat of the City of Angels transmogrifying into a Sodom or Gomorrah through the sins of the All Fool's Night cross-dressers posed a dilemma to the city councilmen: They were torn between the continued need to shore up a sagging economy by attracting tourists to L.A. and the pressures exerted by a mobilized religious Right. The forces of the Right seemed to win out. "The general sentiment of the people of this city is now against permitting the use of public streets as the scene of riotous revelry and debauchery," the Los Angeles City Council declared.[39] The council ordered the city attorney to investigate the California State Penal Code to see whether gender disguise was against the law. The city attorney could find nothing about disguise in the penal code except for an 1874 law, clearly aimed at bandits and highway men, that declared it unlawful to wear "any mask, false whiskers, or any personal disguise" for the purpose of evading recognition while committing a crime. Since that particular law (Sec. 185) could not be easily applied to cross-dressers, the city council asked the city attorney to draft a Los Angeles ordinance that would specifically make it illegal "for a man to masquerade as a women, or a woman as a man."[40] But the council, in their ambivalence, stalled for three years before they considered the ordinance. Finally, in 1898, they inveighed against the "indecencies" All Fool's Night encouraged, banned the festivity along with its drag revelries, and passed Ordinance 5022.[41] This city law forbidding "masquerading" proved to be the bane of drag queens for the better part of the next century and of butch-dressing lesbians throughout the mid-century.

Constraints on gender fluidity did not apply to nineteenth- and early-twentieth-century stage performances, however, and Los Angeles was highly entertained by the gender-benders of the vaudeville and variety stage. Male impersonators particularly were popular figures in L.A. theaters. Despite their young-rake dash and highly sexualized swagger, male impersonators on stage were even considered "family entertainment" (as were female impersonators),[42] since the connection between theatrical impersonation and sexual deviancy in real life had not yet been widely made by American audiences. Ella Wesner, for instance, who had had a long amorous relationship with Josie Mansfield, the former mistress of Erie Railroad millionaire Jim Fisk, was one of the most popular male impersonators of her day. Wesner was described in 1870s newspapers as having "a face quite masculine and jet black curling hair, which she wears cut short."[43] She appeared on stage in formal men's attire, singing songs with lyrics such as:

> *Lovely woman was made to be loved,*
> *To be fondled and courted and kissed;*

And the fellows who've never made love to a girl,
Well, they don't know what fun they have missed.[44]

But at no time during her theatrical career was there ever a public discussion of her lesbianism, Americans still being reluctant to recognize the possibility of sexual deviancy in an attractive woman—even one dressed in drag and singing songs about loving girls. When Wesner conducted extensive theatrical tours in California, her earnings of $200 per week were touted as "the largest salary ever paid to any single star in America."[45] Male impersonators continued to star at top L.A. theaters as late as the 1920s. Kitty Doner, for instance, trumped Fannie Brice as the headliner at the Orpheum and other leading variety theaters. The newspapers described her as "the top-notcher of all male impersonators" and proclaimed that her "delineations of the so-called stronger sex [were] classic."[46]

On stage, men, too, could get away with gender impersonation for a period that extended into the twentieth century. L.A.'s first recorded theatrical female impersonation occurred in 1848 at the American Theater on Temple Street, where, at an opening night performance, General Andreas Pico took a fancy to the lovely woman who appeared as "Lady Elizabeth." The Lady was a man.[47] Throughout the nineteenth century, in L.A., as in many American cities, female impersonators were a staple on the stage, including the ethnic stage. In 1894, for example, when "Gauze," a male singer with the black Georgia Minstrels, appeared at the Los Angeles Theater, s/he was glowingly described in a review as having "a well cultivated voice and much grace as a female impersonator."[48] The Chinese community in Los Angeles also loved theatrical gender-benders. "Chinese female impersonators come high," an 1891 writer observed, "but the Chinese managers [of the Los Angeles Chinatown theaters] must have them." One theater troupe alone boasted of having five female impersonators in its company.[49]

Even into the 1920s, female impersonators strutted on stage, and in film, too. Frederic Covert was famous in Los Angeles theaters and the movies for his drag "vanity" and "peacock" dances. He slyly flaunted his homosexuality through his professional name, Ko Vert.[50] In 1923, Julian

Eltinge, the top female impersonator in America and also a homosexual, was playing to sell-out audiences at L.A.'s Orpheum Theater.[51] As the theater historian Laurence Senelick has argued, before the 1930s, gay men and lesbians were often able to use the stage to "experiment with gender shuffling in a context that won them approbation and indulgence." Drag on stage was seen as art and entertainment.[52]

The Los Angeles antimasquerading ordinance was revised in 1922 to declare that if one dressed in the clothes of the opposite sex on the streets, he or she would be sent to jail for six months and fined $500.[53] However, before the mid-twentieth century, the ordinance (which became Municipal Code 52.51 in 1936) was most often enforced against men. One woman onstage impersonator, Jean Southern, devised a stunt that tested the law (and, more to the point for her, garnered valuable publicity on the eve of her appearance at the Orpheum Theater): Southern, a 1924 newspaper reported, "stuck a cigarette in her mouth, pulled her cap down over her forehead, and walked jauntily out into the street swinging a cane." She then accosted a policeman and engaged him in conversation, waiting to see whether he would recognize that "he" was really "she." The policeman is shown in a *Los Angeles Times* photograph, not very interested in discovering that the "boy" who stands beside him is in fact a girl. Jean Southern was not hauled off to the station. Perhaps gender-bending females enjoyed relative impunity, despite the words of Ordinance 5022, because they were still essentially beneath the radar screen of the law—which was doled out and enforced by men. "There is little in this age of sheiks and shebas a man can do that a girl can't—even to the extent of making the world believe she is a man," the *Times* declared with amusement.[54]

Gender-bending males, on the other hand, could find the courts and community severe, though there were occasional instances of public indulgence, such as the town's response to Billie Dodson, known as "the man milliner of El Monte." According to a 1907 report in the *Los Angeles Times,* Dodson "walks like a girl . . . talks like a girl . . . cooks and sews like a girl." He was a "sissy," the writer bluntly observed, and yet he had "the respect of every man in that little town whose people are direct descendants of the rough old Forty-Niners." Dodson was admired, the article explained, because of his life of self-sacrifice. He had grown effeminate taking care of his invalid mother, and, when she died, taking over the role of mother and housewife for his younger siblings and his bereft father. The writer was also insistent that Billie was not a "degenerate," pointing out that although he entertained college boys at night and his ways were "sissified," he "nevertheless lacked the offensive and unwholesome suggestion that usually lingers about an effeminate man."[55]

However, a more typical response to unusual male gender behavior was a 1911 newspaper column in which effeminate men were branded "Los Angeles Undesirables." "Willie Boys," the columnist called them, and wrote contemptuously of the most overt variety, "Silk Stocking Percy":

He wears his hair à la sow-lick, bedaubs his white lips with rouge and pencils his eyebrows and tucks his pale baby-blue silk kerchief, soused with French perfume, into his coat sleeve. . . . He wiggles like a wild fish when he walks down the street and carries a cane and a pair of gloves to keep him warm.

"Put him down!" the columnist concluded in a sneer.[56]

Flamboyant sissies may have been targeted for public disapproval, but men who actually tried to pass as women were subject to serious legal trouble. Frank Butcher had been working in women's clothes as a cook, but was hauled off to jail when his employer recognized that "she" was a male. In 1913, his transvestism was considered criminal by the authorities, who also questioned his sanity. Butcher was ordered to appear before the Lunacy Commission of the Los Angeles Superior Court. He came corseted, gloved, wearing a large picture hat, and he proclaimed his "overwhelming desire to wear skirts and woman's finery." The court was not sympathetic. The deputy sheriff was instructed to outfit him in male clothing and to lock up his "lady duds."[57]

UNBECOMING "THE WEAKER SEX"

*California is altogether anomalous, and it is not more extraordinary
for a woman to plough, dig and hoe with her own hands if she have
the will and strength to do so, than for men to do all their household
labor. . . never seeing the face of a woman.*[58]

—Eliza W. Farnham, 1856

Both middle-class and working-class nineteenth-century women who
can be viewed as "protolesbian" were attracted to a city like Los Angeles
for similar reasons: the possibility of escaping the pressure of relatives
and the peering of neighbors, the hope of forming a community with
like-minded women who had also run from the constrictions back
home, the dream that work opportunities such as were lacking for
women in more traditional communities might abound in a rapidly
growing new city. Mary Blake, writing in the nineteenth century of leaving New England and going West with another woman, said that even
on the train trip she was already feeling a "release from conventionali-
ties" and "a rubbing off of that dust of conservativism."[59]

Even as early as 1849, "women's righters" such as Eliza Farnham were
advising women without men to "go West." A widow whose most intimate relationships were with other women, Farnham came West with her
children and "Miss Sampson," whom she described as being "at this time
a member of my family," and with whom she labored on the farm they
shared, "rejoicing every evening over the progress of the day."[60] Farnham
told independent women that in California, unlike the rest of the country
that was hidebound by tradition, they might do anything. She bragged of
being her own carpenter, of dressing "à la monsieur" rather than in the
constricting skirts of the day, and of sharing with other women "the
purely sensuous enjoyments" of a pioneering and independent life.[61]

Caroline Churchill, who proudly proclaimed herself a "strong-minded
woman" (a term used by enemies of women's rights to describe both suffragists and "manly women," that is, inverts), observed a generation later,
in 1876, that in California opportunities for "strong-minded women"

abounded, more than anywhere else in the country, because although they were not ubiquitously liked they were nevertheless permitted to go about their business. She wrote of their successes in "money making and other business endeavors," and she claimed to have met several prosperous women physicians in California.[62]

The number of women physicians in the Los Angeles area expanded further with the founding of the University of Southern California, which was opened to both sexes in 1878, when most universities elsewhere in the country still shunned women. The USC College of Medicine was soon flooded with applications from "strong-minded women" who wanted to become doctors, such as the very "manly" Ida B. Parker, who came to Los Angeles from Kansas, graduated from USC medical school, and established a private practice in Southern California.[63] By now, women who wished to escape the constraints visited on them by conservative tradition knew they might find unprecedented possibilities in the young West.

Their opportunities were increased by L.A.'s real estate boom of the 1880s. Many of those who became rich in the boom were single women who had migrated to Los Angeles from other parts of the country. Emma Adams observed in an 1888 book that Los Angeles was unique because it was a "brisk city" of fresh opportunities for pioneers, and it was possible there for "as large a proportion of women as men to increase their fortunes" through the real estate investment business. In Los Angeles, she said, women could attend real estate auctions, boldly bid on property, negotiate sales aggressively—all endeavors that were virtually closed to women, no matter how independent, in most other places in America.[64] Adams observed that of the five single women who happened to be visiting the house where she was at that time residing, every one owned her own home, bought through her own endeavors.[65] So many unmarried women were making a fortune in L.A. real estate during those years that, beginning in 1888, a group of women established what was probably the country's first "Woman's Investment Company."

It was not unusual for such westering women to live their lives with other women, as did Eliza Farnham, though which of them had anything like what our era would call a "lesbian identity" is difficult to know for certain. By the turn of the century, the literate knew that sexologists had articulated the terrible connection between "congenital taint" and the "real inverts"—those twilight crawlers with whom "the respectable" would not wish to identify.[66] In her memoir about a lesbian life in turn-of-the century New York, Mary Casal observed a severe class split among middle-class and working-class women who were homosexual. Once in a while, Casal admitted, she and her woman lover would "go slumming [to] invert resorts" in the Bowery, but always they felt "out of place" among the kinds of people they met there. "Our lives were on a much higher plane than those real inverts," Casal proclaimed, distinguishing herself and her lover from the sorts of lesbians that hung out in "invert resorts."[67] Casal's desire to draw such class distinctions was undoubtedly as pronounced among educated, middle-class lesbians in Los Angeles as it was among those in New York. Genteel women might live together in deeply intimate relationships, but they would not be seen in the rendezvous of the sexual outlaws.

As an early-twentieth-century homosexual police informant, L. L. Rollins acknowledged there was at least one "queer" dance hall in Los Angeles similar to the New York Bowery haunts that Casal describes, where working-class lesbians gathered together with their male counterparts.[68] But though working-class women who were lesbian in early-twentieth-century Los Angeles sometimes shared space with gay men, they appear seldom to have suffered, as the men did, from police entrapment or persecution for their sexual activities. There were multiple reasons for this: Lesbians of any class were less likely to use the sorts of semipublic cruising grounds that gay men favored—such as a dark park (where women had reason to fear male sexual assault) or a tavern (where patronage required discretionary income, which single working-class women did not have in abundance). Because of the facts of physiology that make "quickie" upright sex less appealing to women than to men, female-female sex acts were rarely carried on in any of the other places that were likely targets for police surveillance, such as public restrooms. Also, so few women officers were employed by the police department that schemes to entrap lesbians would have been impracticable; and the notion of sexual pleasure in which a penis was lacking was anyway not taken seriously by many men who made and enforced the laws.

In the middle decades of the twentieth century, lesbians, especially those of the working class, were often charged with "masquerading" by the police, that is, wearing pants and short hair when real women were supposed to wear dresses and tresses. But in earlier decades, city ordinances and municipal codes notwithstanding, law enforcement was surprisingly unpredictable, and even sympathetic, with regard to masquerading women. For example, in 1915, Professor Eugene de Forest, a "well-known teacher of dramatics," had been engaged, according to an L.A. newspaper account, to "a well-known Los Angeles woman," their marriage pending the finalization of Professor de Forest's divorce from the wife "he" had married in 1911. It was discovered that the professor, who would today be called "transgendered," was really a female, and she was arrested for masquerading. But her plea that, though physically a woman, she was "in nature a man" appears to have moved the court. She was never sentenced. Two years later, when the professor fell ill and was admitted to Los Angeles County Hospital, she was even able to convince hospital authorities, who had wanted to put her in the women's ward, that she must be placed in the men's ward.[69]

There were other such remarkable instances of the Los Angeles courts' leniency toward women who tried to pass as men in the early twentieth century. "Lionel Francis Michael Higgins," who had married a woman, was discovered to be a female herself after she misappropriated $12,000 from her L.A. employer. She diverted a jail sentence by claiming "sexual maladjustment." Instead of being imprisoned, she was sent to General Hospital: "The best that can be done is to permit her to continue to be as masculine as possible," the examining doctor told the court.[70]

The Los Angeles courts continued to be surprisingly liberal with regard to masquerading women throughout the 1920s. In 1927, a young woman by the name of Katherine (Kit) Wing posed as a man and married a sixteen-year-old, Eileen Garnett. Two years later, Wing was living as the husband of another young woman, nineteen-year-old Stella Harper. When Wing's bigamy was discovered, she was arrested. But the district attorney ordered her released, declaring that although she had committed technical perjury by misrepresenting the Garnett girl's age at the time of the marriage, "Miss Wing was not otherwise guilty in going through the ceremony or masquerading as a man" since the statutes applied "only where someone [had] been damaged." Wing convinced the district attorney that she had donned masculine attire only because she thought it would enable her to get more work as a barber. "Except for the one matrimony slip, I cannot see that she has done anything particularly out of the way," the DA concluded. He pointed out that "Hollywood girls" sometimes even wore "gob's [i.e., sailor's] clothes at the beach," and that it seemed to him there was "no standard attire for men or women these days."[71]

What can account for that astonishing liberality? Was it because Los Angeles by the 1920s had been feeling the challenge of becoming an important metropolis, of living up to the examples of other sophisticated major metropolises where female gender play was rampant, such as Berlin or Paris?[72] Was it because the advent of the "twentieth century" (after centuries of "teens") had seemed to herald a necessary break from tradition, including old-fashioned gender tradition? Los Angeles in 1900 seemed to brace itself for a break that would be huge: A cartoon of that year showed a couple of the new century, the man flinging his decidedly limp wrists from embroidered mutton-chop sleeves, peering through a monocle under a beribboned hat; the woman wearing a starched collar, suit jacket, and porkpie hat, and leaning on a golf club.[73]

Or had the liberality toward female gender behavior come about because Los Angeles was still reeling from the confusion over the 1911 election, which gave California women the vote eight years before it was bestowed on women in most of America? As in the rest of the country, the nineteenth-century "women's righters" of California had often been treated with disdain, their demands on behalf of women being associated with sexual deviancy. Arguing against inserting a Married Women's Property Rights clause into the first California Constitution, one delegate to the Constitutional Convention voiced the sentiments of many: "The God of nature made women frail, lovely, dependent," he declared. "The doctrine of women's rights is the doctrine of [the tribe of] mental hermaphrodites."[74] Decades later, Los Angeles antisuffragists echoed his hostility, characterizing women who wanted the vote as unfeminine and sexual freaks. L.A. newspapers constantly hammered on the connection between a woman's desire for full citizenship and her gender abnormality.

"She wears her brother's shirt and likewise his suspenders . . . and now she's learning how to vote and lift her voice in caucus. . . . She is that trial to the soul, the modern mannish woman," one article proclaimed.[75] "Woman suffrage should be defeated because it tends to unsex society," another insisted. "Politics is a realm unsuited to the normal woman."[76]

But L.A. women could not be daunted by these tactics, and they continued to pressure male voters to enfranchise them. Suffragists were more successful in Los Angeles than anywhere else in the state. California women won the vote no thanks to Northern California, where the antisuffrage vote was so heavy in San Francisco and Alameda Counties on October 10, 1911, that the *Los Angeles Times* actually predicted on October 11 that the California woman's suffrage amendment had lost.[77] In fact, the suffrage amendment won, but only by 3,587 votes, 2,000 of that margin coming from Los Angeles, where the vote to enfranchise women was 15,000 to 13,000. California became the sixth state in America (following Wyoming, Colorado, Idaho, Utah, and Washington) in which women could vote.[78]

What interpretation could be given to those facts, especially in view of the concerted efforts to depict suffrage women as "manly" and freakish? Neither the majority of men voters in L.A. nor the women who pushed them to vote for suffrage were, apparently, afraid of "unsexing," whatever that meant. The district attorney who could not see that "Kit" Wing had "done anything particularly out of the way" in marrying two women, and who insisted even that old standards of appropriate gender dress no longer applied, seems to have been echoing Angeleno ambivalence of that era about what rules were still pertinent to female behavior. For at least a few years in Los Angeles, the old certainties about how a woman must look and act had been destabilized, or had even disappeared.

Word seemed to have gotten out that women who were disdained elsewhere because of their gender or sexual behavior needed to cross the continent all the way to the Pacific, where they would find not only sunshine but also anonymity and even a modicum of safety.[79] Kit Wing had come to Los Angeles from Springville, Utah, possibly hoping—along with so many women who wanted to escape the scrutinizing eyes of relatives or neighbors—not only that she could lose herself in a distant and growing city but also that she might discover a like-minded community. According to Box-Car Bertha, a hobo celebrity of the early decades of the twentieth century, it was common for lesbian hoboes to ride the rails (often in couples, one dressed in drag so that they might pass as a straight pair) and head for California. There were more female hoboes in California than anywhere else in the country, Box-Car Bertha observed in her memoirs that looked back on the 1920s and '30s.[80]

The Los Angeles newspapers were fascinated by the discovery of odd female immigrants into the city, especially if they passed as men: for example, "Man-Woman Is Seen as Romeo" a 1924 headline declared in telling of a "Paul J. Beach," who was found upon "his" death to be a woman. A picture of Beach in men's clothes and the woman s/he had married in the Midwest, before the couple came to Los Angeles, accompanied the article, as did a love letter from another woman declaring that she dreamt of having Beach's "nice, big, broad shoulder to lean on."[81] "Faint Reveals 'He's' a Woman," another headline announced about Peggy Dolan from Brooklyn, who, posing as a man, had made her way to Los Angeles. Her sex was discovered when "he" was taken to Los Angeles General Hospital after passing out in downtown L.A., the *Los Angeles Times* wrote sympathetically alongside a picture of a smiling boyish Peggy.[82]

SOCIAL VAGRANTS

Disgusting in the extreme was the function described by this young social vagrant . . . which took place a few evenings ago in the richly furnished and perfumed apartments of a wealthy man in the heart of Los Angeles.

—The Fisher Report, 1914[83]

Despite the Los Angeles City Council's attempts to regulate "riotous revelry and debauchery" of the queer variety, an underground gay male subculture took root. Already in the 1880s and early 1890s, there were many places where like-minded men might find one another in the developing city: L.A. moralists complained about the visibility of "sissy-boys on

Broadway," a major Los Angeles boulevard.[84] Night-time trysting places, known only to gay men and police, included Central Park (which in 1918 became Pershing Square) and Westlake Park. There were also traces of a gay subculture in some of the city's numerous saloons. In 1896, a soldier by the name of Holcomb complained to Los Angeles police that he had been robbed of $135 at the Thalia Beer Hall. His assailants were a black man, Charles Berry, and "some of the 'fairies' employed at the Thalia in the capacity of 'beer-slingers' and song and dance artists." The "fairies," the victim claimed, "assisted Berry in getting away with the money."[85] (L.A.'s nineteenth-century underworld appears to have been similar to that of New York, where, according to Earl Lind, a female impersonator who frequented the Bowery, criminal types generally felt comfortable with "fairies" because they knew that society considered homosexuals to be "far worse defilers of the law than themselves." Lind says the "crooks" and the "fairies" were often bed partners.)[86]

Masked balls provided cover for forbidden behavior. One such affair in the summer of 1887 was condemned as attracting "drunken prostitutes of both sexes" who conducted "vile orgies" at Merced Hall.[87] At Turnverein Hall, similar "disgraceful debauches" drew flocks of "prostitutes and their associates, thugs, hoodlums, thieves, and disreputables of all types and classes."[88] Just months after the infamous masked ball at the Merced, British immigrant Frederick Purssord converted the Merced into a lodging house, apparently for homosexual men.[89] Purssord, a colorful character who practiced electrical therapy on nude patients while nude himself, also owned a series of Turkish baths. Police had for years considered him to be "operating as a degenerate." One neighbor complained to a *Los Angeles Times* reporter, "He is the most indecent man I have ever known."[90] In 1913, he was arrested on a charge of "lewd and dissolute conduct" and was reported to have committed suicide in the city jail.[91]

Though the word "homosexual" was never mentioned in California laws, the "infamous crime against nature," which referred primarily to homosexual sodomy, first appeared in the California State Penal Code in 1872. Sodomy, regardless of who the participants were, was punishable by a term in a state prison.[92] As a Los Angeles judge instructed one nineteenth-century jury on a sodomy case, "Every person who assaults another with intent to commit the infamous crime against nature is guilty of a felony, and it is wholly immaterial whether the person so assaulted consents or not."[93] (Clearly, the "assault" was not against the consenting partner but rather against society.) As Los Angeles court records reveal, the Los Angeles police did not scruple to invade privacy if they had reason to suspect that two men were "violating nature." In 1888, police hauled two protesting men at 1:00 A.M. from the bed they shared at a lodging house on North Main Street and took them to the downtown jail. The following morning, Charles Murphy and John Fisher found themselves described in newspapers as "vile criminals."[94]

Fisher, the younger of the two men, escaped charges by testifying against Murphy. The pretrial hearing transcripts reveal a shady L.A. underworld of cheap lodging houses equipped with peepholes for spying, clerks who doubled as prostitutes, and policemen who came running if summoned to witness the commission of the crime against nature. John Fisher claimed to have been introduced to Charles Murphy by a mutual friend. After Murphy bought Fisher dinner, they ended up in a lodging house, where the woman clerk rented them a room for twenty-five cents. In hesitant testimony, Fisher confessed that once they had disrobed and were in bed, Murphy turned him "on my stomach." It was at that point that the clerk (who must have been spying at a peephole) entered their room, lifted her Mother Hubbard dress, and asked, "Do you fellows want some fucking?" She said she charged $2.50 for her services. When Murphy declined, the woman left and fetched the son of the lodging house owner, who testified that he looked through the peephole and witnessed Murphy "on top, just the same as he would be on a woman." He summoned a policeman, who told the court he saw that Murphy's "privates [were] erected" when he arrested the two men.[95]

The clerk who had offered her sexual services for $2.50 was not charged by the court, nor was the lodging house cited for spying on customers. But Murphy was sentenced to a couple of years in Folsom Prison.[96] He can be said to have gotten off lightly compared to the frontier-town treatment of other men who were suspected of sodomy. In 1896, Charles Wheeler was accused of having sex with an adolescent boy.

The boy's father, James Wilde, along with his uncle, tracked Wheeler down, held a knife at his throat to prevent an outcry, and castrated him.[97] The brothers then gave Wheeler a dime and referred him to the county hospital, where he was refused treatment. When the Wilde brothers were charged with mayhem, they expressed astonishment that they had been held accountable for their actions. The judge who tried them agreed. "The facts of the case," he said, alluding not to the brothers' castration of Wheeler but rather to Wheeler's alleged (though never proven) commission of sodomy, "are so revolting that one may well blush for human depravity." He dismissed the charges against the brothers for their rush to judgment and bloody deed and then declared: "The rules I follow can strike terror to no decent man."[98] Such was Wild West judgment of homosexual sodomy when Los Angeles was a frontier town.

—

Sodomy was a felony in California, but oral sex did not appear in the California State Penal Code as a punishable offense until 1915 (though those who were caught engaging in oral sex might be arrested under misdemeanor "vagrancy" statutes or as "lewd and dissolute persons," as was Frederick Purssord).[99] Perhaps because its misdemeanor status diminished the legal consequences, gay men in Los Angeles (as well as gay women, according to a 1914 report)[100] apparently began favoring "the twentieth-century way" once personal hygiene was improved in the city.[101] The oral sex trend may be accounted for by other factors too, such as the invention of the zipper (first introduced in 1893 and produced widely in 1912), which made "quickie" sex possible in parks at midnight—a boon to those homosexual men who lived in urban boarding houses or other dwellings that afforded little privacy.[102]

In 1915, however, California adopted a law that made oral sex as illegal as sodomy.[103] The law was passed as a direct result of the 1914 arrests for fellatio of thirty-one men in Long Beach, a Southern California town near Los Angeles. The arrests of these men unleashed a tsunami of homophobia in the newspapers that described the relationships among them as "a holocaust of vice" and the men themselves as "social vagrants." The incident offers a more detailed glimpse of early twentieth-century gay life in Southern California.

The men were all alleged to be members of two local private clubs. After their arrests, the *Los Angeles Times,* as well as other California newspapers such as the distant *Sacramento Bee,* printed a "List of the Guilty Ones" who, the papers claimed, "were organized for immoral purposes." The men's occupations were listed beside their names so that the public would make no mistake about who they were; and in cases in which the arrestees' occupations were unknown, one newspaper described them as "professional perverted sexualists." The sensationalistic newspaper accounts were fatal for John Lamb, a forty-year-old bachelor who was a banker and an officer in his church. When officers attempted to arrest him, it was reported, he ran for several blocks, "fought them all over Pacific Park," and was led to the station with "his clothes torn and hair disheveled."[104] Released on bail, he swallowed cyanide on a rocky beach near San Pedro. The note he left confirmed that he committed suicide because the *Los Angeles Times* had published his name in its list of "Guilty Ones": "I am crazed by reading the paper this morning," Lamb wrote to his sister. He was not alone in his anguish. So many terrified men sought to buy poison at local drugstores that Long Beach officials temporarily banned the sale of toxic substances.[105]

Southern California was in a frenzy at the notion that widespread homosexual activity was being carried on in the area—at least according to the *Los Angeles Times,* which was bent on fanning the flames by printing hysterical letters such as one from a South Pasadena mother who wrote that she would prefer "having my boy a murderer or a drunkard" rather than one of those "awful vampires."[106] The *Times* assumed the righteous outrage of its readers when it reported that the men had all been members of the "606 Club" and "96 Club" (cf. "69"), which held weekly "drags" where members donned kimonos, powdered their faces, and indulged in orgies to the strains of ragtime piano. The arresting police described these men as "flutters" and "fruiters."[107]

Residents of Long Beach were embarrassed that their town was the site of such scandal, especially since Long Beach was promoting its plan to host what was billed as "the largest religious revival meeting" in

Southern California history.[108] Fistfights broke out over allegations that Long Beach was a home to moral laxness. The newspapers of rival towns such as Venice, another Southern California beach community, mocked Long Beach (à la Mark Twain) as a "Holy City."[109]

It was the overly zealous Long Beach Police Department that triggered the revelations that brought scandal to their own town. During the summer of 1914, the department hired W. H. Warren and B. C. Brown as "vice specialists" to help conduct purity campaigns aimed specifically at men who engaged in homosexual activity. Brown and Warren were central not only in the "606" and "96" cases in November of that year: In a prior sweep, they had been hired by the Los Angeles Police Department and had arrested dozens of men in L.A. Their work appears to be the first instance on record of Southern California police entrapment of homosexuals. Brown, the younger of the two, had delicate features; Warren was said to have rugged good looks.[110] The two men may have been hired partly because the police thought their physical attributes (one femininely pretty, the other masculinely handsome) would entice homosexual men of all tastes to respond sexually, for which these "vice specialists" would then arrest them.

Despite the police badges that were issued to Warren and Brown in Los Angeles and Long Beach, they had had no police training and were closer to bounty hunters than legitimate officers of the law. They seem to have regarded their work as not so much a moral crusade as a lucrative business: They were paid by the head for each man they arrested.[111] Brown boasted of "collaring" up to fifteen "social vagrants" per day, for a bounty of $10 apiece, which would net him $150 for one day's work—a small fortune in 1914.[112] Both Brown and Warren had ambitions about franchising their talents and techniques, and they attempted to sell their services to the police departments of San Francisco, Venice, Santa Monica, and even Portland, with the promise to cleanse those towns of homosexuals just as they were cleansing Los Angeles and Long Beach.

Their tactics were a model for the ways in which Southern California police entrapped gay men for much of the twentieth century. Brown and Warren would hang out in a public restroom or the changing room of a bathhouse and wait "until they saw a man whom they thought to be given to this sort of thing." They would take turns in attracting their mark's attention by putting a finger through a hole in the partition board that divided the stalls. If the man responded by looking through the hole, he would see a mouth close to the aperture. If the man then stuck his penis through the hole, Brown or Warren would stamp indelible ink on it, and then arrest him. The inked penis would serve at the station house as irrefutable evidence of the man's guilt. It is, of course, probable that many of the men arrested in the public toilet—among them cement workers, house painters, bartenders, merchants, and day laborers[113]— were not "homosexual" but "jockers" or "wolves" (men who did not re- gard themselves as homosexual but occasionally had sexual relations with younger or more effeminate men), or they may simply have been tempted by the ostensible offer of quick sexual relief. Nevertheless, the mayor and police chief of Long Beach signed a proclamation that the work of Warren and Brown had "rid the city of a dangerous class which threatened the morals of the youth of the community."[114]

Warren and Brown also played major roles in the trial of Herbert Lowe, a thirty-nine-year-old florist, who was one of the men arrested as a member of the "606" and "96" clubs. Most of those arrested had avoided the further publicity of a trial by quietly paying considerable fines or, if unable to pay, accepting a half-year jail term. Lowe decided to fight the charges against him, which occasioned in the newspapers the raciest gossip since the trial of Oscar Wilde, to whom he was compared. Officers testifying against Lowe said that he had rented to vice specialist Brown an apartment that the *Los Angeles Times* sneeringly called "Lowe's Love Shack." Brown claimed that Lowe visited him at night, in- vited him to the next meeting of the 96 Club, and flirtatiously helped him button up a bathing suit he had borrowed from Lowe.

After he was certain of Lowe's proclivities, Brown said, he arranged for Warren and two other officers to spy while he offered himself as bait. One of the officers stationed himself in the attic, crouching, with his eye to a hole in the wallpaper; another spied through a window. Ex- pecting the arrival of Lowe, Brown climbed into bed. Allegedly, Lowe let himself into the apartment, pulled back the blankets on the bed, knelt, and kissed Brown several times all over his body. It was then, the

Los Angeles Times reported of the courtroom testimony, that Lowe was interrupted by a sharp noise. "Warren or his friend had accidentally betrayed his presence and slipped on the gravel. Lowe looked up toward the window, startled, and arose. Just then Warren and the other officers rushed in and arrested him." The four officers all testified in court that Lowe had confessed to them that he was a "social vagrant" and had offered them a $1,500 bribe in return for his freedom. Lowe denied every allegation.[115]

The public was evidently fascinated by whatever salacious bits of the case they might read, and the *Los Angeles Times* tried to exploit that fascination into a lynch mob mentality by running editorials opining that "degenerates" such as Lowe ought to be "pilloried in the sunlight . . . [to be] abhorred by all mankind." They dubbed the members of the 606 and 96 clubs "devils" and demanded "prominent publication of the name of every wretch convicted of a horrible enormity besides which ordinary prostitution is chastity itself."[116] But despite the public's fascination with the sensational story, the paper's call to pillory fell flat. Los Angeles had undergone something of a change from a generation earlier when Charles Wheeler—the accused but never convicted "sodomite"—suffered a Wild West castration.

Roland Swaffield, Lowe's attorney, was able to put law and order on the defensive, charging that Warren was nothing more than a blackmailer, that his modus operandi was usually to "catch some fellows at the bath house and get all the money they had on them . . . and tell the fellow that he was free and not to come around again."[117] He argued that Herbert Lowe was a well-known and trusted member of the community and that Warren and Brown were outsiders, carpetbaggers. He convinced the jury that a man they saw in their town every day, who looked perfectly harmless, could not be a "degenerate . . . capable of horrible enormity." On top of that, Lowe had not been accused of sodomy—and it was only sodomy that was a felony under the law.

But it was attorney Swaffield's very emotional closing statement that sealed his case before the jury. He heaped on the "vice specialists" whatever guilt the public may have felt over the suicide of Lamb: It was Warren and Brown, Swaffield asserted, who were "dripping with the blood of

John Lamb." In the end, he achieved both sympathy and "reasonable doubt." It took the jury less than half an hour to acquit Herbert Lowe.

"Jury Acquits in Six-O-Six" blared the headline in the fickle *Los Angeles Times,* ostensibly reflecting the public's relief that the popular florist was found innocent; "Stool-Pigeons and Police Given No Credence," the subheadline declared. But the *Times* could not relinquish yet again presenting the specter of the queer peril: Next to the article about Lowe's vindication was printed a full-length portrait of a man in an off-the-shoulder gown and feathered headdress, captioned "Harry A. Wharton, a prominent member of the [606] club, [who] boasted one of the finest wardrobes among the 'queer' people." Nor could the police relinquish their pursuit. They had lost the case against Lowe, but now they were looking for Harry Wharton because they wished to arrest him as a "degenerate."[118] The California legislature, too, was intent on making sure that members of clubs such as the "606" would not get off lightly in the future: Within a year, the California State Penal Code included a new statute, 288a, which turned oral sex into a felony.

—

Lowe's trial had been something of a circus. Hundreds of curious spectators fought for courtroom seats, where they would hear such details as were unprintable even in sensationalistic 1914 newspapers. Those details have been preserved only through the notes and letters of Eugene Fisher, an investigator hired by the *Sacramento Bee's* owner, C. K. McClatchy, to bring him juicy tidbits that he might publish about the wild immorality of Southern Californians. Fisher noted in his letters to his employer (in language that McClatchy could not use in his newspaper) that testimony in court showed that Lowe had "practiced the infamy [of which he was accused] for more than nine years, being the one who will 'go down' on another or will himself willingly and gladly submit to the outrage." He observed further, for McClatchy's delectation alone, that "in the majority of these cases . . . their offense is nothing more nor less than 'cocksucking.'"[119]

Eugene Fisher was also hired by McClatchy that same year to dig for homosexual dirt in Los Angeles. His reports reveal a thriving, socially diverse gay life. "Here in Los Angeles, City of the Angels, boasted center of learning and culture on the Pacific Coast, [homosexual] depravity is growing and spreading like a hideous ulcer, seeking with insidious arts and wiles ever to claim new victims among the boys and girls," Fisher wrote in the inimitable style of the era.[120] The *Sacramento Bee*, reveling in the story of another city's moral turpitude, sensationalized Fisher's reports even further, blaring headlines such as "Vast Scandal in Los Angeles Is Reported as Suppressed"[121] and claiming that five hundred men had recently been secretly arrested for social vagrancy in Los Angeles (though the extant evidence suggests the number was closer to fifty).[122]

Through his notes and letters to McClatchy, Fisher also left a record of the varied gay social scene in 1914 Los Angeles. In the course of his investigations, the police introduced him to L. L. Rollins, who was living in the downtown area of Bunker Hill, already a neighborhood known to police for its queer denizens. Rollins, Fisher wrote, was a "social vagrant"; he offered Fisher firsthand knowledge about the "society of queers," men who cruised at night near the Los Angeles City Hall. Fisher claimed that Rollins also informed him of various other semipublic activities that were already available to L.A. gay men in 1914, such as a party at a Main Street dance hall to which he had gone with two other men, where they had been allowed to stay only because they could satisfy the proprietor that they were indeed "queer."[123]

If Fisher and his informant can be believed, class distinctions among homosexual men in L.A. were already pronounced. "Queer practices" were often conducted in modest apartments that were "scattered throughout the city"; but Rollins also knew about a higher class of "queers," ritzy homosexuals who held soirees in suites at the elegant Alexandria Hotel (where, only a few years later, the gay actor Ramon Novarro was rumored to have had a romance with Rudolph Valentino, who worked there). At the Yale Hotel on Hill Street, Rollins recollected, he had been entertained by a wealthy friend he called "Dad."[124] Young men known as "chickens," Rollins said, were often invited to Los Angeles parties for the pleasure of the socially prominent "queers" in attendance. He described an event, hosted by two millionaires who lived together in Venice Beach, that ended in an orgy of "unnatural practices." Fisher reported with particular relish the details of another homosexual soiree about which Rollins told him—a formal dinner that included next to everyone's plate "a candy representation of a man's privates, which was sucked and enjoyed by each guest to the evident amusement of all."[125]

As the population of Los Angeles grew in the first decades of the twentieth century, homosexual communities and their meeting places also grew. Word of the increasing variety of "queer" venues spread not only to men who desired other men but also to the police who tried to quash them in the service of what they believed was the public will. Homosexual men were victimized by L.A.'s "militant moralists [and] connoisseurs of sin," to use the words of William Huntington Wright. Wright pointed out in a 1913 article in *The Smart Set* that public parks in Los Angeles were now being patrolled, "snooping [was becoming] the popular pastime," and privacy was "impossible." He suggested that L.A. was losing its battle to become cosmopolitan, and he attributed the loss to the recent major influx of migrants from unsophisticated small towns. Los Angeles, Wright said, was being taken over by those who had "brought their Midwestern Puritanism with them."[126] This struggle that Wright characterized between provinciality and sophistication persisted in Los Angeles for some time. It accounts for a virulent tension between the law enforcement officials who would hire men like "vice specialists" Warren and Brown, and a cosmopolitan gay community that burgeoned despite them.

Marlene Dietrich preferred men's suits and shoes in real life, too. *Courtesy of the Academy of Motion Picture Arts and Sciences.*

CHAPTER 2

Going Hollywood

THE INVASION OF A "GREAT SECRET SOCIETY"

A walk along Hollywood Boulevard or any other locale in this mad town will bring any casual observer face to face with the alarming percentage of nances and Sapphic ladies as abound in these parts. Such parties and entertainments as they have are held in their own apartments or bungalows, until for a truth, it seems that they form a great secret society within, yet apart from those they refer to as "disgustingly normal." They come from all parts of the country, and whether the discovery of themselves came in this environment, or whether they knew before they arrived what they wanted, cannot be ascertained.

—"Hollywood Lowdown," 1932[1]

Actors, writers, and designers came to Hollywood largely from vaudeville and the legitimate stages of Europe and Broadway. As artists, they were accustomed to bohemian living, unconfined by the narrow sexual strictures that kept most individuals married and monogamous. The screenwriter Frances Marion recalled that from the beginning, their unconventional reputations preceded them into provincial Los Angeles: When she arrived in 1914 there was already a movement afoot by a committee called the "Conscientious Citizens," made up of "mostly churchgoers," who gathered 10,000 signatures "to force the invaders [those who had come to work in the new movie studios] out of Los Angeles." It was hard for Frances Marion to find an apartment, she wrote in her diary, because tacked over numerous rental signs was the edict "No Jews, actors, or dogs allowed."[2] But the Conscientious Citizens could not succeed in keeping the objects of their disdain out of the area that became Hollywood.

Indeed, by the 1920s people who preferred life on the social edge found Hollywood more attractive than almost anywhere else in America. "The law of the colony is that everyone is entitled to do as he or she sees fit in all personal matters," a Hollywood fan magazine explained in 1921. "If you don't like it you may stay away, but you must not knock."[3] Workers in the movie industry and those who were drawn to the "great secret society" (not mutually exclusive groups) helped to swell Hollywood's population from 36,000 residents at the beginning of the 1920s to 165,000 by the end of the decade.[4] The conscientious citizens' battle with the bohemians did not let up, but the bohemians fought back and even used their new Hollywood prestige to try for a time to raise the sophistication quotient in the rest of America. In 1922, when the Hollywood Women's Club cried for a curfew in the streets, a *Photoplay* magazine columnist shared his outrage with his readers: "Everybody has to be in bed and be good," he wrote in a sarcastic article about the club's curfew campaign. "All wild parties are off. Hollywood [must] become a strictly moral, residential district." He hoped to encourage movie fans everywhere to feel urbane disdain for the Hollywood Women's Club's offer to "aid the police by reporting all unseemly activities and all elements of the kind they want to suppress."[5]

It must have been difficult indeed for the conventional citizenry of what had so recently been a small California town to digest not only the risqué movies being produced in early Hollywood but also the vast changes going on in their neighborhoods. As bohemians who valued nonconformity and adventurous experimentation, many of the men and women of the early film industry would have been anything but perfect 0s ("exclusively heterosexual") on the Kinsey Scale. They were fluid both in sexuality and in gender presentation, and their daring was encouraged: For example, when Julian Eltinge appeared in drag in the 1917 silent film *The Countess Charming,* one of Hollywood's first magazines, *Photo-Play Journal,* described him glowingly as "the celebrated female impersonator, who plays the Countess Raffeisky, a dainty woman of rare beauty";[6] in 1921, *Four Horsemen of the Apocalypse* (Rudolph Valentino's breakthrough film) presented glimpses of lesbians caressing in a café and military officers posing in women's clothes; in that same year, Alla Nazimova not only flaunted her sexual predelictions around town but also announced to the press, "I am to play a boy in my next picture."[7] Throughout the 1920s, the lesbian cavortings of silent film stars such as Evelyn Brent, Nita Naldi, Pola Negri, and Lilyan Tashman were Hollywood's open secret.[8]

The scandalized church groups and women's clubs of Hollywood found themselves fighting a losing battle. Despite the efforts of the Hollywood police who sided with them and the establishment of the Hays Office that tried to force censorship on what came out of (and went on in) the industry,[9] the movie colony continued to be so provocative that even the *New York Times* had to admit that Hollywood was "gayer, newer, brighter, and younger than anything in the history of man."[10] It was with good reason that the gay director George Cukor dubbed the late 1920s and early '30s Hollywood's "Belle Epoque."[11]

In most places in America, the Depression triggered a reactionary mood in which homosexuality was seen as tantamount to evil, degeneracy, perversion, and ugliness. A popular 1931 novel, *Loveliest of Friends*, summed up the widely shared excesses of revulsion for what was sexually unfamiliar: Lesbians were "crooked, twisted freaks of nature who stagnate[d] in dark and muddy waters, and [were] . . . cloaked with the weeds of viciousness and selfish lust."[12] But many movie industry people of those same years, though cognizant of the need to be subtle, continued to think of the sexually unconventional as interesting, provocative, and exciting. In 1932, when Salka Viertel was beginning to write the script for Greta Garbo's film *Queen Christina*, the producer Irving Thalberg asked her whether she'd seen the German lesbian movie *Mädchen in Uniform* (1931). He suggested that Viertel "keep in mind" that Queen Christina's affection for her lady-in-waiting might "indicate something like that" and told her that "if handled with taste it would give us interesting scenes."[13] Marlene Dietrich's early director, Josef von Sternberg, traded on the actress's androgyny in *Morocco* (1930) and *Blonde Venus*

(1931), admitting in his biography that he'd "wished to touch lightly on a Lesbian accent."[14] In 1933, the trade paper *Variety* reported that (in spite of the Hays Office's attempts to censor "sex perversion or any inference to it" in the movies) producers were "going heavy on the panz stuff." *Variety* cited gay touches in several forthcoming films, including *Cavalcade* (based on a play by the homosexual author Noel Coward), *Our Betters* (based on a play by Somerset Maugham, also a homosexual), and *The Warrior's Husband* (a comedy about Amazons).[15]

Those Hollywood insiders not fascinated by homosexuality in this era were at the very least blasé. In that respect, Hollywood was unlike other American cities, where men could be thrown in jail for not being sufficiently butch, as the dancer Danny Aikman recalled about his return to Wichita, Kansas, to visit his ailing mother: "I was just walking down the street . . . wearing this flowered shirt I got in California. They'd never seen anything like it in Wichita. And the police arrested me and charged me with dressing like a woman. Because I wore a shirt with flowers on it!"[16] But within the industry, gender-bending and homosexuality were often treated as in-jokes: "Were you at the Club New Yorker [in Hollywood] the other night when Jean Malin [a female impersonator] announced that he was 'all fagged out'? Whoops!" the "Rambling Reporter" for a Hollywood trade paper quipped in September 1932.[17] The following month he observed Marlene Dietrich walking through the lobby of the Roosevelt (a Hollywood hotel); she was dressed "in men's gray flannel trousers, man's suit coat (with shoulder pads out far enough to make her hips look small), a man's shirt, man's cufflinks, . . . her best mannish walk," and, the reporter added, "she lunched in Bullock's in the same outfit and walk the day before."[18] The "Rambling Reporter" knew that his movie-industry readers would "get" his implications and be pleased with their own sophistication.

Hollywood's relative urbanity in the 1920s and '30s might be explained in part by the influence of the Europeans who came to work in the film industry and/or to escape the emerging fascism of Europe. They brought with them the values of the very tolerant Weimar Republic (where popular nightlife often featured "an enticing line of homosexuals dressed as women [and] a choice of feminine and collar-and-tie lesbians"),[19] or an otherwise Continental attitude toward unconventional sexuality. These immigrants included artists such as Salka and Berthold Viertel, Bertolt Brecht, Joseph von Sternberg, Fritz Lang, Thomas Mann, Billy Wilder, Aldous Huxley, and Christopher Isherwood. Some of them came to Hollywood with a spouse, but their conjugal bonds were seldom conventional. Huxley's wife, Maria, for example, was introduced to female homosexuality in Italy and had an open marriage with Aldous, even helping him to arrange his sexual encounters with other women in Hollywood, which left her free to explore lesbian affairs. As one of her intimates commented, "Maria—like a whole generation of European women of sophistication—never saw the connection between sex and marriage."[20] Salka and Berthold Viertel, as well as countless other Hollywood couples, had similar open arrangements, promoting a notion of sexual freedom in Hollywood that had few counterparts elsewhere in America.[21]

ALL THE VERY GAY PLACES

When I was in Hollywood [in the 1930s] it was considered a wild and, in a manner of speaking, a morally "lost" place. The whole world thought of it as a place of mad nightlife, riotous living, sexual orgies, . . . uncontrolled extravagances, unbridled love affairs and— in a word—SIN.

—Mercedes de Acosta[22]

Despite Mercedes de Acosta's conviction that "the whole world" knew of Hollywood's "extravagances," by the Depression-ridden 1930s the extremes of the movie colony's sexual libertarianism were generally hidden from the outside world. They had by then learned to play "the movie game," which meant creating public images that were generally far more conventional than real—though within the parameters of Hollywood, people were much freer to indulge in the "mad," "extravagant," and "unbridled." Hollywood sexual freedom often played itself out in nightclubs and bars that resembled the colorful nightspots of Europe and the clubs of Manhattan.[23] When Prohibition ended, a decade of underground speakeasy culture had created more than a passing acquaintance between high society tipplers and the social strata regarded as taboo and even criminal. In some major cities, a queer milieu carried over into the new state-licensed bars for a brief but shining moment known in New York as the "pansy craze." In fact, the craze grew so overt in New York that one Broadway nightspot even called itself the Pansy Club.[24] In Los Angeles, the fad was sufficiently established so that the drag entertainer Ray Bourbon could open his own nightclub, the Hollywood Rendezvous. Wags of the period described him as "the Master of the Murky Mouthful, exponent of darting dirtiness . . . [who sings songs] that would make Will Hays [after whom the Hollywood censorship commission was named] screech, 'I *hate* you!'"[25]

Gays, straights, and the sexually flexible—such as Marlene Dietrich, William Haines, James Cagney, Fifi Dorsay, and Mae West—gathered together regularly in post-Prohibition nightclubs that featured gay entertainment.[26] At B.B.B.'s Cellar, the floorshow was called "Boys Will Be Girls," and Fred Monroe did impersonations of the female stars in his audience.[27] At the Bali nightclub on Sunset Strip, the composer and singer Bruz Fletcher, whom the newspapers described as a favorite of nightclub-hopping film stars, entertained the cognoscenti with gay double-entendres in songs such as "Bring Me a Lei from Hawaii," "Keep an Eye on His Business," and "The Simple Things":

> *I want a cozy little nest, somewhere in the West,*
> *Where the best of all the worst will always be.*
> *I want an extensive, expensive excursion*
> *To the realms of "in," "per," and "di"-version.*
> *It's the simple things in life for me.*[28]

The trade papers enthused over the nightclubs' gay shows and the glamorous Hollywood audiences they attracted: For example, they called B.B.B.'s Cellar "the best after-theater spot for the money in town" and "a great drop-in spot for picture names."[29]

The L.A. police were not as tolerant: Their 1932 raid on the Cellar was described by *Variety* as part of "a drive on the Nance and Lesbian amusement places in town."[30] However, since a variety of venues abounded for so-called "Nances and Lesbians," the "drive" met with little success. Men who wished to make gay contact with other men might go, for example, to various hotel bars and the most elegant of the nightclubs—the Mocambo, the Trocadero, Ciro's—which were primarily heterosexual but permitted gay customers to cruise there as long as they behaved with discretion: no touching, no flamboyant clothes, no effeminate gestures.

And, of course, at Hollywood parties, behind the high walls and hedges of private homes, there was freedom either to be openly gay or to dabble in gayness. Several Hollywood historians have suggested that for those who were sexually flexible such parties could further careers. Alla Nazimova's biographer, Gavin Lambert, notes that on Sunday afternoons in her home, which she called "the Garden of Alla," Nazimova hosted poolside parties that were "occasionally mixed, [but] more often 'young girls' only." Lambert implies that Nazimova's lesbian parties served as an entrée for hopeful actresses into the Hollywood scene, whether or not they had previously considered themselves lesbian.[31]

The composer Cole Porter, the actor William Haines, and the directors Edmund Goulding and George Cukor also hosted parties that had similar purposes of providing not only gay social outlets but career opportunities, too, for young men who were (or were willing to play at being) gay and were capable of tight-lipped discretion. Mark Bortles, who worked in the industry during these years, recalls that "getting in with George Cukor or other gay industry figures at private Hollywood parties could help young gay men make a lot of connections." But, he noted, "if you talked the doors got closed."[32] Cukor's parties metamorphosed as the evening wore on. In the early hours, his guests would include heterosexuals as well as close bisexual women friends such as Katherine Hepburn, Greta Garbo, and Tallulah Bankhead, but later at night his hillside home became a gay-male oasis. Over forty years, much of gay Hollywood passed through his parties. Gays flocked there, in the words of the producer Joseph Mankiwiecz, "because George was their access to the crème of Hollywood."[33]

Donald Bogle, a historian of black Hollywood, suggests a parallel social phenomenon in the parties of Ben Carter, an African American casting agent, who was "at the center of early gay black Hollywood." African Americans appeared in Hollywood films during these years almost exclusively as chauffeurs, maids, and extras; but Bogle observes that Carter's frequent gatherings included many young black men, who could promote their limited but relatively well-paying Hollywood careers by opening themselves "for a little [gay] mischief."[34]

Those who worked behind the camera in Hollywood could also make connections at private gay gatherings. Paramount designer Howard Greer, who was responsible for the costumes in highly successful films such as *Bringing Up Baby,* threw gay parties to which "every male dressmaker in Hollywood" came, often hoping to land a job on Greer's staff. His gatherings included a mix of gay Hollywood types of the era—ingénues, muscle men, drag queens, celebrities—as his description of one such party in a 1937 letter reveals: "I flew hither and yon, asking the young, the handsome and the virile," Greer wrote. "On the following Thursday my little villa was thronged with belles. (I'd very carefully asked no women.)"[35] He hired local female impersonators from "a queer night club that ha[d] just started." He rigged up a studio spotlight to illuminate the curve of his stairway, where "really amazing" drag queens portrayed Bea Lillie and Ethel Merman. But the highlight of the evening, Greer says, was "when the torch singer sang one of Mr. Cole Porters' songs, . . . I thought Mr. Porter was going to deficate [*sic*]."[36]

Such private gay parties were a safe haven. When Prohibition was repealed in 1933, law enforcement officers, afraid of losing all vestiges of control over Hollywood nightlife, flexed their muscles by cracking down more often on Hollywood clubs that welcomed the sexually diverse. They were especially hostile to places that offered floorshows in which "men masquerade[d] as women, and women pose as men." When Hollywood Vice Squad officers raided Jimmy's Backyard, they carted off the female impersonators, who were each sentenced to six months in jail.[37] A 1933 *Variety* reported in its inimitable style:

Vigilance of the local gendarmes closed all the pansy joints in Hollywood. Flounce factories had quite a run for the past two years, then the coppers discovered an ordinance which prohibited the appearance of anyone in a café in drag unless employed in the café. That killed the lavender spots.[38]

Variety was wrong. The Hollywood clubs in which those of all sexual persuasions met and mingled continued to flourish.[39] To the end of the 1930s, titillating guidebooks such as Jack Lord and Lloyd Huff's *How to Sin in Hollywood* gave nuggets of advice to readers: "When your urge's mauve" (that is, when you want to visit a "lavender spot"), "go to Tess's Café Internationale [a lesbian nightclub] on Sunset Boulevard at 11:00 P.M." where you can "watch the little girl customers who . . . look like boys."[40] The most popular of the late 1930s clubs was the Baroness Catherine d'Erlanger's Café Gala, which was also called, in the language of Yiddish humor, the "Ca-fegaleh."[41] Beverly Alber, a singer at the Gala, remembers it as "a marvelous gay supper club where straights came to see the entertainment."[42]

But in a milieu in which those who are supposedly gay mix with those who are supposedly straight, lines may easily blur. When unconventional artists were brought together socially during the early decades of the Hollywood industry, many of them dared to be "unstraight."[43] In Hollywood, they could carry on their lives with at least a modicum of openness as long as they played the movie game and hid the fact of their sexual flexibility from their fans. But even if constrained to disguise the root of their sensibilities, these Hollywood artists with their "unstraight" styles profoundly influenced both the heterosexual and the homosexual worlds of their day and ours.

"THE WOMEN EVEN WOMEN CAN ADORE"

She has sex but no particular gender. Her ways are mannish. The characters she played loved power and wore slacks, and they never had headaches or hysterics. They were also quite undomesticated. [Her] masculinity appealed to women, and her sexuality to men.

—Kenneth Tynan, *The Sound of Two Hands Clapping*[44]

In recent years, a whole industry has been created of books devoted to establishing the lesbianism or lesbian experiences of one Hollywood star or another. Many of those books are poorly documented or patently sensationalistic. Some, however, are ostensibly reliable, based on solid evidence such as correspondence or other primary documents, or interviews with narrators who knew the subject well. Cases have been made for claiming as lesbian, or "Gillette blades" (the Hollywood slang for "bisexuals"), or at least "unstraight" numerous Hollywood character actresses, including Spring Byington, Judith Anderson, Hope Emerson, Constance Collier, Agnes Moorehead, Marie Dressler, Patsy Kelly, Hattie McDaniel, Ethel Waters, and Marjorie Main; as well as more glamorous stars, such as Pola Negri, Nita Naldi, Janet Gaynor, Alla Nazimova, Ona Munson, Peggy Fears, Lilyan Tashman, Elissa Landi, Billie Burke, Dolores Del Rio, Louise Brooks, Tallulah Bankhead, Claudette Colbert, Joan Crawford, Katherine Hepburn, Marlene Dietrich, and Greta Garbo.[45]

Why were so many of the female stars of early Hollywood unconventional in their sexuality? In addition to the historical bohemianism of the acting profession, another answer may be that girls who chose the rigorous course of training for a career in the early decades of the twentieth century were already "abnormal" in the sense that they rejected the time-honored prescription that had been laid out for women's lives: to marry young and to procreate. To be ambitious, to wish to succeed outside the domestic sphere—those were considered masculine traits in the previous century, when the early women stars were adolescents. They were not unlike the pioneering women doctors or lawyers, who were also often impervious to socialization into traditional femininity and its concomitant sexuality.[46]

Nineteenth-century sexologists such as Havelock Ellis considered the rejection of women's role a telling sign of "female sexual inversion" that was tantamount to lesbianism. Ellis' case studies in *Sexual Inversion in Women,* which often included the "symptomatic" childhood traits and predilections of typical female "sexual inverts," read strikingly like the early traits and predilections of many women stars of the 1930s. Ellis quotes the recollections of a "Miss V.," for instance: "As a child I loved to stay in the fields, refused to wear a sunbonnet, used to pretend I was a boy, climbed trees, and played ball. . . . When my hair was clipped, I was delighted and made everyone call me 'John.' I used to like to wear a man's broad-brimmed hat and make corn-cob pipes."[47] Katherine Hepburn recollected of her youth (much like Ellis' Miss V.), "From the age of nine to age thirteen, I shaved my head. I called myself 'Jimmy'... [and] loved to wear knickers and [my] brother's shirts."[48] She boasted that "there was not a single tree in town [I] could not climb."[49]

Greta Garbo described herself in her youth as a "strapping boy."[50] Marlene Dietrich admitted: "I used to dress up in boy's clothes when I was a little girl. I have always liked the freedom of men's garments";[51] and when young, she called herself "Paul."[52] "Billie" was the name Joan Crawford preferred as a young person, and she saw herself as "very much a tomboy and a scrapper."[53] Crawford even admitted in a *Modern Screen* interview in 1930 that in her youth she "wasn't like other girls"; she rejected all things feminine, preferring "to shinny trees and climb fences."[54] Examples abound of early women film stars' admissions of their masculine identification in youth.

These women were too complex to be dubbed simply "sexual inverts." (We suspect that many of Havelock Ellis' subjects were also much more complex than his reductive term for them suggests.) Yet they were certainly unstraight. Their androgyny—expressed in their clothes, voice, body language, and the hint of sexual flexibility that was implicit in their gender-bending—was a good part of their allure. Hollywood understood the potential of that appeal when it planned the advertising for Dietrich's first films: The publicity for *Morocco* (1930) featured a picture of the star in black top hat and tails, captioned by the slogan, "Marlene Dietrich—The Woman All Women Want to See." The image of Dietrich in male drag was so successful that she was again dressed in top hat and tails for *Blonde Venus* (1932). When Dietrich went to a private Hollywood party around that time wearing white flannel trousers, a very masculine blue blazer, and a yachting cap, she made such a sensation that the studio took a photo of her in that outfit and planned to issue thousands of copies with the caption, "The Woman Even Women Can Adore."[55]

But part of playing the movie game was to present the glamour actresses' androgyny and all that it might stand for as an indefinable quality rather than patent lesbianism—which would have shocked rather than enchanted the general public. Hollywood's formula was to compel the viewer by a species of sex appeal whose nature was never quite articulated, and thereby to attract both male and female fans. One of Alla Nazimova's women lovers described her as being "like a naughty little boy" when they were alone,[56] but Nazimova was most successful when she understood that her public image needed to be nuanced and ambiguous. "I am a mystery for the Americans, and that is my biggest advertisement," she realized,[57] and like other silent screen stars of flexible sexuality, such as Pola Negri and Nita Naldi,[58] she perfected the vamp image, masking lesbian characteristics in a kind of hypersexuality: The vamp "lolled about on tiger skins and shot glances, seductive or sinister, from beneath hooded lids,"[59] pulling men to her not because she desired them but rather to teach them how weak they were. Nazimova's aggressive sexuality was patently masculine, though its lesbian connections were hidden.

Though fans had little notion of what lay beneath the androgynous screen images that seduced them, behind the high, protective walls of Hollywood, at private gatherings, unstraight actresses felt they did not need to play the movie game. The director Billy Wilder recalled, in a 1988 interview, how fifty years earlier Marlene Dietrich had spoken openly in front of his party guests about her lesbian experiences, declaring: "Women are better."[60] Bankhead and Dietrich even felt safe enough with their Hollywood crowd to conceive a bawdy jest as a comment on local gossip that the two of them were having an affair: They smeared gold dust between them in telling places and appeared thus at a Hollywood gathering, "providing indisputable evidence that the gossips were right," and then "laugh[ing] like schoolgirls over the prank."[61] In 1932, when Paramount briefly considered replacing Dietrich with Bankhead in the tuxedo role in *Blonde Venus,* Bankhead is reported to have quipped loudly at the offer, "Oh, goodie, I always wanted to get into Marlene's pants."[62]

Other women stars, too, felt that they did not need to play the movie game in front of Hollywood intimates; they could reveal themselves. Scott Berg, a personal friend of Katharine Hepburn's, reports that soon after he met her, Hepburn introduced her companion of many years, Phyllis Wilbourn, as her "Alice B. Toklas" (the woman who was Gertrude Stein's lover and literary assistant). When Wilbourn remarked, "I wish you wouldn't say that. It makes me sound like an old lesbian, and I'm not," Hepburn, assuming that Berg, a Hollywood gay man, would appreciate the in-joke, retorted, "You're not what, dearie, old or a lesbian?" But in public, Wilbourn was presented as being merely in Hepburn's employ.[63] Such a guise before the public was common. Nazimova, for instance, played the movie game by calling Glesca Marshall, her lover for the last sixteen years of her life, her "secretary." "She had to," Nazimova's friend Robert Lewis observed. "Employment depended on keeping your nose clean." Hollywood, which Lewis ambivalently called "the dirtiest place in America," was "the most eager to keep everything clean [in front of the public]."[64]

Though Hepburn never ceased to be what her close friend George Cukor called "mannish,"[65] she eventually learned to play the game by being circumspect about her personal life. She dared to express the depth of her feeling for Wilbourn openly only at Wilbourn's funeral, when, as an observer wrote, "Kate suddenly dropped to her knees and sobbed."[66] Perhaps Hepburn had learned to be careful in public when she discovered, shortly after coming to Hollywood in 1932 with the actress Laura Harding (with whom, Hepburn admitted, she was "fascinated"),[67] that their relationship was gossiped about so loudly in Hollywood that "even New York was buzzing with it."[68] Hepburn writes in *Me,* her autobiography, that when she first met Spencer Tracy even he (whom she presents in her book as the love of her life) "imagined that [she] was a lesbian."[69]

One of Hepburn's intimates, Irene Selznick (the daughter of Louis B. Mayer and the wife of David O. Selznick), described Hepburn as "a double-gaiter." When the biographer Scott Berg told Irene Selznick that he was reluctant to make assumptions about Hepburn's relationships with women since Hepburn had always claimed that "nobody really knows what goes on between two people when they're alone," Selznick replied, "That's my point." She then chastised Berg for his naïveté, saying of Hepburn's friends such as Dorothy Arzner, Nancy Hamilton, and Laura Harding, "You're too young to have known all those other women, those single women. I knew them. I knew who they were."[70]

Before she became a movie actress, Hepburn had been married to Ludlow Ogden Smith, a Philadelphia socialite, but the marriage was not a happy one,[71] and a recent Hepburn biographer offers some evidence to suggest that Smith was homosexual.[72] Hepburn left him to go off to Hollywood with Laura Harding. A couple of years later, Hepburn and Laura

Harding flew to Mexico, where Hepburn divorced Smith. The two women continued to live together in Hollywood for years, though Hepburn came to understand that she needed to be very guarded about her unstraight life when she talked to her fans. She did not hide Harding from public view, but she called her in fan magazines, such as *Motion Picture* in 1937, her "inseparable secretary-companion."[73] In later years, Hepburn seemed even more anxious to obfuscate her relationship with Laura Harding, lying about the length of time she and Harding were together, claiming in her autobiography that "after about two years, Laura went back to New York." But as the 1937 *Motion Picture* article indicates, Laura Harding, who came to Hollywood with Hepburn in 1932, was still there with her five years later.

The fan magazines much preferred, of course, that stars play the movie game by giving them an exciting story about a heterosexual romance rather than one about an "inseparable secretary-companion." The magazine writers seemed to breathe a collective sigh of relief when the androgynous Hepburn, whom movie critics were describing as having "a strident, raucous, rasping voice" and "a broad-shouldered, boyish figure,"[74] became a party to "the most celebrated Hollywood love story of the century."[75] They glommed on to the story of Hepburn's love affair with Spencer Tracy with delight; that Tracy was a married man who said he couldn't divorce his wife because he was Catholic made little difference. Several Hollywood historians, such as Richard Gully in *Vanity Fair* and Anne Edwards in *Publishers Weekly,* have suggested that Tracy was, in fact, bisexual, and that he and Hepburn, who were undeniably close friends, were also "beards" for one another.[76]

Fandom did not want to be bothered with complex truths, nor with being forced to analyze the nature of the tremendous appeal to both women and men of the Dietrichs and Hepburns and other sexually flexible, gender-bending stars. Most fans would not have wanted to learn that the styles they admired in those stars were actually rooted in a particular subculture, the name of which they could not have brought themselves even to whisper. But those who lived their lesbian experiences in 1930s Hollywood, and communicated in their films the styles that were iconographically lesbian, were a powerful influence across

America. Josef von Sternberg, the director of Dietrich's early films, recalls in his biography that he had not realized it would "stimulate a fashion" when Dietrich, a transvestite off the screen, too, appeared in men's attire in *Morocco;* but he was astonished that that was precisely the effect the film had, that it caused multitudes of straight American women for the first time in history to "ignore skirts in favor of . . . male attire."[77] It was the influence on American women of Dietrich (as well as other androgynous actresses such as Garbo and Hepburn) that the songwriters Richard Rogers and Lorenz Hart had in mind when they wrote "I'm One of the Boys":

I've always had a passion
To wear the latest fashion.
That's why I have to look like this today.
I'm one of the boys, just one of the boys.
I go to the tailor that Marlene employs.
No dresses from France are so modern as these,
And under my pants are BVD's.[78]

The new look and comportment popularized by the androgynous, unstraight women stars of the 1930s truly alarmed reactionary forces in America, who soon reacted. By the mid-1930s, the film industry, already financially hit by the Depression, had reason to panic about the pressure that churchly groups were exerting on the studios to make movies that were "100 percent pure or else,"[79] as the *Hollywood Reporter* lamented after a Catholic boycott spread across the country. The efforts to shut down the sinful film industry continued throughout the decade. Censorship advocates were opposed to anything in movies that smacked of human sexuality, but they were particularly vehement against homosexuality. "Don't go near the films. You must do without them if you want to save your soul," Cardinal William O'Connell, the archbishop of Boston, hysterically admonished "all good women, Catholic and non-Catholic" in 1938. What bothered him more than anything else about the movies of the 1930s, he revealed in a speech to a Congress of Catholic Women, were their lesbian and feminist messages: "Just as there is something queer in being an effeminate man, it is equally queer to find a mannish woman. There is something abnormal in a woman attempting to dress in men's clothes," he proclaimed, concluding that the "modern pagan ideas [in the movies] shattered the ideal . . . that women's first and principal place is in the home."[80]

But whether or not such pronouncements frightened off heterosexual women, the unstraight across America must surely have taken heart from those alluring androgynous images of stars who, they could sense (despite fan magazine lies), were somehow like them. Young women who loved women could learn how to look and act "lesbian" even without access to an urban lesbian subculture. As the author of a 1933 book supporting movie censorship observed disapprovingly, the movies were giving young females lesbian ideas: He quotes a sixteen-year-old girl who happily proclaims, "I have one girlfriend that I love a good deal. . . . It is on her that I make use of the different ways of kissing that I see in the movies," and a seventeen-year-old who reports that she practices with her girlfriend the love scenes they see in movies: "We sometimes think we could beat Greta Garbo."[81]

The early women stars who played out their sexual flexibility and androgyny in the private setting of the Hollywood community—and then subtly communicated who they were through Hollywood films—have always fired the imagination of the unstraight everywhere. The 1930s images showing Garbo kissing her lady-in-waiting in *Queen Christina,* Marlene Dietrich flirting with women in *Morocco* and *Blonde Venus,* and Katherine Hepburn in her boy clothes in *Sylvia Scarlett* form what has been called "the foundation of lesbian film culture."[82] These films became icons of lesbian history not only because of the unstraight characters they presented but also because lesbian viewers intuited the complex sexuality of the women who played those characters. And the lesbian viewers did not have to rely solely on intuition: Despite the stars' attempts to play the movie game and keep confined to their Hollywood circles whatever was not straight in their lives, the secrets were whispered among lesbians in Chattanooga and Boise as well as in New York and Boston. Hollywood gay gossip has somehow always jumped the town's boundaries.

THE FRATERNITY

Jim soon had a well-defined and well-interpreted picture of Holly-wood and the abnormal underworld which here existed closer to the surface than anywhere else in America. It was said that of all the handsome leading men all but a few were abnormal and even these few were under constant surveillance by the others, waiting for a single indication to include them in the fraternity.

— Gore Vidal, *The City and the Pillar* [83]

When it became widely known in Hollywood that Cary Grant and Randolph Scott (who had been lovers for years) were leaving their wives on weekends to spend private time together at their beach house, RKO executives, fearing that the gossip would leak beyond the industry borders, gave Grant an ultimatum: He must choose between continuing the relationship with Scott and having his contract renewed.[84] In contrast, when Janet Gaynor and Mary Martin, who were also lovers, took a vacation together (leaving their homosexual husbands at home), fan magazines considered it "charming for them to enjoy some time for 'girl talk'"—as their desire to be alone was naively dubbed. Gender ambiguity and "romantic friendships"[85] such as female stars could enjoy without suspicion were verboten for male stars, who were pressured to conform to the "red-blooded" image of virility that Hollywood manufactured and marketed.

But the film colony was a bohemian and artistic world that offered unprecedented opportunities for gay expression.[86] As William Mann has pointed out in *Behind the Scenes,* men with gay sensibilities were well represented among the shapers of early Hollywood—as set and costume designers as well as actors, directors, and screenwriters.[87] Nevertheless, the coercion to be discreet, to play the movie game, was severe. The male gay "underworld," as Gore Vidal characterized it, may have "existed [in Hollywood] closer to the surface than anywhere else in America"; but before the 1950s (when women, too, started to come under suspicion and scrutiny), it was far more important for gay and unstraight men than it was for lesbians and unstraight women to keep the secrets of their extraordinary world hidden from those outside the industry enclave. Even inside Hollywood, gay men were often much more nervous than their female counterparts. Noel Coward, who had come to Hollywood from London to write screenplays, warned his friend, the aspiring photographer Cecil Beaton, "Your sleeves are too tight, your voice is too high and precise. You mustn't do it. It closes so many doors . . . I take ruthless stock of myself in the mirror before going out. A polo jumper or unfortunate tie exposes one to danger."[88]

Malcolm Boyd, who worked as a publicist and producer, recalls being forced to similar discretions: "If you wanted to stay, the rules were quite clear. I didn't let my guard down." When gay men did relax their guard, they paid for it with anxiety, Boyd suggests; he recalls a romantic dinner in a restaurant following an afternoon in bed with a lover: "I wasn't thinking, and we were actually holding hands. Then one of the top journalists in town walked up, with his wife. I felt panicked. I woke up fast. It killed the romance—the entire night was ruined. I had let my guard down."[89]

Leonard Spigelgass, a screenwriter, observed that within the industry enclave there was an "awful ambivalence" about male homosexuality. It "was held in major contempt." And yet it was also "the most exclusive club." Those who were strictly straight in Hollywood were kept out of it—to their ostensible envy, because they were thus barred from the cultured world of Cole Porter, Larry Hart, George Cukor, Somerset Maugham, and Noel Coward: "On the one hand, if you said, 'They're homosexual,' 'Oh, my, isn't that terrible' was the reaction," Spigelgass recalled. "On the other hand, if you said, 'My God, the other night I was at dinner with Cole Porter,' the immediate reaction was, 'What did he have on? What did he say? Were you at the party? Were you at one of those Sunday Brunches?'"[90]

If any suspicion of homosexual behavior leaked out beyond Hollywood, the popular media could be merciless in its language of shock and disgust. When the director William Desmond Taylor arrived in Hollywood in 1915, he kept his private life discreet to the point that he was considered "mysterious"; but his houseman was arrested in Westlake Park for procuring boys whose services only the director could afford.[91] When an unknown assailant murdered Taylor in 1922, panicked Paramount representatives, fearing that an investigation would reveal Taylor's homosexuality, hurried to the murder scene. Desperate to avoid a scandal, they tried to remove all gay traces before the police arrived. According to some accounts, they even planted "evidence" suggesting that Taylor had numerous girlfriends.[92] But they could not avert the suspicions of the popular media. Newspapers around the country reported that Taylor belonged to an "unnatural love cult . . . comprised entirely of men";[93] that his houseman and his former secretary were "both said to be 'queer persons'"[94] and that Taylor's companions were "people of doubtful character—men who sew and crochet and embroider, women of queer reputation."[95] There was also much speculation about whether Taylor was "abnormal himself." The newspapers angrily complained of a Hollywood cover-up when the *Los Angeles Times* suppressed the rumors about Taylor's homosexuality: "It is quite true the movie world would prefer the thing handled in silence, even ignored," one reporter declared. "The movie interests would spend millions of dollars not to catch the murderers; but to prevent the real truth from coming out, to avert the exposure of Hollywood, to squelch before it is born the scandal of the century."[96]

The reporter was right about the studios' willingness to pay those with the power "to prevent the real truth from coming out": The Motion Picture Production Association made generous "contributions" to city officials; moonlighting police officers were hired to guard movie productions at good salaries. They helped the studios continue to hush up scandals for at least the next half-century: As an L.A. police historian, Joe Domanick, points out, studios "needed to protect [their] stars and other key players from career-destroying scandals. . . . Carousing wild men like Errol Flynn and homosexual stars were constantly being picked up by the LAPD, but never booked."[97]

Behind-the-scenes connections could not, of course, protect every star. Suspicions of homosexuality caused a mini-riot in El Porto, a small beach community south of Los Angeles, where the movie star William Haines and his lover Jimmy Shields had summered for years and hosted parties for their gay film friends. The Hollywood trade-paper columns had factually noted such parties: "George Cukor, Billy Haines, and a lot of others are week-ending at Laguna these week-ends";[98] but the small beach community was not as blasé as Hollywood appeared to be. In the summer of 1936, Haines, Shields, and several friends (Cukor possibly among them) were attacked by a mob that alleged Shields had molested a minor. The crowd hurled tomatoes at the men, beat them, and booted them out of town. The scandal effectively ended Haines' career. To protect his own reputation, Cukor ceased to see Haines for years; Shields left the country for a time.[99] Hollywood gay elders remember to this day the horror of "Billy Haines being tarred and feathered out at the beach."[100]

But despite the dangers outside of Hollywood, "the fraternity" was ubiquitous within Hollywood. In 1932, the columnist for the "Hollywood Lowdown" snickered, "Discretion forbids particular mention of names in this case, but at least two prominent young men of the films owe their rapid rise to such arrangement with older men in the picture game who are not averse to helping young boys along."[101] Harry Hay, a gay man who was an actor in the 1930s, recalled that "the sexual path to the screen was more than fifty per cent," though he added that, in his experience, gay social connections could be as valuable as sexual ones: "I knew a couple of producers from underground gay scenes and got parts occasionally from them—never from my agent."[102] The career of Ralph Graves, a handsome silent-screen actor, was also helped along by gay connections—though Graves himself was unstraight rather than gay. He admitted to the film historian Anthony Slide that he'd "been in bed with a couple of fairies," including Noel Coward and Somerset Maugham during their Hollywood stints; and that he'd spent "two years of my life, every day, every night" in an "unholy relationship" with the comedy director Mack Sennett.[103] A young Tyrone Power, according to his biographer, "was approached by several wealthy homosexuals" when he first hit Hollywood, and he became a "kept boy,"[104] as Gary Cooper was said to have been in the 1920s.[105] Though male homosexuality was met with opprobrium by the outside world, within a secret Hollywood enclave, men who were open to it had a decided advantage.

⌐

Paradoxically, as despised as male homosexuality was in much of America, gay style, as it was presented through Hollywood personalities, had an influence on American men, just as lesbian style did on American women. Perhaps the most notable purveyor of gay style in the early decades of the twentieth century was Rudolph Valentino. "The Great Lover," as he was known, was so attractive to women fans that a top-selling brand of condoms was hopefully named "Sheik," after his eponymous role in *The Sheik* (1921). But women were not the only ones who found him attractive, as one of his contemporaries coyly suggested in describing "the spell Valentino cast over the entire female population—and some others."[106]

Valentino's style—his clothes, his grooming—were iconographically queer, and they created an absolute panic among homophobes, as a *Chicago Tribune* column revealed in 1925 when Valentino visited Chicago wearing what the writer sardonically described as "a symphony in green." But Valentino's green suit was only one of his items of apparel that caused the *Chicago Tribune* columnist to write hysterically, "Our gorge rises; our back hair prickles; we want to chew tobacco and spit; we want to . . . assert our masculinity." There was also the beaver collar on Valentino's coat and his slave bracelet. "What in the name of all things masculine is a slave bracelet?" the writer wailed. The worst of Valentino's offenses against butch America, according to the column, was that he was a style-setter, and his style was decidedly gay:

> It gives us a horrible sinking feeling at the pit of the stomach to know that within the next few days tailors and clothing stores will be swamped with requests for green suits, that overcoat buyers will demand beaver collars, that jewelers will be besought for slave bracelets— whatever they are—"just like Valentino's" (spoken with a lisp). Sadly we acknowledge to ourselves that this will happen.[107]

The following year, when Valentino's style-setting did not abate, he was again attacked in the *Chicago Tribune,* where the writer opined, in a column titled "Pink Powder Puffs," that someone ought to "quietly drown" Valentino because he encouraged men not only to pomade their hair but also to powder their faces. Valentino's deleterious influence, the columnist insisted, was even responsible for the installation of powder vending machines in men's washrooms, where men could now "hold a kerchief beneath the spout, pull the lever, then take the pretty pink stuff and pat it on their cheeks in front of the mirror!" If one had to choose between male and female homosexual styles, the writer concluded with angry resignation, "better a rule by masculine women than by effeminate men."[108] Valentino's justified fury at the *Chicago Tribune* column created only another occasion for media mockery. Even the *Los Angeles Times* sneered at the actor's effeminacy with comments about his "pounding, indignant heart beneath a fresh gardenia," and headlines such as "Rudy's So Sore, It's Just Awful" and "Why, He Wants to Fight Duel with Vile Detractor."[109]

Valentino's threat to the nation's masculinity was exacerbated by various rumors about his affairs with his fellow actor Ramon Novarro and later with the French actor André Daven.[110] His wives, Jean Acker and Natacha Rambova, had both been romantically involved with Alla Nazimova (who was said to have orchestrated their marriages to Valentino);[111] and both his wives' sexuality and gender behavior (Jean Acker drove a motorcycle) helped to fuel further speculation that he himself was gay. It was also widely known in Hollywood that Acker did not spend her honeymoon night with Valentino, and that she left him the day after her marriage to resume a lesbian relationship with Grace Darmond.[112] The only other well-publicized "heterosexual relationship" Valentino had in Hollywood was with Pola Negri, who, after a dramatically staged mourning for him when he died, went on to live the rest of her life in a lesbian relationship.[113] Though the jury is still out among Valentino biographers about whether the actor was truly gay,[114] the popular press had little doubt that he was, and that his flamboyant style, rooted in homosexuality, was posing a clear threat to the traditional definition of the American male.

LAVENDER COUPLING

. . . our neuter relationship
(Publicized as "super" in Movieland):
So—between films, while he romped with men . . .

I drew plans and built a new suite
Apart from my would-be mate. . . .
("On your left, you see the great movie star's
Gorgeous Garden of Alla without an 'h'.")

— From Alla Nazimova's 1926 poem, "Not That It Matters,"
on her "lavender marriage" with the actor Charles Bryant[115]

Already by 1921, in the wake of the Fatty Arbuckle scandal about his alleged rape and murder of a young woman, studios were beginning to include a "morality clause" in their contracts; in effect, these clauses said that "an actor who commits any act tending to offend or outrage public morals and decency will be given five days' notice of the cancellation of his contract."[116] Though the morality clause was instituted in response to heterosexual wrongdoing, homosexuals had reason to fear it. Once the movies became a wildly lucrative business, studio bosses, who had a great deal to lose monetarily if a star's personal life "offended or outraged" the fans, became absolutely dictatorial about the public image of their stars, on screen as well as off. The studio bosses believed that in return for fat contracts, their stars were under obligation to appear—if not actually to be—"moral." If homosexuality was immoral in the mind of the general public, gay and lesbian actors needed to convince the public that they were straight, even to the extent of concocting pap for the media about their personal lives.[117]

Fan magazines adored articles about who was dating or marrying or pining for whom, and actors were usually happy to cooperate, whether or not their romances were real. The straight storybook love affairs gay actors invented not only kept them from coming under fire but also garnered great publicity, which was life's blood to Hollywood stars. Lesley Ferris dates bogus Hollywood couplings back to the 1920s, suggesting that the studios were as desperate then as they were in later decades "to cover up and divert attention from same-sex relationships."[118] Hollywood insiders adopted an extensive secret vocabulary to describe publicity pairings that involved nonheterosexuals, such as "twilight tandems," "beards," "front dating," and "lavender marriages."

Some of these actors married repeatedly. Cary Grant, his long-term affair with Randolph Scott notwithstanding, was married five times, generally in great unhappiness.[119] Tyrone Power's two marriage attempts were likened by his biographer to the attempts of a light-skinned black person to "pass." While married, Power patronized Smitty Hanson, a discreet gay hustler who was trusted by a number of Hollywood actors.[120] The more successful a gay or unstraight actor became, the more intense grew studio (and self-imposed) pressures on him or her to hide true proclivities. But Hollywood front marriages were not limited to the actors. Even a power player such as Mike Connolly, whose "Rambling Reporter" column could make or break reputations, might feel the pressure. Connolly, a gay man, often made homophobic quips in his columns, such as referring to gay men on Fairfax Avenue, a predominantly Jewish neighborhood, as "gefilte swish." Connolly had lived in a long-term relationship with another man, but, inspired by the successful ruse of Rock Hudson's front marriage to Phyllis Gates, the lesbian secretary of his agent, Connolly, too, arranged to marry a woman friend. He called off the "engagement" when he realized it would bring more attention to his homosexuality rather than less: A rival columnist had queried, "Which columnist with a raised pinky is going to shock all of Hollywood and get married?"[121]

Male actors, even those who played character roles, could never afford to risk fandom's knowledge of their homosexuality, though character actresses felt freer. The comedian Patsy Kelly, for instance, whose walk was characterized by one fan magazine writer as being "as near a sailor's roll as the swagger of an old salt,"[122] dared to declare in the fan magazine *Motion Picture* that she had been living for several years with another actress, Wilma Cox. Obviously, she was not free to use the "L" word in the 1930s, but she could say that the home she'd made with Wilma was decorated in blue and white because those were Wilma's favorite colors; that instead of dating, "often Wilma and I have a few folks in for the evening," and that she had no thoughts of marrying because "I'm having too much fun as I am. . . . I like my life. I'm happy."[123] No male actor would dare make such declarations in the 1930s.

The screen director, Dorothy Arzner, who appeared on sets almost always in virtual drag, openly attributed her ability as a director to her "masculine characteristics," as she told *Motion Picture Studio Insider* in 1937.[124] Though she, too, certainly never admitted in print to being a lesbian—no one among her contemporaries did, except for the author of *The Well of Loneliness*—neither did she feel compelled to hide the fact that she had lived for almost half a century, until death did them part, with a woman, Marion Morgan, who was the director of a highly successful dance troupe and choreographer of Arzner's first four films.[125] Though Arnzer was not totally unscathed by her openness (Lucille Ball's biographer claims that Ball was "embarrassed by widespread gossip about Miss Arzner's lesbianism" and was unhappy about working with her),[126] nevertheless, by virtue of her "masculinity," Arzner was taken seriously in what was considered a man's profession. She was the only woman to have a significant career behind the megaphone from the 1920s to the 1940s.

Though androgyny was sometimes part of their appeal, glamour actresses usually strove to make the public think of them as heterosexual—notwithstanding Tallulah Bankhead's revisionist wisecrack in the 1950s that she became "a Lez" when she was younger "because I needed the publicity. I had to get a job, [and] in the '20s and '30s, a Lesbian was tops in desirability, especially with a girlfriend as a side dish."[127] Alla Nazimova realized that—in contradiction to the complex sexuality she communicated through her screen image—she had to pretend for the fans that in "real life" she was uncomplicated and traditional. For years she claimed to be married to actor Charles Bryant, though the marriage was never legalized and Bryant apparently preferred his own sex, as Nazimova's 1926 poem suggests (see above). She felt compelled to take publicity photos that showed her sitting on Bryant's knee, leaning against his shoulder, and smiling up at him in adoration.[128] When Nazimova forgot herself, acting out too publicly her lesbian relationship with Glesca Marshall, the "Rambling Reporter" reminded her, through a snide reference to "a certain foreign actress" and her "wife," that indiscretion robbed her of the charm of mystery.[129]

Gay and lesbian actors who were buddies sometimes paired up, genuinely liking one another enough to spend years of their lives cohabiting, though continuing to have homosexual relationships that were well hidden from the fans. The silent-screen star Lilyan Tashman, whose lesbian life has been documented by several Hollywood historians,[130] was married to gay actor Edmund Lowe. Together they were the darlings of the fan magazines and gossip columnists, cooperating often for articles such as *Photoplay's* "How to Hold a Husband/Wife in Hollywood":

> He: "I like elegance. There's always a delicate odor of sachet about my shirts and handkerchiefs. Lilyan puts it there."
>
> She: "A woman can easily learn how to make herself attractive, how to make her home attractive."[131]

Sleek and sophisticated Tashman, who was described by the movie magazine writer Gladys Hall as "the most gleaming, glittering, moderne, hard-surfaced, and distingué woman in all of Hollywood," even told Hall in a 1931 interview about her joyous anticipation of "maternity, nursing bottles, formulas, layettes, obstetricians, and teething problems."[132] She never gave birth to a child. As the Hollywood historian William Mann explains about such public pretense, stars like Tashman and Lowe were merely following "the protocol of the times."[133] They accepted the fact that their Hollywood careers demanded they play the movie game by appearing to be heterosexual, regardless of where they fell on the Kinsey Scale.

But even stars who resisted the game were made a party to it: Not even Greta Garbo, who was notoriously disgusted by the media's attempts to pry into her personal business, could escape. In the privacy of Hollywood, Garbo made little attempt to mask her life. Aldous Huxley recalled the first time he went to Garbo's home, where he met her lesbian lover, Mercedes de Acosta, and then Garbo herself, "dressed like a boy."[134] In the early 1930s, Garbo permitted her affair with Mercedes, as well as her perpetual transvestism, to be common Hollywood knowledge. The *Hollywood Reporter* regularly ran items such as "Greta Garbo buys men's suits for herself—from Watson, the Tailor,"[135] and discussed her "self-made man" look. The "Rambling Reporter" called Garbo "ambidextrous," referred to Mercedes as her "new love," and noted her visits to "lavender" speakeasies.[136] When Mercedes de Acosta was replaced in Garbo's affections by Salka Viertel, the *Hollywood Reporter* even carried an item hinting at their triangle.[137]

But such gossip seldom escaped the confines of Hollywood, and Garbo's letters to Mercedes show that she worked to keep hints of their relationship from leaking out to fandom. Garbo's nervousness about being "outed" outside of Hollywood was so intense that she often admonished Mercedes with words such as "You must not put my name on any letter. . . . And please be sure to glue envelopes well together as your letters usually come opened."[138]

The fan magazines were complicitous in keeping Garbo's secret because they knew that moviegoers wanted desperately to believe that Hollywood's hottest star was uncomplicatedly and romantically heterosexual, and they were overjoyed when they were able to report an ostensible affair between Garbo and John Gilbert. (Gilbert claimed privately that when he proposed marriage to Garbo, her response was, "Ah, you don't want to marry one of the fellows.")[139] Garbo did have heterosexual relationships—most biographers agree in placing the director Reuben Mamoulian, the conductor Leopold Stokowski, and the actor Brian Aherne among her lovers; but in their zealousness, fan magazines as well as gossip columnists for the nontrade papers also matched her with her gay male buddies. Hedda Hopper, writing in the *Los Angeles Times,* for instance, exuded about Garbo's road trip with the health guru, Gayelord Hauser (who was, in fact, in a long-term domestic relationship with another man, Frey Brown): "Those marriage rumors are again being revived. I do know that [Greta and Gayelord] took a picnic lunch and spent the whole day sitting together on a piece of land, trying to make up their minds whether a home should be built on it."[140]

As years went by and Garbo married no one, the fan magazines, scrambling for an explanation to give their readers, put out the word that it was because she never got over a youthful love for the Swedish director Mauritz Stiller (who was dead and had been gay).[141] "Why is it that the most alluring woman on the screen today has never married? What strange reason exists which keeps the most excitingly beautiful Garbo from committing matrimony?" one fan magazine asked, then informed readers that "the answer to the riddle of why Garbo never married . . . [despite her romance with John Gilbert] that thrilled the whole world" was to be found "in that far away grave in Sweden."[142] It is not improbable that Greta

Garbo's famous wish to "be alone" was born of her disgust with such constant attempts to place her in heterosexual dyads, her distaste for the movie game, and her fear that the public would discover that her real predilections were much more complex than *Photoplay* could process.

A LOSING GAME

"I think a woman wants to be dominated by a man. Men are much cleverer than women. A dominating woman cannot be happy."

—Marlene Dietrich, *Los Angeles Herald Examiner*, July 15, 1951

During the postwar years, while Joseph McCarthy baited reds and gays and women trotted back to nurseries and kitchens, the movies and the tastes of fans changed dramatically. As Gary Carey observed in his biography of Louis B. Mayer: "More and more pictures were dedicated to upholding the dignity of motherhood, family life, and other sacred values of middle-class America."[143] The girlish foppery of Armand as played by both Rudolph Valentino and Robert Taylor in Hollywood productions of *Camille* (1921 and 1936) would have caused bloody riots in the movie houses of the 1950s. The studios would have thought it suicidal in the 1950s to make films such as *Morocco* or *Queen Christina* in which the leading ladies were dressed as men. In 1937, Hepburn's "hoydenish" appearance[144] was considered charming by the fans, but twenty years later, in 1957, the fan magazines were complaining that "she allowed herself to be photographed without make-up . . . and, even worse, dressed hideously in mannish garb—sloppy slacks, sweaters, and men's trousers and suits."[145] Androgynous women stars such as Hepburn, Dietrich, and Garbo were out, and superfemmes such as Marilyn Monroe and Jayne Mansfield were in. Gay actors such as Rock Hudson were typed as heterosexual wolves (despite the open secret in Hollywood that he was a homosexual wolf). Gay fans may have continued to discern who was unstraight in Hollywood, but heterosexual moviegoers were more snug than ever in their oblivion, unless, that is, scandal magazines called homosexuality to their attention. The stars and studios did all they could to keep the fans in the dark.

Though actors and actresses had to play the movie game in earlier eras too, in the 1950s it became very serious business: To convince the public of their normality they stooped to such absurd utterances as Dietrich's hypocritical statement, quoted above, about a woman's place. Studios exacerbated the actors' anxieties to appear "normal" by routinely admonishing them that they must be accompanied by a person of the opposite sex at all public appearances, and they must never be seen at gay bars.[146] They must, above all, keep themselves out of the scandal magazines—*Confidential, Whisper, Blast, Uncensored, Rave, Top Secret,* and a host of others—which had suddenly emerged and enjoyed vast circulation in the 1950s. (*Confidential's* readership, for example, was about 5 million in 1957,[147] outstripping both the *Saturday Evening Post* and *Look.*) Unlike the fan magazines, which had avoided stories that readers would find shocking (and thereby protected the stars), the scandal magazines traded in shock. Before the proliferation of scandal magazines, what happened in Hollywood behind high walls and hedges would stay there. But the scandal magazines' staff pounced on the film colony, scaling barriers that could never be fortified enough against them, and produced salacious, career-sabotaging headlines about infidelity, divorce, legal trouble, alcohol and drug problems—and especially about homosexuality, which, in the 1950s, was thought to be more scandalous than all the other topics put together. The actor George Nader, who was part of the mid-1950s gay circle around Rock Hudson, recalls: "We lived in fear of an exposé, or even a veiled suggestion that someone was homosexual. Such a remark would have caused an earthquake at the Studio. Every month, when *Confidential* came out, our stomachs began to turn. Which of us would be in it?"[148]

Hollywood powerbrokers sometimes found ways to protect their "star assets," even gay ones, from the perils of scandal magazines. The agent Henry Willson, himself a homosexual, was one of the most powerful players in 1950s Hollywood, known as the man who "discovered, named, represented, promoted, pimped and protected"[149] a stable of male stars. Willson invented the "postwar hunk," including Tab Hunter, Rock Hudson, Troy Donahue, and dozens more. Not only did Willson hire Los Angeles Police Department (LAPD) off-duty "goons [and] leg-breakers" to silence the ex-lovers of his clients who threatened to sell their stories to the tabloids but he also engaged in deals with those tabloids. For example, he negotiated with *Confidential* in 1955 to protect his prize client, Rock Hudson, from a ruinous gay exposé by feeding them Tab Hunter instead (who had by then left Willson for another agent): Willson informed *Confidential* about a police report on a gay party in Glendale where Hunter had been arrested with twenty-six other men for same-sex dancing.[150] *Confidential* was happy with the exchange: They luridly characterized the incident as a "gay pajama party." (In his memoirs, published when he was seventy-three, Hunter admitted his homosexuality but denied there was anything other than harmless drinking and dancing at that particular party.) But studio heads, too, could and did maneuver to save a star: Hunter found himself "magically" rescued by Harry Weiss, the attorney who, he says, "was on call to agents, producers, and studio bosses."[151]

Gay stars who were not under a powerful protective wing had good reason to be terrified of Robert Harrison, the publisher of *Confidential,* because he was absolutely obsessive in his preoccupation with revealing their homosexuality. According to Steve Govoni, the son of *Confidential*'s managing editor, Harrison would spend many thousands of dollars if necessary to check facts and line up witnesses who would corroborate the stories of Hollywood's homosexual peccadilloes. Govoni claims that the magazine never simply made up a story out of whole cloth. *Confidential,* as well as most of the other scandal magazines, hired spies in moving companies (to tell them who was moving in or out of a dwelling), among sales clerks (who informed them of tidbits such as Dan Dailey's purchase of a dress for his own use), and in houses of prostitution. They had paid informants among waiters and hatcheck girls and hotel maids and bail bondsmen; and they employed an army of private detectives, wiretap experts, and hidden-microphone specialists.[152]

Against such forces, stars were helpless. In the sexually conservative and suspicious 1950s, women were under as much scrutiny as men. Lizabeth Scott was very much a Dietrich type; she had cool, blonde good looks and what Hedda Hopper described in various columns as a "caramel contralto" voice[153] and "a million dollar figure."[154] She was selected in 1946 as one of *Modern Screen* magazine's "Stars of the Month," and she made eighteen pictures in nine years, four of them in 1947. But she was not wily in playing the movie game, and she failed to produce a requisite "beard." In a 1946 article, she claimed to have no time for romance, and by 1949 Dorothy Manners was profiling her before the public as a "confirmed career girl."[155] In a 1951 interview that Hedda Hopper titled "Star By-passes Romance for Career," Scott knew enough not to be entirely dismissive when Hopper snooped for a man in the actress's life: In answer to the question, "What about romance?" Scott replied (much as Patsy Kelley did in the 1930s), "Right now, I'm having a ball, Hedda. I wouldn't give it up for anything"; yet she was quick to add, "Tomorrow is another day. I may meet that certain guy and flip completely."[156] But her attempts to pose as heterosexual were too perfunctory.

Robert Harrison was thus alerted to search for dirt, which he found and blared to millions of readers in a September 1955 *Confidential* article: "Lizabeth Scott in the Call Girls' Call Book." The article presented Scott not only as a lesbian who wore pants and was called "Scotty" but also as a habitué of an exclusive Los Angeles house of prostitution, where she enjoyed the services of "a trio of cuddle-for-cash cuties." Instead of ignoring the article, as Dietrich had done two months earlier when *Confidential* ran a story that exposed her lesbianism ("The Untold Story of Marlene Dietrich"), Lizabeth Scott sued the magazine. Papers around the country carried news of the suit and, of course, the reasons for it. *Confidential's* allegations thus reached not only the magazine's audience but tens of millions of newspaper readers. Scott's career was effectively ended. She made only three more pictures, two in 1957 and one in 1972. It became clear through her fate that stars could no longer assume that their gay secrets would be protected by Hollywood's high walls and hedges.

Fronting in the 1950s: the lesbian and gay "Cufflink Crowd," sitting boy-girl-boy-girl, at a straight nightclub. *Courtesy Tom Gibbon.*

Lovers Tom Gibbon and Bob Clark, members of the "Cufflink Crowd," who were careful never to attend all-male parties. *Courtesy Tom Gibbon.*

CHAPTER 3

L.A. Noir

THE UNDESIRABLES

The door opened silently and I was looking at a tall blond man in a white flannel suit with a violet satin scarf around his neck. There was a cornflower in the lapel of his white coat and his pale blue eyes looked faded out by comparison. The violet scarf was loose enough to show that he wore no tie and that he had a thick soft brown neck, like the neck of a strong woman. . . . He had the general appearance of a lad who would wear a white flannel suit with a violet scarf around his neck and a cornflower in his lapel.

—Raymond Chandler, *Farewell, My Lovely,* 1940[1]

As the 1940s began, Los Angeles literally darkened. Following the 1941 attack on Pearl Harbor, cities on the West Coast instituted blackouts, fearing they would be the next target. City dwellers were instructed to blacken windows and to cover with dark paint their skylights and the top halves of automobile headlights.[2] Wartime cast shadows everywhere. This period that was so dominated by darkness and dark suspicions introduced a long era in which the unfamiliar was despised and persecuted, even by public officials whose job it was to protect. The literary and film style of "noir," marked by shadowy lighting and a theme of urban corruption, reflected a new L.A. reality.

Within weeks after the Pearl Harbor bombing, 23,000 Japanese Americans from Los Angeles alone were sent to relocation camps.[3] But most other minorities too, including homosexuals, were deemed outsiders, dangerous to the "real" citizens of Los Angeles, and they were thus targets for police harassment, false arrest, and beatings. The LAPD even turned a blind eye to assaults by others on these outsiders, allowing, for instance, enlisted servicemen to beat scores of Mexican American youths with impunity during the 1943 "Zoot Suit Riots."[4] Survivors of the era who witnessed both racism and homophobia by the police are hard put to say which was worse. Stella Rush, a white gay woman who was close friends with a black man, recalls their being followed by the police after leaving a gay bar: They were stopped, questioned, and bullied— under suspicion not only that they were "a lezzie and a fairy" but also (simply because they were a black man and a white woman together) that he was a dope pusher and she was his victim, or that he was a pimp and she was a whore.[5]

The LAPD's increasing nervousness about "undesirable" populations was exacerbated by L.A.'s sudden and massive expansion. The war demanded ships and planes. Huge ship-building facilities and aerospace plants such as Lockheed, Douglas, Northrup-Grumman, and Hughes were soon established in the Los Angeles area. Hundreds of thousands of migrants came into L.A. to fill the newly created jobs. More than 230,000 workers, most of them men initially, were employed in the aerospace industry alone.

As the men were drafted into the military, women came to take their places, making more money than ever, wearing pants, learning independence, and generally becoming very different people than they'd been before. With increased job opportunities for women, the number who had the wherewithal to live as lesbians multiplied.[6] Gay male activity in Los Angeles also expanded during the war, as gay men who lived in L.A. at the time attest: Because L.A. has a port and vast numbers of soldiers landed there, far from watchful eyes "back home" and yearning for rest and recreation, they enjoyed unprecedented opportunities for gay experiences. Kenneth Marlowe observes that during wartime Pershing Square "was even gayer than its regular scene. And servicemen who couldn't find an available female date could always find physical satisfaction waiting for them. Many took advantage of it."[7]

The military tried to prevent the inevitable, officers warning their soldiers about big-city homosexual snares before they hit the shore: "We were solemnly told that all the queers in California wore red neckties and hung out at the corner of Hollywood and Vine," a former marine remembers.[8] The military even attempted to keep its men away from L.A. gay spots by posting bold-lettered signs on the doors of the Hollywood Boulevard bars, Slim Gordon's and Bradley's; the downtown bars, the Gay Inn, the Gayway Café, and Smittys; and every other venue they suspected drew a gay crowd (eventually including, for servicewomen, the gay girls' bar, the If Club): "OUT OF BOUNDS TO MILITARY PERSONNEL," the signs proclaimed. But there were many places that military officials missed, and before the war was over, more than a dozen gay bars were doing business on or near Hollywood Boulevard alone. The bars were a huge success with soldiers looking for gay life. For example, at the men's bar of the downtown Biltmore Hotel, which had been a cruising spot even before the war, uniformed soldiers would be "packed three-deep," according to a gay patron.[9]

The war eventually helped to foster the building of permanent homosexual communities in Los Angeles. By one estimate, a quarter million "war migrants," both straight and gay, settled in Los Angeles during the first eight years of the 1940s. When military men and women completed their tours of duty, more came back to Los Angeles than to any other city.[10] Most returned for its sunshine and space and economic opportunities. But servicemen and -women who were gay found L.A. especially attractive because its size promised both anonymity and the possibility of being able to find a community. L.A.'s gay underground expanded greatly with the influx of these new populations, as did places where gay people could meet one another.

For symbolic and functional reasons, the beach was especially attractive to gay people. It represented the very edge of the continent, far away from "back home." It was an ideal cruising ground, where one could legitimately wear minimal clothing and look at others who were similarly unattired. During and after the war, veritable oases of gay life could be found in the open at many Los Angeles beaches, where the atmosphere was celebratory, carnival-like, even lawless.

Lesbians remember congregating and sunning at a stretch of Venice Beach near a popular gay girls bar.[11] In Santa Monica, "Bitch Beach," as it was campily called, was, according to Jim Kepner, "a square mile of lesbians and gay men, being free like nowhere else I'd seen." Gay bars fronted the boardwalk; and lesbians and gay men of the era remember especially the Tropical Village—dubbed "the TV" by its regulars—an indoor-outdoor beach bar with a Polynesian décor that, as Kepner wrote, always attracted a huge crowd, "hunky beach boys in swim trunks, gentlemen in suits and ties—lesbians in equal number, hunky butches, some in male drag, femmes off *Vogue* covers."[12] One patron recalls that the singer Johnny Ray not only drank there, but occasionally stood up and performed for the crowd.[13]

At Muscle Beach in Venice, an open-air seaside gymnasium, Bob Mizer, a shy man who lived with his mother in Los Angeles, found eager models for his Hollywood-studio-style homoerotic photography.[14] Mizer established the Athletic Model Guild (AMG) in 1945. His pictures capitalized on the image of the "California boy," always tanned, frequently blond, and sporting little more than a mischievous grin. Many of his models were gay Hollywood hopefuls, though some—like Steve Reeves, who played Hollywood's Hercules—were straight. In exchange for their modeling services, Mizer supplied them with the photos they needed for their professional pursuits. By advertising his glossy beefcake prints in a magazine that he established, *Physique Pictorial,* Mizer helped to create a huge underground gay market and to sell the promise of a gay male paradise in Los Angeles. *Physique Pictorial* also provided the first national outlet for other gay photographers, including Bruce of Los Angeles, and artists such as Tom of Finland and "Art Bob."[15] Mizer also influenced later gay artists, such as David Hockney, who said that AMG photographs motivated him to settle in Los Angeles and inspired his own famous paintings of blond boys basking in the sun.[16]

Despite Mizer's successes, however, he found himself in trouble with the law. He was arrested on obscenity charges in 1947 and sentenced to six months in prison. The authorities were shocked by his photos of men in Roman wrestler stances with oiled bodies and generously padded posing straps, antique-looking columns in the background, a modern Southern California swimming pool in the foreground.

To Chief of Police William Parker, the galloping growth of the city and the changes it brought in the years after the war were extremely troubling. Joe Domanick, the LAPD historian, observes that Parker nervously gave his police force terse orders: "Confront and command. Control the streets at all times. Always be aggressive. Stop crimes before they happen. Seek them out. Shake them down. Make that arrest."[17] For Los Angeles' gay men and lesbians, along with people of diverse racial and ethnic groups, life became much harder with the advent of Chief Parker ("Wild Bill Parker" gays and lesbians called him)[18] since they were the ones most often being sought out, shaken down, and arrested. Under Chief Parker's ascendancy, arrests for "sex perversion" crimes, involving primarily male homosexuals, jumped dramatically.[19]

For homosexuals, LAPD's persecution had also been exacerbated in the years after the war by the chilling medicalization of their "state" through the influence of the police department's leading criminal psychiatrist, Paul de River. De River believed that homosexuals, men and women, were a grave danger to society: They were seducers of children, he opined, and in their "wild sexual orgies" they even committed murder. In his book *The Sexual Criminal,* which became a text for police officers nationwide, it was claimed that he had examined "carefully and scientifically more sex perverts than any other person in the United States at the present time."[20] He recommended preventative treatment for those he called "sexual criminals" by imposing on them Spartan living, hard work, and—most important of all—electric shock therapy, "a minimum of two shocks a week."[21]

In an article titled "Increase in Sex Crimes Laid to War Influence," the *Los Angeles Times* reported that L.A. police claimed to have accumulated records on "10,000 . . . known sex offenders."[22] Politicians who seemed to believe that persecution of homosexuals gave them political capital encouraged LAPD hounding: Police sweeps of gay bars and arrests of both gay men and lesbians on the streets were invariably worse immediately before elections, as if to demonstrate to the public that the incumbents were "cleaning up" sin and crime. Politicians' war on homosexuals was manifested in other ways as well. An Assembly Subcommittee on Public Morals for Southern California recommended that eight Hollywood and Sunset Strip establishments be closed because they were "gathering places for perverts." The subcommittee also recommended that the legislature "prohibit the sale of liquor in taverns to unescorted women," which meant that bars that catered primarily to gay women would be put out of business entirely.[23] The Los Angeles City Council, mindful of the subcommittee's recommendations, then enacted stringent laws "to drive degenerates out of public places, especially bars."[24]

The politicians, like their henchmen the police, insisted that merely by virtue of their homosexuality all gay people were outlaws. However, the more liberal California Supreme Court ruled against several legislative and police actions regarding gay life and gay venues. For example, when a bar's license was suspended in 1951 because the owner permitted "persons of known homosexual tendencies to congregate," the California Supreme Court "set aside" the suspension, decreeing that homosexuals had the right to patronize an establishment as long as they committed no overt acts of sexual misconduct on the premises.[25] In 1956, the California Legislature tried to challenge the supreme court's decree by passing a law that prohibited the licensing of gay bars on the grounds that they were "resorts for sexual perverts"; but in 1959, the court, citing its earlier finding, declared the 1956 law unconstitutional.[26]

In Los Angeles, too, the court was far more liberal than local politicians and the LAPD. For example, the 1898 city ordinance, passed to prohibit All Fool's Night masquerading, was used by the LAPD in mid-century to prosecute gay men as well as gay women who dressed in drag or in any way that was not considered gender-appropriate: The clothes Marlene Dietrich, Greta Garbo, and Katherine Hepburn wore regularly in the 1930s could have landed a woman a jail sentence during L.A.'s noir years. Arrests under the old ordinance were challenged twice by gay women in 1950: Both actually won their cases, the courts declaring that a woman cannot be found guilty under the ordinance simply because she is wearing "slacks together with a coat similar to that commonly worn by men, plus the fact that her hair is worn short instead of long," unless there is "further evidence of an intent to conceal her identity."[27] But despite the court's declaration, which was published in the Los Angeles Municipal Code book and must surely have been known by the LAPD and the politicians who encouraged them, cross-dressing lesbians continued to be treated as criminals throughout the 1950s: They were harassed, arrested, and thrown into the city jail's "Big Daddy Tank" (just as gay men were thrown in the "Fruit Tank" of the same institution).[28]

THE MEN'S STORY

Young and good-looking policemen . . . go into a gay bar, act as they think a gay fellow should act, and wait for someone to talk to them. They offer someone a ride or accept a ride and that does it. Some of them play fair, inasmuch as they wait for the gay one to make a pass at them, but many others wait only long enough to get in the car before declaring the arrest. The officer's word, of course, will be taken as true, and they always count on the victim not wanting publicity. They know he will pay the fine and be quiet.

—Helen Branson, owner of a 1950s Hollywood gay bar for men[29]

Los Angeles, the newcomers said, was paradise. Jim Weatherford, who came to L.A. from West Virginia, likened it to the tropical island of Aruba, where he had guarded oil refineries during the war. William Bryan, who came from Cleveland, was sold on the balmy weather, which, he says, allowed him to wear his most successful cruising outfit, a Milkes-brand athletic undershirt, year-round. Malcolm Boyd, who entered the city via the broad boulevards and manicured gardens of Beverly Hills before finding a cramped Hollywood room for $5 a week, called it Babylon.[30] But while Los Angeles was a virtual paradise for post–World War II gay newcomers from other parts of the country, it held distinct danger.

Marvin Edwards remembers one night in 1950 when he learned first-hand about the danger. He'd arrived the year before from Detroit with

Dorr Legg, his older lover, who would soon become a legendary homophile organizer. When they parted after about a year together in Los Angeles, Edwards began to frequent a bar they'd previously visited as a couple: the Crown Jewel, located in downtown L.A., on 8th Street near Olive, not far from the central public library. Outside, over the door, a glowing neon crown beckoned. Patrons recall the bar as dark, elegantly appointed, and popular. Those who were respectably employed in downtown offices regularly packed the place after work. In contrast to rougher gay bars in the area, the Crown Jewel had a coat-and-tie dress code that customers were expected to follow.

That night in 1950 when Edwards returned to the Crown Jewel, he struck up a long conversation with an attractive man, and eventually they left the bar together. They weren't aware of it, but officers of the Los Angeles Police Department tailed the two men to Edwards' rented cottage. Edwards was lucky to be spared the worst of the traumas that many gay men endured at mid-century—arrest, booking, pleading, sentencing, and even jail time. But the officers informed his landlady that he'd brought a man to spend the night under her roof. She told Edwards that she could not tolerate that sort of thing. He would, of course, have to leave. Homeless, young Edwards left L.A. permanently.[31]

Harassment such as Edwards suffered was common. As Mike Rothmiller reports in his book *L.A. Secret Police,* officers were given specific orders to "go after" homosexuals.[32] Vice Squad officers often staked out homosexual bars, both gay and lesbian, and wreaked havoc on the lives of the patrons. Sometimes they raided the bars, carting selected patrons to the police station. Sometimes Vice Squad officers noted the license plate numbers of cars parked near a bar and informed the hapless patrons' employers. Job loss was common in such cases, and for those whose contracts included "morals clauses," such as teachers, or those who worked in L.A.'s booming aerospace industry, which required a security clearance, entire careers could be lost.

Harassment was only one of the techniques that the Vice Squad used to carry out its homophobic policies. Entrapment, such as that described by men's gay bar owner Helen Branson, was the squad's most pernicious method. Law enforcement departments across the country practiced entrapment, using undercover officers to respond to and even solicit sexual come-ons, which would permit them to make an arrest. But LAPD officers were said by victims to excel in this cruel practice because "Hollywood rejects," attractive would-be actors who failed to find work in the movies, were employed by the vice squad to carry out entrapment scams.[33] Their looks and histrionic training enabled them to play the role of decoy especially effectively, as those who were fooled by them still remember.[34]

Some undercover Vice Squad officers became known among gay men, who would caution one another about familiar faces. Tom Gibbon says he narrowly escaped an all-too-typical nightmare one afternoon in the early 1950s: "I was at a bar called Johnny Frenchman's in Malibu. I'd had a few belts and went to use the can." On his way, he spotted two good-looking men sitting at a table who, he thought, had been previously pointed out to him as being from the LAPD Hollywood Division Vice Squad. He recalls that while he was using the small restroom's toilet, "suddenly I hear this voice say, 'Hi, how ya doing?'" His instinctive feeling was that it was one of the Vice Squad officers:

> I immediately thought, "Oh shit! There it goes—the job, the whole thing." When I leave the toilet, I'm careful not to look directly, because that can mean immediate trouble, but out of the corner of my eye I can see that the guy was standing at the urinal, jacking. As I head for the door, he turns, dick hard, and stands in my way. So if I try to leave the bathroom, I'd actually have to touch it, which would be a sure arrest. I didn't know what I was going to do. Somehow, I pushed his shoulder and threw him off balance just long enough to get out of there.[35]

When Gibbon made his way back to the bar, the bartender belatedly tipped him off that the man who had been in the restroom with him was indeed a Vice Squad officer.

Stanley Markowitz was not so astute and thus not so lucky. Markowitz recalls a 1957 incident at the Hollywood Greyhound station: "There was a very good-looking guy standing at the urinal, pulling on himself. He started asking was I a student." When Markowitz admitted that he took classes at Los Angeles City College, the man mentioned the names of specific teachers and spoke of the classes he had recently taken at the college. "I thought for sure he was a student. When he asked what I liked to do with guys, I told him. And bam—out came the cuffs. I bolted, ran smack into a wall. Broke my wrist, but still got arrested."[36] He later found out that the man was a legendary undercover officer, especially prized by the Vice Squad for his ability to gain the trust of gay men and to lead them into admitting their homosexuality—for which he would arrest them.

Charges might be trumped up with no provocation against men whom Vice Squad officers found in places the LAPD knew as "resorts of homosexuals." Rudy Ruano, a Guatemalan who aspired to become a ballet dancer, moved to Los Angeles where he quickly discovered the gay bars. One night he was in a crowded bar: "This gorgeous man came over and started talking to me. Absolutely gorgeous," Ruano remembers. Naïve to potential danger, he appreciated both the attention and the chance to practice his English. "He bought me a beer, then a second one. After an hour and a half, we were talking so much, then he said, 'Excuse me, I'll be right back.'" The man left and, moments later, returned with several uniformed police officers. "He said, 'This one and this one, and you'—pointing at me."

On the word of his accuser, an undercover Vice Squad officer, Ruano was jailed in the Glass House, the newly constructed downtown police station. Unable to afford an attorney, he endured two terrifying days waiting for a public defender. She urged him to plea-bargain. She told him the officer said that Ruano had proposed performing oral copulation on him. "I couldn't believe it. I told her, 'I can hardly speak English that well.' She said, 'It's your word against his.' So I agreed. They changed the status of my charge from lewd conduct to disturbing the peace." Ruano managed to stay employed and productive, but he feels that the arrest imposed four decades of anxiety on his life. "It's been difficult for me to arrange citizenship because of that. I want to become a citizen, but because of that little thing, it caused a lot of damage."[37]

"Entrapment was absolutely common," Duncan Donovan says, recalling many friends who suffered that fate throughout the 1950s and '60s.

Donovan remembers that frequently the phone rang late at night in the house he shared with his partner, Thomas Patrick, the deputy district attorney for Los Angeles County. "Always some young man who'd gotten picked up in a park, in a bar, in a restroom. We'd get up, get dressed, and drive across the county to help him out." Though Patrick was, of course, closeted, as his job required, his name was known as someone who could be of assistance to gay men in trouble. According to Donovan, Patrick would counsel men about whether they needed legal aid and how to deal with their arraignments. In doing so, he knew that he was taking an enormous career risk. But he had won some of the city's most explosive cases, such as the 1951 "Bloody Christmas" scandal, in which eight LAPD officers were indicted for severely beating Latino detainees; and he banked on his clout in the DA's office to help him survive those risks.[38]

But most gay men who were arrested in L.A. were not lucky enough to have Patrick's assistance. Jack had been an award-winning teacher in the Pasadena School District in the 1950s. But because he was arrested on a "Vag Lewd" charge, he lost not only his job but also the right ever to teach again, anywhere. Not yet forty, he moved hundreds of miles away to run a family motel, the only work he could find. His profession, his friends—his entire life—were virtually wiped out.[39] John Rechy remembers a friend, new to gay life, who was also ruined. Ed, who had never before had a gay sexual relationship, went to his first gay bar where he met a man who began flirting with him. When Ed suggested they "get together," the man, a Vice Squad officer, arrested him for solicitation. Rechy's friend was taken to jail. The judge before whom he appeared declared him mentally unstable. Ed was forcibly institutionalized and not permitted to communicate with anyone for six months. In the mental institution, he was threatened with shock therapy. "He was forever emotionally branded," Rechy says, "and he became a recluse for the rest of his life."[40]

Gay people who were brought to court could be in very serious trouble. Until 1975, oral and anal sex were felonies in California. Oral sex could be punishable by up to fifteen years in prison; anal sex could earn an offender a life sentence. But the most common charge against gay men was "lewd and lascivious conduct"—"Vag Lewd" under antivagrancy statutes. The notorious section 674 of the California Penal Code was termed by the gay press in the 1960s as "the catch-all that catches all."[41] Two subdivisions of 647 particularly targeted gay men: 647(a) prohibited soliciting or engaging in lewd or dissolute conduct, and 647(d) prohibited loitering in or around a public toilet for the purpose of soliciting or engaging in lewd or dissolute conduct. (The other subdivisions addressed prostitution and begging.) Though 647 offenses were misdemeanors, those convicted under the statute were required to register as sex offenders for the rest of their lives. Gay men of that era say that a 674 arrest was often tantamount to "being ruined." Some tell stories about their depression and alcoholism following such an arrest. Some remember the suicides of others who had been arrested.

Defendants who plea-bargained in 647 arrests were usually given two years' probation and were forbidden to associate with known homosexuals or frequent places where known homosexuals congregate. So intimidated were gay men at mid-century that many believed that even private gay gatherings were illegal: Some Angelenos of that era tell stories of jumping out of the windows of private homes if the LAPD arrived at a gay party, as police sometimes did with the excuse that neighbors had complained of loud music or drunkenness.

Sometimes, arrests were the result not of entrapment but rather police discovery of real homosexual trysts in semipublic places. To gay men, these midnight-hour encounters could seem safer than bringing a sexual partner home, where one risked the discomforts and dangers of being turned in by snoopy neighbors. L.A.'s gay hunting grounds became legendary for the ease with which men found each other for connection and release. The homosexual poet Hart Crane, visiting California in the 1920s, declared of Pershing Square: "The number of faggots cruising around here is legion." (Crane even encountered a movie personality who regularly made homosexual contact in Pershing Square.)[42] The square had a "national reputation" among gay men,[43] and visitors staying at the adjacent Biltmore Hotel knew through the gay grapevine that they would find what they were looking for in the Pershing Square underbrush. For years, in daylight hours, too, as one 1960s writer observed, the Square continued to be a premier homosexual spot, and it even attracted tourists who would "come down and walk through it just to see all the loud, swishing, painted queens who were parading noisily up and down the walk and carrying on with vile disregard for the 'other people.'"[44]

L.A.'s year-round good weather and growing gay population made possible the establishment of numerous outdoor trysting places, such as Echo Park Lake, Westlake Park, and North Hollywood Park. At Griffith Park, which encompasses five square miles, wild orgies involving scores of men were common. The orgies could even take place in daylight because Griffith Park had vast areas where the overgrown scrub provided a venue that was like a veritable outdoor gay bathhouse for "sex-hunters," as John Rechy calls them. Rechy, who explored gay cultures all over America in his autobiographical novel *City of Night,* observes now that he knew of no other city in the 1960s "that had a daytime scene as thriving as Los Angeles did in Griffith Park."[45] The LAPD often made arrests in such semipublic trysting places, but they could not dent the exuberant gay male eroticism there for long because as the numbers of gay men in L.A. continued to increase, the Vice Squad could not keep up.

Aside from the men's semipublic sexual encounters, there is no question that acts that were considered to be merely a social nuisance when engaged in by heterosexuals were treated as criminal when engaged in by homosexuals. Straight couples caught petting in a park or a "lovers' lane," for example, were likely to be shooed away, but gay couples were inevitably arrested. Even the most innocuous behavior was criminalized. At mid-century, bars that catered to lesbians and gay men could be shut down by the LAPD if same-sex couples were dancing there, or even simply sitting with an arm around a shoulder. To evade such harassment, at mixed gay-and-lesbian bars such as the Canyon Club in Topanga Canyon it was understood by the patrons that if the Vice Squad should make an appearance on the property, the management would flash lights on the dance floor to signal to the same-sex couples that they must switch to a partner of the opposite sex.[46] At Gino's, a gay club in Hollywood, an advance warning system would change the music selection to the "Star Spangled Banner," which effectively ended dancing.

Gay men learned that not only would they be persecuted by the police (who called them "fruits"),[47] but that even in direst need they could not count on them for protection. Steve Hodel, a retired LAPD homicide detective, recalls one of the worst examples, which happened in the 1960s: A gay man who had been stabbed called the police as he was dying. The responding LAPD officer ridiculed the man's vocal mannerisms and mocked his dying breaths. The policeman was not disciplined, Hodel says, even though his unprofessionalism and cruelty were captured and preserved on tape.[48] Gay men could not escape the knowledge that the LAPD regarded them not only as laughable but also as ultimate criminals. Even those who were blackmailed often felt they had nowhere to turn. Without recourse to justice, it was not uncommon that they would be bled broke.[49]

The Crown Jewel, the downtown bar in which Vice Squad officers spotted Marvin Edwards and then tailed him and his new friend, was owned by Harry Weiss, the proprietor of two other gay bars and a lawyer since 1941. In the 1950s and '60s, Weiss regularly defended gay men who were arrested for homosexual activity. Though he was himself homosexual, many gay men perceived him as being unsympathetic to the plight of his clients. According to Tom Gibbon and James Miller, who knew the mid-century L.A. gay scene well, Weiss had friends in high places, from the police department on up, and there were widespread rumors about the intricate complicity between Weiss and the law.[50] Gibbon and Miller believe to this day that, in true "noir" fashion, Weiss often tipped off officers about whom to arrest; then arresting officers handed their prey a business card bearing attorney Weiss' name and number; and—to complete the circle—Weiss kicked back part of his substantial legal fees to the arresting officers.

Though Weiss was closeted, his flamboyance—including a penchant for white linen suits, fine fedoras, and other affectations—made his homosexuality evident to those in the know, even judges. Bill Regan recalls an incident in which a judge in open court referred to Weiss as "the faggot lawyer," meaning not only that he defended "faggots" but also that he was himself one.[51] But gay men in trouble put aside their worries and flocked to him. They grudgingly agree that he was effective. Weiss was "the top gay attorney," says Aristide Laurent. "He had a bad reputation, but he also had a reputation for being well connected, which meant your best chance for beating the charges."[52] He was "the go-to guy [for] all the boys who were arrested," recalls Guy Richards. "He'd help them get out of jail; then he'd go to the judge and say, 'due to lack of evidence currently available,' or some such thing, until he got the case postponed and postponed—and finally got the judge that he wanted: another queen." If the judge that Weiss managed to have assigned to the case was indeed a gay male crony, Weiss would campily tell his client, according to Richards, "*She'll* save you."[53]

Despite the various criticisms of Weiss among gay men, his business flourished, for it was not easy to find an attorney in Los Angeles who would help a gay man in trouble. Perhaps most attorneys were reluctant to take gay clients because they feared that the stigma of defending an accused sex offender could damage their professional reputations. In any event, of the thousands of local attorneys practicing then, only two were popularly known for defending homosexuals.

The other was Gladys Towels Root, who had for years been called the "Defender of the Damned." Root began practicing law in 1929 and was rumored to have defended more sex offenders than any other attorney in the United States. She, too, was a flamboyant character, as tall as Weiss was short, with a theatrical appearance that may have been calculated to disarm. In the style she regularly wore to court—opera gloves, hat towering as high as three feet above her head, rings set with stones only a little smaller than hens' eggs—she looked like the drag queens she often defended on masquerading charges. (Duncan Donovan once rode with her in an elevator that could barely accommodate her hoop skirt.) Her office was equally extravagant: paneled with mirrors and carpeted in pink; her pink draperies were embroidered with her initials in sequins, all setting off her wide desk, which was fashioned entirely of mirrors. But Duncan Donovan's partner, Thomas Patrick, the deputy district attorney for L.A. County, observed her often in the courtroom and declared her "brilliant."[54]

Both Root and Weiss earned considerable fortunes for stooping to represent a friendless, pariah community. Though some gay men who remember the 1950s characterize both attorneys as "wonderful advocates [in the court room], . . . who shamed the justices into seeing their point of view,"[55] others still resent that Root and Weiss grew rich off the entrenched homophobia of the legal system to which all gay men were vulnerable. The average fee they charged their homosexual clients, from $2,000 to $3,000, was, for many in the early 1950s, a huge burden—the equivalent of a year's salary. Some who were defended by them also questioned their insistence that a client plea-bargain (regardless of the facts of the case), which meant that even a defendant who might be totally guiltless ended up with a record as a sex offender. Most of their clients went along with this tactic to avoid the scandalous publicity of a trial and the strong possibility of a felony conviction (a plea generally meant getting away with a misdemeanor charge). And in most cases, of course, they despaired of fair treatment in the system anyway. As many older gay men still insist, the police, who were always believed over an accused "degenerate," were very willing to practice perjury on the stand. Duncan Donovan, who was present for numerous courtroom proceedings involving charges against homosexuals, says, "Vice Squad officers had memorized what they should say. . . . They would hit the points of what should have occurred in order to get a conviction. 'Improper touching.' 'Offer to provide sexual services.' 'Solicitation of sexual services.'"[56]

Many homosexual men shrugged off these terrible legal hassles as part of the cost of being gay, and most were lucky enough to stay one step ahead of the heat. But some began to question whether they really deserved to suffer the threat of police harassment and the expensive legal price tag that accompanied it just because they were homosexual. Their realization of their essential innocence—the innocence of a human being who pursues innate needs that hurt no one else—became the start of homophile organizing.

THE WOMEN'S STORY

When I went to gay bars I always drank something nonalcoholic, because I thought, "If they raid the place I don't want to be so stupid drunk that I don't know what I'm doing." So I would order a 7-Up or something.

— Lisa Ben, on going to L.A. gay girls' bars in the 1940s and '50s[57]

In Los Angeles before World War II there were only a few places that catered primarily to lesbians, and they were very different from the many bars that emerged in the years after the war. The prewar bars were usually in the tradition of the upscale nightclub, and they promoted an exotic glamour, much like the lesbian bars of Weimar Berlin. They included Jane Jones' and Tess's (called in its various iterations Tess's Continental and Tess's Café Internationale). The eponymous Jane Jones was a big woman with a basso profundo voice who'd been a singer in movie musicals.[58] Tess's was owned by Tess—a woman who dressed in basic black, pearls, and a great deal of makeup—and her partner Sylvia—who looked like Radclyffe Hall and always carried around a long cigarette holder. Both Tess's and Jane Jones' featured male impersonators such as Tommy Williams and Jimmy Renard, tall, broad-shouldered women singers who wore tuxes and bow ties and had tenor voices. Gay women who frequented those nightclubs remember still Jimmy Renard's rendition of "Tonight We Love" and the evening that Tommy Williams brought Marlene Dietrich to Tess's and sang to her.[59] Unlike nightclubs such as Jimmy's Backyard and The Barn that had a large gay male clientele and featured female impersonators, Jane Jones' and Tess's suffered neither raids nor closings by the police because the phenomenon of the lesbian was not yet taken very seriously in 1930s Los Angeles.

Even into the mid-1940s, upscale lesbian nightclubs were still relatively safe. At the Flamingo in Hollywood, Beverly Shaw entertained wearing drag on her top half—a man's jacket and bow tie; and sexy-lady clothes on her bottom half—a short skirt and high heels. At the Gypsy Room on the Sunset Strip in those years, women could be openly demonstrative with one another, as Dottie remembers: "There were a lot of women in tuxedos and a lot in beautiful gowns. Dancing was the thing. We could hug our partner and dance as close as we wanted. We never worried about the place being raided."[60] Perhaps the Gypsy Room patrons were not harassed by the law (as waltzing male couples undoubtedly would have been) because it was still socially acceptable for two women to dance together in the 1940s, and there were so few of these elegant women-only nightclubs that they may have been beneath the notice of the LAPD.

But lesbian nightspots multiplied in the years after the war, their clientele boosted by the many gay women who had come to Los Angeles to work in the defense industries and then stayed on. Working-class beer-and-pool-table bars for gay girls were soon scattered around many of the poorer areas of Los Angeles. They were different from the Sunset Strip and Hollywood nightclubs in that their patrons were regulars: women who "hung out" there and sometimes imposed on newcomers stringent rules that governed butch/femme dress and behavior.[61] Their working-class style and lingo felt alienating to middle-class lesbians. Terry DeCrescenzo, who had been a social worker, remembers that when she walked into the If Club, "a stereotypical dyke bar," as she describes it, the butches there called to each other, "Here comes a dish of ice cream." She was terrified. "I was in there for eight minutes," she says.[62] Middle-class lesbians generally stayed away from such bars, just as middle-class heterosexuals stayed away from those bars' straight equivalents. As Min, who was a business woman, and her partner Marion, who was the director of nursing in a Los Angeles hospital, now recall of their one foray into a gay girls beer bar:

> Some friends sent us to this place in Torrance—probably as a joke. We took one look around and then almost knocked each other over trying to get out. It was a different socioeconomic group. First of all, we didn't want beer, and we didn't want to play pool. We wanted a cocktail and to listen to nice music. And secondly everyone there was either a stomping butch, dressed like a man, or a frou-frou femme. We sure didn't fit.[63]

But for many working-class lesbians ("the industrial set," as Rikki Streicher, a lesbian bar owner, called them),[64] those bars were a haven to which they retreated often—so that by the 1950s, there was a considerable choice of nightspots where L.A. gay girls might go: the Lakeshore near Westlake Park and the If Club on 8th and Vermont, both of which had started in the decade before but continued to flourish; the Cork Room, the Star Room, and the Paradise Club, where butch-and-femme couples less fashionable than those at the Gypsy Room could dance; the Pink Glove in the Valley that imposed a $5 cover charge on straight customers to keep them away; the Redhead in East L.A., which welcomed only Mexican American lesbians; the Open Door (just across the street from the If Club) where lesbian blue-collar and pink-collar workers rubbed shoulders with prostitutes—and M & M, a bar with a similar mix that catered primarily to Latinas, where Nancy Valverde remembers being dressed "very butch" when a john said to her, "If you weren't so pretty I'd pop you one," and a femme waitress coming to her defense by throwing a beer bottle and an ashtray at the man.[65]

Lesbians did not suffer from sexual entrapment by LAPD Vice Squad decoys, but the relative indulgence they had once enjoyed in Los Angeles had quite disappeared by mid-century. The upheavals of the war, when females took on freedoms and responsibilities formerly relegated to males, made many in the postwar years long for a return to an imaginary past, when all women were homemakers and, "by nature," nurturers of men.[66] The mere concept of the lesbian mocked that longing. Thus gay women living in the mid-century were aware of the danger that awaited should their lesbianism become known. Those who dressed in masculine clothes or frequented bars were often harassed by overzealous and hostile police officers, but even those who were not bar habitués or cross-dressers or visibly homosexual in any way worried about the increased opprobrium in which lesbians were held. No matter how moral or socially productive they were as citizens, they knew that they were also outlaws and were cognizant that even their private acts of love could send them to prison under California law.[67] They felt they needed to be constantly looking over their shoulders, keeping their lives secret from all but a trusted few, devising ingenious ways to disguise their lesbianism.

For middle-class lesbians, especially those who were employed in the few professional positions open to women at mid-century (for example, teacher, nurse, social worker), social life was most often carried on in private homes because they knew that in the main public venue for lesbians, the gay girls bar, they would be vulnerable to police harassment. As Maggie, a former physical education teacher, recalls, after narrowly escaping a Vice Squad raid at a gay bar on Santa Monica beach in 1952 ("I was at the window, and I jumped out onto the sand and ran"), she never again went to a public place where gay people gathered: "I'd worked too hard to get where I was, and I didn't want to jeopardize it."[68]

But working-class and young lesbians who lived with their families or in dwellings too small to host social gatherings did not have the luxury of rejecting the bars if they wanted to find partners, or enjoy community, or merely be in the presence of their peer group. "The bars were the only place to meet women. There was no other place," Liz, who was born in 1926, recalls about the 1950s and '60s.[69] K.C. remembers a Gardena beer bar where white and Latina lesbians mixed in camaraderie during the early 1960s: "It was like going to a friend's home or a community center." The bar was the hub and starting point of all her social activities, she says, even her softball playing, which was sponsored by the bar.[70] Sharon A. Lilly says of Anna's, a Silver Lake bar where she spent her weekend nights in 1962, "It was always packed—all of us young people, nobody over twenty-three or twenty-four, dancing together. I loved it."[71]

But what was to lesbians a community center was to the police as bad as a bawdy house, and they worked hard to find ways to shut the bars down. Though lesbians may not have been entrapped sexually, the LAPD Vice Squad did not scruple to entrap them and the proprietors of their bars in other ways. For example, gay girls bars would be closed down on the charge that they had "served liquor to an intoxicated person"— though, as a transcript of a 1959 court hearing on a lesbian bar raid indicates, the liquor had been *bought for* that intoxicated person, a lesbian, by an undercover Vice Squad officer.[72] Undercover officers might return to a bar repeatedly before finding a reason to call for a raid of the premises, as they did at the Party Pad, a gay girls bar on Vermont Avenue. The Party Pad was declared "injurious to public morals" when the undercover officer testified that he "observed a female dressed in a man's attire place her arm around the body of a female dressed in female attire, pull this person to her, and kiss her on the neck and face."[73]

Proprietors of gay bars tried various ways to avoid trouble with the police: Some encouraged a mixed crowd—lesbians, gay men, and sympathetic straights—so that the nature of the bar would be less obvious.[74] At the Star Room, a lesbian bar on the edge of Watts, where women were permitted to dance together, the owner circulated on the floor and shone a flashlight between couples, admonishing them that if a beam did not appear on the opposite wall they were dancing too close and would get her into trouble with the Vice Squad.[75] But despite various precautions, the Vice Squad might still pounce, and patrons might still be dragged off in paddy wagons and booked on trumped-up charges.[76]

From all accounts, bar raids were utterly terrifying. The methods and manners of raiding officers seemed close to those brutal Gestapo tactics against which America had recently been fighting. Though she never learned the reason for the raid, Stella Rush remembers that in 1948 she witnessed a police invasion of the Tropical Village:

> The cops burst in. There were at least six of them. They shoved us off in corners, demanding names, IDs. Losing your job was on everyone's mind . . . and finding money for a lawyer.
>
> I said to the cops, "What's the charge?"
>
> One cop answered, "We haven't charged anyone yet." Another one shouted at me, "None of your business. We're asking the questions." They interrogated you with the utmost contempt, grilling you like you'd committed some terrible crime.[77]

Police brutality, mysterious and false charges, humiliation of innocent bar patrons—all continued throughout the 1950s and into the '60s, as Eileen Cusimano recalls. Early one evening after work, she and her partner had stopped to have a beer at a gay girls bar:

The place was raided. The police came in. Everyone froze. They walked around the room, indiscriminately arresting people. They arrested my girlfriend. I think they chose her to arrest because she was tall and good looking and stood out in the crowd. "Because you're drunk in public," they told her.

I said, "That's a lie. We only had one beer."

This policeman yelled at me, "You shut up or we're taking you in, too."

They shoved six of the women into a paddy wagon, and then they took them to Lincoln Heights jail. They booked them all for public drunkenness. None of them was drunk. It was strictly terrorism. I couldn't get my girlfriend out until the next morning. They all had to go to court. The charges were dismissed for all of them, but what a horrible time they went through.[78]

Arrests in lesbian bars seldom led to extended sentences, but the primary goal of police harassment seems to have been to intimidate the women and frighten them away from such meeting places. It was the job of officers of the law to keep them in check, keep their numbers down, and control the proliferation of their bars—which, ironically, were burgeoning in mid-century. In the 1960s, as L.A.'s population continued to grow and the city and county to spread out, such bars began cropping up even in small communities and neighborhoods to serve local gay girls who preferred not to travel the freeways—Joan's Place in Long Beach; the Bull Dog, the Big Horn, and the Hialia in the Valley; the Big Candle in Inglewood; the Westwinds in Venice; the Daily Double in Pasadena; Arnie's on Washington and Dee's Merry-Go-Round on Manchester and Vermont, which attracted mostly black gay girls; the Plush Pony on Alhambra, which attracted mostly Chicana gay girls.

As the number of gay girls bars continued to increase, so did police harassment in them increase. Eileen Leaffer, a sociologist who studied L.A. lesbian bar society in 1967, observed that LAPD Vice Squad officers hung around gay girls bars so often that bar regulars could distinguish them from tourists or "fish queens" (men whose preferred sex act was cunnilingus, and who hoped to meet lesbians in the bars who would be amenable). The regulars in the bars were careful to warn new patrons as soon as they befriended them about the plainclothes officers in their midst ("He's not kosher. You know . . . Vice").[79]

LAPD harassment of lesbians outside the bars increased as well. By the 1950s, a woman's presumed homosexuality alone seems to have been sufficient justification to flash the badge. Masculine-looking lesbians, or those congregating around a lesbian bar, or a butch-and-femme couple simply walking down the street together were slapped with charges that were often as false as those devised in bar raids. Meko, an African American woman, says that she and her friends were "hauled in" by the LAPD regularly on weekends—sometimes just for standing in front of the If Club or the Open Door: "They'd lie and say that we were prostituting, and they'd take us off to jail. We'd have to stay there until we got bailed out." Sometimes, Meko remembers, they were arrested just for walking in pairs, going from one bar to another on 8th and Vermont, especially if one of them was a "hard dresser" (the term among black lesbians for a woman who wore masculine clothes): "They'd say that we were 'fondling' each other. We'd have to pay a fine for 'fondling,' which was a misdemeanor."[80]

Driving was no safer: Many patrons of gay girls bars now recall that they did not dare even to park their cars in the vicinity of a bar: "The police might see it and wait for you to come out. Then they'd follow you and arrest you for anything."[81] Mid-century LAPD officers all seemed to share the conviction that a woman's mere *status* as a lesbian was tantamount to her criminality.

‍

The most common reason for police harassment of lesbians on the streets of Los Angeles in the mid-century was "masquerading"—wearing clothing that was deemed appropriate only for men. It is difficult to imagine in our day how disturbed some people have been in the past, even in a major metropolis such as Los Angeles, at the mere sight of a woman in pants (Garbo, Dietrich, and Hepburn notwithstanding), and how intense the efforts were to keep ladies garbed in skirts. During the war years, as many women donned trousers to work in defense factories, a panic gripped traditionalists. Fletcher Bowron, the mayor of Los

Angeles, declared to his city council in 1942 that he loathed "to see masculine women much more than feminine traits in men." It was bad enough that women were losing their womanliness in defense factories; City Hall, at least, must be free of gender desecration, he said. Bowron admonished the council members not to let the war "undermine these things we like to consider feminine and ladylike." "Good taste and good sense" must prevail, the mayor decreed, exhorting the council to pass a regulation that would prevent female employees at City Hall from wearing pants.[82]

The 1950s witnessed even more concern over the undermining of things considered feminine and ladylike; and cross-dressing women were a visible emblem of how some females refused to assume their traditional roles, stubbornly continuing to claim male prerogative. The forces of reaction came down upon them. Despite the two 1950 court decisions that found that women who dressed in men's clothes were not breaking the law, throughout the 1950s cross-dressing women were more persecuted in Los Angeles than they ever had been before. Up to World War II, female transvestites had apparently continued to be treated with relative tolerance in L.A.: In 1940, a woman barber who was en route to buy supplies for her shop was arrested by the Vice Squad and charged with being dressed to impersonate a man. But the businessmen in her neighborhood came to her defense by testifying that she was not "impersonating" because they all knew she was a woman as well as a person of fine character; and—as one sympathetic newspaper reporter (erroneously) stated—there was anyway "nothing in the statute books which prohibits a woman from donning men's clothing." The felony booking charge against her for impersonation was dropped.[83]

Women who cross-dressed in the postwar years were not as lucky. Like the woman arrested for "male impersonation" in 1940, Nancy Valverde was also a barber, but her run-ins with the law fifteen years later were brutal. During the time Nancy was a student in barber school, she was arrested "almost every weekend" because she wore short hair and men's clothes: "Drapes I'd get off the rack and a tailor would alter them. A sweater with tweed in front and wool in back that cost me twenty-seven dollars. The cops would get me for masquerading and then add on stuff, like they'd say I was drunk too, even though I was cold sober." Usually the police would take her to Lincoln Heights Jail, where she would spend a night or two before her case was heard in court the following Monday. "The cops would bring my clothes in as Exhibit A. Sometimes they'd sit behind me, goading me, laughing, saying things like, 'Better not fuck around with my wife.'"[84] Valverde says the police worried her so much that "whenever I'd see a black-and-white I'd run and hide until they were gone." In 1959, tired of repeated jail stays when she didn't run fast enough, she went to the Los Angeles County Law Library on Hill Street, checked the penal code, and found that the courts had already decided in 1950 that women were not breaking the law simply because they wore men's clothes. She provided her lawyer with that information and he used it in her defense. Finally, she says, she stopped being thrown in jail.

But though her arrests ceased, malicious police harassment did not. Once she became a barber, her neighborhood policeman found an extralegal way to trouble her, and even to threaten her livelihood: "He'd walk his beat where I worked. He just didn't like the way I dressed. He'd knock on the barbershop window with his nightstick, really loud, and my customers would jump to the ceiling. It's a good thing I had steady hands or I would've nicked their ears off lots of times."[85]

Valverde admits to having been defiant in her younger years when she was repeatedly accosted by the police: "They used to tell me, 'I want to see you in a dress.' I said to them, 'Sit down and wait 'cause you're gonna get tired.'"[86] But it was not her defiance alone that caused the police to persecute her. Even if a butch woman complied with the rules of dress and did nothing to challenge law officers, she ran the risk of police harassment anyway, sometimes for surprising reasons. Frankie Hucklenbroich, who stood at five foot eleven, tells of dressing up in a skirt, high heels, a woman's blouse, and a tailored jacket when she was job hunting one day in 1957. At the end of the afternoon she'd gone to meet her girlfriend at Coffee Dan's, a restaurant in Hollywood whose clientele included gay people and oblivious heterosexuals:

And suddenly these cops are descending on me and telling me to get up and step outside. They wanted to arrest me. I kept asking, "What have I done?" I hadn't a clue. Everyone was looking. Finally one of the cops said that I was a man dressed up in women's clothes! "No! I'm a woman!" I kept telling them. They ended up calling a police matron who took me into the ladies room and made me prove that I wasn't a guy.[87]

Frankie's story may be uncommon, but the stories of mid-century lesbians who were arrested for cross-dressing—in all big American cities—are not. An urban myth soon emerged in lesbian communities that had little basis in legal reality: The police could not arrest a woman for masquerading if she was wearing three articles of women's clothing. Flo Fleischman believed the myth, just as most gay women did: "In those days," she says "if you were dressed in drag you went to jail; so though I'd wear mostly men's clothes, I'd also be sure to be wearing a bra and girl's underpants and some other thing—nail polish or earrings or a man-tailored shirt that buttoned like a blouse or maybe pants that zipped up on the side."[88] Gay women held on to the "three articles" myth as though it were a talisman. But it did little to help them avoid capricious arrests.[89]

Because the police were so hostile to them, lesbians often internalized the notion of their criminal status and saw themselves as outlaws, separate from much of the human community, regardless of who they really were and what they really felt about their fellow beings. The costs of that outlaw self-definition could be dear, to themselves certainly, but also to the larger society. One Los Angeles woman illustrates those costs by telling the sad story of an incident that occurred in 1965:

I'm driving on the freeway. . . . It's about empty . . . sunset . . . and this VW bug is in the fast lane. I'm in the right lane. I don't know if the guy had a heart attack or what happened. He came careening across at a right angle and smacked into the concrete. I had all this paranoia that if I [stopped and called Emergency] the cops are going to pick up a dyke and stuff like that . . . so I was afraid to stop. I always regretted it. I don't know what happened [to the man]. I panicked and got the hell out of there because I was dressed like a dyke.[90]

The memory and her sense that—because of police hostility against people like her—she had failed her own rules of responsible and decent behavior have haunted her ever since.

——

Some middle-class gay women in the 1950s and 1960s did risk occasional forays into the L.A. gay girls bars, and even played with being outlaws, donning a "noir" persona for a night out, though the experience was never without at least a twinge of discomfort. Violet, who was a graduate student, recounts how in the first years of their romance, she and her lover, Ruth, a nursing administrator, sometimes enjoyed the feeling of going incognito to a forbidden place such as the Cork Room or the Star Room, where they could dance together: "There was an element of thrill to it. Not only were we doing something 'decent citizens' wouldn't like, but there was also the danger . . . a double thrill."[91] They were aware of the huge price they'd pay should their nighttime selves be discovered; and though they liked being in a roomful of lesbians, they did not dare befriend anyone there because it was impossible to know whom they might trust. A night out at the bar was like a parenthesis in the line of their lives that they strove to make as conventional as possible. Violet retained her ex-husband's last name, calling herself "Mrs."; and she and Ruth dressed conservatively in the daylight, hiding their other personae beneath a mask of tasteful makeup.

Even the potential thrill of being an outlaw for the evening could not outweigh the fear of the Vice Squad and the discomfort with bar habitués that middle-class gay women generally felt. A couple of upscale nightclubs did open in the late 1950s; both were in the more-hidden San Fernando Valley rather than on the Sunset Strip, where such places had been prominent earlier: "Beverly Shaw, Sir," who had been at the Flamingo in the 1940s, resurfaced at the Club Laurel, singing "songs tailored to your taste" in sultry and stylish imitation of Marlene Dietrich; Joanie Presents was presided over by Joan Hannan, an exotic blonde who'd made a name for herself among lesbians as the drummer in the movie *Some Like It Hot*. Such places felt a bit safer to some middle-class gay women, not only because those clubs were, like the Sunset Strip nightclubs of the 1930s and '40s, more elegant than the bars but also because of their location: "They were out of the City of Los Angeles. They were in the County and that was less risky. I'd be fired by my agency in a snap if I'd been caught in a bar raid in the City," Betsy, who was a television ad executive, explains.[92]

Most middle-class Los Angeles gay women at mid-century avoided public lesbian venues wherever they were located, and they felt they had to find other ways to construct a social life. But it was a challenge for a gay woman who did not go to bars to find a community or even a few close friends: How could you carry on trusted friendships when you feared you couldn't risk revealing your secret? How could you even meet others like you when you and they felt compelled to hide? Harriet Perl recalls that when she taught at Hamilton High School, she and her partner played poker every weekend at the home of another couple of women teachers. "We were pretty sure they were gay because we used to put our coats in their bedroom, and we saw they had only one bed." But though the two couples met for poker during a period of six or seven years, "never, never, never did we dare admit anything to one another, not them and not us."[93] Because they could not chance telling the truth about their most important relationship, the friendship stayed superficial.

The need to hide also placed lesbians in painfully ludicrous situations. Donna, who had been a physical therapist, remembers that though most of the women in her department at the Downey hospital where both she and her partner worked were gay, they all went to great lengths to pretend they were "spinster ladies":

We bought our first house, but we decided we'd better let people think Adele was living elsewhere. She actually kept a room on the hospital campus, though she never stayed there. The supervisor of the physical therapy department was in the same kind of situation. She lived with a woman on the nursing staff. Even though most of us knew about them, they'd arrive at work with the nurse crouched down on the floor of their car so that nobody would see them driving in together. Then the nurse had to wait until she thought no one was looking before she could sneak out of the car.[94]

Such demeaning fear of exposure was universal among professional women who were gay in those years, so forming friendships through work, as heterosexuals often did, was not an option for many of them. As Harriet Perl characterized it, in the 1950s, "being gay, even in L.A., was like being on the outskirts of civilization. It wasn't any easier to be gay in L.A. in those days than it would have been in Amarillo, Texas, or South Bend, Indiana."[95]

But in a metropolitan area as large and diverse as Los Angeles, there were certainly gay women who were able somehow to find compatible circles of lesbian friends. Mary, who was a social worker, found a tightly knit network of women who would come together regularly for house parties in her home in the hills of Silver Lake. The group called itself the "Hilltop dancing girls" because romantic dancing (such as they would not have risked in the public space of lesbian bars in the mid-century) was a prominent part of their private social get-togethers. Mary recalled in "Old Trees with White Blossoms," a 1998 ethnography about elderly lesbians, that through the decades and into old age, she and her friends continued as "a crucial support system" for each other when they became ill or lost their lovers.[96] Myra Riddell, however—another mid-century social worker who also found a group of gay professional women with whom to socialize—remembers that though it was a relief in one sense ("Here you could shake off the mask you wore at work") there was still discomfort: She characterizes her gay women friends as having been "up-tight, scared to death, always careful never to admit to anyone outside your little circle who you were." No matter what else you were in your life, it was virtually impossible at mid-century to escape the feeling that if the world knew you were a lesbian, you would be regarded first and foremost as a criminal.[97]

HIDING IN PLAIN SIGHT

Our closest friends in the '50s were two gay men, a couple like us. We did the straight world with them—parties, dancing at the Coconut Grove. My partner and I would have loved to go places we could dance together, but the gay bars were too dangerous. We had

a dear friend, a gay man, who'd lost his teaching credential because
of an incident at a bar. You had to be realistic.

—Dr. Mandy B., a medical doctor in the 1950s[98]

The old Hollywood tradition of lavender coupling was still popular in mid-century L.A., particularly among those lesbians and gay men who needed to present a front to the world.[99] Gay men and lesbians would take one another to work-related holiday parties, dinners with the boss, homes of relatives who had asked uncomfortably often, "When are you going to find a nice girl [or nice boy] and get married?" They would go together to fancy restaurants and theaters and straight nightclubs, or on vacations to exotic places, where women without male escorts couldn't get in and male couples would not be welcomed. Millie remembers that she and her partner would "dress sexy," in high heels and fur stoles, and go to dinner at Freres Taix or the Biltmore Hotel and then concerts at the Philharmonic with two handsome gay men who worked, as they did, for a real estate firm. "When we got out of the car, Bob would say, 'Okay, boy-girl, boy-girl.' He'd take my arm, and Michael took Sylvia's arm. Then, when we got back into the car, he'd say, 'Okay, boy-boy, girl-girl,' and Sylvia and I would cuddle together in the back seat all the way home."[100] In addition to being convenient, front dating permitted gay people to be in control over what was potentially hurtful. They could deceive the hostile straight world that was so sure it could "spot a queer anywhere."

Another charm of these friendships was the secret fun gay men and women shared about their challenge to gender orthodoxies. Mayor Fletcher Bowron and his ilk may have loathed "masculine women" and "feminine traits in men," but role reversals often became a source of humor for male and female homosexuals. Beverly Hickok, who worked as a riveter in L.A. during the war, says that she and her girlfriend went to gay beaches and to casual restaurants with Leon and Joey, a gay male couple. Their reason for being together was not that they felt they needed to pass as straight but that they simply liked each other and enjoyed the in-jokes that revolved around gender reversal. Joey, a hairdresser, was "effeminate," and he gave Beverly her first short haircut, a boy-style bob. He would tell her he couldn't understand why she liked to work as a riveter; she would tell him she couldn't understand his interest in hairstyling. "We really loved camping together," Beverly remembers.[101]

Norman Stanley recalls with great affection that in the late 1940s and the '50s he "ran around with this little dyke named Peggy." She was, he adds, "cute as hell and she used her masculine charms effectively on everybody." He relishes the memory of the amusing times they had in making people believe that they were heterosexuals. When they were with their partners, Patricia and George, Norman says, "We were, for all the world, two straight couples." But one New Year's Eve they didn't want to play that role, and the four of them went to a gay nightclub on La Cienega. They were refused admission. "The doorman said, 'No straights allowed!' George got us in by saying, 'If you don't let us in, Mary, I'll slap you with my purse!' For weeks we talked about how we'd become straight!"[102]

The fun in these friendships might come also from a contradictory game—being able to act out conventional gender behavior without the annoying concomitant of raising romantic (heterosexual) expectations. Jo Duffy says she and her partner loved going to restaurants and bars with gay male friends: "They were so solicitous of us. They treated us always like we were proverbial queens."[103] A gay man might have felt that he was misleading a straight woman if he opened the car door or lit a cigarette for her, or played at being chivalrous in any other way; but with a lesbian he could engage in such traditional masculine behaviors with pleasure and impunity. Millie recollects that because she and her partner were "socialized to be so girlie," it was in fact very useful to have Michael and Bob in their lives since they would "come help with the 'man chores' around the house—fixing wiring or lifting heavy things."[104] The women felt they could allow themselves to be feminine with gay men, and the men could be knightly or butch with lesbians, because such role playing in each other's presence led to no awkward expectations: There was a mutual understanding between them that conventional gender behavior (assumed or discarded at will) was divorced from conventional sexual desire.

Twilight tandems between lesbians and gay men were generally based on socioeconomic similarities, shared cultural interests and social concerns, and the chemistry necessary for any good friendship. Gay people of color often banded together in friendship groups because they perceived a double discrimination against them in public gay venues; they were subject not only to police harassment but also sometimes to discrimination by other gay people. Saundra Tignor, an African American woman, remembers that shortly after coming to L.A. from Washington, D.C., she and her partner visited the Canyon Club, which, she says, "definitely had a racial policy." The two women were seated right away, but after a few minutes the manager came to them and told them to leave. When Saundra asked, "Is it because I'm black?" he admitted that was indeed the reason. "I was shocked . . . out here in this land of palm trees and honey. It was very hurtful."[105]

The solution that some middle-class African American gay people found was to create private clubs for both men and women that would meet in people's homes. Mynun and Gayle talk about occasionally going to bars where there were some African American lesbians, such as the Sugar Shack; but other bars, they say, seemed less welcoming: "I never wanted to go someplace and be rejected," Mynun remembers. "So because we weren't going to pay to be mistreated, we quickly fell in with a crowd of gay people, men and women, and we entertained together on a big scale." Their group was about 80 percent African American, and the rest American Indian, Latino, and white. Their parties were more than amusements, they say. Men, women, and their children from previous heterosexual relationships, too, created an extended family together:

Anything you wanted to eat or drink. . . .

Great dancing. . . .

All the women dressed up in cocktail dresses and pearls or good slack suits; the men in tuxes or other fine clothes. I never saw a pair of jeans at one of those parties.

But the added good thing was that we didn't have to farm our kids out—we could have the children at the parties too, and everyone was respectful of them. Some of the men were nellie, but they weren't going to do drag at our parties.

I loved the men. They were such fun to be with. They tell Miss Thing she looks good when she looks good.

We loved each other; we really cared about each other.[106]

To many gay people, who were (realistically) worried in the homophobic mid-century that they could lose their jobs and even be thrown into jail if their homosexuality became known, it also seemed that heterogenderal friendships helped keep them safe. Tom Gibbon and his partner Bob Clark both worked for corporations. When Gibbon was suddenly picked up by the LAPD and questioned most of one night about whether he was "queer," he and Clark feared that the police had had them under surveillance. So they decided in 1950 that, for the sake of their jobs and general well-being, they must never again attend gatherings at which only men were present. They created what they called the "Cufflink Crowd," a "tight social circle" of lesbian and gay male couples who were of their class and shared their interests. Most of his crowd preferred to stay away from gay nightspots because they were "in the closet," Gibbon says. "You had to be if you cared about your job." Usually they entertained in their homes, but even at their private parties they were careful to look "appropriate"—the men always wearing coats and ties and the women wearing dresses; and the group's forays into public places of entertainment were always arranged to appear "boy-girl, boy-girl," as is illustrated by the picture of the Cufflink Crowd's visit to a Las Vegas hotel to see Pearl Bailey perform at a dinner show. As convenient as their heterogenderal arrangements were, however, fronting ultimately became less important than genuine friendship. Gibbon says that most of his "Cufflink Crowd," who are now in their eighties, "remained friends for life" and still see one another.[107]

The mid-twentieth century was the bleakest period in L.A. history for homosexuals: Police persecution and the popular prejudices of a reactionary era made gay men and lesbians aware almost always of being threatened and excluded by the straight world. If you were a gay person, it was difficult to escape the feeling that you were forced to live in hiding, to keep the dearest and most important part of your life a deep, dark secret. But through fronting and friendships, some gays and lesbians found creative ways to expand their social parameters, bring some light into the noir, and foil the bad guys.

The Mattachine founders in a rare group shot: (clockwise) Dale Jennings, Harry Hay, Rudi Gernreich, unidentified, Bob Hull, and Chuck Rowland. *Photo: John Gruber.*

CHAPTER 4

Organizing Underground

LITTLE BEGINNINGS

Considering Mattachine, Bilitis, ONE, all seem to be cropping up on the West Coast rather than here [in New York]. . . . What is it in the air out there? Pioneers still? Or a tougher circumstance which inspires battle?

—L[orraine] H[ansberry] N[emerov], 1957[1]

In 1942, a circle of lesbian friends pooled their money and purchased a row of rental houses in Los Angeles. They created an early lesbian enclave in the heart of the city, constructing communal areas, such as a swimming pool, where they would meet each other regularly; and the homes in which they did not live, they leased only to other lesbians. They were not consciously political. They "just thought it would be pleasant to live next door to friends" and to form a community that would serve as an extended family. They provided not only fellowship for one another but also social services. For example, when a sixty-year-old resident of the community suffered a ruptured aneurysm, and doctors, observing severe impairment, wanted to institutionalize her permanently, her lesbian neighbors organized constant rotating shifts to dress and undress her, feed her, and keep her stimulated by conversation. Against the doctors' dire predictions ("She will survive as a vegetable"), she recovered normal speech and became fully functioning after three years.[2]

Such an instance of community was possible in Los Angeles long before the start of a gay movement because the homosexual population had reached a critical mass. Los Angeles by the 1940s was already largely a city of immigrants, people who came from somewhere else in search of what they could not find back home. Of course, Los Angeles would have been particularly attractive both to those who sought fleeting homosexual sex and to those who saw themselves as *being* homosexual. The city promised the sophistication and panache associated with Hollywood, the freedom that comes from relative anonymity, and the urban-area odds of meeting others who shared one's interests.

Edythe Eyde (who later became known as "Lisa Ben") came to Los Angeles as a young woman in 1945 for the same reason many were attracted to the city—to escape a stifling family back home.[3] In Northern California she'd had intense crushes on women, but she had never heard words such as "gay" or "lesbian," nor did she have any notion that there were millions like her. In Los Angeles, she soon met gay girl neighbors who took her dancing at the If Club and to softball games where most of the players and fans were lesbian. In the bar, Eyde recalls, she could not allay her fears that the police would burst in and "take me off in a paddy wagon and put me in the pokey."[4] Hoping it would help her meet gay girls in a less dangerous setting, she decided to publish a small periodical. She chose the name *Vice Versa: America's Gayest Magazine* because, she says, gay life was considered a "vice" and "the opposite of the lives . . . approved of by society."[5] Though in Berlin in the 1920s there had been three magazines directed at lesbians—*Die Freundin, Frauenliebe*, and *Garçonne*—in America, there had never before been anything like it.[6]

Production and distribution of *Vice Versa* were elementary affairs. Eyde was employed as a secretary for a minor executive at RKO, and he'd told her that even when he had no work to give her she must look busy. She was thus able to produce a hand-typed issue of *Vice Versa* every month, from June 1947 to February 1948, with a run of twelve copies per issue (an original and five carbons typed twice). Her underground readership was much larger than twelve, however, because readers passed the magazine on to other lesbians after they'd read it. The first issues of *Vice Versa* were mailed to friends or distributed at the If Club, until Eyde was told by a more seasoned patron of the bar, "Hey, you shouldn't bring those things in here because if [the Vice Squad] catch you with them they'll put you in jail." Eyde recalls that until then she'd been utterly naïve about the danger of distributing a lesbian magazine:

> I said, "Why? There's no four letter words or dirty stories in it."
>
> She said, "It doesn't matter. If it's gay they'll put you in jail."
>
> So that tipped me off. I didn't do that anymore. I used to blithely mail them out [too]. . . . But these girls made me wise. So then I would just hand them out personally to people whom I would meet somewhere else.[7]

Eyde wrote each issue almost singlehandedly, the only repeat contributor being a straight male friend who was sympathetic to lesbians.[8] She never used her own name, nor any other name, in *Vice Versa,* nor did she even identify the magazine's provenance[9] (though her reviews of L.A. theater productions made its origin obvious). Despite her care about secrecy, however, Eyde was astonishingly militant for her day, even something of a cheerleader for the gay girl and lesbian life. She echoed Radclyffe Hall's 1928 British novel, *The Well of Loneliness,* in writing that "the third sex must be recognized as equally 'honorable' as those who are heterosexual," but her early gay pride was a sharp contrast to Hall's moroseness. Eyde dared to take on, as she described it, the "self-styled judges, who smugly carve the standards for society,"[10] to proclaim vehemently, "the Third Sex is here to stay," and to anticipate the lesbian feminism that would come three decades later when she declared: "A woman may live independently from a man if she chooses and carve out her own career. Never before have circumstances and conditions been so suitable for those of lesbian tendencies."[11]

In creating *Vice Versa,* Eyde was addressing an imaginary community, one much broader than what she saw at softball games or at the bar—a widespread gay women's intellectual and political community such as had not yet come into existence in America. Her idea to hand produce a little magazine may have been triggered when she attended meetings of the Los Angeles Science Fiction Society, whose members

(including several gay men) sometimes wrote for what she has described as "homemade [science fiction and fantasy] magazines."[12] Perhaps she was also inspired to create a magazine for lesbians when she
saw on the RKO lot actresses such as Liz Scott "flouncing around . . .
with a girlfriend, arm and arm, real cozy."[13] In Los Angeles, such interesting images abounded like nowhere else in the country and could fire
the imagination of a romantic young woman, as Eyde was. Though homophobia and the paranoia that homophobia sometimes provoked
were very present in the L.A. of the 1940s, so were unique stimuli that
could permit a gay girl to envision a homophile magazine.

When Howard Hughes bought RKO in 1948, Eyde lost her job. Though
she found work at other movie studios, it was usually in a secretarial pool:
"I could read what they were typing and they could read what I was typing," she recalls.[14] By then she knew she'd been engaged in risky business.
Vice Versa came to an end. But the shortlived Los Angeles magazine
stands as an icon that marks the beginning of homophile publishing in
America.

BEYOND THE "LEGION OF THE DAMNED"

Yes, your title [for the science fiction magazine Toward Tomorrow]
*has my eyes turned "toward tomorrow" also. What lies ahead? Can
we incorporate ourselves? Can we first organize into a defensive
body to fight for our rights?*

— from a gay correspondent, "Walt" [Wally Jordan],
to Jim Kepner, March 19, 1943[15]

Long before the 1969 Stonewall Rebellion, gay men were fantasizing
about the possibility of banding together to fight for their rights. During
the war years, when those in the military had the opportunity to make
contacts with others like them from far-flung cities and towns, it helped
embolden some enough to dream of themselves as an underground legion. In the summer of 1943, an air force sergeant who signed his letter
only "George" wrote to Jim Kepner in Los Angeles about the "Legion of
the Damned," a group to which he believed Kepner belonged: "I am very

much interested in joining this organization if it will better my unfortunate status and give me the rights and privileges that I feel all bisexuals are entitled to." George acknowledged that an organization of homosexuals might come under police scrutiny, but he was willing to take the risk: "If I knew that [the Legion of the Damned] was backed by the right kind and number of other nerve-torn individuals such as myself, it would be a great relief to me. . . . Please write me as soon as possible."[16]

George had heard about the Legion of the Damned from Wally Jordan, another serviceman, who lived in a small town in Wisconsin. Jordan, Kepner's science fiction pen pal, had tried to enlist him not only in the fantastical Legion but also in the "Sons of Hamidy," which he'd described as yet another underground homosexual organization. It had been founded in 1888, Jordan wrote, by "a few socially and politically prominent men [who] decided that a Universal Union of all Hamidy's men . . . would benefit mankind greatly."[17] Named for a Greek hero, Harmodius,[18] the group, Jordan claimed, was reactivated in 1934 and had "operatives" in major cities. A fund had even been established to pay those who "brought another H in for enlistment." Some bad recruits "almost blew the lid off," Jordan said, complicating the plot of his story as any good science fiction/fantasy writer might, but now a plan had been set to make the Sons of Hamidy a national group: "Any member of our klan" would be eligible to join; "heteros," "criminals," and "degenerates" would be kept out.[19]

Kepner sought information on the Sons of Hamidy for decades but was finally forced to conclude that it, as well as the Legion of the Damned, was a figment of his correspondents' imaginations. However, the idea of a homosexual organization was indeed in the air. In the late 1920s, in his native Minnesota, an adolescent named Chuck Rowland (later a key figure in Los Angeles homophile groups) read an article about homosexuals in *Sexology* magazine and decided that it was "perfectly obvious that what we have to do is organize."[20] In fact, there had already been attempts to organize: In Chicago, a German immigrant, Henry Gerber, had joined with a handful of other men in 1925 to create a group he called the Society for Human Rights, a name inspired by Magnus Hirschfeld's Scientific-Humanitarian Committee, which had started in Berlin in the 1890s.[21] Gerber hoped to gather a large base of homosexuals and to educate them, as well as lawmen and politicians, through lectures and a newsletter. He felt his way carefully, devising a purposely vague charter, which was actually registered with the state in Illinois. But despite his care, Gerber's efforts were cut short when members of the group were arrested and subjected to lurid headlines naming them homosexuals and thus criminals. Though the charges were ultimately dropped, Gerber conceded defeat: "We were up against a solid wall of ignorance, hypocrisy, meanness, and corruption. The wall had won."[22]

But after World War II, male homosexuals began to make serious efforts to attack the wall again. In 1945, gay ex-GIs in New York formed an underground social organization, the Veterans Benevolent Association.[23] By 1948, the center of action had moved west along with the burgeoning migration, as the writer Joseph Hansen reports. In that year, he was approached by a man on a Hollywood street who invited him to join "an association of homosexuals that would hold meetings in each other's houses to talk over the ins and outs and highs and lows, the gaiety and grief attached to living such a life and to perhaps come up with ideas to make things better." Hansen, like many homosexual men at the time, quietly dismissed the idea as "pathetic."[24]

In that same year, Harry Hay, who had been an aspiring actor and screenwriter, wrote his first homosexual rallying cry. It was a manifesto in which he drew an alarming comparison between the murder of homosexuals in Nazi Germany and the recent firings of gay men in a homosexual purge at the State Department, which had already come under the influence of McCarthyism.[25] Hay had been well seasoned in movement strategies through the Communist Party, which he had joined in the 1930s, in rebellion against his affluent family. In the hopes of pleasing the party he had even married a woman who was a fellow member; however, after ten years of marriage he came to realize that his homosexual desires would never dim, and he was ready to devote himself to what was still practically unimaginable—a political movement of homosexuals.[26]

In his manifesto, Hay announced that he wanted other men to join him in an organization he would call Bachelors Anonymous. Like the imaginary Sons of Hamidy, who, according to Wally Jordan's fanciful account, wore silver signet rings bearing the initials SOH,[27] members of Hay's equally imaginary "International Fraternal Order of Bachelors" would wear lapel pins so that homosexuals could discreetly recognize one another in public. The name he chose for the group was calculated, of course, to mask its nature. During the postwar era, secret fraternal organizations, a nineteenth-century craze, had enjoyed a surge in popularity, and Hay believed that such a structure provided both privacy and a sense of brotherhood that would not only defuse fear but would also appeal to homosexuals and encourage organizing. By 1950, Hay's new lover, Rudi Gernreich (who would become the well-known fashion designer), embraced Hay's manifesto, and within a year a nucleus of founding members had come together in L.A. to bring the group into being.[28] Hay then decided to call the new organization "Mattachine," which referred to medieval folk jesters who always wore masks when they performed in public. The masked Mattachine, Hay believed, would be an appropriate mascot for the organization because a mask hid identity.[29]

Unlike Gerber's earlier Society for Human Rights and other brief attempts to organize homosexuals in America, Mattachine managed to grow over many years and marked the beginning of the national homophile movement.[30] Hay's Hollywood-honed charisma and training as a stage actor were useful to the group's establishment. Early members of Mattachine's inner circle were swept up not only by his vision but also by his ability to communicate that vision dynamically.

The group exercised extreme caution. They used the word "homophile" to deflect the criminal- and mental-illness connotations of "homosexual." ("Phila" means "love.") They were super-careful in bringing others into the organization. In such venues as the basement of the First Unitarian Church of Los Angeles, the group conducted semipublic discussions on the problem of homosexuality. Many of the homosexual men who attended were so nervous about even being caught listening that they brought along a female "date" as a beard. The Mattachine leaders observed their audience: Only guests who evinced particular enthusiasm for the subject were quietly invited to join the secret society. Mattachine also adopted a cell structure, which was designed to protect members from exposure and ruin.[31] No master lists were kept. The leaders and the rank-and-file were separate, and the latter did not know who the former were. Secrecy was key to Mattachine's existence, as was crucial at a time when homosexuals had much to fear.

Though Mattachine operated under the realistic conviction that extreme discretion was necessary to avoid the fate of Gerber's group, secrecy also had its own charm. An interracial group of homosexuals that was formed in Los Angeles about the time that Hay began Mattachine—the Cloistered Order of Conclaved Knights of Sophisticracy (more commonly known as the Knights of the Clock)[32]—modeled their elaborate rituals on groups such as the Masons. They conducted a solemn, candlelit installation ceremony, ending in the words: "May each of us then search his heart and find there gifts deep and fine to bring to the service of his brother Knights."[33] The Knights, primarily a social club (though Harry Hay recalled they were also known for sex parties),[34] aimed to offer social services, too, such as helping interracial gay couples find housing.[35] But the Knights remained a small group. No one among them had the charismatic leadership ability and visionary eloquence of Mattachine's Harry Hay.

Initially, Mattachine had a hard time growing. The fear and loathing of the homosexual at mid-century had left a terrible mark. John Gruber remembers that those who came to the early meetings often harbored such self-hatred that they "had to start at a pretty low level of group therapy" such as "'We're not ill. We're not insane.'" Even that basic premise was too much for some, who ran from the meetings in sick terror. But others bravely stayed. Gruber still recalls that people were standing up and saying, "'This is my second time here. I swore the first time I'd never come back, but you got me thinking.'" He adds, "So we were doing something right."[36]

The organization did not grow rapidly, however, until word spread of an incredible, unprecedented legal victory: In the spring of 1952, Dale Jennings, one of Mattachine's core members, was arrested on a morals charge, and he admitted that he was a homosexual. But, he said, he'd been entrapped by a member of the Los Angeles Vice Squad, who was lying in his accusation that Jennings was guilty of lewd conduct. Jennings' plea was in marked contrast to that of Herbert Lowe, the man who had been caught forty years earlier in the Long Beach sweep and was exonerated only because he emphatically *denied* that he was a homosexual. Mattachine seized the opportunity to fight the entrapment battle openly. Hay found Jennings an attorney, and the group held fundraisers to pay his legal expenses. Jennings' acquittal caused a sensation on the gay male grapevine. A dozen Mattachine chapters immediately proliferated in Southern California and then quickly spread to Northern California and beyond.

But the organization's frenetic growth heralded the demise of its leadership: The new rank-and-file soon rebelled against the secret-cell structure, which had been central to Hay's conception of security. Jim Kepner, who was brought to his first Mattachine rank-and-file meeting in 1953 by one of the organization's few women members, Betty Perdue, recalled complaints that Harry Hay was a mysterious, shadowy figure who sat in some unknown realm and pulled the strings. "Everyone quotes Harry Hay but no one ever sees him," the new members said with resentment.[37] Worse, rumors of the founders' communism ran rampant just as McCarthyism was reaching a boiling point in the national consciousness. The rumors were inflamed through an attack on Mattachine by the L.A. columnist Paul Coates, who wrote of the organization as a "strange new pressure group" with Communist ties.[38] At two tumultuous conventions in the summer of 1953, tensions reached a crisis over the issues of secrecy and communism. Harry Hay and other early Mattachine founders, including Rudi Gernreich, Dale Jennings, John Gruber, and Chuck Rowland, resigned when they were dubbed Communists who "would disgrace us all."[39]

It was not only Communists that Mattachine feared would "disgrace us all." From its very beginnings, the organization eschewed men who affected a "swishy" style because the Mattachine founders, as radical as they were, felt compelled to present a conservative public face. Jamie Green remembers the emphasis placed on "presentability." "To be invited to Mattachine," he says, "you had to be wearing a Brooks Brothers three-piece suit. Those who were unusual dressers or had unusual hairstyles were not invited. If you made the mistake of bringing someone who was too flamboyant, you could be asked to leave."[40] John Gruber says that though the organization was "so mindful of freedom for the dispossessed, at the same time we knew there had to be limits for the movement to survive."[41]

The prohibition against those who were "loud in voice or dress" was unwritten. It clearly extended to "queens"—a broad term that included gay men who were effeminate as well as "drag queens"—those who dressed and identified as women, and who would probably be regarded as "transgendered" today. Miss Destiny, a mid-century L.A. gay man who achieved fame as the fabulous queen in John Rechy's *City of Night*, observed that queens were "outcast among outcasts."[42] But queens, including drag queens, believed themselves to be part of the gay world, and before more sophisticated ideas about gender were conceptualized they all simply called themselves "gay."

It is ironic that the city's emerging gay rights movement shunned its queens; they had, after all, been the most targeted for social opprobrium and legal harassment at least since 1895, when the Los Angeles City Council put an end to All Fool's Night because the revelries encouraged drag queens. In 1914, the newspapers, outraged against the men of the 606 and 96 Clubs, expressed particular disgust that they "wore kimonos and powdered their faces." In the 1930s and '40s, a main reason that the LAPD gave for raiding clubs where homosexuals congregated was that those places attracted "female impersonators and their following."

But despite consistent harassment and scant help from their fellow gays, queen culture flourished in Los Angeles. Jim Kepner remembered that when he arrived in 1943 he found an ongoing society of queens; he had a sexual encounter with one of them, having been "snatched into Vaseline Alley off Angels' Flight downtown by Carioca, a mad Latin queen who said she was chosen successor to venerable Wilhemina, Queen of Bunker Hill."[43] A generation later, Tony Albanese, who came to L.A. hoping to live as a woman, frequented downtown gay bars on Main Street such as Harold's, the Waldorf, and the 1-2-3, where he encountered some males in garish drag, others indistinguishable from real women, all resembling, as he ambivalently characterized them, "creatures of another world" with their "cacophony of psychedelic patter, falsetto laughter, screeching and cackling."[44] Albanese fell in with a group of transgender immigrants from Hawaii and Samoa who lived in a downtown apartment replete with "female clothing strewn all around and noxious perfumes."[45] One of the Hawaiians introduced Albanese (who by then had adopted the drag name of Denise D'Anne) to a wealthy older man who kept company with beautiful "girls." His home in the Hollywood Hills was called the "Girl Factory," and he had already helped four males become "girls" by sending them to a sex-change clinic in Casablanca, Morocco.[46]

Miss Destiny, who championed the mid-century queen world, seemed to be commenting directly on Mattachine's disinclination toward those who were "too flamboyant" when she wrote that a political movement among the sexually different would not succeed "until we stop hat[ing] the types that we are not comfortable with." "After all," she added, "how can any homosexual afford to be intolerant? All adjustments that hurt no one else ought to be accepted and understood—at least by homosexuals."[47] But it would be another generation before the community embraced the idea of unity through the concept of "GLBT."

Los Angeles Mattachine never recovered from the loss of its founders. Though the organization continued elsewhere, in L.A. it lost members because it lost direction. In 1956, throwing out the founders' common sense along with their Communist taint, Mattachine's president stated: "We do not advocate a homosexual culture or community, and we believe that none exists." The group's research director reported that his aim was "to help professional researchers find the cause of homosexuality and end the problem."[48]

However, L.A. Mattachine's early flame was not extinguished. It had already started burning in a torch of a different kind. In October 1952, a Mattachine group in West Hollywood had begun talking about creating the first homosexual magazine in America that would have national distribution. The following month, they met at the Studio Bookshop in Hollywood and chose the name "ONE, Incorporated" for their new group.

They referred to themselves often as "the Corporation"—a "capitalist" mask that was calculated to put to rest the putative connections between Communists and the homophiles. Their official name, ONE, suggested by an African American member, Bailey Whittaker (a.k.a. Guy Rousseau), came from Thomas Carlyle's line, "A mystic bond of brotherhood makes all men one." Several members of the group had been members of Knights of the Clock, the pointedly interracial homophile organization. One of the signers of ONE's incorporation papers was the partner of Don Slater, Antonio Reyes, who came to L.A. when he was sixteen, and under the tutelage of Rita Hayworth's uncle, Eduardo Cansino, became a celebrated flamenco dancer. (Reyes and Slater met while cruising in the underbrush of Pershing Square and became lovers for the next fifty years.) Merton Bird, an African American accountant, and John Nojima, a Japanese American survivor of the Manzanar Relocation Camp, were also founding members of ONE, Inc., though race was not among the primary issues ONE addressed.

ONE Magazine began publication in January 1953 with a bland first cover that could have adorned any literary quarterly, but it quickly became more and more daring. By the fourth issue, the editors made the magazine's real purpose evident on the cover, with a mock red-scare headline: "Are You Now Or Have You Ever Been a Homosexual?" By November, the phrase "The Homosexual Magazine" appeared on the cover, signaling to gay people that at last here was a periodical that dared to speak directly to them.

Against heavy odds in the midst of the reactionary McCarthy era, *ONE* made a considerable impact nationally, appearing on newsstands in several U.S. cities and selling about 5,000 copies a month, many of which passed through multiple hands.[49] By articulating issues in cover stories, such as "Homosexual Marriage," "Homosexual Servicemen," and "Religion and the Homosexual," *ONE* set a community agenda that would last for the next fifty years and more. It changed its subtitle to "The Homosexual Viewpoint," hoping to speak for homosexuals everywhere. It also provided a public address for often-desperate homosexual correspondents all over the country. An overwhelming refrain in the letters *ONE* received from male readers was about police entrapment "wherein a plain clothesman will approach a person and pose as a fellow-sufferer," as one correspondent sadly phrased it.[50] Many correspondents who had endured such entrapment experiences turned to *ONE* for legal advice as well as solace.

The "Corporation" rented two rooms on the second floor at 232 South Hill Street, a deteriorating area of downtown Los Angeles. The office, with its beat-up creaky wooden floors and its ceiling-high orange-crate bookshelves, was as shabby as the neighborhood.[51] The men and the few women who staffed the magazine labored with great devotion and scant pay. Jim Kepner, typically, was working full-time at a milk-carton factory and volunteering an equal number of hours writing for *ONE* under at least five pen names. As the magazine's presence became more known, the staff was harassed by visits from police and even FBI officers. Others visited too, believing that ONE's expertise with homosexuals could be put to good use, such as the two Chicago priests who made their way up the creaky stairs bearing a letter of introduction from the Cook County sheriff. The priests assumed that ONE was like Alcoholics Anonymous—that is, that ONE aimed to help unfortunates recover from their homosexual addiction. "They asked if we could send two staff members to Chicago at county expense to run [recovery] groups for gay prisoners and [to train] counselors in their parishes." (The ever-fiery Don Slater, judging them unenlightened, ordered them from the premises.)[52]

The threat of the law was the most troubling to *ONE*'s editors. The Comstock Act of 1873 forbade the mailing of materials that were "obscene, lewd, lascivious or filthy," and the mere mention of homosexuality, which was illegal throughout the country when *ONE* began publication, could be considered all those things. Subscribers, too, worried: Simply by receiving a magazine which dealt openly with homosexuality they were engaging in a dangerous enterprise. Almost two-thirds of the subscribers chose to pay an extra $1.00 a year (a subscription was only $2.00) to have *ONE* mailed to them first class, in a sealed envelope, with no return address.[53]

The editors and subscribers were right to worry. As Stella Rush, who had just joined the staff, remembers, in August 1953, seven months after *ONE*'s beginning, "a couple of men suddenly showed up to search our office. They confiscated our pure, sanitary little magazine," she says, astonished still. "Maybe they were looking for guys going down on guys in the toilet. But nobody had time for that. It was a very busy and business-like place."[54] The intruders had been sent by the Los Angeles postmaster, Otto Oleson, whose order to confiscate the magazine came from federal post office authorities in Washington, D.C.[55] The August issue had sported a cover that announced the lead article was titled "Homosexual Marriage?"

ONE's staff sought the legal aid of Eric Julber, a twenty-nine-year-old heterosexual attorney just two years out of Loyola Law School. He had recently made the newspapers when he presented evidence that the LAPD had brutalized his client, a black man accused of drug possession. Julber got him acquitted.[56] Julber recalls now his visit from a *ONE* delegation, which was made up of Dorr Legg, Dale Jennings, Don Slater, and Jim Kepner. They asked him to help them get back from the post office the seized copies of the magazine. "I told them, 'I never had anything to do with gay people, know nothing about that way of life. . . . But I do know about one thing—civil liberties and the right to be free from censorship.'" Julber says he agreed to work with *ONE* gratis, recognizing that this was potentially a "landmark case" that could make his reputation as a civil rights attorney. But he did not have the opportunity to show his skills in court: The solicitor general in Washington determined in three weeks that the August issue was not obscene, and the confiscated copies were returned.[57]

The *ONE* seizure case certainly did not enhance Julber's reputation; instead, he had to suffer the jaundiced view of his fellow attorneys, who, when they heard that he had agreed to help *ONE,* remarked, "You're kidding! What are you doing? People are going to think you're one of them."[58] Nevertheless, Julber continued working pro bono with *ONE,* reviewing each issue before publication, making sure—in a paradox that represented the era—that the homophile magazine did not advocate homosexuality. In the October 1954 issue, he wrote an article explaining what the law considered obscene, opining in that article that the subject of homosexuality among women could be treated "with greater freedom."[59]

Ironically, it was that issue of *ONE* that the post office seized once again, naming as the most obscene piece a (dismayingly innocent) story about lesbians, "Sappho Remembered." Two other pieces in the October 1954 issue were also named obscene: an advertisement for a Swiss homosexual magazine, *Der Kreis,* which alluded to the magazine's "beautiful photos," and a playfully satiric poem, "Lord Samuel and Lord Montagu," which hinted at homosexuality in British history. Again Julber agreed to take the case gratis. Afraid that his own expertise about obscenity cases was insufficient, he tried to "get some heavy-weight backup from the ACLU." He told a director of the Southern California branch, "I think there's a violation of the First Amendment. How about becoming co-counsel?" To Julber's astonishment, the director's answer was, "I don't think we'd be interested in a case like that."[60]

Julber carried on alone. He appeared before Federal District Judge Thurmond Clarke, whom he remembers as "a beefy former USC football player," who declared in 1956 that the October 1954 issue of *ONE* was unmailable because it contained "filthy and obscene material." The judge flatly concluded, "The suggestion advanced that homosexuals should be recognized as a segment of our people and be accorded special privileges as a class is rejected."[61] *ONE* and Julber then took the case to the Ninth Circuit Court of Appeals, only to get similar results: In February 1957, the three-judge panel of the court of appeals deemed the magazine issue under question "morally depraved and debasing." Jim Kepner characterized the verdict as "a crushing decision so broad we could hardly continue the magazine if it stood." Having no alternative but to press ahead, they asked Julber to try to take the case to the United States Supreme Court.[62]

It is utterly amazing that at a time when a federal district court refused to recognize homosexuals as "a segment of our people," the Supreme Court, which had never before heard a lawsuit involving homosexuality, would listen to *ONE*'s case. It is even more amazing that the Supreme Court agreed that the post office, by imposing "stricter standards" on the magazine than would be imposed on a nonhomosexual magazine, was "discriminating" and denying *ONE*'s staff "equal protection." On January 13, 1958, the Supreme Court reversed the lower courts. Mere homosexual content in a magazine was no longer obscene, and a homosexual magazine could be sent through the U.S. mails.[63]

How could *ONE*'s editors not gloat over the huge victory? "We took on the whole federal government for a period of four years—and they spent big money, with top lawyers brought from Washington, to squish us," Dorr Legg remarked. "And they didn't! We won."[64] But as Don Slater wrote in the next issue of *ONE*, it was not the magazine alone that achieved a victory: "*ONE Magazine* has made not only history but law as well and has changed the future for all U.S. homosexuals. Never before have homosexuals claimed their rights as citizens."[65] The Los Angeles magazine's unprecedented win in the Supreme Court was a turning point for homosexual America that would be crucial to the gay movement that was to come: No homosexual publication could ever again be declared obscene merely because it was about homosexuality.

—

ONE, Incorporated, expanded its reach with each passing year. In the summer of 1956, ONE began a second publication, *ONE Confidential,* directed at "members of the corporation" rather than the general subscriber. That same summer saw the development of a new branch of the corporation that caused great excitement (and which eventually caused catastrophic division). Dorr Legg, the business manager and main mover and shaker behind ONE, Incorporated, had been a visionary since his participation in the Knights of the Clock, when he hoped to establish social services for interracial homosexual couples. Now he continued to dream of homophile activism that would have long-range impact. As manager of the corporation, he lamented the "tremendous gaps existing in higher education . . . concerning the homophile's place in history and his true status." Legg hoped to close the gaps.[66] He found strong support for his project among the erudite but self-taught Jim Kepner, the college-educated Julian "Woody" Underwood, and Merritt Thompson,[67] a retired dean of education at the University of Southern California whose academic credentials provided prestige and legitimacy to the venture. Gerald Heard, a much-published British philosopher and a friend of Christopher Isherwood's, joined the core group to hammer out the curriculum. The ONE Institute of Homophile

Studies,[68] the first gay studies program in the country, began offering courses in the fall of 1955.

The founders credited themselves with outstripping even Hirschfeld's Berlin Institute for Sexual Science in attempting "a specialized study of the whole field of homosexuality,"[69] including history, biology, psychology, anthropology, sociology, law, religion, philosophy, world literature, and "problematics"—which taught students how to apply their new knowledge to create strategies and goals for the homophile movement.[70] Saturday afternoon classes in these topics were offered to the public at ONE, Inc.'s office. (Kepner noted that classes, though earnest, were not large, and that "constant off-key singing, or caterwauling screeches" from an elderly singing teacher down the hall "often interrupted our classes, producing a levity out of sync with the content or tone of our lectures.")[71] ONE's educational division gave rise to yet another publication, *ONE Institute Quarterly of Homophile Studies,* and to a series of annual conferences, known as ONE's Mid-Winter Institute, which was held at various downtown L.A. hotels—another first for a homosexual group—though when the hotel staff approached, the participants were sure to lower their voices so that the nature of their discussions would not be overheard.

ONE was also becoming *the* place where homosexuals knew they could turn when in trouble or perplexity—virtually the first "gay center" in America. Charles Rowland, a member of ONE, soon took the idea of a gay center even further. In the Southern California tradition of "thinking big" and establishing new churches, he began the Church of One Brotherhood, which for a brief period hosted ecumenical Sunday morning services at the Hill Street office. Through the church he also tried to raise money for a freestanding building that would be called the "Walt Whitman Guidance Center," where homosexuals would be provided with all the elements of a social service agency, such as counseling, employment assistance, legal referrals, and medical service. Rowland estimated that hundreds of homosexuals arrived in Los Angeles monthly, including many gay teenagers whose dreams of stardom drew them to Hollywood. They became part of a legion of homosexuals "without jobs, without funds, without friends, without adequate job training or education." The Walt Whitman Guidance Center was to be their lifeline.[72]

It would be another generation before something resembling the prescient Rowland's Center could be built; nevertheless, the ever-increasing demands for help forced ONE to create a "Division of Social Services" in its two-room office, led by the indefatigable Dorr Legg. Despite slender resources, the "division" offered a gamut of services, including job placement for gay people. Surviving case forms also show that families of homosexuals, too, turned to ONE when in need: For instance, a mother used ONE's social service when her twenty-year-old son, an air force officer, faced a court-martial. The fact of his homosexuality had been leaked by a gay acquaintance who had been caught and grilled by military authorities. The mother believed her son was "unwilling to face [the] actualities of the case and [the] need for vigorous, drastic action," and solicited ONE's help.[73]

The little office was soon deluged. There were letters, such as those from small-town gay men asking whether ONE could assist them in moving to Los Angeles. There were long-distance calls from all over America from homosexuals or their families seeking advice.[74] There were "the Talkers" who "come up to the office and Talk and Talk and Talk," as the staff lamented. "It slows work down. . . . [But] they must find an outlet somehow, apparently, so we listen and listen."[75] The nation's only openly homosexual office had become a Camelot. Volunteers labored selflessly, as Dale Jennings, honored in 1953 for his work with ONE, recognized in his praise for fellow workers, "sitting there in unsuspected glory. Each of us here tonight is a hero, each has a place in history."[76]

But as revolutionary and remarkable as these "heroes" were, their organization did not escape numerous crippling problems, which foreshadowed those that were to plague the gay movement throughout the generations that followed. The sheer volume of work and simmering tensions over what "the homosexual viewpoint" should be brought intense pressures to the idealistic staff. Jim Kepner, who devoted his life to homophile causes, described his labors at ONE as "a diet of bitterness."[77] A struggle over power and over the very purpose of the organization itself created an ultimate schism for ONE, Inc. Personal tensions heightened. Some members of ONE's board were leery of Charles Rowland's enduring

Red-tinged militancy; or they were harshly critical of his far-reaching plan for the Walt Whitman Guidance Center, deeming it pie in the sky.[78] Dorr Legg, always the dominant force at ONE, Inc.,[79] lost interest in the magazine and advocated that the corporation expand its educational function, which riled Don Slater, who had been *ONE Magazine*'s creative mainstay. Slater also accused Legg of unethical tactics when he trumped Slater's bid in 1965 to win a majority on the board. Slater then mobilized his supporters, rented a truck, and removed ONE's furniture, business files, and library, claiming that *his* group was "ONE." The corporation sued Slater et al. Slater then formed a new group, the Homosexual Information Center, and published a gay magazine he called *Tangents*, lifting the name from Jim Kepner's column in *ONE*. Though Slater and his allies eventually signed an agreement promising to return all ONE business records to Legg, he kept many of them until his death in 1997.[80]

For several years the funding issue was just as thorny as the personality issues at ONE because huge donors, such as emerged a generation later, were scarce at mid-century. But though the personality problems went unresolved, the funding problem was eased when ONE received a windfall through an eccentric multimillionaire named Reed Erickson. The small-boned bodybuilder who wore a red pompadour and flaunted a pet leopard was born Rita Erickson and had been the first woman to graduate from Louisiana State University in mechanical engineering. Erickson, through sex-change procedures in 1965, was a pioneering female-to-male transsexual. After working with Harry Benjamin, the sex reassignment guru, Erickson, who had inherited a family fortune that he parlayed into $40 million, decided to use the wealth to fund a nonprofit educational foundation that would serve those whose "human potential was limited by adverse physical, mental, or social conditions." For twenty years, beginning in 1964, he poured millions of dollars into the gay/lesbian/transgender movements. Many of those dollars went to the ONE Institute for the Study of Human Resources. Eventually, Erickson purchased for ONE the Milbank Estate in L.A.'s Country Club Park. Now ONE could offer the academic programs such as Dorr Legg and his supporters had only dreamed about—in a twenty-seven-room mansion surrounded by lush acreage and worthy of its proximity to Hollywood. (In more recent years, the mansion has been the setting of films such as *Rumor Has It* and *Running with Scissors*.)[81]

—

In addition to establishing a homophile movement, L.A. members of Mattachine and ONE played another vital role in gay American history as subjects in the first study to look at homosexual men outside a clinical context. In the 1940s, when Evelyn Hooker was teaching psychology classes at UCLA and performing experiments on neurotic rats, Sammy From, a gay man who was one of her brightest graduate students, befriended her. He introduced Hooker to a circle of several other gay men and two lesbians who shared a Silver Lake house; he took her to gay bars and drag clubs; he took her to parties where she met such gay luminaries as Paul Goodman and Christopher Isherwood.[82] He had made it his mission to introduce Dr. Hooker to a broad swath of gay society before he proposed that she study "people like us," that is, functional gay men who had no need for psychotherapy. When Hooker mentioned From's proposal to a heterosexual colleague, he encouraged her to take advantage of a veritable open field: She could gather empirical data about homosexual men, which had never before been done. Hooker began collecting male homosexuals' life histories and Rorschach test results in Los Angeles, but changes in her own life took her away from the city and her nascent study. She returned in 1951, still feeling, as she characterized it, "absolutely haunted" by the study she had not finished.[83]

It was then that Hooker applied for a grant from the National Institute of Mental Health. She proposed to compile data on men who were a 6 on the Kinsey scale, that is, exclusively homosexual. (As a control, she would administer the same tests to an equal number of Kinsey 0s, exclusive heterosexuals, mostly fireman and police officers.) Hooker received the NIMH grant only after federal investigators came to visit; she suspected that, because they feared a homosexual would not be impartial, only by eyeballing and interviewing her could they confirm her claim to heterosexuality. She apparently passed their test, though Hooker, nearly six feet tall and sometimes described as mannish, had occasionally been mistaken for a drag queen, as happened when a police officer tried to prevent her from using the women's restroom at a Halloween drag ball in Santa Monica because he assumed she was really a man.[84] She took the dangers of her work in stride but used sensible precautions: Anticipating being swept up in a raid in the course of her gay bar visits, she carried a signed letter from the chancellor of UCLA describing the nature of her research.[85] By 1956, Hooker was ready to publish her first study, "A Preliminary Analysis of Group Behavior of Homosexuals,"[86] for which she had relied primarily on members of Los Angeles Mattachine and ONE as "an [established] pool of people she could dive into."[87]

Her research with gay men continued. Hooker had used her contacts in homophile organizations to locate other L.A. gay men whom she could use in her studies. Skip Foster, who later worked for her as a graduate researcher, first met her when the two sat together at a ONE banquet in a downtown hotel. He recalls how this "cultivated and interesting" mind zeroed in on him. She wanted to know about Foster's social network: Not only was he very familiar with L.A.'s gay bars, he also had a long-standing group of nearly two dozen gay friends who played volleyball together at Will Rogers State Beach on weekends. Hooker supplied him with a new Webcore tape recorder, which he used first to interview his beach companions; then (as Foster's lover at the time often complained) he hung out in the gay bars until closing time for a full year, earning his living by pursuing interviews through last call. "She wanted to know everything," he says—about people, bars, and all the gay institutions that were hidden away from the straight world.[88] Her work culminated in *The Hooker Report* in 1969.

The research that Hooker did in Los Angeles had national consequences. By concluding that homosexuality was not a mental illness, her studies provoked a series of attacks in the 1950s, but they played a pivotal role a generation later in the American Psychiatric Association's decision to remove homosexuality from its list of mental diseases. Judd Marmour, a psychiatrist and a leading advocate of the APA's 1973 reform, recalled that it was Hooker's L.A. studies that were "the reference point we always went back to."[89]

OVERCOMING "GOOD MANNERS"

If you mind your own business and use "good manners" you will not get into any trouble at all.

—"Attorney Stresses Nothing to Fear," *The Ladder,* 1957[90]

The women's story in Los Angeles was not the same as the men's when it came to mid-century organizing because, though lesbians and gay men often shared friendship and social life, their biggest battles with the outside world were different. Middle-class lesbians, like homosexuals of any class, suffered the threat of being rejected by family and friends, but they had little occasion to worry about the police. They were not entrapped by "Hollywood rejects" hired by the LAPD. They did not run the risk of being busted for public cruising or T-room sex. They were seldom stopped by policemen on the streets. Their greatest enemy was generalized "homophobia," which was a much more amorphous adversary than the LAPD and one that seemed impossible to tackle in such repressive times. Middle-class lesbians had good reason to worry about being fired from those very few professions that were open to females at mid-century if their sexuality became known. But, as the attorney for the *The Ladder* (the magazine of the first American lesbian organization) stressed in 1957, if they "mind[ed their] own business and use[d] 'good manners,'" they had "nothing to fear." To mind one's own business was, of course, the diametrical opposite of participating in a homophile movement.

Working-class lesbians in Los Angeles had considerable reason to be concerned that the police might arrest them in a bar raid or for masquerading, but as female and poor they also had to worry about everyday survival. They were in no position to see themselves as a united political force,[91] and middle-class lesbians were certainly not inclined to take up the battle for their working-class sisters. (Unlike middle-class gay men who, through their sexual tastes, were sometimes brought close to working-class men, homosexual women of different social classes seldom mixed.) What could bring lesbians together in a political organization?

Formal organizing among lesbians at mid-century was also hampered by other factors. Women as a whole were still political neophytes who had been voting in America for only three decades when the homophile movement emerged. Collectively, lesbians, no less than heterosexual women, had little experience in joining organizations the aim of which was to fight political battles. Their reluctance to take a public stance as homophiles was exacerbated by the fact that those who came of age in the postwar years were of the cohort dubbed the "Silent Generation." Activism was foreign even to most men of that cohort, but for women, who had been doubly repressed by virtue of their gender, it was generally inconceivable. That even a few lesbians managed to fight the good fight in the 1950s homophile movement is astonishing.

Neither Mattachine nor ONE was able to politicize more than a few lesbians. To most women, the organizations seemed irrelevant, to say the least. First of all, they were male-founded, male-dominated, and male-focused, and even their rhetoric of "brotherhood" seemed to exclude women. Even worse, women viewed the organizations' defense of gay men's penchant for semipublic sexual encounters in the same way that many members of Mattachine had viewed the Communist issue: It was a Trojan horse that threatened to discharge trouble on all homosexuals, but lesbians could avoid it simply by dissociating themselves. Many lesbians had little sympathy anyway with gay male sexuality, which seemed to them so different from female sexuality. The attorney Herb Selwyn recalls that when he warned a Mattachine group in the 1950s about Vice Squad stakeouts in the parks, one of the few lesbian members present observed with disdain: "The boys are so horny. They just can't wait."[92]

The homophile organizers in L.A. did try from the movement's inception to include lesbians. Like the leaders of early European cogendered homosexual organizations—who argued in the nineteenth century that the presence of homosexuality among women as well as men proved that it ought to be regarded as a "natural state" rather than criminal behavior[93]—Mattachine leaders understood the political value of a cogendered organization. Rudi Gernreich, who knew of the earlier European homophile groups from his youth in Vienna, brought "Flo," a lesbian fashion model with whom he'd worked, to the first organizing meeting. (Harry Hay remembered that Flo was "very pessimistic" about the possibility that homosexuals could organize, and she did not return).[94] Gernreich later brought another of his lesbian models, Catherine Cassidy, but she, too, did not last long in the organization. Ruth Bernhard, a bisexual who later became one of the most noted photographers of the female nude in America, was recruited as well, and she became the lone woman among seven men who formed part of the inner circle of leadership. (Bernhard left the group in 1953 and went to San Francisco, where she worked with Ansel Adams and Imogene Cunningham.)[95] From time to time, other lesbians joined Mattachine and occasionally even played substantial roles in the organization.[96] But without a burning reason to organize formally, such as gay men who suffered police entrapment had, few Los Angeles lesbians were convinced of the group's significance to their lives, and the number of women members remained miniscule.

Daughters of Bilitis, the first lesbian organization in America, was founded in San Francisco in 1955 and had a bit more success attracting women in Los Angeles than did Mattachine or ONE, though middle-class lesbians seldom joined Daughters, either. Del Martin, a founder of Daughters, pointedly complained that lesbians who had "some measure of professional status" not only refused to support homophile groups but even "damned [them] for bringing Lesbianism into the open, fearing that as the public became more aware, people might take a second look at them."[97] The accusation certainly held an element of truth: The more homosexuality was discussed in public, the more difficult it would become for two mature, unmarried women to pass as "housemates."

However, it was not merely fear of exposure, nor all the other factors mentioned above, that kept middle-class lesbians away from Daughters of Bilitis. The declared aim of the organization—to "integrate the [lesbian] into society" by "educating" her and helping her "make her adjustment"—was patronizing to middle-class lesbians, as were the preachy articles in *ONE*, such as "Café Saturday Night," which appeared in 1954. "Why the fly front pants?" the lesbian writer taunted butch lesbians:

[Why] the men's shorts (you brag that you wear them) and the men's jackets that always look too big in the shoulders? Your answer—a hundred times over from 100 different people—would be, "I'm more comfortable this way. I never could stand women's clothes. I've always dressed this way!" (You must have looked adorable at age 7 in your bow tie and long chain!).

The author concluded with a proclamation for her lesbian readers: "We are accepted or not, THRU OUR CONDUCT! Our homosexual SOCIETY can be accepted and approved—it's up to YOU![sic]"[98] But the middle-class lesbian at mid-century had already learned very well how to comport herself in the outside world; she did not require an organization to "adjust" her. If she was able to maintain her middle-class status, it was because such survival techniques had become second nature to her. She would brook no condescending edicts from the homophiles.

But perhaps lesbians who were middle-class professionals rarely joined homophile organizations in the 1950s mostly because they lacked what political scientist Doug McAdam has identified as being crucial before minorities can organize formally—an understanding that they might have some sort of "latent political leverage."[99] "Political leverage" of any kind was unimaginable to those whose very livelihood depended on their success in hiding. In lieu of homophile organizations, however, what the Los Angeles middle-class lesbian had (if she was lucky) was a social group on which she could depend for the long haul, such as the circle of lesbians who became neighbors in 1942 and pulled together to help one of their number recover from her aneurysm; or the "Hilltop dancing girls" who met to dance in the Los Feliz area from the 1940s until death did them part;[100] or the extensive Malibu Canyon friendship circle of lesbian real estate brokers, architects, veterinarians, social workers, entertainment executives, and professors, who met in one another's homes for lavish catered parties. ("We were the A List," a member of the group now recalls.)[101] Such companionable communities offered security in the knowledge that one was not alone. It took a couple of decades more and a revolution in consciousness before middle-class lesbians were finally able to band together politically in feminist organizations.[102]

Even Daughters of Bilitis had not been formed with the intent of being a political organization. Rather, the founding members, made up largely of pink-collar and white-collar workers, wanted to establish a social alternative to the dangerous bar scene. Once the group named itself, enlarged the membership, and began discussing the social discrimination from which lesbians suffered, its purpose broadened beyond the social.[103] A year after Daughters' founding in San Francisco, Del Martin sought to expand the organization and turned to L.A. first as the most likely city outside the Bay Area where such a group might take hold. She found several lesbians who agreed to establish a chapter,[104] though it was only when a founding member and past president of San Francisco Daughters, Helen Sandoz (a.k.a. Helen Sanders or Sandy), moved to Los Angeles in 1958 that a chapter was finally formed. The woman who became her partner, Stella Rush (a.k.a. Sten Russell), remembers that Sandoz arrived in L.A. with a list of likely-prospect names and that the two of them drove all over Los Angeles County trying to convince other lesbians to join the fledgling organization.

Finally, about fifteen women came to the early meetings, which were usually held in Sandoz and Rush's living room. Rush recalls those meetings as being like pioneering consciousness-raising groups combined with group therapy: "We'd talk about our problems and fears—like how we risked losing our jobs if we didn't lie about who we were. We'd assure each other that it was society that made us lie, and not that we were bad people because we weren't allowed to be honest."[105] For the first time in Los Angeles, a group of white-collar and pink-collar lesbians were regularly gathering together to discuss systematically the problems that were visited on them by a homophobic society.

Ann Bannon (the author of the Beebo Brinker series), who lived in Los Angeles from 1956 to 1962, attended those early Daughters' gatherings, and her memories give insight into why women would have found the meetings salubrious, but also why they did not join in great number. She remembers that Daughters' meetings were a great relief after the dark, stifling gay places she had known in New York:

In Greenwich Village I'd met people mainly in smoky bars. In L.A. everything seemed so expansive and beautiful. It seemed to spill over into the gay community [and Daughters]. We sat in a real home—a bottle of wine, a plate of cookies, all those attractive women, talking about real things, like how do we counteract society's refusal to know we drink orange juice and eat cereal in the morning, just like them.

But for her, the meetings were, paradoxically, more dangerous than the bars because in the bars she could be anonymous; at Daughters, where everyone soon learned a great deal about everyone else, she had no cover; and she feared the news that she was a lesbian could leak to her husband, who might claim their two small children. Bannon says she admired the group's desire to address publicly the difficult issues with which lesbians had to contend: "They discussed social change. Some of the women had been in the military, and they were angry at the hypocrisy of military policies about lesbians. I remember them even talking about would we be able to get a group together, to demonstrate. But," she says, "because of my circumstances, it was too scary for me, I couldn't join them."[106]

In fact, Daughters did not take their grievances to the streets in those years. To the extent that the consciousness-raising of their discussions made the Daughters understand the ways in which homophobia impinged on their lives, the L.A. organization may certainly be said to have been political; but the women of L.A. Daughters had no consensus about an immediate and dramatic struggle they needed to undertake, such as Mattachine men did in fighting the LAPD's nefarious entrapment policies. L.A. Daughters, like all the other branches of the organization that sprang up in the late 1950s and through the early '60s, was plagued by a fogginess of purpose. Barbara Gittings, who became a founding member of the New York branch, remembers, "Our motives were pretty hazy. We didn't have any clear sense of what we were going to do. It just seemed enough that Lesbians were getting together. . . . The discussions were awfully vague and groping. We kept seeking for ways of making the meetings interesting, without having clearly said to ourselves, 'What exactly are we meeting for?'"[107]

That unspoken question was apposite. To take on the whole world for its injustice was too overwhelming. Thus Daughters lacked an immediate political raison d'être, such as Mattachine had when it challenged Dale Jennings' prosecution. The women's group could effect no dramatic victory. For those reasons, unlike Mattachine, it would have no spectacular growth spurts.

Helen Sandoz tried valiantly to make L.A. Daughters grow by expanding its political meaning—associating her group with the larger homophile movement, insisting that the fate of the lesbian was inextricably linked to that of the gay man because they were both "homosexuals." To that end, she circulated to Daughters' members extensive legal and medical literature on homosexual men. (Little attention had been paid to lesbians in such literature at that time.) And she tried to get members to attend ONE-organized lectures, which were usually about problems specific to gay men. So strongly did Sandy believe that lesbians must make community with gay men that in the late-1960s, while *The Ladder* and other Daughters chapters were becoming feminist,[108] she refused to join forces with the women's movement, claiming that she appreciated its goals but "did not approve much of the rhetoric," and that she wanted anyway "to concentrate on getting rights for both gay men and lesbians in the homophile movement." Her good intentions alienated many members. Stella Rush recalls: "We had a number of girls whose experiences with men had been so bad that they wouldn't even come if we had a male speaker or met jointly with the guys [from Mattachine or ONE]."[109]

Sandy also tried to expand the base of the membership by bringing more working-class lesbians into the organization. But, as in most of the homophile movement, Daughters was dedicated to the proposition that all lesbians ought to look "respectable," which meant that in public meetings, especially those with heterosexual speakers, Daughters members were obliged to "dress appropriately," that is, in skirts or dresses. Stella Rush remembers "one poor butch" who owned nothing but pants when she joined Daughters, and who had no notion of how one dressed to look "appropriate": "She got the president of Daughters to go shopping with her for a woman's suit that she could wear to attend some big meeting with an outside speaker."[110] But working-class lesbians generally had no desire to be as accommodating to the Daughters' rules as this woman was, and they did not regard the organization as a safe space.

⸺

ONE Magazine also had mixed success in attracting L.A. lesbians. *ONE's* guiding hand, Dorr Legg, was determined, as the Mattachine founders had been, to make *ONE* cogendered. He supported a February 1954 all-lesbian issue as well as a regular feature, "The Feminine Viewpoint: By and About Women." As a representative of *ONE Magazine* and ONE, Inc., he reached out to Daughters' members not only in California but in New York and Chicago as well; he also promoted *The Ladder* when it began publication, and he helped with its Los Angeles distribution, hoping to demonstrate ONE's willingness to make common cause with lesbians.[111] The other editors of the magazine were equally anxious to appeal to women. They brought a lesbian couple, Ann Carll Reid (née Irma Wolf and nicknamed "Corky") and Eve Elloree (née Joan Corbin), onto the editorial board with four men. Elloree, whose clever and charming drawings lent sophistication to the magazine, was made art editor. Reid was also elected the "chairman" of ONE, Inc.; the other eight board members were all men.

Ann Carll Reid shared the goal of Legg and the others at *ONE* to involve more women in the magazine. As an editor and frequent author of the "Feminine Viewpoint" columns, she made impassioned pleas for women contributors in the pages of *ONE,* trying to shake lesbians out of their complacency: "Why are we, the women, reluctant to express our viewpoint?" she challenged. "Fear? Shame? Indolence? Snobbery? Which?"[112] But so reluctant were lesbians to be contributors to *ONE* that the magazine was reduced to publishing stories about lesbians written by men under women's pseudonyms to improve the ostensible gender balance of *ONE.* Even "Sappho Remembered," the lesbian short story that became a cause célèbre when the Los Angeles post office's seizure of the magazine led to a Supreme Court trial, was written not by "Jane Dahr," as the magazine announced, but by James Barr, the author of a much-publicized 1950 gay novel, *Quatrefoil.*[113]

To rephrase Ann Carll Reid's question, why did she and Eve Elloree "*not* feel fear or shame or indolence or snobbery" about "expressing their viewpoint" in a homophile magazine? Their courage in working at *ONE* is beyond question, but it is interesting to speculate about the reasons they (and the few other lesbians who contributed regularly to *ONE*) could jump in where others feared to tread. Surely their familiarity with *Vice Versa*, Edythe Eyde's little Los Angeles magazine, had helped "prepare the way," as a ONE, Inc. publication declared in 1956: Both women had been avid readers of *Vice Versa* in the 1940s, and so the concept of a magazine by and about homosexuals was not as startling to them as it would have been to most lesbians in the early '50s.[114]

But the subtleties of class and the imperatives under which middle-class professional women lived at mid-century—even in expansive Los Angeles—explain a good deal as well. Reid, described by Eyde as "a dear, elfin, little girl, real cute,"[115] was a white-collar worker at a downtown advertising agency who often held lunch meetings with her ONE board at a nearby coffee shop.[116] Elloree, who had been a student for a couple of years at San Jose State College before coming to Los Angeles to make a home with Reid, worked only as art editor for *ONE,* an unpaid position.[117] Both women, Elloree later recollected, felt free to hang out at the If Club and keep company with "a Hollywood crowd."[118] Stella Rush, writing under the name Sten Russell, was *ONE*'s other most frequent contributor. Like Reid and Elloree, she had some college education, but she did not work in a professional job—she was a draftsman. There is no doubt that producing a homophile magazine in the reactionary mid-century demanded great courage of anyone. Yet all three women were fortunate to feel freer to do such work than did those who, as Del Martin wrote, "had some measure of professional status" and were terrified of losing it in the midst of the McCarthy era.

But regardless of what enabled the women at *ONE* to do their work, its value was uncontestable, as the many letters to the magazine confirm. Only about 10 percent of *ONE*'s correspondents were female,[119] but over the sixteen years of the magazine's existence they wrote numerous letters, asking for advice, bemoaning their loneliness, pleading for an introduction to other women like them. Their letters were often poignant, such as the one from a Philadelphia woman: "I have been miserable these last few months because I have no one to discuss my problems with. But now that I have found your magazine I feel much better about my whole situation."[120] Sometimes the letters were utterly desperate, such as the one from a woman who asked for the name of "understanding lawyers in the Chicago area" because she could not "relate my true reason behind my difficulty" to her present lawyer. *"Very Urgent—Danger is involved,"* she wrote at the bottom of the page.[121] A married women in Granby, Quebec, confessed her lesbianism to the person she addressed as *ONE*'s "Feminine Editor" and lamented that "in this Province it is very difficult [for two women] to get together and live together, as our laws are very strict." She begged the "Feminine Editor" to "pass along my name and address to someone or a Club" who might exchange correspondence with her.[122] A New Britain, Connecticut, lesbian, after imploring the editor to "find me someone to correspond with as I am helpless in my own vicinity for reasons that you can readily understand," closed with a P.S.: "Please excuse my [hand]writing as I am very nervous."[123] It was no light thing for a lesbian to write to a homophile magazine in the 1950s.

Ann Carll Reid responded gently to all such letters, though she had to tell those writers who requested introductions to other women that the "postal authorities" would charge *ONE* with "inciting to illegal acts" if it served as a pen pal club.[124] But she, as well as the other editors, generally offered the magazine's crew as social service workers at a time when a social service organization for lesbians was inconceivable. "If you feel that any of the members of the staff of *ONE* can be helpful to you, please feel free to write to us,"[125] the editors told the women correspondents, and even coaxed them: "Please my dear friend, come out of that shell . . . and we will gladly help you in every way we possibly may."[126] The L.A. magazine's mere existence in itself was already, according to lesbian correspondents, a huge help for those who dared to read it. They looked to ONE in the 1950s to envision for them a freer world and to promise it would come to pass.

By the next decade, the outlines of such a world were appearing. The women's movement, which worked to better women's lot and also to overthrow their political reticence, was bringing about significant change; and lesbians—who as independent women suffered most under sexism—were in the forefront (as they had been in the first wave of the women's movement, during the nineteenth and early twentieth centuries).[127] They led feminist groups and they established lesbian groups. Feminism even miraculously revived L.A. Daughters by the end of the '60s. As *The Ladder* reported, the Los Angeles branch, after being dormant for a while, had "come to life like a fabled sleeping giant, with a large and very active group." Its president was a Latina, Delia Villarreal.[128] Villarreal's tenure was short-lived; but in 1971, another young Latina, Jeanne Cordova, became president, and her energy allowed the group to hold on even as other organizations for feminist lesbians were proliferating. L.A. Daughters opened the first lesbian social services center in the country, ambitiously offering "educational, recreational, and sociopolitical services, activities, and actions on behalf of our community" every night of the week in a little building it had procured on Vermont Avenue. "Our community," as Jeanne Cordova now defined it in the L.A. Daughters' newsletter she edited, had spread its concerns beyond lesbians: As its feminist goals now mandated, it was "dedicated to the personal and social liberation of all women."[129]

Gay men in Los Angeles were also changing with the times, and public perception of them was beginning to change, too. By the mid-1960s, the efforts of the homophiles to educate the straight world about homosexuality finally seemed to be producing traces of national impact. *ONE,* which had labored for more than a decade to bring homosexuality into the public forum, had reason to feel it had succeeded in 1964, when *Life* magazine ran a two-part feature on homosexual men, "Homosexuality in America: A Secret World Grows Open and Bolder," citing Los Angeles as the birthplace of the homophile movement. The *Life* article created tremendous visibility for the love that had dared not speak a name ever since the European invasion. Though the writer of the article was not precisely sympathetic to male homosexuals, he did attempt to be somewhat evenhanded, unlike the national media, which had seldom been fair when discussing homosexuality in the past.

What was more significant, the *Life* article announced to the public that the old perception of homosexuals as cowering in the twilight was in need of drastic revision, that a serious transformation was beginning. The writer of the *Life* article observed that the Los Angeles Police Department had arrested 3,069 men for homosexual offenses the previous year, but even the LAPD could not help but notice that a minirevolt was already occurring on the streets: "The pervert is no longer as secretive as he was," Inspector James Fisk despaired, inadvertently prophesying a sea change that was soon to come. "He's aggressive, and his aggressiveness is getting worse."[130]

II: THE BOLD ONES

Defiant gay activists from The Patch inside the LAPD Harbor Division Station, October 1968. This was one of two sustained Los Angeles public protests against gay bar raids prior to 1969. Troy Perry at far left. *Courtesy Lee Glaze.*

CHAPTER 5

Rumblings of a Gay Revolution

While it is possible that [the new morality] might lead to corruption and collapse, we have every reason to believe that what will ultimately emerge will be stronger, freer, and more decent than anything we knew in the past.

—Myron Roberts, "Our Changing Morality,"
Los Angeles Magazine, 1963[1]

THE "AGGRESSIVENESS" of Los Angeles homosexuals that Inspector James Fisk observed in 1964 was trivial compared to what it would become in the wake of a vast social upheaval that mounted throughout the decade. The 1965 Watts riots, the first race riots in which whites rather than blacks ran for cover, captured worldwide headlines and helped set off a new radicalism among black people all over the country. "Black Power" became a dramatic rallying cry as militants rejected the nonviolent rhetoric of Dr. Martin Luther King, Jr., and the gradualism of liberal schemes such as President Lyndon Johnson's War on Poverty. Ignited by images of a city burning and the rhetoric of righteous anger, the politically dispossessed of all stripes—including opponents of the war in Southeast Asia, Chicanos, students, hippies, the New Left, and radical feminists—adopted the stance of militancy for their own causes. In Los Angeles, Chicanos rejected the assimilationist

"Mexican Americans" and proclaimed themselves members of "La Raza." They formed organizations such as the Brown Berets and captured attention by dramatic demonstrations not only against the Establishment's war in Vietnam but also against discrimination, oppression, and malign neglect.[2]

Fueled by the nearby examples of Watts and the Chicano movement, as well as the attention of the Hollywood media that loved the color and drama of the new "youth culture," the disaffected young in L.A. also grabbed headlines.[3] In the fall and winter of 1966, thousands of them, dubbed by the *Los Angeles Times* the "Disturbing-the-Peace Corps,"[4] gathered nightly on the Sunset Strip for nearly a month; they protested the curfew laws that ordered them off the streets by 10:00 P.M. as well as the arbitrary arrests of long-haired boys and unconventional dressers. When the number of young protestors swelled to 2,000, the police called in bulldozers and tanks to clear them away.[5]

Among the protestors were many young gay people who relished the freedom to blur gender lines in the unisex drag that the counterculture now encouraged. "We used to dress up in the most outrageous outfits on weekends, and the [hippie] styles gave cover to us gay kids," Lee Mentley recalls. The young gays with whom he ran would start the evening by listening to records at Wallach's Music City on Sunset and Vine, and then make their way down the Boulevard among the hippie kids (who were often sexually flexible), stopping at the Whisky A-Go-Go, Gazzari's, the Fifth Estate Coffee House, and Pandora's Box, and ending up in the nearby gay bars such as the Farm.[6] "It's the freaks who walk up and down the streets that cause the problems," a city official complained of the boys who dressed as girls used to, with their long hair and jewelry; and the girls who dressed as boys used to, with their Levi's jeans and T-shirts.[7]

Despite the 1966 bulldozer-and-tank police assault, the young continued to flock to L.A. from small towns and cities to try their fortunes or to escape the narrowness of "back home"; and they continued to haunt the perennially flamboyant Sunset Strip, where they would meet their own kind and could savor the arty cutting edge, such as the new music scene that drew huge crowds of the countercultural young. Gay kids who

had no place to go but the streets—the runaways and throwaways—
were legion among the newcomers. (They would become a chief reason
for the establishment in 1972 of the Los Angeles Gay Community Services Center.)

The hip and high and gay who marched up and down the Strip and
found crash pads here and there in West Hollywood or Silver Lake or
Venice Beach rejected the sociopolitical rigidity of the noir years and fervently embraced new politics and a new consciousness. Influenced by
sensitivity marathons, Eastern mysticism, and mind-expanding drugs,
which fueled utopian visions, they became part of the countercultural
"flower children" of the "love generation," and they believed themselves
destined to bring "enlightenment" and radical reform to the troubled
world they were inheriting.[8] They had a champion in the *Los Angeles
Free Press,* which had been established in 1964 as a community alternative to the major media that avoided stories of interest to progressives.
The news about the city's campaign to drive nonconformists, including
homosexuals, from Pershing Square, for example, was virtually ignored
by the *Los Angeles Times,* but it merited front-page headlines in the *Free
Press.*[9] The militancy of the *Free Press* about progressive issues alternated with laid-back permissiveness. The *Free Press* would even publish
overt "Personal" ads, not yet welcomed in the mainstream media, including ads from "Groovy Guys" (which had become a new slang term
for "gay men") and "Gay Girls." The *Los Angeles Free Press* was the voice
of young hippies who rejected the conventionality of their parents' culture and identified with the "different." "What if all the minorities, both
born and voluntary, got together to cooperatively rent houses, shops,
ballrooms, coffeeshops, ALL over town?" a writer for the *Free Press*
asked in 1967, dreaming of a community of the "different."[10]

The great population of social and sexual nonconformists in 1960s
Los Angeles was often visible at the Human Be-Ins, held regularly in
Griffith Park and Elysian Park, where the inhibitions of convention were
enthusiastically challenged. "Man, everybody TOUCH!" a counterculture poet demanded at a Griffith Park Be-In. "We are too many and only
this rapport can make us one." He called out to "L.A. hippies, angels,
freaks, heads, old hairs, long hairs, Mods, Minis, mendicants," telling

them, "We have a communion to build!"[11] This "communion," in which "TOUCH" was literal as much as figurative and old notions of appropriate and sanctified behavior were vehemently rejected, helped not only to foster the Sexual Revolution but also to loosen old taboos against same-sex touch.

In fact, the loosening of taboos that ushered in the Sexual Revolution had begun in Los Angeles even by the end of the 1950s, when laws regarding "obscenity" were challenged: A book dealer was arrested for selling the lesbian pulp novel *Sweeter Than Life*, and he fought the city ordinance that made it a crime to stock "obscene" books. The United States Supreme Court found in his favor in 1959. Justice William Brennan, speaking for the Court, declared that such a city ordinance "inhibits constitutionally protected expression [and] cannot stand."[12] But it was the Hollywood film industry that was especially instrumental in spreading a developing new ethos all over America. As early as 1961, film censorship, which had been codified by the Hays Commission in the 1930s, was compromised when the Motion Picture Association of America declared: "In keeping with the culture, the mores, and the values of our time, homosexuality and other sexual aberrations may now be treated with care, discretion, and restraint."[13] The Motion Picture Association of America ceased to pronounce any film "prohibited"; instead, it "advised caution" or recommended certain films for "mature audiences only." Through Hollywood, censorship was on its way to meeting its demise across America.

HOLLYWOOD A-GO-GO

I see gay guys dancing their souls out, their faces sweating. . . . I see queens stepping out of their closets and finding the world outside isn't as bad as they thought. . . . THEY ARE OUT! I see them taking the banner from the "free people" (I mean the hippies or flower children. . .) and wearing the most beautiful feathers they can find.

—Sam Winston, *Los Angeles Advocate*, July 1968[14]

In 1961, an estimated 140,000 homosexual men and women lived in the greater Los Angeles area.[15] The sheer numbers of homosexuals who were congregated in L.A., combined with the example of the widespread militancy of groups that had once been tractable, would soon make its gay revolution inevitable. Already Los Angeles was one of the easiest cities in the world in which one might be "different"—which included being gay. Milton, who was employed at Universal Studios, recalls a sign he saw on the lot that had been posted in the mid-1960s, which at that time probably had no equal on the planet: "Universal Does Not Discriminate Against Gays."[16]

Though Hollywood had always been a haven for homosexuals, in the 1960s it became more overtly gay than ever. According to a 1968 book titled *Hollywood, Gay Capitol of the World,* it was now nothing short of a lavender paradise: "If he wanted," the writer proclaimed, "the gay individual in Hollywood could spend just about his entire life, perform nearly every function, entertain and provide for himself, in a purely gay milieu."[17] In 1969, according to one source, the male homosexual population in Hollywood alone was 25,000.[18] Lesbians, too, had formed residential enclaves by the 1960s (generally in less affluent areas such as suburban North Hollywood) where they might spend much of their lives in company with one another. In the early 1960s, North Hollywood had a dozen lesbian softball teams sponsored by various bars, as well as numerous bowling leagues, restaurants, and private key clubs.[19] Lesbians were also brought together during these years as fans at sports events such as the Roller Derby—televised weekly in Los Angeles—which featured dashing women skaters who were almost all gay.[20]

The growth in the male homosexual population in Los Angeles did not go unnoticed by the straight media, though lesbians generally continued to remain beneath the media radar. In the early 1960s, L.A. newspapers still damned gay men as pariahs. The worst media treatment of gay men came in 1963 from a small paper, the *Hollywood Citizen-News,* which launched a muckraking assault on "sexual deviates"—coining the term "S.D."—in a four-part series based on little that was actually news. The "exposé" was triggered apparently by the newspaper's discovery of the Los Angeles homophile movement: "These S.D.'s are organized," the writer complained. "They have their own newspapers, picture magazines, and code."[21] "SEX DEVIATES MENACE L.A.," the first headline of the series blared. The article declared that homosexuals posed the "greatest threat to health and morals in the Southland," and it distorted statistics on the venereal disease problem among gay men. The article also accused gays of being responsible for 60 percent of crime in L.A. and (bafflingly, without a shred of evidence) declared them all to be "potential killers."[22] The *Hollywood-Citizen News* called on the state legislature to make it easier to close gay bars since they were the main "S.D." meeting places.

In the midst of the newspaper's assault, an unlikely ally leapt to the defense of the beleaguered "S.D." Paul Coates, the columnist who bashed the Mattachine Society in the 1950s, recognized by the '60s that news of homosexuals in Hollywood was no news. Coates scoffed at the *Hollywood Citizen-News*'s "discovery" that Hollywood's "star-studded streets are being gingerly trod by coveys of quaint young men." "It should come as no surprise," he added with surprising understanding, "that the cinema hamlet is a traditional mecca for homosexuals. . . . They came here for a kind of social acceptance. And they found it."[23]

The *UCLA Law Review* also leapt to the defense of homosexuals in the mid-1960s. An exhaustive study, "The Consenting Adult Homosexual and the Law: An Empirical Study of Enforcement and Administration in Los Angeles County," demonstrated gross police and legal injustices against homosexuals and recommended the elimination of unfair laws.[24] The study team, led by Jon Gallo, interviewed dozens of judges and prosecuting attorneys, and were told by most of them off the record that "the legal system was behind the social mores of the day" and "[homosexual lewd conduct cases] were a waste of judicial time, prosecutorial time, and police time." "If they had their 'druthers,'" Gallo observed, "they'd rather not be dealing with such cases."[25] Obviously, for many Angelenos, citizens and officials both, times had already changed dramatically since the 1950s. The Sexual Revolution, the mass of young people who were rebelling against the conventionality of the reactionary decade in which they grew up, the alternative media and meeting spaces that supported them, and the old L.A. flamboyance all made the rhetoric of moral crusades such as that of the *Hollywood Citizen-News* seem to many to be anachronistic.

But the police, as untroubled by anachronism as was the newspaper, continued to hound homosexuals, both men and women, throughout the 1960s. Bill Stephens recalls the "Barbra-Streisand sweep" one evening in 1967, when LAPD officers raided gay bars and made mass arrests on lewd conduct charges. Stephens, who was among those arrested, says that there had been a Barbra Streisand television special that evening, and after watching it, he had gone to meet friends for a drink at the Ram's Head, a Silver Lake beer bar. He ended up at the police station: "They took sixty of us out of five gay bars," Stephens remembers. (He added that it was that harrowing experience that radicalized him. He decided to go to law school and spend his professional life defending gay people.)[26]

Connie Eddy recalls another night at her favorite Pasadena bar, the Daily Double: She'd gotten up from her table to go to the restroom just as three sheriff's deputies came in, and she had to pass by one of them as he stood near the pool table. By the time she returned and resumed her seat there was a strange hush in the room because "everyone was too afraid to talk." The deputies were going from table to table, questioning the nervous patrons. The deputy she'd passed earlier came to her table and asked her name. She told him.

He said, "Stand up, please."

I said, "Why?"

He said, "I want you to come outside with me."

"Why?" I asked again.

"Do what I tell you," he said. "I want you to get in the car. I'm taking you to the police station, for bumping into me—for harassing me when you walked by me at the pool table."

She insists she had not even touched the officer when she walked by. But he handcuffed her, though she begged him not to and assured him she was not resisting arrest. She was taken to Temple City Jail in a squad car and booked. Then she was put in a jail cell with women who had been arrested on drug charges. She was kept all night. "I was frightened to death. They let me out the next morning, and I called my mother to come pick me up. I had to go to court. They gave me a public defender who said to plead 'no contest.'" The commissioner admonished her: "You swore at the officer. You won't do that again, will you?" She dared not answer anything but no. Her case was dismissed.

Connie says she went back to the bar to talk to the owner, wanting to figure out why the deputy had picked on her. The owner speculated that Connie had been singled out only because she'd caught the officer's eye since she was femininely dressed. "It was like 'Who are we going to pick up tonight?' And I was the straightest-looking person there. They wanted to scare the hell out of me."[27] For the LAPD, nothing had changed since the noir years.

But despite such harassment, bars for lesbians and gay men proliferated dramatically all over Los Angeles and its outlying areas as more homosexuals came to the city and felt freer to show themselves in semipublic places. It was a game of cat-and-mouse, and the mice were growing bolder. In 1966, there were 119 bars that catered to gay men and lesbians in and around Los Angeles.[28] In 1969, the number of bars in those areas had risen to 162.[29]

Gay men's bars have always been more numerous than those exclusively for lesbians, but the number of lesbian bars and those in which lesbians were welcomed grew larger than ever in the 1960s. Through the hippie movement, which rendered whatever was bourgeois a target of disdain, many young lesbians who had come from the middle class had declassed themselves. They were unworried about finding jobs that were "respectable" and "worthy" of their class, and they took risks that their 1950s counterparts had feared to take. Sharon A. Lilly (who became a high school principal years later) remembers that while she was still in high school, in the early 1960s, she and a gay male friend, their phony IDs in their Levis' pockets, would hang out at Anna's, a bar on east Sunset Boulevard, where Latinos, blacks, and whites mixed. "It was filled with boys and girls our age—sixteen to twenty-four. Flamboyant kids. We'd dance and dance and dance. Boys and boys. Girls and girls. Girls and boys."[30] Unlike McCarthy-era middle-class lesbians who felt especially vulnerable because they worked at jobs funded by the government (for example, teacher, social worker) the declassed hippie was not terrified about confronting "the pigs" in bar raids. Francesca Miller, a middle-class African American woman who dropped out of college in the 1960s because she was "into having fun and doing drugs," remembers that in 1969, when the police raided the Farm, a West Hollywood gay bar frequented by young gay men and lesbians, the saucy patrons "blew kisses at them."[31]

~

Though some lesbian and gay teenagers managed to procure borrowed or forged IDs that would represent them as being over twenty-one and thus old enough to enter bars, for those who could not pass as adults, a new spate of coffee shops served as a sort of community center where they might socialize with other young gay people. During the 1950s on Hollywood Boulevard, gay teens hung out at coffee shops, such as the Marlin Inn, that catered exclusively to homosexuals, and those such as Coffee Dan's where an oblivious straight crowd sipped their coffee and nibbled their BLTs alongside drag queens and butches.[32] In the 1960s, more and more coffee shops opened where young gay boys and occasionally gay girls congregated. Some attracted a mixed crowd, as an Angeleno who had been a teenage habitué recalled of a Melrose Avenue coffeehouse, the 8727 Club, which catered to "gay, straight, hip, and the 'gee, I dunno' group."[33] The mix was a good cover. The proprietors of coffeehouses that had an all-gay clientele sometimes felt constrained to be as careful as bar owners: Bill Stephens, whose hangouts as a gay teen were the St. Genisius on Hollywood Boulevard and Alberto's in Westwood, remembers that the management at both, disturbed by frequent police visits, forbade the kids to booth-hop. But they carried on anyway by "sending a cup of coffee or a soda through a waitress to someone you liked," Stephens recalls. "Then you might meet and talk on the street. You could also send notes through the waitresses."[34]

Gay coffee shop hangouts were by no means limited to teens. Older gay males sometimes frequented such places to find teenage boys who were looking for adult companions. The over–twenty-one crowd of lesbians and gay men had their own coffee shops, such as the Gold Cup on Hollywood Boulevard and Arthur J's on Santa Monica Boulevard. Francesca Miller remembers Arthur J's as a phenomenally popular all-night hangout where gay people flocked after the bars closed. Arthur J's was thought by gay men to be a great place to score. Aristide Laurent, who was a regular in the 1960s, recalls that the sexual carryings-on had been so rampant in the men's rooms at Arthur J's that the waitresses were ordered to toss a cup of ammonia on the floor hourly so the fumes would preclude anyone from spending more time than was required to use the toilet.[35]

The Sexual Revolution was clearly not lost on homosexuals. Inspired by the topless craze that was sweeping high fashion and low nightclubs, gay clubs, such as Goliath's on Melrose Avenue, featured nude male go-go dancers. Some gay men felt nudged to liberation by the phenomenon: "I remember going into one of those clubs, which was absolutely packed, and seeing a naked boy dancing up on the bar. It felt like a new wind of freedom was blowing through the place," one man recalls.[36] Sexual freedom became a major issue in L.A. gay male culture in the 1960s, and there were bars for every variety of sexual tastes. The Red Plume aped *Playboy* by appropriating its icon for outrageously gay usage: Customers were waited on by male "bunnies" wearing little more than a bow tie and a smile.[37] Madness Inc. served the leather trade. At Cannibal, the patrons could witness live sex acts.[38] Drag came back to the Sunset Strip and Hollywood. Ciro's nightclub on the Strip, which had long been shuttered, reopened as a gay venue featuring the young female impersonator, Jim Bailey. "Drags have gone mod," the author of *Hollywood, Gay Capitol of the World,* said in 1968 of miniskirted and vinyl-booted queens in the Hollywood bars.[39]

Sexually charged gay motorcycle clubs also multiplied in Los Angeles during the 1960s. The Satyrs had been the only gay motorcycle club in America when it was established in L.A. in 1954, but now the Blue Max, Oedipus, and the Kingmasters clubs all competed with the Satyrs in bringing men out of the bars and to the campgrounds of the San

Bernardino and Santa Monica Mountains, where they explored literal new heights of sexual and personal freedom.

OLD GAYS IN NEW TIMES

Homosexuals reading the "non-discrimination" clause in Government contracts, which sets the official key for employment policies through-out the nation, might wonder with some reason whether the term "sexual orientation" should not be added to those specifying "race, creed," etc., and thus become a part of those conditions which should have no relevance to employment opportunities for every American.

—Robert Gregory, ONE *Magazine,* 1961[40]

Though some Los Angeles homophile groups remained quite timid throughout the roaring '60s, others became bolder, defining themselves unequivocally as members of a minority and asking for the rights that were opening up to racial and ethnic minorities, as did *ONE's* managing editor, Robert Gregory, in his claim that homosexuals should be added to the government's list of protected groups. But for the most part, there was a split between "old gays" who brought into the 1960s their 1950s fears, and "new gays" who observed the social upheavals that were taking place in Los Angeles and the world and wanted to force change even among the homophiles.

Jeanne Cordova, briefly the president of Los Angeles Daughters of Bilitis, recalls that the "old gays" in Daughters, who were generally mid-dle-aged, were uncomfortable with the feminist thrust that she and the few other women in their twenties tried to impose on the organization. The older lesbians were still afraid that if they appeared too subversive they would be more vulnerable to their enemies, and they were annoyed when Cordova invited a group from "Women Against the War" to ad-dress Daughters. Cordova recalls that the old gays were especially "furi-ous" with the in-your-face title that her "new gay" editorial committee had selected for the Los Angeles Daughters' newsletter, *Lesbian Tide* (cf. *The Ladder*).[41] By mutual agreement, the *Lesbian Tide* soon became independent. Daughters of Bilitis had been the only organized precursor to the lesbian-feminist movement, but it was unable to hold on to young members in the 1970s because it could not overcome sufficiently its birth in a very different era. With the rise of lesbian feminism, L.A.'s Daughters dissolved for good.

Other homophile organizations fared better because they reflected more of the ethos of the 1960s. ONE's dream of a big donor, which had miraculously come true in the person of Reed Erickson, the female-to-male transsexual multimillionaire, was realized in a milieu very different from that of the 1950s, when ONE had been born. Erickson's Educational Foundation announced in its brochure—in very 1960s flower-power rhetoric—that "the foundation of the Foundation is Love," and that one of its chief goals was "to bring to awareness of Love Reflecting Through in the lives of those (the children, the animals, and some of the 'lepers' of our society) who have become accustomed to rejection and cruelty."[42] With Erickson's money, the ONE Institute for the Study of Human Resources could fulfill its mission, couched in New Age language, to "assist gay people and members of other sexual minorities to attain their fullest potential in our society." ONE became the first institution to offer graduate degrees in gay studies, and it was eventually accredited by the state.[43]

Some Los Angeles groups that were founded in the 1960s began by sounding like their 1950s predecessors, but their rhetoric and purpose became increasingly aggressive. The Society of Anubis, its purported eight hundred members equally divided between lesbians and gays, tamely declared when it began in 1967 that "the membership . . . strives to present to the public a true picture of the homosexual as a worthwhile member of society."[44] Gradually, however, Anubis became bolder. When the organization received a state charter two years later, the lesbian president, Helen Niehaus, boasted, "What makes it even sweeter is the specific purpose for which we are chartered." The group had made it clear on the application that a primary intention was "to support legislation for the enactment of just and enlightened sex laws."[45] Though

Anubis (named after an Egyptian god who was a "balancer of the scales" and a "healer") was hardly a radical organization, it caught something of the temper of the times in its willingness to fight. After two female undercover agents infiltrated the organization in 1969 and, at a birthday party for an Anubis member, returned with Vice Squad and Alcoholic Beverage Control officers to stage a raid, Helen Niehaus blocked their cameras with her body. She was threatened with arrest but stood her ground. No arrests were made, though Anubis was cited for selling alcohol and permitting dancing without a license.[46] The experience made Anubis even more political, and members were regularly reminded that their "voting potential" as lesbians and gays "could be pivotal."[47]

A few Los Angeles homophile groups were even bolder. In 1966, thousands of bemused Angelenos witnessed the first gay parade on record, which was part of the "First National Homophile Protest" to end the ban on gays in the military.[48] On May 12, a long line of cars bearing on their hoods signs four feet tall that declared "Ten Percent of all GI's are Homosexual" and "Write LBJ Today!"[49] wound a twenty-mile route from downtown Los Angeles to Hollywood. The protest, one of five demonstrations in cities across the nation, was planned by the National Conference of Homophile Organizations, though Los Angeles was the only city to stage a parade. The energy behind the march came from the old homophiles: Don Slater, who had been an editor of *ONE Magazine* and, after a bitter dispute with Dorr Legg about movement priorities, founded *Tangents* (a magazine that was a cross between homophile and new gay),[50] provided his office as headquarters for the caravan. Harry Hay, the deposed founder of Mattachine, acted as president of the Los Angeles committee. A core of homophile stalwarts provided most of the manpower in raising the money and driving the parade cars. As *Tangents* reported, "Almost nightly from Topanga Canyon on the North to Long Beach on the South, teams of workers placed fliers under windshield wipers of cars parked in the vicinity of bars known to cater to the gay crowd."[51]

The parade got a nibble of attention from the media. The CBS affiliate in Los Angeles ran a brief film clip of the caravan, and Slater, Hay, and his partner, John Burnside, were interviewed on local television and radio.

Though the impact of this first gay parade was minimal—and more than forty years later gay people were still fighting the same battle over homosexuals in the military—Harry Hay observed that the homophile movement had "never had so much news coverage before." [52] The coverage was inconsistent at best. For example the *Los Angeles Times* declined to send a reporter to cover the parade "unless someone was hurt." [53] Homophiles, however, coming from an era in which the media would keep mum about them if there was nothing bad to say, were thankful for crumbs of attention that were not unmitigated vilification. The homophiles did not understand what the gay revolutionaries of the next generation would figure out brilliantly: how to manipulate the media.

A NEW ROAR: THE GAY REVOLUTION BEGINS

John Q. Public has to wake up to the fact that he has to accept us. We exist. Straights have to learn to live with it. . . . If they close up our clubs we'll all have to take to the streets.

—Lee Glaze, quoted in the *Los Angeles Advocate*, August 1968[54]

Gay leaders emerged in Los Angeles during the 1960s who understood that different times called for different approaches. A few of the radical founders of the L.A. homophile movement joined them; indeed, they jumped eagerly into the new radicalism that the social climate now permitted. Jim Kepner wrote for daring journals such as the early *Advocate*, and he joined younger gay militants in actions such as a 1967 protest about police harassment at an L.A. gay bar, the Black Cat;[55] Don Slater hosted the first meeting of the Los Angeles Gay Liberation Front at his *Tangents* office on Cahuenga Boulevard. But the new gays were inventive in ways that would have been inconceivable to the older generation.

For example, gay activist Vernon Mitchell (a retired aircraft engineer) opened in West Hollywood the nation's first free clinic that would serve "homosexuals, hippies, and others reluctant to go to the Health Department [to] get reliable VD exams and treatment."[56] Gay men had often feared that if they sought treatment for venereal infections they and their sex partners would be reported to the Health Department and, since most forms of homosexual sex were illegal in California, be accused of committing a felony. Mitchell's clinic (which would have been inconceivable almost anywhere else at the time) was a product of L.A.'s vibrant alternative culture in which the dispossessed, despairing of the Establishment, were finding their own solutions to problems.

—

The most notable organization that formed in Los Angeles in the mid-1960s, PRIDE, was far more radical in rhetoric and action than any of the earlier homophile organizations had dared to be.[57] PRIDE (probably the first application of the word to gay politics) was an acronym for Personal Rights in Defense and Education. Members of the organization called their opening meetings "Pride Night" and referred to the Hub, the gay bar that hosted them, as "Pride Hall." PRIDE was founded in 1966 by Steve Ginsberg, who was determined to disassociate the group from what he perceived of as the stodginess of the homophile movement. "The main hang-up is the difference between the activist militant groups, which take to the streets, like our organization, and the prissy little old ladies of some of the older groups," Ginsberg proclaimed (with the brashness of youth) to the *Los Angeles Free Press*.[58] In the context of the 1960s' sexual revolution, PRIDE's leaders adamantly refused to obfuscate their sexuality. Ginsberg, who was a twenty-seven-year-old landscape gardener, wore leather to meetings, emphasizing the determination of a new breed of gay male activists to claim freedom by flaunting rather than buttoning down.

Instead of dismissing young bar-goers as "riffraff" and shrinking from them, as Ginsberg believed the homophiles had, PRIDE hoped to embrace gay youth of all classes as part of a vital gay community. The September 1966 PRIDE newsletter proudly announced, "Ours is a young group. . . . We have great contact with the kids in the bars, who have always been neglected by the other groups."[59] But though PRIDE defended the bars, and even hoped to attract to their organization "the kids [from] the bars," they also believed that gays needed a variety of social outlets, including "a healthy atmosphere to meet in."[60] PRIDE aimed big, announcing its immediate goal—which was revolutionary in its day—to open a gay community center.[61] Pot-of-gold donors such as Reed Erickson were still scarce, however, and the group never succeeded in raising the necessary money for a gay center, though it did organize "healthy" community activities such as a hiking club and a bowling league, and even provided "marriage" counseling for gay people—anticipating by years activities that eventually became common in many urban gay areas.

But PRIDE's most revolutionary contribution was to organize angry protests against those who tried to rob gay people of pride—most notably, the Los Angeles Police Department, which had not ceased its attacks on gays. PRIDE was behind one of the earliest demonstrations against the police harassment of homosexuals. The response to a Vice Squad raid in the first moments of 1967 at two gay bars in the Silver Lake section of Sunset Boulevard anticipated the Stonewall Rebellion by two and a half years: Twelve plainclothes Vice officers had positioned themselves in a large crowd at the Black Cat to observe the goings-on. At 11:30, when a costume contest ended at New Faces, a bar down the street, dozens of men in drag crowded into the Black Cat. As the Rhythm Queens, a trio of black women, sang a rock version of "Auld Lang Syne," balloons fell from the ceiling and gay men exchanged the traditional midnight kiss. That was when uniformed police, who had been alerted by the undercover officers, rushed in and began to swing billy clubs, tear down leftover Christmas ornaments, break furnishings, and beat several men brutally.[62] Sixteen customers and employees were arrested and forced to lie face down on the sidewalk until squad cars came to take them away. Plainclothes officers chased two men across Sanborn Avenue to the New Faces bar. There, the officers knocked the woman owner down and beat her two bartenders unconscious.[63] One of the bartenders, Robert Haas, suffered a ruptured spleen from the beating. He remained in critical condition for days, and when he recovered, was charged with felony assault on an officer.[64] Six men were charged with lewd conduct: They were seen kissing other men on the lips for up to ten seconds.[65] A jury found them all guilty.

But after a couple of years of witnessing other minority groups demand their rights, and even take to the streets for them, many Los Angeles homosexuals were now unwilling to absorb such outrage without response. PRIDE spoke for them, organizing multiple protests outside the Black Cat.[66] Hundreds of onlookers supported the parading pick-eters, and activists passed out 3,000 leaflets to motorists explaining why they were there.[67] Though this may have been the first gay protest in America to attract significant numbers, the demonstrations never caught the attention of the media, and the Black Cat did not take the role in gay history attributed to the Stonewall Rebellion two and a half years later. Topography played a role in the significance of both events: Los Angeles is an area spread out over 450 square miles, where (unlike New York's Greenwich Village, the site of Stonewall) people seldom take casual walks. The Black Cat protests attracted multitudes of people who drove across town to participate, but chance passers-by (such as many of the Stonewall protestors had been) were scarce.

Nevertheless, the Black Cat protests continued for several days. Fund-raising efforts for the convicted six eventually drew support from San Francisco as well as from New York.[68] Herb Selwyn, a heterosexual lawyer and longtime supporter of gay causes, acting on behalf of two of the six men, Benny Baker and Charles Talley, appealed their convictions based on the equal protection clause of the Fourteenth Amendment: Two heterosexuals, he argued, who might be briefly kissing in a bar on New Year's Eve, as the gay men had been, would not have been subjected to police harassment, beating, and arrest. His brief reached as far as the United States Supreme Court, though the Court finally declined to hear the case.[69]

But a new activism had begun in gay L.A. Gay-Ins, inspired by Be-Ins, started in Los Angeles in March 1968. At the second Gay-In, held in Griffith Park in July, the speakers became political, exhorting huge crowds that LAPD entrapment practices must be tolerated no longer.[70] The response to a police bar raid several months later showed that L.A. gays were ceasing to accept harassment as part of the built-in cost of being gay. The Patch, owned by the comedian Lee Glaze, whose tag was "The Blond Darling," attracted many gay men and some lesbians (in-cluding the women who skated in the Roller Derby). Glaze had been warned by the police commission that if he wanted his bar, in the L.A.

suburb of Wilmington, to stay in business he had to prohibit not only drag but also groping, male-male dancing, and more than one person at a time in the restrooms.

Because business dropped dramatically after Glaze tried to comply, he boldly reinstated dancing, telling the *Los Angeles Advocate* that "homosexuals have got to start taking stands on these issues," and that he was "confident that bans against male-male dancing will be declared unconstitutional if a case ever gets before the Supreme Court."[71] As Glaze now recalls, "The cops were harassing me up one side and down the other." He responded in his inimitable way: Whenever Vice Squad officers came in to inspect the bar, Glaze, who knew them all by sight, would put "God Save the Queen" on the juke box to warn customers.[72]

One weekend night in August 1968, when the bar was packed with five hundred or so patrons and the dancing was wild, Vice Squad officers burst in with half a dozen uniformed policemen behind them. They stomped around to intimidate the patrons, demanded to see IDs, and made arrests. Glaze jumped on stage and shouted, "It's not against the law to be homosexual, and it's not a crime to be in gay bar!" The raid swiftly became a political rally. Glaze urged the patrons to band together and fight for gay rights. "We're Americans, too!" a man shouted.[73] Glaze announced to the cheering crowd that The Patch would pay for a bail bondsman for those who had been arrested. They marched to a flower shop belonging to one of the patrons, and Glaze bought all the gladioli, mums, carnations, roses, and daisies (but not pansies). At 3:00 A.M., demonstrators carried huge bouquets into the Harbor Division Station and staged a flower-power protest as they awaited the release of the arrested men.[74] With irrepressible camp, Glaze announced that he was taking out an injunction against the Bolshoi Ballet because sometimes its director permitted acts of male-male dancing. The officer behind the desk called for reinforcements.[75]

Despite the rising militancy in Los Angeles, gay people remained largely obscured to the public eye—except, of course, when homosexual men were being attacked in the mainstream press. Alternative newspapers such as the *Los Angeles Free Press* were cropping up in urban areas throughout the 1960s, but there was no national media that spoke directly to young urban gay people who were observing minority militancy everywhere and were perplexed by, and impatient with, the gentlemanly rhetoric of the homophile publications such as *ONE* and *Tangents,* which were considered stuffy and outdated. To communicate with the world—and, more important, with each other—a new gay movement needed a media infrastructure.

That infrastructure began with a periodical that continues to this day and enjoys the largest circulation of any gay publication in America. It was born in an unlikely place: the print shop that produced scripts for the daily soap operas at ABC Studios. Richard Mitch, the driving force behind the periodical, had joined PRIDE in 1966 after being arrested at the Red Raven bar under the preposterous charge that he had performed oral sex on the dance floor. Mitch was a writer for a chemical industry journal, and he volunteered his skills to help put together PRIDE's mimeographed newsletter. Over the summer of 1967, Mitch and his lover, Bill Rau, conceived of the idea of upgrading the newsletter to a real newspaper. Their production could proceed openly because all the men in the print shop, where Rau worked with Sam Allen and Aristide Laurent, were gay. They undertook to make the newspaper look more professional than the newsletter by typing it in columns on an expensive IBM electric typewriter and setting the headlines in press type.[76] Five hundred copies of the paper's premiere issue were printed in the ABC Studios basement.[77] They chose to call the new paper *The Advocate* because the name sounded "forward-going and legal."[78] That 1967 issue contained a front-page headline that was the first use on record of the slogan "Gay Power."[79] When dissension in the PRIDE organization imperiled *The Advocate,* Richard Mitch negotiated to buy the publication for $1.00.[80] *The Advocate* eventually spread far beyond Los Angeles, becoming the first national gay news publication.

Like many gay people at mid-century who were concerned about their "day jobs," Mitch hid his identity in the gay world under a pseudonym—Dick Michaels.[81] Michaels hoped to create a paper that would provide in-depth factual coverage of news related to gay men. (Though the paper attempted to include some lesbian coverage, it was perfunctory and generally limited to cultural items such as reviews in 1968 of the play *The Killing of Sister George* and the film *Therese and Isabelle*.) Michaels' personal obsession, triggered by his false arrest, was to investigate LAPD abuses whenever possible, and articles with such titles as "Anatomy of a Raid" and "The Fine Art of Entrapment" became staples in the paper, which included lighter fare, too, such as an April 1968 article about L.A.'s first "Gay-In" in Griffith Park, described as "a throng of about 200 wild fairies having a festive affair."[82]

Michaels was also an astute businessman who realized he might create a wider appeal for his product if he included columns about everyday-life interests such as might be found in the *Los Angeles Times:* a fitness column, "Body Buddy"; amusing features such as "Cooking with Auntie Lou"; advice columns such as "Smoke from Jeannie's Lamp," written by a heterosexual woman, Jeanne Barney; and "Astro-Logic" (an astrology column by Aristide Laurent, who confesses today that he "knew nothing about astrology").[83] Michaels also appealed to his gay readership through a large all-male personal ad section, "Trader Dick" (a play on the sexual slang terms "dick" and "trade," and the Pacific Coast chain of restaurants, Trader Vic). The Trader Dick section of the paper became increasingly provocative and—of course—popular and profitable.

Despite the sexual daring of his newspaper and his willingness to be confrontational in his attacks on the police, Michaels often betrayed a surprisingly conservative nature, both personally and in what he wanted to be the tenor of his paper. Not only was he adamant about keeping his real name a secret throughout his years at *The Advocate,* but also he refused to permit his picture to appear in a gay context and he stayed away from gay events for fear he would be photographed.[84] Though a paper such as *The Advocate* probably could not have existed were it not for the radical milieu into which it was born, Michaels preferred to feature gay men who were clean-cut and moderate in their demeanor. For instance, Troy Perry, the founder of the Metropolitan Community Church (and dapper in or out of his clerical collar), enjoyed frequent coverage in Michaels' newspaper; but Morris Kight, a prominent spokesman

for the L.A. Gay Liberation Front and an old hippie in style, had a difficult time getting the notice he merited.

For about two years, the paper's official name was the *Los Angeles Advocate,* and its beat was local. However, because "local" was Los Angeles
and included Hollywood, *The Advocate* sometimes reported on stories
that were also covered in the national press. It was *The Advocate*'s mission to rescue such stories from homophobic distortions. For example,
the 1968 murder of the silent film star Ramon Novarro by two brothers
working as hustlers made lurid headlines all over the country, but the
only gay-sensitive (and factual) account of the trial was in *The Advocate,*
where Jim Kepner wrote that the prosecution "seemed less concerned
with [the murderers] than with convicting the semi-retired screen star
of homosexuality."[85] *The Advocate* also doggedly challenged the authorities as other papers feared or neglected to do on homosexual issues. In
1969, for example, when a slight-of-stature male nurse named Howard
Efland died after injuries sustained at the hands of LAPD Vice officers, a
coroner's inquest described the death as "excusable homicide" due to
Efland's resisting arrest; the *Los Angeles Advocate* was the only paper
that recorded outrage at the law enforcement officials' patent lie.[86]

Shortly before the paper dropped the geographic modifier from its
name, Mitch hired Rob Cole, a seventeen-year veteran at the *Dallas
Morning News* and its former city editor, to infuse professional journal-
ism standards into the newspaper. *The Advocate* was soon widely recognized as "the news arm of the gay movement."[87] Gay readers everywhere
saw it as the source to which they might go for crucial stories that were
blacked out of the mainstream press.

Dick Michaels, who had paid one dollar for ownership of *The Advocate* a few years earlier, sold the paper in 1974 to investment banker
David Goodstein for $350,000.[88] Its initial print run of 500 copies had by
then swelled to an audited circulation of 44,000 per issue,[89] and *The Advocate* was changing with the rapidly growing readership. Goodstein
soon fired the original staff. Jeanne Barney, who continued to write for
the paper, recalls that Goodstein announced to the staff that he wanted
the paper to appeal to "the upwardly mobile homosexual who has a
home in the hills, drives a luxury car and orders alcohol by brand." (Her

reaction: "That's all very nice—but what about the rest of us?"[90]) Aristide Laurent, who had been with *The Advocate* since its beginnings as the PRIDE newsletter, recalls that he felt as though "[his] country ha[d] been taken over."[91] Goodstein moved *The Advocate* headquarters to the affluent area of San Mateo in Northern California. It came back to Los Angeles ten years later in a much altered form.

Homosexuals understood at mid-century that their greatest adversaries were the churches, which dubbed them sinful; the mental health profession, which dubbed them sick; and the law, which took its clues from the other authorities and thus justified their cruelty. Though activists waited until 1970 to try to change the mental health profession, they embarked on a well-organized campaign to educate the churches in 1964. A group of homophiles in San Francisco started the Council on Religion and the Homosexual, an interfaith coalition under the sponsorship of the powerful Glide Memorial Church, formed in the expectation that if the churches could be made tolerant of homosexuals, law enforcement would follow suit. The following summer, an independent group calling itself the Council on Religion and the Homophile was established in Los Angeles. The Council on Religion and the Homophile argued that the public's "misunderstanding of and mistreatment of homophiles" was "unchristian," and that "open communication between churchmen and homophiles" was necessary to end intolerance.[92]

A few Los Angeles churches had long been sympathetic to homosexuals. Even during the 1950s, Stella Rush recalls, the Unitarian church to which she belonged was so concerned with police harassment of both progressives and gays that it instructed all the parishioners about what they should do if they were ever accosted by the police: "We should never say where we worked. 'Give only name, rank, and serial number.'"[93] But such liberalism was rare among the churches. In a city with more church denominations than any place else on earth, lesbians and gay men who were religious had few safe harbors at mid-century, though in the midst of the 1960s Sexual Revolution, some ministers were gradually coming to understand that they were obliged "to reexamine their traditional attitudes toward all sexual matters, including male and female homosexuality," as one clergyman wrote.[94] But most homosexuals who wanted a church affiliation still had to be closeted.

JJ Vega, who as a teenager in the 1960s had been a member of Assembly of God, a Pentecostal church in La Puente, remembers that six or seven of her friends at church were also teenage lesbians. Though some of them, like JJ and "George" (née Nancy), felt painfully awkward when forced to be feminine, they were told they must always wear dresses, could not use masculine names, and must do the "altar call" in order to have their demons chased out of them. JJ quit the church, but church members continued to pursue her. When she began living with another woman after she graduated from high school, they paid her harassing visits, telling her she was "living in sin" and must leave her partner.[95] Her experience was all too typical for gays and lesbians who were hungry for spirituality and had nowhere to turn but the established churches.

The raid at The Patch in 1968 was at least indirectly responsible for the establishment of a new church in L.A. that would eventually provide safe harbor to many lesbians and gays worldwide. Troy Perry, a Pentecostal minister who was expelled by his Tennessee congregation because he was discovered to be gay, had moved to Southern California and had found work as a manager in the yardage department at Sears. The night of The Patch raid, he had come to the bar with a date, Tony Valdez, who was one of those arrested. After Valdez's release, Perry tried to comfort him with talk of God, but Valdez would not be comforted: "We're just a bunch of dirty queers," he said. "God doesn't care [about us]." Perry believes the incident was an epiphany for him, stirring him to the realization that he must found "a church for all of us who are outcast."[96]

Chuck Rowland had tried to found the Church of One Brotherhood years earlier, in 1956, but that era was not ready, and Rowland's efforts were short-lived. Twelve years later, the times were right. Such a church would have been inconceivable in Baptist and Pentecostal Tennessee, or almost anywhere else, but Southern California had been home to countless cults and tiny denominations as well as gigantic single churches built around one charismatic figure, such as Aimee Semple McPherson and the Angelus Temple that she founded in the 1920s. Thus the idea of a gay church was credible—though not to everyone: Perry recalls that he presented his plan to a friend, who scoffingly asked, "How are you going to organize a bunch of queens, and get them to follow any religion . . . or do anything together?" Perry was himself uncertain, but he took out an ad in *The Advocate*.

Twelve men and women responded, and in October 1968, in the living room of his rented Huntington Park house, Perry conducted the first service of the Metropolitan Community Church, named for its birth in metropolitan Los Angeles.[97] Milan Charles, who had been a member of Rowland's failed Church of One Brotherhood, at last found a spiritual home: He became one of the early members of the Metropolitan Community Church.[98]

Perry had hit on the way to fill a gaping need of the many lesbians and gay men who had been thrown out of their churches or, like JJ Vega, were made to flee, but still longed for a spiritual life. From the initial dozen worshippers, the congregation grew so rapidly that Perry had to scramble almost every week to find a larger venue. "You better attend church every Sunday if you want to know where the Church is going to be," the congregants would quip.[99] When Perry obtained the 385-seat Encore Theater on Melrose Avenue for Metropolitan Community Church services, that, too, filled. The services were seriously Christian, but not without gay levity. For instance, Lucia Chappelle recalls that the music director, Willie Smith, "all dressed in white, would just fly out on the stage holding a microphone and shout, 'All right you queens! On your feet for Jesus!'"[100] Perry performed some of the first public gay wedding ceremonies in the country, beginning with the wedding of two Latino men in 1969.[101] In addition to tending to the spiritual needs of its parishioners, the Metropolitan Community Church offered a spate of social services, including a Crisis Intervention Counseling hotline and an "Alcoholics Together" group.[102]

Perry wanted to bring gay and lesbian community diversity into his congregation, and he was especially receptive to women and people of color. He welcomed as ushers butch women in formal dress suits;[103] he eventually helped to establish De Colores, an all-lesbian group within the church; and he encouraged the ordination of lesbians as ministers in MCC. Flo Fleischman, who was a counselor in the church's Crisis Intervention Counseling Program, recalls that when her group was planning a conference, a gay male psychologist asked, "How many of you women will do the cooking?" She went to Troy Perry to complain and was delighted with his response: "The next Sunday in his sermon, he chewed the guys out. . . . 'I want you men to know that the women are not here to cook and clean for us!'"[104]

Perry's faithful parishioners soon made it possible for the church to purchase a large building in the West Adams district, and attendance at Sunday services swelled to more than 1,000.[105] The phenomenon did not escape national attention, and Perry was soon being interviewed for *Time* and *Newsweek,* and even appeared on Regis Philbin's celebrity television show, together with Vincent Price and Sal Mineo.[106]

Troy Perry was far from radical in his style or politics. (Lucia Chappelle remembers that the church was so conservative that she found only one other church member who openly opposed the Vietnam War.)[107] But his conception that homosexuals deserved a church where they would not be damned as sinners was radical in the 1960s, as were the gay activist causes in which he encouraged his parishioners to participate. When the Los Angeles Gay Liberation Front was formed in 1969, Perry became a member and an unlikely bedfellow of the radical, hippie activist, Morris Kight.

—

The culminating event of the decade came with L.A.'s May 1969 election in which City Councilman Paul Lamport lost his bid for a second term because gay people united to defeat him. Lamport's biggest accomplishment had been his campaign for the "Walk of Fame" tourist attraction— blocks and blocks of movie stars' names etched on the sidewalks of Hollywood Boulevard.[108] He also proudly counted among his achievements the passage of an antiloitering ordinance, aimed primarily at chasing male homosexuals, whom he referred to as "molesters and troublemakers," from the streets of Hollywood.[109] Some gays were convinced that Lamport, who was endorsed by the LAPD chief, Tom Reddin, was "the man behind" the Silver Lake bar raids of New Year's Eve, 1967.[110] His 13th Council District encompassed not only Hollywood but also Silver Lake and Echo Park, a cumulative area that contained perhaps the greatest concentration of gay population and gay businesses in the nation.

Lamport's election defeat is one of the earliest instances of the power of the gay vote. *The Advocate,* which Lamport denounced for producing "a steady stream of filth and perversion,"[111] along with the gay-friendly *Los Angeles Free Press,* had united with "assorted militants"[112] in order to promote Lamport's challenger Bob Stevenson and, as *The Advocate* vowed, "to really swing an election."[113] "It's inconceivable to me that these characters presume to attempt control of an election in our district," Lamport told the media, complaining that homosexuals were so rampant in the area that he was "afraid to let [his] twelve-year old son walk through Hollywood to attend a Boy Scout meeting."[114]

The coalition to defeat him succeeded. Bob Stevenson won the election, and when he died suddenly in office, his wife, Peggy, who was voted in to replace him, made the rising gay community integral to her political machine. From the May 1969 election on, candidates realized that they could not win the 13th Council District without gay support. Even Paul Lamport came to that realization: In the next election, 1973, hoping to recapture his seat, he campaigned in gay bars of the 13th District, such as the Butch Gardens in Silver Lake. He admitted to the media that in the 1969 election the gay community had defeated him: "I didn't know anything about [the gay community]," he said in a mea culpa, "I'd never taken it seriously. Now, I do."[115]

—

The young radical gays in L.A. who stridently rejected what they saw as the overly cautious approach of the homophile generation that went before them were perhaps no different from many of the young, past and present: Lacking historical memory about how bad things once were and how much had already been overcome, they crassly characterized their warrior predecessors as being no more vigorous than "prissy old ladies." But, in fact, the homophiles who emerged in the 1950s and the new gays who emerged in the '60s each helped move the political center with regard to homosexuality as far to the left as it might go in their respective day. The new gays could shake their sabers somewhat louder and push left somewhat further because Los Angeles had metamorphosed by the 1960s to sanction the rumblings of a revolution.

Most of those who would found L.A.'s radical gay groups as well as its radical lesbian groups at the end of the 1960s and in the early '70s began as political and social left-wingers (as did their 1950s predecessors). They cut their teeth on the 1960s Vietnam and civil rights struggles and the counterculture, where they learned to theorize doubts about the infallibility of society's wisdom pertaining to issues of war, race, and morality. Before they began their work as gay liberationists, the new gays learned to conceptualize minority oppression not as a problem for the oppressed individual to suffer alone but as a social ill that a mass movement might eradicate. As one veteran of civil rights and union organizing, who became a gay activist, recalled: "All of us, to a person, had been involved in other struggles." Finally, they asked, "What about *our* liberation?"[116]

This picture of Lee Heflin, Stanley Williams, and John Platania of the Gay Liberation Front appeared in *Life* magazine in 1971. *Photo: Grey Villet/* Time *and* Life *Pictures/Getty Images*

CHAPTER 6

Into the Streets

A little theory may have gotten whipped up in Boston, but in Los Angeles we put it into effect. Lesbians and gays did a lot of marching and demonstrating in the streets of L.A. because here you can do it all year round, like you can't in the East with their long cold winters.

—Jeanne Cordova, 1970s organizer[1]

SUPERFICIAL OBSERVERS of Los Angeles have delighted in characterizing the city as a kind of Land of the Lotus-Eaters in which the residents spend their days puffing pot while soaking up the sun's rays or lolling on white couches decorated with egregious zebra-hide cushions—as a New York lesbian claimed of her 1970 visit to L.A.: "These surfer girls weren't political, at least not in the New York feminist sense I was used to," she wrote with East Coast chauvinism about L.A. lesbians, quipping that the 1970 gay pride parade down Hollywood Boulevard did not start until 7:00 P.M. because "no one wanted to forfeit another good beach day; it was a challenge to be political and to stay tan, too."[2] (In fact, the parade was scheduled to start at 7:00 P.M. only because the hostile LAPD, hoping for its failure, would not permit the marchers to begin earlier.)[3]

Radical gay men and lesbians who lived in Los Angeles during this time bristle at such feeble satire at their expense. They say L.A. was a hub of passionate politics long before Stonewall. Not only had PRIDE brought modern radical gay activism to Los Angeles by the mid-'60s, but lesbians in L.A. who came of age in the uninhibited and politically lively 1960s were very different from their postwar "Silent Generation" lesbian predecessors. Though a bit slower to fight for their own rights as lesbians, they were on the front lines of L.A.'s civil rights, antiwar, and feminist movements. Even in Venice Beach, the area of Los Angeles where the New York visitor claimed that in 1970 the sole interest of the lesbians she met was in getting a full-body tan, lesbians were in fact helping lead radical grassroots actions such as "Free Venice," a campaign for rent control and against the gentrification that was forcing poor people out of area.[4] Early in the 1970s, Venice Beach was where lesbians were soon in the forefront in establishing the Westside Women's Center, with, as Ariana Manov characterizes it, a "'fuck-you-and-the-establishment-you-rode-in-with' attitude." Lesbians at the Center published the first West Coast feminist newspaper, *Sister*, and they fashioned groundbreaking programs, such as the Fat Underground, the training of women to work in the building trades, and the Radical Therapy Collective—all in the service of women in general and lesbians in particular.[5]

The Westside Women's Center had as its model even earlier L.A. grassroots groups that offered social services to lesbians. The Los Angeles Women's Center on Crenshaw opened in 1969 (its building decorated by a red-and-white sign of the woman symbol, with a clenched fist in the circle signifying radical feminism); the Daughters of Bilitis started a center in December 1970; and the Gay Women's Services Center was founded in February 1971 by Del Whan, a lesbian who had been in the Peace Corps and had spent the 1960s in the civil rights and antiwar movements. The Gay Women's Services Center became the first organization in America that was incorporated as a social service agency exclusively for lesbians.[6]

The Gay Women's Services Center, which hoped to meet the needs of those in direst straits, expanded its services in 1971 and '72 under the leadership of a lesbian couple, Sharon Raphael and Mina Meyer. The Center's staff bailed gay women out of jails, rescued them from mental institutions, and provided shelter until they could get on their feet again; but the Center also served women who were not facing calamity: Activities were offered every evening of the week—rap groups, dances, a music night in which women brought their own instruments and played together—all of which provided welcomed alternatives to gay women who would otherwise have spent their nights in the bars. The Center was staffed entirely by volunteers. To keep the facility afloat and pay the rent ($95 a month), they held a spaghetti dinner once a week and passed the hat.

Because they thought it essential for gay women to be able to find the Center, the leadership battled the telephone company over its refusal to print the word "gay" in the phone directory. The Center prevailed with the help of a phone company administrator who happened to be a lesbian: "Gay Women's Services Center" became the first telephone book listing of the G-word in L.A. (The word "homosexual" first appeared in the Los Angeles phone directory in 1968, when the Homosexual Information Center was listed.) The Gay Women's Services Center also announced its existence to potential clientele by sporting signs on its doors and windows that announced here was a "Services Center" for "Gay Women"[7]—a heroic public proclamation for 1971.

THE L.A. GAY MOVEMENT AND THE LEFT

In the Gay Liberation Front we were all radical, antiwar, antigovernment, anticapitalist soldiers. We said that gay liberation was just one of the many battles against the existing power structure. . . . We were in solidarity under the greater umbrella of "revolution" against the system, on all fronts, worldwide.[8]

— Sharon A. Lilly, a member of the Gay Liberation Front in 1970

McCarthyism had been dead for almost a decade, and the opprobrium in which homosexuality was held had so lessened during the liberal 1960s that the Left could afford to be more receptive to gay radicals than it had been to their homophile counterparts in the 1950s, when it was expunging homosexuals from its organizations. But because the Left had been unsympathetic to homosexuals it was initially hard for some gay leftists to claim the gay struggle as one for *"our* liberation." Morris Kight, who ultimately became a principal leader of the radical gay movement in Los

Angeles, first dipped his toe gingerly into gay politics: He carried a sign at various left-wing demonstrations that proclaimed himself to be a "Heterosexual in Support of Gay Rights."[9]

However, after the huge media focus on the New York Stonewall Rebellion in June 1969, the gay cause became a cause célèbre among the Left, and Leftist gays everywhere suddenly felt free. Autonomous chapters of the Gay Liberation Front sprang up across the country.[10] Morris Kight helped found the Los Angeles chapter a few months after the riots at the Stonewall Inn. The L.A. Gay Liberation Front, which defined itself as "the militant arm of the gay movement,"[11] borrowed the language of the Left for its slogans: "Gay Power to Gay People. Right On with the Revolution. All Power to All People." The very name "Gay Liberation Front" proclaimed the organization's roots in the Left, as did the rhetoric of their newsletter, *Front Lines:* The gay people's struggle for freedom, Morris Kight declared in a 1970 *Front Lines* editorial, had "in its wake the freedom of all those crippled by a racist, sexist, imperialistic system, [and gays would] soon break the chains."[12]

The Los Angeles Gay Liberation Front's intense commitment to a gay revolution was rooted in more than mere rhetoric. In 1970, the Los Angeles Gay Liberation Front (GLF) had opened a little thrift shop on Griffith Park Boulevard; its profits were to be funneled into GLF causes. "Gaywill Funky Shoppe," its sign proclaimed. It was run by Ralph Schaffer, a volunteer who lived in the store's back room. It was there that he was found murdered, his hands tied behind his back. His comrades believed that he had been martyred because of the sign that announced the shop as gay. Their determination to make the world a more hospitable place for gay people became profoundly personal, and their anguish over his murder radicalized them further.[13]

But GLFers considered themselves soldiers of the broader revolution, too. The group pointedly elected as its first chair Greg Byrd, an African American. Morris Kight had worked in the Bureau of Indian Affairs and was in the forefront of the protests against Dow Chemical Company's production of napalm; John Platania had registered as a conscientious objector and had worked with the United Farm Workers Union. Don Kilhefner had served in the Peace Corps in Ethiopia and was active in the Peace and Freedom Party. Some of the earliest meetings of GLF were held at Revolution House, a mahogany-paneled, oriental-carpeted mansion dedicated to revolutionary people as a "safe house" by a wealthy anonymous donor. At Revolution House, all the revolutionary causes—social, economic, racial, and sexual—were represented. The Gay Liberation Front melded well: Its members were invited by other Revolution House groups to join their antiwar demonstrations and even to be openly gay at the Revolutionary People's Constitutional Convention. John Morgan Wilson recalls the frenetic enthusiasm among GLFers. Their excitement as young revolutionaries was palpable. "There was such a flux and a flow and an energy," he says. "Everyone was growing in leaps and bounds."[14]

Lesbian feminism, too, emerged from left-wing organizations in Los Angeles and employed the language of the Left. "We'd talk revolution—about how things had to change totally, and revolution was the only way," Sharon A. Lilly, a member of GLF and later a founding member of the Lesbian Feminists, remembers. "Revolution became like a religion for all of us."[15] Simone Wallace says that all the women at the Los Angeles Women's Center to which she belonged were—even *had to be* (if they were to fit in)—"very Maoist."[16] Sue Talbot and Liebe Gray, who were also habitués of the Women's Center, says they were really "Trotskyites."[17] All agree that they were very much to the Left, and that just as lesbian feminism grew out of the Left, women in the Left often grew into lesbian feminism. The Socialist Feminist Network, for instance, had been formed to address the ills visited on women in a capitalist society; "sleeping with the enemy" soon came to be regarded as a cause of those ills, and lesbianism (a political choice any woman could make) as a solution.

Though the gay and lesbian movements shared their Leftist genesis with the homophile movement that preceded them, their approaches to battling a homophobic society were very different because their times were very different. The homophiles were amazingly courageous for their day; but the insouciant, colorful antics such as "kiss-ins" and "gay-ins," which became almost routine in the next generation, would have caused immediate arrests and shut down organizations in the 1950s, when bravery was required simply to attend a private Mattachine or Daughters meeting. By the 1970s, lesbians and gay men could, and did, stage the wildest of public larks, often using the Leftist revolutionary technique of guerrilla theater to inform the "het" population that "we're coming out, and you better get used to it."

In Los Angeles, they did it with special élan. When Marsha Salisbury and her lover Debby Quinn were told by the manager at an International House of Pancakes that they'd have to leave if they continued holding hands at their table, they left—and brought back with them a dozen other women who staged the first lesbian kiss-in.[18] Lesbian kiss-ins soon flourished in L.A., as did gay-men's kiss-ins. To express their displeasure at the omission of women and lesbian artists at the Los Angeles County Museum of Art, Joan Robbins and other lesbian activists called the local television stations to announce the "First National Lesbian Kiss-In," to be held right in front of the museum. The women made the evening news—as they had hoped they would.[19]

GUERILLA TACTICS

The time will come when we will march, arm in arm, ten abreast down Hollywood Boulevard, proclaiming our pride in our homosexuality.

—Charles Rowland, in the 1950s,
predicting the future of L.A. homosexuals[20]

Gay men and lesbians in the L.A. Gay Liberation Front believed that flamboyant militant actions were indispensable tools for bringing about social change. By the first months of 1970, GLFers, in an incredible burst of energy, were making themselves felt everywhere. They slapped day-glo stickers of crossbones superimposed on the head of a pig (i.e., "police") on telephone poles and in restrooms to warn cruising gay men about police surveillance. They staged noisy demonstrations at the *Los Angeles Times* because it refused to publish positive news about gay people. (The paper soon changed its ways, even running a sympathetic five-part article titled "The Woman Homosexual" in June 1970.)[21] They ceaselessly picketed Barney's Beanery, a famous West Hollywood eatery, on whose wall hung the illiterate sign, "Fagots Stay Out." It had been a fixture at

Barney's for two decades, but now it came down (though it later went up again before it was removed for good in 1984).[22] They targeted offensive presentations of gay people on television, protesting the appearance of Gay Gaylord, a recurring character on the *Carol Burnett Show* in the sketch, "As the Stomach Turns." The show's producers eliminated the character and expressed unprecedented contrition for the entertainment industry's hypocritical public homophobia, writing to GLF, "We hope you will accept our apology for having offended you."[23]

The Gay Liberation Front also battled against the L.A. gay bars' antiquated rules against touching, which dated back at least to the 1950s when the Alcoholic Beverage Control would revoke a bar's license if same-sex couples on the premises were caught merely placing an arm around a shoulder. Terrified still of having their liquor licenses pulled, many bar owners continued to enforce the taboo throughout the 1960s. But gay militants now proclaimed such rules to be discriminatory: "Our bars shouldn't be any harder on us than the heterosexual bars are on their customers, and I have been to straight bars where they have almost had sex on tabletops," observed the Reverend Troy Perry.[24] The Gay Liberation Front took on the fight, aiming at a West Hollywood bar, the Farm. The Farm's proprietor, Eddie Nash, a Lebanese immigrant born Adel Nasrallah, owned a half dozen other West Hollywood bars that attracted a gay clientele.[25] Nash tried to enforce the "no touching" rule rigorously, even though on any weekend night the Farm would be packed with more than five hundred people, hip to groin. One gay Liberation Front activist made an appointment to confront the Farm's manager. "I explained to him that with his 'no touching' policy, he was trampling on the civil rights of the very people that made his business possible. . . . He said to me, 'You don't know who you are dealing with,' and with that he put his thumb down on the desk and twisted it as though he was crushing an ant." The activist, frightened but furious, says he conjured up his nerve and raised the threat: "You don't know who you are dealing with. We will bomb your bars."[26]

On September 8, 1970, armed with nothing more lethal than fliers and posters, a crowd of determined GLF men and women descended on the Farm and launched a pacifist attack. When they proceeded to hold hands they were "86'd," that is, kicked out of the Farm. "This is blatant oppression by a bar we gays frequent and support with our money," GLF proclaimed in the fliers that the "Radical Caucus Committee" distributed as they marched in front of the Farm every weekend for a month.[27] "Why Can't We Hold Hands in Our Own Bars?" the fliers asked. "We Can—There Is No Law Against It!" they answered.[28] After nearly a month of noisy demonstrations, the owner of the Farm capitulated and met with Morris Kight to negotiate. Activists nailed a triumphant sign outside the bar: "GAY PEOPLE'S VICTORY! THE FARM IS LIBERATED!"

On subsequent fliers, GLF informed Los Angeles gays that because the Farm was a "liberated bar," GLF was now urging gay patronage. Eddie Nash had learned to understand the power of gay organizing so well that he became a major contributor to the Gay Community Services Center when it was established the next year by former GLF leaders.[29]

A major goal of the Gay Liberation Front was to pull homosexuals out from the shadows—where they'd been relegated by a hostile society and their own fears—and into the sunshine. The GLF organized three "Gay-Ins" in 1970, each attracting thousands of frolickers who dared to be openly gay under "GAY POWER" and "GAY IS GOOD" balloons and banners.[30] Some Dionysian revelers went even further, painting their bodies with slogans such as "Fuck Forever."[31] The LAPD assigned large contingents of policemen and Vice Squad officers to patrol and intimidate Gay-In participants. But the times had already changed so much in Los Angeles that GLF was able to get a lawyer to file a temporary restraining order claiming violation of civil rights.[32]

When GLF staged the first Los Angeles gay pride parade in June 1970, the police again tried to interfere: GLF was denied a parade permit by the hostile chief of police, Ed Davis, who told newspaper reporters that he would approve a march of "thieves and burglars" more happily than one of homosexuals; but the Gay Liberation Front managed to convince the American Civil Liberties Union (ACLU)—which had refused to help the homophiles in the 1950s—to come to their aid in 1970.[33] On June 28 of that year saw the fulfillment of Chuck Rowland's 1950s prophecy about the proud day to come when homosexuals would march, "arm in arm, ten abreast, down Hollywood Boulevard"—though Chief Davis was able to get one last lick in by preventing the parade from starting before 7:00 P.M..

One of the most effective Gay Liberation Front actions of 1970 was staged in October at an international Conference on Behavioral Modification, at the Biltmore Hotel in downtown L.A. As Carolyn Weathers recalls, she, together with other GLF members, "interspersed our hippie-clad selves among the suited psychiatrists." In the midst of Phillip Feldman's presentation on an aversion therapy cure for homosexuality that used electric shocks, one GLFer rose up and cried, "Are we going to stand for this shit?" The others shouted, "Hell, no!" and stormed the stage, grabbed the mike, and screamed at the audience, "We're sick all right—sick of having ourselves defined by sexist straight psychiatrists." Don Kilhefner, who counseled gay youth for the Gay Liberation Front, told the stunned doctors, "You have imprisoned us in your mental institutions and brainwashed us into hating ourselves. I'm working with a teenage boy right now who wants to kill himself because of you people—and you're going to, by God, sit there and listen to us for a change." Several of the doctors rose up to support them, and a dialogue ensued. The 1970 incident in L.A., one of the first in which gays challenged the mental health establishment's classification of them as "sick," helped lead to the removal in 1973 of "homosexuality" from the American Psychiatric Association 's diagnostic manual of mental disorders.[34]

Despite the explosion of unprecedented activism that some GLFers described as "a demonstration a day," the mainstream media largely ignored the Gay Liberation Front. Because this lack of visibility severely limited GLF's social impact, the group looked for an action that the mainstream media could not possibly ignore. In summer 1970, when Don Jackson, a Gay Liberation Front member, proposed a scheme in which gay people would take over a small county, GLF found a way to break through the media impasse: The organization announced that 479 homosexuals were prepared to relocate to Alpine County, a Northern California mountain community of 1,000, whose motto was "A Great Place to Raise Children." A new law had just shortened voting requirements from a year's residency to only ninety days, which meant that within three months, gay people might become a political majority in Alpine. GLF's scheme created "utter terror" and "a shock wave through the whole State and beyond,"[35] which made the Gay Liberation Front gloat in its newsletter, *Front Lines*:

> The lid really blew off the establishment's teapot when the GLF-LA told the world about the plans for taking over the tiny county of Alpine, California. Everyone in the State power structure from Ronnie Reagan to the Board of Supervisors of Alpine to "Dr." Carl MacIntire, organizer of the recent "Victory in Vietnam" fiasco in Washington, D.C., have been running around like lunatics trying to find some legal (or even not so legal) way to prevent the takeover of the otherwise insignificant area by gays.[36]

Did GLF really intend to move gay people to Alpine en masse? Members of GLF were not always positive themselves which of their actions were serious and which were pulling the collective leg or yanking the chain of their enemy. As John Platania characterized it: "There was always an aspect of fairyland non-reality in what we did, but there was always a potential of some reality. Our vision sounded like madness. People would sometimes look at me like, 'That boy has had one tab too many.' Some people took it seriously. They saw the possibility." Without a clear consensus about whether Alpine was in earnest or a hoax, GLF devised precise procedures for their "invasion," and even obtained bids from two consulting firms to draft detailed building plans for the gay occupation—for which they could never have paid.[37]

But their scheme tested the limits of democracy and threw down a gauntlet before any who had been critical of GLF's tactics: "The entire plan is to be carried out in a totally legal manner," they proclaimed. "If the establishment really means what it says about working within the system, this is the time to prove it."[38] GLF leadership encouraged gays to prepare for a tough winter in Alpine, and Don Kilhefner and others called a news conference and deadpanned deadly seriousness about the gay takeover, pointing out what homosexuals had been denied in America because of discrimination:

> It would mean gay territory. It would mean a gay government, a gay civil service, a county welfare department which made public assistance payments to refugees from persecution and prejudice. It would mean the establishment of the world's first museum of gay arts, sciences, and history, paid for with public funds.

Kilhefner added, to ratchet up the jolt to heterosexual America, "Almost any state in the union has an Alpine."[39]

The Establishment fell for it: Carl MacIntire, a fundamentalist minister, even announced on his radio program, which was aired on numerous stations around America, that he would lead a group of "good Christians" into Alpine to prevent this "disgrace to our country." "Christian" jabs encouraged the future settlers (or hoaxers) further. "This time, the lions will win, Dr. McIntire," GLFers jeered. [40]

MacIntire was not alone in giving the Gay Liberation Front plenty of exposure. The *Los Angeles Times* ran half a dozen stories about the Alpine takeover; major magazines and national networks followed suit. But after an actual visit to Alpine (accompanied by an FBI undercover spy whose identity all the GLFers knew),[41] GLF hinted that the group had been perpetrating a hoax and called the action off.[42] For as long as it lasted, though, the "zap" gloriously fulfilled the Gay Liberation Front's desire to attract the attention of the national media.

———

Agitation such as the GLF perpetrated sometimes did affect the democratic process and promote social change—if only because it made less radical demands seem reasonable by contrast. But perhaps, too, agitation forced society to reexamine antiquated notions, as happened with Penal Code 288a, the 1915 California law that had made oral sex a felony punishable by a sentence of up to fifteen years in a state prison.

In fact, the law had seldom been enforced against consenting adults in their own homes; but it was nevertheless a Sword of Damocles over the heads of all homosexuals, since even if it had not been used against them, it *could* be.[43] Albert Gordon, a Los Angeles attorney, agreed to work with Morris Kight in 1974 to devise a plan to challenge the hypocritical law. They enlisted in the battle against the oral sex statute a gay male couple, a lesbian couple, and a heterosexual couple. Gordon, who had left his job as a janitor and started law school at the age of fifty after one of his two gay sons was entrapped, had by now become the leading pro bono lawyer to L.A.'s gay community. He asked each member of the couples to sign a confession that stated: "On or about May 8, 1974, in the County of Los Angeles, State of California, we did participate in the act of oral copulation with each other."

In what Gordon admitted was "a little circus," he informed the Los Angeles Police Department that the "felons" would be available for arrest on June 13—at the L.A. Press Club. Needless to say, the cameras were poised, and no policemen showed up. Anticipating a no-show by the LAPD, Gordon had arranged for Morris Kight to make a "citizen's arrest." Kight drove the "Felons 6," as they called themselves, to the Rampart Division Police Station—with the press in attendance. But the police would not bite; the station commander refused to make the arrests: "We didn't see the crime in action" was his excuse.[44]

The next stop for the Felons 6 and their media entourage was the office of the assistant district attorney, who issued a statement such as the Long Beach men whose lives had been ruined in 1914 would have dearly loved to hear: "It is the policy of our office not to file criminal charges where consenting adults, in private, engage in sexual acts which might be considered violations of the penal law."[45] If that was the district attorney's policy, Gordon and other lawyers who fought for gay rights could argue that California Penal Code 288a—which read, simply, "Any person participating in an act of copulating the mouth of one person with the sexual organ of another is punishable by imprisonment in the State prison for a term not exceeding fifteen years"—was misleading and must be changed.

And it was changed: In 1975, Assemblyman Willie Brown, who had long been sympathetic to gays, authored a Consenting Adults Bill, and all California laws against consensual homosexual acts were revoked.[46]

"OH, YOU LESBIAN FEMINISTS!"

We lesbians had to march in the gay pride parade together with the guys who were dragging a twenty-foot papier-mâché penis down Hollywood Boulevard!

—Brenda Weathers on the 1971 gay pride parade in Los Angeles[47]

Though men and women managed to work together on some crucial issues in groups such as the Gay Liberation Front during the 1970s, the merger was not always a happy one. Encouraged by both a very articulate feminist movement and the gay movement, lesbians, after generations of virtual silence, now dared to speak up in large numbers. But, as many complained, gay men seemed deaf to their voices. Lesbians in the Los Angeles gay movement said they often felt as though they were being asked, in spirit if not in fact, to make the coffee and take the minutes.[48] Their feeling of inconsequentiality was exacerbated because Gay Liberation Front men often lived together in all-male collectives, where meetings might be held informally. Lesbian GLF members were resentful because it seemed to them that sometimes important decisions were made at these meetings. On top of that, the women complained, they had devoted themselves to many Gay Liberation Front actions that had little direct relevance to them, such as the month-long protests at the mostly-men's bar, the Farm—and yet they could see no reciprocal efforts from gay men. About lesbian concerns, the gay movement seemed largely mute.

But the most unbridgeable gap between them was sexuality. The women were troubled that, despite radical rhetoric, the new gay movement was spending too much of its energies on battles that were no different from those of the old homophile movement (such as fighting the LAPD's hostility to gay men's semipublic sex encounters). Some of the women were deeply annoyed, too, that they felt forced to witness gay male sexual displays. "The big thing that drove us nuts," they recall of GLF's joint gay and lesbian dances, "was the men's promiscuity. To the men it was liberation finally to be able to grope each other in public. But the women were put off by this nonemotional sex flaunting."[49] The men resented the women for mischaracterizing their newfound freedom and trying to squelch it.

Many lesbians were now deciding they had less in common with gay men than with straight women, that heterosexual feminist gripes about the male of the species were little different from their own. But perhaps the coup de grâce to lesbian participation in GLF came with the men's decision that the GLF would form a coalition with the Black Panthers. Though the Gay Liberation Front women had understood from the start that GLF intended to be in solidarity with all revolutionary groups, they came to resent not only that lesbian concerns were too often placed on the back burner but also that the issue of the Panthers (quintessentially macho with their values of muscle and power) now seemed to have more significance for male GLFers than any issue raised by their GLF lesbian sisters. "The men invented this idea and were entirely behind it," Michele Ross, a GLF member, wrote angrily in the *Los Angeles Free Press* in October 1970. "The women were not. We feel we must find our own identity and our own causes as gay women."[50]

For a while, the lesbians in the Gay Liberation Front continued to try to attract more women to the group, hoping that if they were better represented at meetings they might be able to modify the male-dominated agenda. Brenda Weathers wrote in the GLF newsletter:

Attendance by the sisters [at Gay Liberation Front meetings] has been at best very sparse. The most frequently voiced reason for this seeming lack of enthusiasm seems to be that the meetings and committees are male dominated and oriented. Often I have heard sisters say, "there's no place for me there." Well . . . GET OUT OF THE BACK SEAT, SISTERS, AS WELL AS OUT OF THE CLOSETS![51]

But despite her pleas, lesbians persisted in staying away from GLF meetings. (So meager was lesbian attendance that some former GLF men today erroneously recall the organization to have been all male.)[52]

Like lesbians in the 1950s, the women could not see the relevance for them of a male-directed gay organization, but they also had other reasons for staying away. Many lesbians had become feminists by now, and they had a choice of political homes in L.A. In October 1970, most of the GLF women split from that organization and moved to the Los Angeles

Women's Center, which welcomed lesbians. The former Gay Liberation Front members started the "Gay Women's Liberation" group.[53]

———

The women who became refugees from GLF chose the Women's Center and not the National Organization for Women because they found the Center's radical Leftist politics more compelling—though L.A. NOW, founded in 1967 by women who had been active in the peace movement, was, in fact, the most radical chapter of the organization in the country.[54] Unlike New York NOW, which had purged its lesbian president, Ivy Bottini, in 1970,[55] Los Angeles NOW that same year elected as its president Toni Carabillo, a magnetic woman who also happened to be a lesbian. Other lesbians, such as Carabillo's partner, Judy Meuli, held key leadership positions in NOW. Though they were not officially "out," in L.A. NOW their lesbianism was an open secret, known to all the lesbians and to any straight women in the organization who cared to know.[56]

But that it should have been any kind of secret was abhorrent to radical lesbians. They would never join so tame a group. However, they were determined to make NOW deal openly with the lesbian issue. Nancy Robinson recalls that Gay Women's Liberation, to which she belonged, invaded a NOW meeting and performed guerilla theater tactics in an effort to push NOW to change: "We stormed in, all marching behind our lesbian banner, passing out our literature, shouting that they had to read it."[57] Though the radical lesbians had disrupted a speech by Assemblyman Mervyn Dymally, they were invited to stay and tell the NOW audience about the reason for their rage.[58] It was that meeting that led directly to L.A. NOW's drafting a powerful resolution in support of lesbians. The resolution declared in part:

> Whereas, the lesbian is doubly oppressed, both as a woman and as a homosexual . . .
> Whereas, the prejudice against the lesbian is manifested in the courts as well . . .

> Whereas, because she is so oppressed and so exploited, the lesbian has
> been referred to as "the rage of all women condensed to the point of
> explosion" . . .
> Therefore Be It Resolved . . . that NOW acknowledges the oppression of
> lesbians as a legitimate concern of feminism.

Ivy Bottini, who moved to L.A. after she had been ousted as president of New York NOW, conjectures that such a resolution could only have been written in Los Angeles. Life in L.A. was freer, she says: "The women in the New York chapter who were lesbians had high-powered jobs and were terrified of losing them. The women of L.A. NOW weren't so afraid to deal with the lesbian issue because they had more creative jobs, where they knew there was a lot of freedom and acceptance."[59] Not all members of L.A. NOW worked in creative jobs, of course. But what is certain is that L.A., at the far western part of the continent, felt freer to challenge NOW's East Coast founder, Betty Friedan, who had declared lesbians to be the "lavender menace of the women's movement." At the 1971 national conference, which happened to be held in Los Angeles, NOW invited an attractive heterosexual actress, Eve Norman ("Eve Normal" she was jokingly called by the L.A. lesbians of NOW),[60] to read the lesbian-rights resolution at a plenary session. The national delegates to the conference, far from the watchful eye of Friedan, resoundingly rejected her intolerance, and the resolution was adopted as national policy.[61]

Yet despite L.A. NOW's pro-lesbian stance, radicals continued to regard the organization as much too button-down. Though most of them, like the NOW members, had been raised in the 1950s as children of the staid middle class, in their romance with militancy during the 1970s they declassed themselves with a vengeance. They loathed what they described as the "polyester pant-suit crowd" of NOW. True radicals sported jeans and flannel and, unlike middle-class lesbians of the earlier generation or the more restrained lesbians of NOW, they declared their lesbianism loudly and proudly, whether they saw themselves as "gay women" or as "lesbian feminists."

Both "gay women" and "lesbian feminists" believed by 1971 that "the women had to do it for themselves." Until huge crises arose later in the decade that demanded that gay men and lesbians work together against a common enemy, lesbians' collaboration with gay men became minimal. But not only did they split from the men; "gay women" and "lesbian feminists" also split from one another. In this era of identity politics, identities came to be defined more and more finely (or narrowly): Del Whan, who had spent the 1960s fighting as a radical for minority rights, believed that homosexuality was a civil rights issue rather than a feminist issue, and that she'd been most deprived of rights not because she was a woman but because she was gay. She had joined the Gay Liberation Front in late 1969 and then the Los Angeles Women's Center, but her realization that she preferred to work in a "gay women's movement" where she could promote gay women's causes led to her renting the Echo Park storefront that became the Gay Women's Services Center.[62] Brenda and Carolyn Weathers and Sharon A. Lilly, who had started out, as did Del Whan, in the L.A. Gay Liberation Front, soon became radical feminists at the Los Angeles Women's Center. They despaired about working in the male-dominated gay movement, but they also did not want to work with women's organizations such as NOW that had large heterosexual memberships. They changed their name to the "Lesbian Feminists" in February 1971 when, according to Marsha Salisbury, "a straight woman from NOW saw us stage [a kiss-in] and said, 'Oh, you lesbian feminists!' We liked that name, so we had a vote that decided that's what we'd call ourselves."[63] The name became a term used by radical lesbians everywhere.

Lesbian Feminists hoped to devote their energies to developing new cultural institutions that were both lesbian and feminist. Throughout the 1970s, an unprecedented variety of lesbian-feminist institutions and experiments spoke to the social, political, and even health needs of lesbians.[64] Many of those institutions and experiments that began in Los Angeles capitalized on what was distinctive there, such as the weather or a willingness to explore what more traditionalist cultures considered far out and even "crackpot."[65] The Feminist Women's Health Center, staffed largely by lesbians, helped women take control of their bodies. They were taught by the staff how to do their own speculum exams, what homeopathic remedies to use for vaginal infections, and how to get rid of an annoying period in one fell swoop through menstrual extraction. A radical feminist educational group, the Califia Community ("Califia" in honor of the namesake of California, the legendary queen of golden-armored women warriors), was established in 1975 by two lesbians, Betty Brooks and Marilyn Murphy. Califia drew women to Malibu Canyon and other forest camps for bare-breasted retreats. There, imbued with utopian ideals, they labored seriously at finding solutions to problems such as class prejudice and race prejudice.[66] As "Southern California" as phenomena such as the Feminist Women's Health Center and Califia were, they caught on and spread elsewhere: The women's self-help health effort that the Los Angeles group began inspired a national movement and the eventual founding of the Federation of Feminist Women's Health Centers,[67] and Califia was one of the earlier prototypes for the outdoor lesbian mass gatherings that soon became popular all over the country.

Lesbians in 1970s Los Angeles developed a culture that had commonalities with that of urban-American lesbians elsewhere; but it was distinct, too, because it was shaped in part by the artistic and creative talents that Los Angeles has always attracted in abundance.[68] In 1973, the Woman's Building opened in L.A. in an elegant old edifice of the former Chiounard Art Institute. It became the birthplace of a new lesbian-feminist art movement in America. Though not all those who patronized its galleries, studios, classrooms, coffeehouse, bookstore, theater, and travel agency were lesbian, all were feminists and lesbian-friendly. (Cheri Gaulke and Sue Maberry, who met at the Woman's Building in the 1970s and are partners still, say that "the *energy* of the Woman's Building was absolutely lesbian.")[69] Founded by the lesbian artist Arlene Raven, along with Judy Chicago and Sheila de Bretteville, the Los Angeles Woman's Building was intended primarily as a venue for women artists and writers from all over the world who would work there to create a new women's culture.

Gaulke, a lesbian performance artist who came to L.A. in 1975, says she was drawn to the Woman's Building because of the liberty it offered to develop new kinds of art. The New York art world, Gaulke says, was more rigid than L.A.'s because it was fixated on a male-dominated gallery system and obsessed with male-defined "success." Los Angeles artists could be looser because they had been disenfranchised anyway from the "marketplace of art" that the New York gallery system imposed. "In many ways that was a good thing," Gaulke says, "because it meant that they had the freedom to be more daring. The lesbian-feminist artists in Los Angeles could really enjoy that freedom." The effect on her and other lesbians was transformational. "The Woman's Building became a research and development lab. And what they developed was not just art; it was a whole movement."[70]

Those who were there exude still about how "thrilled the women were to find themselves finally in a lesbian environment that had nothing to do with the bars," how fabulous and important it seemed to be engaged in forming a "women's culture" that would be unique to the history of the world.[71] Women's culture (by which was usually meant "lesbian culture") was truly one in which "the women had to do it for themselves" at the Woman's Building, from defining art and the role of the artist to deciding what should and should not go into Woman's Building space and how to raise the money to keep it all afloat. Among the courses offered was a "Program of Sapphic Education," the goal of which, Terry Wolverton recalls, was "to inspire art-making" and "to help us figure out our ethics and purpose as a lesbian people."[72] Instructors and students pioneered in art forms that were revolutionary in the 1970s—performance art, autobiographical art, collaborative projects—which, in good part because of their efforts, are now considered legitimate artistic expressions.

One of the most ambitious attempts to contribute to lesbian culture by the artists of the Woman's Building was the 1977 Lesbian Art Project, affectionately called LAP. Wolverton explains that those who worked on LAP wanted not only to study lesbian culture but also to reshape it, to rescue it from the "oppression mentality" that it had fallen into during the dark decades. "Why do lesbians gather in dark and dismal bars?" they asked. "Why do they dress so drably?" LAP artists tempered their politics with Hollywood dash, resurrecting the sophistication of a bygone era by staging events such as the 1978 Valentine's Day "Dyke of Your Dreams Dance," where the participants dressed like Ginger Rogers and Fred Astaire, or like the tuxedo-and-gown lesbian set who used to frequent the Sunset Strip night clubs in the 1930s and '40s.

The women of the Lesbian Art Project foreshadowed by almost a decade the Lipstick Lesbian veneration of style, which first took hold in L.A. in the later 1980s. Wolverton says LAP craved to promote "glamour, elegance, joie de vivre." In a gesture of playful nose-thumbing at more somber lesbian feminists, the women named themselves the Natalie Barney Collective, after a wealthy and very fashionable lesbian of the early twentieth century. They hoped to "revolutionize" anew the lesbian's conception of herself by getting her out of her very proletarian, very 1970s, plaid-shirt-and-jeans uniform and into the costumes that Hollywood thought of as glamorous:

> We tried to change the atmosphere of the lesbian social event. We put our artistry to work. We designed beautiful invitations that would highlight the specialness of the occasion. We flew gorgeous banners. We enclosed the dance floor with hanging panels that pictured women outlined in glitter. We encouraged an atmosphere of playfulness—women dressed in antique evening gowns, tails, top hats. 'Delightism' is what we tried to foster. 'This is what we should give to ourselves,' we were saying.[73]

The lesbians of the Woman's Building were not alone in their desire to promote glamour among L.A. lesbian feminists while, paradoxically, not doing violence to radical lesbian-feminist values. The Women's Saloon and Parlor, a popular restaurant that opened in 1975 on Fountain Avenue in East Hollywood, was run by Colleen McKay, whom former patrons describe as "tall, willowy, elegant . . . like Romaine Brooks," the early-twentieth-century artist who was Natalie Barney's lover.[74] The very name "Women's Saloon and Parlor" was an attempt to capture all-in-one the upscale connotations of "salon," the genteel connotations of "parlor," and the working-class hangout connotations of "saloon." Lesbian-feminist patrons came to hear lesbian-feminist poets read their poems and musicians such as the New Miss Alice Stone Ladies Society Orchestra play their retro-ragtime. Those who were there remember the setting as "classy" and "arty," with a décor designed by women artists.[75] "Beautiful, 'Hollywoody' women" composed the clientele, Simone Wallace recalls.[76]

But Colleen McKay made it clear that "Hollywood" was not all that the Women's Saloon and Parlor was about; she said that she opened the establishment "as a way to invade society and reinforce what feminists believe."[77] Any patron with a thin wallet was welcome to work off her drinks by washing dishes.[78] When workers picketed against the Gay Community Services Center (see chap. 7), the Saloon's staff refused to serve anyone who crossed the picket line.[79]

Women's music also flourished in Los Angeles. Olivia Records had started in 1973 as a lesbian collective in Washington, D.C., but before the release of Olivia's first album, Meg Christian's *I Know You Know,* the collective decided to move to Los Angeles. Ginny Berson, a founder of Olivia Records, recalls that before Olivia settled in Los Angeles she and Meg Christian had made an exploratory trip to the West, and they were awed by L.A.'s difference from D.C. In Washington, heterosexual feminists were actually "hostile to lesbians," according to Berson. In L.A., lesbians were integral to "everything that was feminist."[80] But the company chose to settle in Los Angeles "first of all, because L.A. was the center of the record industry." Berson also explains, "While we might have found a center in Nashville or New York, we didn't think a lesbian record company would do very well in Nashville; and in New York, the entertainment industry was one of many big things; in L.A. it was *the* big thing."[81] Olivia, women-owned-and-operated (from the technicians to the talent), soon opened the music industry to lesbians in ways it had never been opened before.

⟶

The number of lesbians in Los Angeles multiplied exponentially during the 1970s, when radical women who had ostensibly been heterosexual opened up to the notion of lesbianism as a political choice that any radical feminist might make. Simone Wallace, who was married when she started attending the Women's Center, remembers the Center's "Gay-Straight Dialogues," where she heard and saw, for the first time she was aware of, women who called themselves lesbian. "I felt, 'this is a world I know nothing about.' It was scary, disturbing. But it was also tremendously exciting and interesting." She eventually concluded, as did many at the Women's Center, that "my [heterosexual] lifestyle was not in keeping with my politics." She came out as lesbian.[82] "At one point, all the women were straight,"

Donna Cassyd recalls of the Los Angeles Women's Center, "and then suddenly we were all lesbian. It was like . . . 'Who did it happen to today?'. . . Lesbians were popping up like California poppies," she says.[83]

In the 1970s, women came out as lesbian into a world that would have been inconceivable to the generations that preceded them. The title of the 1955 nonfiction lesbian pulp *We Walk Alone* ("Of the love that dwells in twilight . . . in Lesbos Lonely Groves," the cover announced) encapsulated how many lesbians felt at mid-century, but such wails of loneliness were inconceivable to the "new lesbians." They knew themselves to be part of a vast community. Their knowledge was supported by a flourishing lesbian press in Los Angeles[84] as well as all over America. They had retreats and national conferences with thousands of participants, which made them feel, at least for the duration of the event, that the world was lesbian.

Los Angeles pioneered in such vast gatherings, beginning with the 1971 Gay Women's West Coast Conference, which attracted to its Metropolitan Community Church venue "gay women" (including a large Daughters of Bilitis contingent) as well as "lesbian feminists" and (to the surprise of the organizers) delegates from not just all over the West Coast, but also the East Coast, the South, and the Midwest. Jeanne Cordova, organizer of the conference, remembers that the "old gays" and the "lesbian feminists "were shocked to see each other."[85] The daughters of the Silent Generation were encountering the daughters of the Sexual Revolution. What might the generations make of one another? The lesbian feminists took off their shirts and danced about wildly and freely, in weaving circles, as at a bacchanal,[86] while the old gays looked on, bemused.

The splash of the first conference made Cordova dream of an event even more ambitious. A 1973 West Coast Lesbian Conference was national and international, attracting to its UCLA venue almost 2,000 women from twenty-six states and several countries—"the largest single gathering of lesbians known in history" to that date.[87] As was perhaps inevitable in bringing together so many diverse people, conflicts were epidemic in these conferences. One of the first political conflicts over transgenders took place at the West Coast Lesbian Conference when some lesbian attendees wanted to stop a male-to-female transsexual singer and guitarist, Beth Elliot, from performing. The Los Angeles organizers of the conference "didn't care about transsexuals one way or another," according to Jeanne Cordova. "L.A. activists weren't purists, and we certainly weren't threatened by transsexuals' participation. There were so few of them."[88] But many of the conferees from elsewhere insisted that male-to-female transsexuals like Elliot had not only enjoyed patriarchal power over women but also continued to exude "male energy." According to Cordova, a contingent who called themselves the "Gutter Dykes of San Francisco," led by "two orange-headed dykes with crew cuts," gathered near the stage and started a protest: "They were screaming, 'That's not a woman! He's a fake! He's a transsexual!' It was like an earthquake—at first a little earthquake. Then an 8.5," Cordova remembers now.[89] Robin Morgan, a keynote speaker, exacerbated the fury with an impassioned harangue, excoriating Beth Elliot as "an opportunist, an infiltrator, and a destroyer—with the mentality of a rapist."[90]

Nor was the Elliot incident the only war of the weekend. The subtitle of the conference had been billed as "Lesbian Oppression—What Are Our Solutions?" and many of the participants aired their own feelings of oppression with immense anger, often at the lesbians sitting right beside them. For example, when the women from a lesbian mothers workshop complained that the child-care arrangements at the conference were insufficient, another lesbian yelled at them, "You should have thought about that before you fucked him."[91]

Yet the conference brought together lesbians from all over the country, and many made political coalitions. A Lesbian Mothers Union, for example, was started at that same contentious lesbian mothers workshop. The conference was also very meaningful to women on an individual level. Those who were not embroiled in the various battles remember it still as a turning point in their lives. Mary Margaret Smith says that though she'd been a lesbian for years, she had never seen more than two lesbians together before, "and at the UCLA Conference there were two thousand, women of all ages, all colors." She remembers, "Someone had handed me some kind of flier. I hid my face in it and cried because I was so overwhelmed."[92] Donna Cassyd, who had thought of herself as a heterosexual feminist on the first day of the conference, recalls now that the conference helped her find a new identity: "Being there was so wonderful, incredible, joyful. We took our shirts off and listened to women's music. I thought, 'This is so amazing.' Everything about myself that had felt isolated was affirmed now. It made sense then to add 'lesbian' to 'feminist,' to become a lesbian-feminist."[93]

INSTITUTIONALIZING

We were demanding a place at the table. Once we had it, there was no reason to stand outside demanding it.

—John Platania, a Gay Center founder[94]

Members of the Gay Liberation Front, imbued with the romance of the Left, had been cynical about the possibility of effecting social change without a revolution. But to their astonishment, it was happening. By the early 1970s, it began to seem that "the system" was actually opening up a bit— that the law was not always hostile, that those in power might listen, that demands might be granted. Leftist GLF was faced with a dilemma: It could either deny the success of its labors or take credit for victory. GLF chose the latter. In announcing that the Gay Liberation Front was disbanding in September 1971, Morris Kight proclaimed, "Many of the goals that the Gay Liberation Front of Los Angeles started out to achieve have been achieved."[95] Though some GLFers were astonished at Kight's autocratic pronouncement, it did indeed appear to be time to move on to a new phase.

In this new phase, the leaders were no longer focused on the outside world—hoping to shock heterosexuals out of their complacency by guerilla tactics; rather, they directed their attention inward, to the lesbian and gay community—trying to figure out what it needed to do to improve its collective and individual quality of life. To that end, members of the Gay Liberation Front, led by Morris Kight, John Platania, and Don Kilhefner, used GLF's "Survival Committee" to set up social services very much like those that Chuck Rowland had dreamed of in the 1950s. They established the Van Ness Recovery House, a rehabilitation facility that would serve gay alcoholics. They set up Liberation House, which provided "crisis housing" to indigent gays, mostly young runaways and throwaways.[96] Then, John Platania, who had worked for the L.A. Community Development Agency, drew up a detailed development plan for a nonprofit corporation. His plan was the start of the Los Angeles Gay Community Services Center.[97]

The Gay Community Services Center began with Leftist rhetoric that was like that of GLF. The Center's purpose was "to meet the real needs of an oppressed minority." The word "Community" in the Center's name, according to early organizers, signified "having that kind of relationship to others in a group of people in which a person receives according to his/her needs and gives according to his/her ability." All volunteers were to understand these principles. For instance, the medical clinic was to be staffed completely by gay doctors, nurses, and technicians "who welcome the opportunity to serve their brothers and sisters."[98]

But such lofty ideals were sometimes compromised by the realities of "institutionalization." The L.A. Gay Community Services Center became the first gay entity to be granted nonprofit status by the Internal Revenue Service, thanks to Alan Gross, a heterosexual Los Angeles attorney who served pro bono as the Center's legal counsel. Gross made numerous visits to the IRS in Washington and was able to convince the feds by 1972 that the Center qualified as a "nonprofit."[99] When that status came up for review, the founders, formerly the most fiery radicals of the GLF, realized they must play the system's game: In defending the nonprofit status, Don Kilhefner, the Center's first executive director, informed the IRS: "The Center *does not advocate any* sexual orientation or lifestyle. It is common in our Gay Awareness groups to have several participants increase their ability to enjoy heterosexual relationships."[100] The ploy, purposely misleading, worked. The leadership was so successful at such maneuvering that in 1975 the Los Angeles Gay Community Services Center became the first institution with the word "gay" in its name to receive federal funding; the Center was also granted licensure by the state of California—all in an era of official antigay policy.[101]

Despite the founders' necessary practicality, however, the Gay Community Services Center's early clientele recall that in its first years it remained "hippie radical."[102] The Center's first building, a dilapidated Victorian on Wilshire Boulevard and Union Street where rap groups, planning meetings, and a variety of services were conducted, was certainly hippie shabby, with its creaky, steep stairs and rooms furnished only with old sofas and pillows.[103] Fund-raising, recalls Steve Lachs, was Morris Kight calling him or other affluent gays to say, "We seem to be unable to see our way to meeting the phone bill this month," and asking Lachs, or any of the other "suits," whether he could offer a check for the needed amount.[104] It was rumored that in particularly desperate times, young male board members would even hit the Boulevard to turn tricks and thus be able to cover the Gay Community Services Center's rent.[105]

Gay people were willing to give their money (and perhaps even their bodies) to assure the Center's survival because they perceived it as, what one observer called, a wonderful, exciting "beehive" of "boisterousness and serendipity,"[106] with an incredible panoply of effective social programs for a community that had always been malignly neglected. No obstacle seemed to slow it down. During the Gay Community Services Center's first year, its staff reported that 1,700 to 2,500 gays and lesbians passed through its doors each week, numbers that grew even higher as word spread of this institution that had no equal anywhere.[107]

Shabby as it may have appeared, the mere existence of the Center was considered a major victory for the community. John Morgan Wilson remembers "a complete sense of celebration in that house."[108] The frenzy of activity that had characterized GLF now characterized the Gay Community Services Center. Someone was always on duty to welcome visitors. A crisis hotline received calls twenty-four hours a day. The venereal disease clinic for gay men is illustrative of the Center's luck and pluck in creating something remarkable with practically no money in these years. Benjamin Teller, a physician and the founder of the VD clinic, had read about the L.A. Gay Community Services Center in a 1971 underground paper in Atlanta, Georgia, during his stint as a public health physician. When he came to Los Angeles, he not only volunteered to run the Center's free clinic without pay but also managed to persuade pharmaceutical companies to donate drugs; and, as the founders dreamed, he recruited doctors, nurses, lab techs, and administrators who were willing to work pro bono to "give back" to their community. (Some did it despite their worries for their careers: One of the doctors would sign only his first name on charts—though eventually he mustered the courage to become an open activist.)[109]

In creating a venereal disease clinic in which gay men felt comfortable, the Center addressed the long-standing crisis of the spread of venereal disease among gay men, which County of Los Angeles officials had never been able to solve.[110] Dr. Teller's master strategy was to create an ethic: Gay men must take personal responsibility for being tested periodically so that the chain of transmission could be broken. To achieve this ethic, a gay-positive culture had to be created. Teller dreamed up a poster of two bare-chested, good-looking, long-haired men embracing under the banner "Don't Give Him Anything But Love." He proposed to the Los Angeles County Health Department that if they would agree to do all the Center's lab work free of charge, the Center would provide a safe space for testing; this meant that sexually transmitted diseases might be identified and treated earlier and the long-run cost to the county would be reduced. Ed Edelman, who was the county supervisor for the Hollywood and West Hollywood areas, recalls that because the Center was thus saving the county money, he felt justified in becoming a strong ally and helping it obtain government funding.[111]

The most important services for the gay community, which had long suffered vilification and discrimination, were in the area of mental health. Individual counseling by mental health professionals was available to anyone in the gay community, but nonprofessionals were also trained by Betty Berzon and Don Clark, both professional therapists, in how to facilitate "consciousness-raising groups specifically for lesbian and gay people." The most basic of guidelines had to be formulated, since they were not self-evident in 1971: for example, "Use the weight of your authority to approve homosexual thoughts, behavior and feelings, in general, when reported by your client. This is important to counteract past experience with disapproval of authority figures."[112]

John Morgan Wilson describes himself as having been "a guy in a lot of confusion and pain" who was "drinking and doing a lot of drugs." The Center's therapy groups, which he attended when he was in his early thirties, provided him with a "safety net," he says. "That old Union Street Center saved my life."[113] Older clients shared that sense of salvation. "Most of my gay friends were not interested in 'being gay,'" says Ken Bartmess, who had been a dancer twenty years earlier, in the 1950s. The groups at the Center helped him build "a positive gay identity"—a concept that was completely new.[114] Veterans of less fortunate times were being healed.

The Alcoholism Center for Women, which rose from the ashes of a bitter strike against the Gay Community Services Center in 1975. *Photo: Denise Crippen/Courtesy Carolyn Weathers.*

CHAPTER 7

Big Battles

WHEN THE man who would become the first openly gay judge in the world announced to a friend that he would march down Hollywood Boulevard in the 1971 gay pride parade, the friend cautioned: "Steve, you can't. You have a career."[1] But Steve Lachs was not the only person with a "career" to come out as a homosexual in the early 1970s. Suddenly, in the wake of gay visibility that the radicals had succeeded in effecting, and the Sexual Revolution that acknowledged that sex was not always connubial, a whole new group of men and women were daring to admit publicly that they, too, were gay. They were not hippies or radicals who had dropped out of society, but professional and business people who were invested in the system. Because they wanted to forge a new image for the group to which they had secretly belonged, one of a "respectable" and "responsible" gay community, they had to begin by coming out, one person at a time.

Then, as they learned, to be effective—to make their impact felt as gay citizens and consumers; to create a community such as had never been, one served by a multiplicity of gay institutions and businesses—they also had to build a broad-based public presence. Thus they had to find ways to work together with diverse gays, such as radicals who had little interest in their "respectability." Coalition building was far from easy. Homosexuals would find that, other than attraction to the same sex and the threat of persecution, as a group of individuals their similarities could be illusions and their differences could be enormous. In

ethnicity, socioeconomics, aesthetics, politics, temperament, philosophy—they were as unlike one another as members of any random
grouping might be. How could these differences be put aside in favor of
a common good?

No collection of diverse individuals can find it uncomplicated to work
together for an extended period toward a huge objective. But among
some gays and lesbians the difficulty may have been further exacerbated
because society had for so long oppressed them for their sexual desire or
sexual identity. Now, suddenly, in the course of a general social liberal-
ization, it appeared that they might have their day in the sun—that is, if
other gays or lesbians did not elbow them out and claim the best rays for
themselves. Internecine battles flared between personalities as well as
classes, races, genders—between every conceivable grouping in the
Tower of Babel that was the L.A. gay community. The community's up-
setting tendency to "eat its own" was so prevalent that it was dubbed
"oppression sickness."[2] It was only when enemies appeared at the gates—
as happened when Senator John Briggs attacked California homosexuals
through a deadly ballot initiative—that the entire gay and lesbian community seemed able to put aside its differences and work together toward victory.

INTERNECINE WARFARE

*"Unfortunately there were bits of personal friction involved in this
misunderstanding . . . and a resentment at feeling that I, and others,
were often being manipulated like puppets."*

—One of several resignation letters by Jim Kepner to ONE Inc.[3]

Even the earliest movement for homosexual rights in Los Angeles had
suffered from internecine battles, such as the 1953 revolt against Harry
Hay and his fellow radicals by the Mattachine Society.[4] In the early
1970s, "respectable" lesbians and gay men who entered the movement
were upset by the ragged revolutionaries because they presented an
image more disheveled and an agenda more radical than the "respectable" wished to promote. When the GLF sought donations from

those they called the "capitalist pigs" in the Hollywood Hills, some mon-eyed gays muttered to one another that access to their resources "was not going to [those in] tie-dye shirts."[5] From their earliest days of found-ing the Gay Community Services Center, GLFers dreaded the time when "the gray suits would finally come [in] and take over," even though they acknowledged that it must eventually happen if the Center was going to thrive and expand.[6]

Arguments over politics and approach also erupted constantly in the Los Angeles movement: What was the right public image? What should the gay agenda include? What were the right strategies for winning? Who had the authority to speak for a diverse community? How ought activists to treat one another to salve the wounds of being outcasts? How could lesbians and gay men work together effectively?

Though all wanted to believe that "an army of lovers shall not fail," sometimes the lover aspect caused the worst arguments of all and inter-fered with the army's goals. John Platania says that he and the other founders of the early Gay Community Services Center "were all sleeping with each other." Employees of the Center recall that sex was not un-common in the men's rooms and did not raise many eyebrows.[7] For gay people in those days before the AIDS epidemic, every transgressive affair was a personal affirmation and a political act. (As one 1970 poster pro-claimed, "Gay Liberation. Dig it. Do it.") Among lesbians, too, the heady excitement of working together toward revolutionary change could be mistaken for attraction or love, though the women generally had fewer sexual encounters than their male counterparts. The emotional vulnera-bility and erotic rivalries triggered by intimacy between movement workers easily hampered the important labors at hand.

All manner of conflicts were inevitable at all levels—from the most committed leaders to the rank-and-file folks who provided bodies for demonstrations—because each was, after all, an activist who had taken a profound personal risk in publicly supporting a gay cause. Each wanted to put his or her proverbial two cents worth in, and each felt that his or her contribution must be respected—no matter how paltry, contentious, or offbeat. One woman at a gay pride parade organizational meeting in the mid-1970s claimed to abhor the mealy-mouthed euphemisms "gay" and "lesbian." Instead, she vehemently insisted, the parade should adopt the terms "men who suck cock" and "women who eat pussy." "And she was absolutely serious," recalls Rob Wray, who covered the meetings for *NewsWest*.[8] In contrast, a correspondent to the newsletter of the Southern California Women for Understanding, an organization of homosexual business and professional women, was uncomfortable with the in-your-face connotations of the word "lesbian"; she argued that women had a right to reclaim the term "gay," which had once been the preferred term of homosexual females as well as males. "Why should the men get it, and scot-free at that?" she asked angrily.[9]

Human foibles and egos abounded. The question of who would emerge as a leader in the relatively open field of gay power could take on almost comic overtones. Mike Manning recalls an early 1970s gay press conference in which he witnessed a discreet shoving match between Troy Perry and Morris Kight, each hoping to capture the eye of a rolling television camera.[10] Morris Kight's dedication and prodigious activism earned him the nickname of L.A.'s "gay godfather" for more than three decades; but despite wide regard for Kight, his faults could not escape notice. The writer John Rechy, who knew Kight over the years, observed that "his sense of self-importance approached megalomania." When Rechy appeared on a television panel to which Kight had not been invited, the activist, furious about the slight, called the author the next day and proclaimed, "The gay community is very angry at you," as though Kight and community were one.[11] Kight was by no means unique. A growing cadre of alpha types had emerged, each righteously certain of his or her queer convictions and promethean destiny.

Throughout the 1970s and into the '80s, lesbians who were political had their own points of internecine contention. Grievances such as those that simmered constantly around the radical lesbian-feminist community came to a boiling point at the West Coast Women's Music and Comedy Festival in 1981. As the feminist newspaper, *Off Our Backs,* described it: "Over 400 women of color, Jewish women, and whites gathered in the dark, . . . shouting at each other, without mikes or organization, trying to gain the floor and be heard." The Latina lesbians complained that "there was racism (conscious or not) among women attending the festival and the festival planners," evidenced by the fact that the Latin American Solidarity Day speeches "had to compete with the nearby proximity of . . . a crafts' fair and lake." Though women who could not afford to pay for a ticket were allowed to do a work exchange, leftist contingents complained, using anti-Semitic taunts against the producer, Robin Tyler, that the $65 admission for the four-day festival was excessive and that she was making too much money.[12] Flo Kennedy, a black activist lawyer who was an emcee at the festival and came to Tyler's defense, was called by other people of color an "elitist nigger." When Tyler repeatedly made the plea, "Please don't trash the festival," she was drowned out by the angry mob's continued protests that the festival was racist and classist.[13] Battles such as these devastated countless lesbian efforts and many of those who dared to emerge as leaders in the radical lesbian community.

The worst internecine battle, however, came at the Gay Community Services Center after it had enjoyed for several years the status of jewel in the crown of the Los Angeles gay and lesbian community. The battle evolved from a series of skirmishes that had been pitting leftists against "suits"; people of color against whites; and especially radical lesbian feminists against gay men, whom they accused of male chauvinism. For example, in 1972, Mina Meyer, a member of the board, became an administrator at the Gay Community Services Center and worked to establish the first lesbian clinic in the world—though it came into being only after a characteristic struggle. Meyer, part of the new generation of lesbians who vehemently refused to be submerged in gay male concerns, says that when she took the job at the Center there were few programs explicitly for lesbians, and she resented having to fight to create them:

> For instance, I asked the men who hired me about a women's clinic.
> They said, "Women don't get VD."
> I said, "If you're going to have a clinic for men, I want one for women."
> They said, "Okay. Find a woman doctor."
> Everything I wanted to do for lesbians was like pulling teeth.
> When the guys wanted to open the men's clinic, it was the whole Gay

Community Services Center that worked on it. But I had to put the women's clinic together on my own.

Nevertheless, she found a physician, Jane Patterson, who was willing to volunteer her time at a clinic for women and even to be trained by the Feminist Women's Health Center in self-help procedures so that she could teach her lesbian patients. Meyer also got lesbian nurses and technicians to volunteer their time, and eventually three more women physicians joined the staff. Despite her disgruntlement with the men at the Gay Community Services Center, Meyer believes that the women's clinic there was a huge boon to the lesbian community. "Women came in who were in their forties, fifties, sixties," she says. "They'd never had a pap smear because they didn't want a male doctor messing around with them. Now, finally, they could be safe with a lesbian doctor."[14]

The Gay Community Services Center was also home to women who did not need to avail themselves of services such as the clinic. It was what PRIDE in its pioneering vision had dreamt of years earlier—a safe and healthy place. Sylvia Rhue, an African American woman, recalls, "I didn't drink, smoke, dance, or like loud music"; the Center suited who she was much better than the lesbian bars where, she says, she once saw "this woman on her knees from a drug-induced stupor." She adds, laughing, "I always thought I'd rather have a woman on her knees in prayer. A Boinkable Bible Babe." The lesbian rap group she joined at the Center was "like this wonderful brave new world," she says. "There we were, all together, talking seriously, trying to understand one another." For her, the Center extended beyond its services: It was there she found her social group as well as romance.[15]

Nevertheless, trouble was brewing in paradise. Those who felt unjustly treated in one manner or another sometimes tried to suppress their complaints for fear of broadcasting the stereotype of gay people as divisive or bitchy, but that merely exacerbated tensions.[16] Many internal memos were addressed in a rhetoric of total harmony to "Brothers and Sisters"; reports were often concluded with "lovingly submitted." But discord was a daily reality. Some of the greatest tensions were over money: The Center began as a labor of love that had been staffed by volunteers, but when grants made it possible to pay workers, the social ecology changed. Jaime Green recalls the anguish he and others felt when that happened. "The activists were pushed out by the professionals when the salaries began," he says. "I remember when people started having job descriptions. Job descriptions?! That's when the activists started drifting away."[17]

Tensions came to a head in 1975. The conflict that almost became the coup de grâce for the Gay Community Services Center began when Lillene Fifield, a lesbian on the University of Southern California staff, volunteered her grant-writing skills and presented a proposal to a federal agency, the National Institute for Alcohol and Alcohol Abuse (NIAAA), which succeeded in netting the Gay Community Services Center's Alcoholism Program for Women a three-year grant worth $1 million. It was a windfall absolutely unprecedented for any gay group in the world. Now, with a fortune suddenly coming in, it seemed to the Center's fiscal director that it would be right to funnel some of that money out of the women's program and spend it on pressing institutional problems: The men's VD clinic was always short of funds, he pointed out, and also money was needed for the Center's new home because the ancient ramshackle Victorian in which it had been housed was condemned and would be demolished.

The director of the Alcoholism Program for Women, Brenda Weathers, who had assisted Fifield in writing the grant proposal, discovered the fiscal director's intent. She stormed into Don Kilhefner's office, protesting that the federal grant was earmarked for the women's program. To Weathers' outrage, Kilhefner tried to placate her, saying, "We're all brothers and sisters here, so when we get this kind of money we have to spread it around so everybody benefits."[18] When the Center management persisted in diverting the funds despite her vehement objections, Weathers notified Washington. Federal investigators were sent to examine the Center's books. Kilhefner preempted further actions by agreeing that Weathers and her program should be permitted to take the money from the Center's jurisdiction and establish a separate facility to serve women (primarily lesbians) with alcoholism problems.[19] The federal agency then transferred the grant to Weathers' new nonprofit, called the Alcoholism Center for Women, which continues to this day.[20]

The fight over the grant money emboldened those in charge of various programs to articulate their own growing discontent over issues of money and power. People of color complained that few nonwhites were given authority. The lesbians believed that the overwhelmingly-male board had formed a power bloc that was, psychologically if not in fact, made up of "reactionary gray suits," men who had no compunction about stealing funds from a women's program to shore up programs for men. Several program directors published an in-house newsletter, *It's About Time,* decrying the "deplorable conditions" at the Center.

When *It's About Time* fell into the hands of Supervisor Ed Edelman's gay aide, David Glascock, he warned that the Gay Community Services Center's internal squabbling must cease or it would lose its public charter as well as the federal revenue-sharing funds that Edelman's office had helped the Center obtain. The "insurgents" were then asked by the management to sign a "statement of fidelity," which they refused to do because it seemed too much like signing a loyalty oath. Eleven of them were fired—six lesbians and five gay men.[21] This was barely the beginning of the Center's problems.

Those fired did not go away. They called themselves the Gay Feminist 11, and a defense coalition was formed to support them. The coalition demanded that the Gay Feminist 11 be reinstated immediately, that the Center's "bureaucracy" meet with them in an open community forum, and that no "scabs" be hired to replace the fired workers. When the management was not responsive, a strike was called in front of the Gay Community Services Center's new facility on Highland Avenue.

The socialist Lavender and Red Union, which met at the Center, pushed itself to the forefront of the strike and promoted it as a workers' issue,[22] complaining that "the workers" were underpaid and overworked and could no longer tolerate the Center's "patriarchal management systems" or its "racism, sexism, and classism."[23] Michael Weinstein, who was a leader in the Lavender and Red Union, says that his group "came together with the strikers [in] fighting for the heart and soul of the community, and trying to have the community embrace an agenda of activism, equality, radicalism."[24]

They believed that the Gay Community Services Center was straying from those principles that were central to its founding and its very mission, and they made utopian demands, such as equal pay for all workers, from the highest supervisor to the lowest janitor.

Jeanne Cordova, who was one of those fired, says that she and some others of the Gay Feminist 11 fought the strike proposal for which the Lavender and Red Union agitated. The Gay Community Services Center "wasn't a supermarket," she argued. "It's the place my baby gay brother might go to ask for a bed when my Catholic parents throw him out. It's a place for kids who are beaten by their fathers for being faggots." But despite the reluctance of some of the Gay Feminist 11, the strike went forward: Picketers demanded the unionization of the Center, forbade "scabs" to cross their line, and sang union songs such as "Solidarity Forever." Because some of the strikers were people of color, the Center's administrators were dubbed racists and "capitalist pigs." (The charges were particularly galling to the Center's founders. Don Kilhefner had been known as a Maoist. Morris Kight was assumed to be a Communist. Gay Liberation Front wags had called them "Peking and Moscow."[25] Just a few years earlier, they had hurled the "capitalist pig" epithet at others.)

Cordova writes that she kept protesting: "This is not a labor issue. Our fight is about lesbian feminism versus male-dominated hierarchy." But the fight generally continued to be presented to the public as a "workers' protest." She complains that the strike was set up by the socialist faction, which was less concerned for lesbian and gay welfare than interested in "bringing down capitalism."[26] (Lillene Fifield agrees that the strike had been set up—but by the Right rather than the Left: arranged by the FBI, who wanted to destroy the first and largest gay center in America. She speculates that a handsome young habitué at the Center, who claimed to be gay though he socialized with no one, was a plant, a provocateur, who agitated with "lefter than thou" rhetoric and maneuvered the strike.)[27]

Regardless of the strike's purpose or the fired staff members' grievances or whether the strike was manipulated, it created a civil war within the community that almost succeeded not in "bringing down capitalism," of course, but in bringing down the Gay Community Services Center. Three of the four physicians who staffed the women's clinic refused to cross the picket line, effectively closing the clinic.[28] Contributions to the Center dried up. Mary Margaret Smith, who had been a donor, heard that a group called the Gay Feminist 11 was striking because they'd been mistreated. "I didn't want to be caught up in controversy," she says, "And I certainly didn't want to give them my money if they weren't treating women right."[29] Others who had been contributors had absolutely no idea what the strike was about but knew only that there was discord at the Center and refused to donate until it was settled. The strikers' angry chants such as "Shut it down or we'll burn it down!" drove supporters farther away.

The lesbians on the staff who did not strike attempted to explain their position in a sixteen-page broadside, "Women Speak Out About the Gay Community Services Center," in which they declared that though they were dedicated "to providing services for the lesbian/women's community—not the gay community," at this time the Center was "the only viable means of transmitting those services in Los Angeles."[30] But their explanation met with little sympathy among radical feminists and leftists, who composed much of the activist community at the time. All those who crossed the picket line to work at the Center were ostracized as strikebreakers.

The conflict rent the lesbian community in two. *Lesbian News* (which was to become the major L.A. lesbian publication) was started by Jinx Beers during the strike in an effort to present a moderate voice after some of her friends were ejected from the Westside Women's Center because they were "scabs." A riot almost broke out the evening a group of women who continued to work at the Center went to the Women's Saloon for dinner. "'Gunfight' at the L.A. Saloon," the headline of the first issue of *Lesbian News* read. They were refused service, and the Saloon's proprietor, Colleen McKay, shut down for the night rather than tolerate their presence.[31]

Lillene Fifield, who had obtained the million-dollar grant for the Alcoholism Program for Women, was, ironically, punished the most by strike sympathizers. Fifield says now that the men at the Center had indeed been capable of being "very oppressive" to women; but she believed the Center was precious because it was where gay men and women who'd been abused by society "would begin to heal," and she thought it inappropriate for the staff to "air our dirty laundry for all the world to see." She thus chose to continue in her post as the director of women's programming, despite the strike. She says she was "made a villain" at every workshop and community event. "I was thrown out of everywhere. Even at the Woman's Building. I was told I was not welcome." Strikers overturned her car and slashed the tires.[32]

The boycott of the Gay Community Services Center continued for three years. Josy Catoggio says that when the Center received money from the Comprehensive Employment Training Act (CETA) in 1978 and hired her to be the office manager for women's programming, she was called a scab by other lesbians even though there was no longer a picket line in front of the Highland Avenue building.[33] Finally, however, in the fall of 1978, the dispute was settled out of court. The Center revised its personnel policies and procedures "in an effort to insure that the rights of present and future workers will be secure," and the strikers were awarded "token reparations" ($90 apiece). The Center capitulated further by making a public apology to them in the L.A. gay papers.[34] That year, the Center's board, sensitive to the accusation that women were not given important positions, appointed Carol Nottley as the head financial officer and Susan Kuhner as the Center's assistant director.[35]

The male-heavy board truly did try to placate lesbians over the next few years, hoping to stave off serious trouble before it took root. After a group of young women led by Christi Kissell climbed the Center's roof in the middle of the night and painted the word "Lesbian" on the Gay Community Services Center sign, the board, understanding the temper of the times, voted to make the change permanent. In 1982, in a move to cut costs, the board briefly entertained the idea of eliminating the Women's Resource Office because supposedly all the Center's departments served women. But when the board's meeting was invaded by five angry lesbians who demanded that the Center offer more, not fewer, programs geared specifically toward women, their demands were quickly met: The board established Lesbian Central—an office run by a paid administrator devoted exclusively to lesbian concerns, as well as a meeting space and a library.[36]

But class, gender, and race problems reoccurred with regularity. Money was often behind these difficulties. The Center had grown rapidly because of the generous Democratic administration of President Jimmy Carter. It was federal money from the Department of Housing and Urban Development that permitted the Center's board to pay off the last $250,000 of its mortgage on its Highland Avenue home, and it was Comprehensive Employment and Training Act money that permitted the rapid expansion of Center programs. But with the advent of the Reagan era, such government support was cut off. Another way had to be found to fund a Center that was dedicated to social services for gay people. That way—the only way, board members insisted—was to convince private donors that the Gay and Lesbian Community Services Center was a serious, "respectable" institution.[37] They sought to hire as the Center's executive director someone who would convey that impression and would also have the ability to charm major donors (who were almost invariably men since women tended to be less affluent, not yet having made real progress anywhere in America in their fight for equal pay).

Steve Schulte, who had received a political science degree from Yale before coming to L.A. and had worked for the Los Angeles City Council, was hired as executive director in 1979. His talents were not only executive. He had moonlighted as a nude model for Colt Studios, and his beefcake pictures were wildly popular. On his first day at the Center, one employee remembers, "every man in the building ran out of his office" to get a look at the Colt legend.[38] Even board members called him "eye candy."[39] Schulte was given a dual mandate: to "clean up" the Center[40] and to raise big bucks. Under Schulte, the pull away from the Center's radical roots became downright deracination.

It was clear that the Gay Community Services Center needed "a certain sense of structure, order, and credibility" and "could not remain this ragtag, spontaneous agency," Schulte recalls. "We were moving to become a mainstream social service institution." The gay center was making its final transformation from a culture of community activists to one of corporate management.

Schulte was determined, first of all, to create a more professional work environment by ending the "casualness about dress and rules" (which for many of the Center's staff and clientele had surely been part of its gay charm). "I'll never forget," he says, "a guy named Mike at the info desk . . . a very attractive black guy who had a great body and who worked shirtless at the front desk" (where he was the first sight of all visitors to the Center). "I had to tell him he could no longer work shirtless."[41]

During Schulte's years as director, administration burgeoned at the Center, which created further conflicts with the volunteers and low-paid staff. Cosmo Bua, who ran the information desk after "Mike," voices the complaint of many of the workers of that period by saying that the administrative offices, housed on the upper floor of the new building, swelled to the point that "if the Center was a boat, it would tip over. There was too much on top." Bua says that because so much money was spent on administration, basic services, which had been crucial to the initial concept of a "gay community services center," were eliminated, such as the hotline to counsel gay people facing crises. "People would call, suicidal, and there'd be nothing. It was appalling."[42] For the first time in the Center's history, a "minimum donation policy" was instituted, so that clients would realize, as an internal memo said, "the value of the services they are receiving."[43]

Schulte believes that, these criticisms notwithstanding, he never lost sight of the real goal, to "end up serving more people."[44] Some who worked at the Center in those years believe that that is precisely what happened. JJ Vega, who was a Center caseworker from 1982 to 1985, talks, for instance, of "the hoards of gay kids who came in from Hollywood Boulevard" who were given food, clothing, and shelter at the Center, treated by the physicians and psychologists, and "taken to museums, camping, things they never before knew."[45] But to that end, raising money was crucial. Steve Schulte considered it part of his job "to go to Trumps [a fashionable West Hollywood restaurant owned by Sheldon Andelson] and wine and dine someone and get their money" for Center programs. His sexual charisma was a not-inconsequential aid to the robust donor program that the board instituted in order to free the Center from the vicissitudes of government funding.

The board of directors courted those who were affluent enough to join a group such as Friends of the Center or the Silver Circle and commit themselves to donations of at least $1,000 a year. Terry DeCrescenzo, one of the few women who served as chair of the board during those years, recalls that at a 1981 dinner held to attract donors six hundred people quickly signed up to join the Silver Circle.[46] The *Center News,* the Gay and Lesbian Community Services Center newsletter, often read like the society page of a metropolitan newspaper, as an announcement for one of the Center's annual fund-raisers illustrates:

> Vintage Hollywood extravagance will be on tap for this Summer's 8th Annual Lawn Party, to be hosted at Wolf's Lair—a dream castle perched high in the hills above Lake Hollywood. Celebrating the theme "Camelot in White," the lawn party site at the home of Bob Crane and Tom Mc-Clay features spacious gardens, sunny terraces and luxurious decorator touches. The affair will be catered by Trumps, which promises a sumptuous hors d'oeuvres and cocktail buffet.[47]

Potential donors were also wooed by candlelight dinners at the homes of the board members or were taken on tours of the Center, which was redecorated so that they would be impressed that nothing at the Center was "ragtag."

—

Yet another bloody battle brewed when the position of executive director became vacant once again because Schulte left to run for the city council. This battle combined all the major points of dissension: class, race, and gender—and even included the issues of "looksism" and ageism to boot. The board continued to believe that because money-raising must be the executive director's major task, it should hire for that position someone who could excel at bringing in the dollars. Women, it was long thought, would have less success in appealing to affluent male donors than someone with the impressive charms of a Steve Schulte.

Del Martinez, a lesbian who was a licensed social worker and the recipient of a prestigious award from the National Social Work Association for her successes as a community organizer, made it to the shortlist of candidates to succeed Schulte. But the board ultimately rejected her for the position because, as one member complained, "She's not polished enough to reach out to our major donors."[48] When Terry DeCrescenzo, who was board president in 1983, continued to urge Martinez's appointment, DeCrescenzo's failure to consider appearance and style was met with great consternation. One of the most powerful members told her, "I recommend you stand down. You don't have our confidence." Another member said bluntly, "We have to face it! Fat and Mexican don't play in raising money!"[49]

Martinez's supporters did not have to be present at the board's executive sessions to know that she was rejected because she was middle-aged, Latina, and a woman with working-class style. Many of the lesbians who worked at the Center or used its services had hoped that if Martinez became executive director, she would pay more attention to lesbian interests than the gay male directors had been willing to do. They felt that despite the concessions of Lesbian Central and the Center's name change to include "Lesbian," women were still getting short shrift. So they were furious when Martinez was passed over by the board in favor of John Brown, a man in his thirties, whose credentials were far inferior to hers: Martinez says, angry to this day, "It was a mockery."[50] Many of the women staff members, including the director of Lesbian Central, Lauren Jardine, agreed. They resigned in outraged protest.[51]

Jardine then approached Martinez about forming an all-lesbian center, one that would speak to lesbian needs, first and foremost, as the Gay and Lesbian Community Services Center never had. Since private donations were absolutely crucial to the success of her ambitious plans, Martinez and Jardine threw themselves into fund-raising efforts. They named the center they were designing "Connexxus" because it was to serve as a nexus that would "connect us" all, that is, all members of the lesbian community. An upscale lesbian organization, Southern California Women for Understanding (SCWU), agreed to help with a generous stipend and a sponsorship, which would permit Connexxus to raise money under SCWU's own nonprofit status. The vision that Martinez and Jardine shared for Connexxus was unique. They wished it to be all things to all lesbians, to reach out to "the baby dykes"[52] as well as to those who would go to a Connexxus-sponsored event at the Sheraton Universal Hotel to hear a white lesbian attorney and an African American lesbian entrepreneur discuss the topic "It Doesn't Take a Lot of Money to Make Money."[53]

Though there had been earlier lesbian centers in Los Angeles, Connexxus was the first to attempt to become a funded institution and to involve so broad a spectrum of the population. It was the first to operate with the unalloyed blessings of a bona fide city, West Hollywood, which provided space and even some funding. Because Connexxus was located in West Hollywood, far from many areas where lesbians who needed social services lived, Martinez worked to establish neighborhood satellites. (Connexxus's Centro de Mujeres was opened in East Los Angeles and continues to function there still.) In grand Hollywood manner, Martinez also planned—as she told potential donors—that Connexxus would eventually develop a business/services/entertainment complex for lesbian-owned businesses, professional offices, arts organizations—even a health club.[54] For a time, Connexxus seemed to be succeeding. It was reportedly serving 15,000 women yearly and finding ways to meet its annual budget of $240,000.[55]

But it was forced to shut down in 1990. The problem of money, which had been of such concern to the Gay and Lesbian Community Services Center, plagued Connexxus as well; but, unlike the Center, Connexxus could not find solutions. Though its programs directed at the diversity of the lesbian community had become increasingly elaborate, the funds to make those programs viable dried up. Most lesbians, like most women, enjoyed less discretionary income than men, who could spend more on charitable giving and were more used to being donors. Try as they might, Connexxus could not find ways to persuade women to open their wallets wider. After the first great flush of excitement over a center exclusively for lesbians, donations dropped. The horror of the AIDS epidemic, which soon occasioned the government's pouring of money into the Gay and Lesbian Community Services Center, also diverted private donations, as well as governmental support, from an all-lesbian institution because lesbians were the population least likely to be threatened by AIDS.

Sadly, what Martinez and Jardine had hoped would be the greatest strength of Connexxus, that it would "connect us," became one of the reasons for its failure: The diverse socioeconomic and ethnic groups that made up the huge lesbian community of Los Angeles ultimately found (once again) that they could not happily share space—neither on the board nor at the Center. Working-class lesbians and many lesbians of color refused to stifle their conviction that Connexxus was too white and too middle class, that it catered too much to the affluent (who could afford to donate to the institution); and middle-class lesbians believed that Connexxus was not only too radical but also "downwardly mobile,"[56] and they were not inspired to donate.

Before disbanding, Connexxus distributed the money that was left in its coffers to the June Mazer Lesbian Collection, a repository and archive that it had helped fund, and to the Centro de Mujeres, which was determined to keep going despite the death of its parent agency. Torie Osborn, who had become executive director of the Gay and Lesbian Community Services Center in 1988—the Center's first woman executive director since its establishment seventeen years earlier—vowed to provide at the Center all the services for lesbians that had been available through Connexxus.[57]

It had been the tragic AIDS epidemic, which was destroying a generation of male leaders, that finally made "lesbian ascendancy" possible at the Center and in gay organizations everywhere. Torie Osborn, who had run Holly Near's Redwood Records and had come to Hollywood to "get into mainstream show business," was a perky, attractive young woman with enough charm and charisma to be acceptable to the Center's Board and acceptable to the grassroots women as well. (One of them, so delighted over Osborn's appointment, spray painted "It's a Girl!" in front of the director's parking space.) Though Osborn was not precisely a Steve Schulte, she did not disappoint: For the first time, lesbians became donors in significant numbers. They were especially encouraged by an annual "Women's Night," a Hollywood gala, often replete with celebrities, the brainchild of Osborn and Jean O'Leary, a national lesbian leader who had settled in Los Angeles. (Women's Night presently raises about a half-million dollars for the Center in the course of one evening.) Osborn also ingratiated herself with male donors, and many of those who died of AIDS remembered the Center in their wills. Resources and budget doubled in her four years at the helm.[58] The taboo against a woman executive director at the Center finally vanished, bringing at long last détente about the gender issue. To date, all the subsequent executive directors at the Center have been women.

THE ENEMY AT THE GATES

Lesbian separatists worked with men; street people with stockbrokers. . . . People who would hardly speak to each other learned to put aside their own goals—and their anger—to work together. . . . Although the whole campaign is one we shouldn't even have had to fight, it's given us a sense of common purpose that we lacked.

— Gayle Wilson on the "No" on 6 Campaign[59]

Despite constant internal battles, for nearly a decade there seemed to be no stopping gay progress in Los Angeles. Since the 1969 city council election victory in which gay activists were instrumental in replacing homophobe Paul Lamport with gay-friendly Bill Stevenson, gays had gained steady political momentum. Remembering Lamport's defeat, some candidates began to campaign in gay bars. Bob Geoghegan, a member of Councilman Ed Edelman's staff, recalls that politicians were still sometimes attacked by their political opponents if they addressed themselves to the "untouchable community";[60] but these attacks did not stick, and gay Angelenos handsomely rewarded the attention of gay-friendly politicians. By the early 1970s, there was a political pool to

The very "manly" Dr. Ida B. Baker, who established a private practice in Southern California. *Author's collection.*

Harry Wharton, who "boasted one of the finest wardrobes among the 'queer people,'" 1914. *Courtesy Sacramento Archives and Museum Collection Center.*

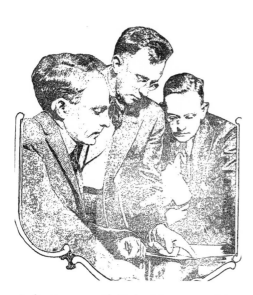

Left, attorneys with Herbert Lowe, one of dozens of men accused in a "social vagrant" scandal in Southern California; right, B. C. Brown and W. H. Warren, bounty hunters of homosexuals. These pictures appeared in the *Los Angeles Times* in 1914.

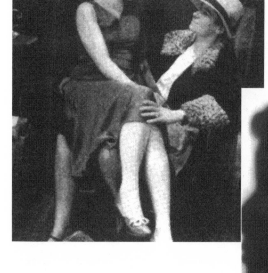

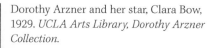

Dorothy Arzner and her star, Clara Bow, 1929. *UCLA Arts Library, Dorothy Arzner Collection.*

On screen and in private, several "unstraight" Hollywood women, such as Katharine Hepburn, dressed as men and lived as they wanted. *Author's collection.*

In the 1920s, Rudolph Valentino cast a spell "over the entire female population—and some others." *Author's collection.*

The guidebook, *How to Sin in Hollywood*, told tourists where to go to see lesbian "boy-girls." Drawing by Lloyd Hoff, 1940

. . . the little girl customers . . .

At quiet backyard parties, a gay movie queen and a gay director mingled with gay worker bees: George Cukor (in glasses), Tallulah Bankhead, and two unknowns (1937). *Photo: Rex Evans/courtesy Jim Weatherford.*

Rock Hudson, pressured by fan magazines to marry, wed lesbian Phyllis Gates. *Courtesy of the Academy of Motion Picture Arts and Sciences.*

Attorney Gladys Towels Root, "Defender of the Dammed," 1950s. Herald Examiner *Collection/Los Angeles Public Library.*

Jimmy Renard, male impersonator in L.A. nightclubs during the 1930s and '40s. *Author's collection.*

Marvin Edwards, all too briefly enjoying Los Angeles, 1949. *Author's collection.*

Nancy Valverde was regularly stopped by the LAPD for "masquerading." *Author's collection.*

"Lisa Ben," editor-in-chief of *Vice Versa. Courtesy of the ONE National Gay and Lesbian Archives.*

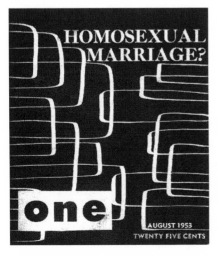

From "gay pride" to " gay marriage," *ONE Magazine* predicted the gay agenda by half a century. *Author's collection.*

THE FABULOUS

Butch-femme '50s style: a member of the
Satyrs motorcycle club; Miss Destiny, on
the cover of *ONE* magazine. *Photo left: John
Gruber/ photo right: Author's collection.*

Meko and Juanita, at the Open
Door, early 1960s. *Author's
collection.*

Members of one of L.A.'s numerous Lesbian
softball teams. *Author's collection.*

Transgender millionaire Reed
Erickson (center) on a date, early
1960s. *Courtesy of the ONE National
Gay and Lesbian Archives.*

Stella Rush, one of the few lesbians
to write for *ONE Magazine,*
published under the name Sten
Russell. *Author's collection.*

Morris Kight (far left) and Don Kilhefner (bearded) were known among GLF wags as "Moscow and Peking." *Courtesy of the ONE National Gay and Lesbian Archives.*

Old gays in new times: Joan Hannan of "Joanie Presents" and Lee Glaze of "The Patch," 1969. *Courtesy Lee Glaze.*

A new twist on Hollywood glamour: artists William Moritz and Robert Opel prepare to go out on the town. *Photo: Philip Stuart/Author's collection.*

L.A. Golden Boys circa
1970. *Courtesy Bruce Reifel.*

"Oh, you lesbian feminists!": Sharon
A. Lilly and Brenda Weathers.
Courtesy Sharon A. Lilly.

The Lesbian Tide Collective
(right) helped promote a
movement of kiss-ins and dances.
Photo courtesy Jeanne Cordova.

THE GAY WOMEN'S SERVICE CENTER
BRINGS YOU 2 MORE
WONDERFUL

GAY DANCES

FRIDAY, APRIL 16 & 23
AT   8:30 - 12:30

TROUPERS' HALL

JUST   1625 N. LA BREA
$1.50 BEER-   UNDER 21 OK
SODA
ALL SISTERS & BROTHERS

Early 1971. *Courtesy Carolyn Weathers.*

Standing together at the Gay Community Services Center on Wilshire Boulevard: Chris Brownlie and Mary Adair on right. *Photo: Tony Barnard/UCLA Special Collections.*

New power players: from left, Judge Rand Schrader, Sheldon Andelson, Theresa DeCrescenzo, Betty Berzon, Steve Schulte, Judge Steve Lachs, and Duke Comegys. *Courtesy Theresa DeCrescenzo.*

Openly gay councilman Steve Schulte.
Courtesy of the ONE National Gay and Lesbian Archives.

Lawyers and lovers, MECLA leaders
Roberta Bennett and Diane Abbitt
Courtesy of the ONE National Gay and Lesbian Archives.

National gay leader and adopted Angeleno, Jean O'Leary. *Press photo.*

Richard Deacon of *The Dick Van Dyke Show* (center) with Ah Men Founder Don Cook; unidentified man at left. *Courtesy of the ONE National Gay and Lesbian Archives.*

Beth Chayim Chadashim
president Davi Cheng with
scribe Neil Yerman,
repairing a rescued Torah.
Courtesy Davi Cheng.

Comedy team Patty Harrison and
Robin Tyler. Their contracts were
dropped by the ABC network when
word got out that they were lesbians.
Courtesy Robin Tyler.

West Hollywood's first mayor, Valerie
Terrigno. *Courtesy of the ONE
National Gay and Lesbian Archives.*

Rudy Ruano, before
leaving Guatemala in
the early 1960s.
Courtesy Rudy Ruano.

A 1991 cover of *Lesbian News*, which began in L.A.
as a two-page mimeographed newsletter in 1975.
Courtesy Ella Matthes.

Ivy Bottini, a leader in the women's movement, gay rights struggles, and gay eldercare.
Courtesy Ivy Bottini.

Designers and costumers came out from behind the scenes for the AIDS fight. *Photo: Craig Collins.*

Charlene Nguon sued her southern California school district for outing her as a lesbian. *Courtesy ACLU of Southern California.*

Butchlalis de Panochtitlan: Nadine Romero, Mari Garcia, Raquel Gutierrez and Claudia Rodriguez. *Photo: Evelyn Reyes.*

Robin Eans and Sandy Sachs, the owners of Girlbar in West Hollywood, where the term "lipstick lesbian" was coined. *Photo: Dean Keefer, Courtesy Sandy Sachs.*

After years of working in the shadows, gays themselves finally became the focus of a Hollywood classic in *Brokeback Mountain. Photo: Kimberly French/courtesy Focus Features.*

splash in, and groups such as the Gay Community Alliance were formed:
As Mike Manning, one of the founders of the Alliance, recalls, its approach was multileveled. The organization reached out to all gays—not
only those who might donate campaign money but also "the kids in the
bars"—to register, vote, and think of themselves as a political force. They
developed a voter slate and a dedicated team of campaign volunteers.
They raised funds for printing and mailing leaflets that would help convince gay people that their vote was crucial if gay power was to be taken
to "the next level."[61]

Such efforts paid off throughout the 1970s. In 1973, Burt Pines won
his campaign for city attorney with the help of a large gay constituency, which he had wooed in part by campaigning in gay bars.[62]
Pines recalls, "Once I learned how [gay people] were being treated, it
really troubled me. It seemed so unfair."[63] He fulfilled his campaign
promises, making a seismic shift in the official response to homosexuality with two rulings: the first, that the city attorney's office would no
longer prosecute people for holding hands, dancing, or making sexual
propositions "just because [the act] occurs in a gay bar";[64] and the second, that the Los Angeles Police Department not only would cease to
harass homosexuals but also would be *required* to hire qualified homosexuals as police officers.[65]

Ed Edelman, a two-term city councilman, followed Pines' campaign
trail through gay bars in 1974 ("I never weighed the risk," he recalls)[66]
and won a seat in the supervisorial district that encompassed Hollywood, West Hollywood, and Silver Lake. It was then that Edelman kept
his campaign promise to hire David Glascock to serve as a liaison with
the gay community, making one of the earliest openly gay political appointments in the nation. Glascock had been a driving force behind the
Gay Community Alliance; he had also been convicted for a homosexual
act, and he had tended a bar on Cahuenga Boulevard, where drag queens
congregated. But if the media thought they could use that information
to shame the new supervisor, they were wrong. The days were dead in
L.A. when a politician could be made hysterical if it was discovered that
a homosexual was on his staff: "We hired [Glascock] because we knew
he was a homosexual," Edelman bluntly told reporters. "If we're going to

solve our problems in the gay community, we want someone who understands those problems."[67]

On the Los Angeles City Council, too, there were members who were very friendly to the gay community. Peggy Stevenson held on to the seat in her largely gay district, which she had inherited from her husband. Joel Wachs, elected in 1971, was a "perennial bachelor" who remained closeted during all his twenty-eight years on the council, but he invariably served as a powerful ally to gay interests. Some elected officials in L.A. were gay-friendly in part because they had come to understand their own lesbian and gay relatives. One of Mayor Tom Bradley's daughters is a lesbian.[68] Ed Edelman, who became known as the "archangel of the center" for his help in securing government funding, acknowledges that he has a sister who is a lesbian.[69] David Russell, the son of Councilwoman Pat Russell, became the lover of the *Advocate*'s publisher, David Goodstein.[70] Though officials of that day never joined Parents and Friends of Lesbians and Gays, family sympathy made a difference in their political understanding.

Considering the positions taken by the city attorney and the gay allies on the Board of Supervisors and the Los Angeles City Council, Police Chief Ed Davis had good reason to know that the LAPD's antigay witch hunts would no longer fly. Even the *Los Angeles Times* seemed to be against him: Chief Davis sent the newspaper a bitter letter complaining about its "strong editorial support of homosexuality" and canceling his subscription.[71]

But despite changing times, "Crazy Ed," as the chief of police was called in the gay community, refused to relinquish his hostility. In 1975, the same year Governor Jerry Brown signed the "consenting adults" bill to legalize gay sex, Davis orchestrated what may have been the most expensive (and silly) gay raid in history. John Embry, the publisher of *Drummer* magazine, had invited members of what he called the "leather fraternity" to the Mark IV bathhouse on Melrose Avenue for a private party to benefit the Gay Community Services Center. The entertainment included a mock slave auction. Val Martin, the rugged star of the SM movie *Born to Raise Hell,* offered to serve as auctioneer. (Martin, a

Colombian immigrant, worked both as an actor and an SM hustler with a pioneering specialty in fisting. His business card read, "Give me a call and I'll give you a hand.")[72] Martin had just "sold" the first gay volunteer to Terry LeGrand, who in turn gave him to Jeanne Barney, the heterosexual woman who was at that time an editor for *Drummer* magazine, to do her yard work. Then a massive police assault began.

Records indicate that 105 police officers participated in the raid (though the LAPD would not admit to more than 65).[73] Helicopters, dozens of squad cars, and a bus surrounded the bathhouse—the bus had been specially chartered as a mammoth paddy wagon. "There was total chaos and pandemonium," recalls Aristide Laurent. "I tried to leave and saw cops coming over the walls. . . . There were lights, a helicopter, and just so many cops." Jeanne Barney, who helped coordinate the event says, "No one could believe the helicopters. Then the loudspeakers. Then sheer terror." She shudders as she remembers that the police packed forty men into the bus; they took Barney in a separate car.[74]

The busload of arrestees, all shackled with plastic handcuffs, waited for hours in a crowded holding cell before they were processed at the police station. Laurent remembers one man who had a tragicomic cause to panic: "He had a dildo in his pants 'for effect,' and he was afraid of what would happen if the cops—or other inmates—found it. So he had to get behind a couple of us—all of us are in handcuffs—and we had to, without looking, get his pants open . . . unzip them . . . pull the dildo out, and kick it under the candy machine in the holding cell."[75] Sheer terror of another order set in when the charges were filed: The LAPD booked all forty men on an 1871 statute for trafficking in human slaves, a felony.

Furious with the LAPD's overkill, the community mobilized. "For the first time . . . I saw people really come together," says Jeanne Barney. "Everyone was so incensed at this: We got the West Hollywood sweater queens, the leather queens, the drag queens, the Morris Kight people . . . an amazing show of solidarity."[76] Morris Kight organized a town meeting at Troupers Hall in Hollywood, where Troy Perry raised money for the arrestees' defense by defiantly auctioning off more volunteers. (The heterosexual attorney, Al Gordon, who took the case pro bono, stepped up to the auction block and was immediately purchased by his wife.) A liberal councilman, Zev Yaroslavsky, showed up and denounced the arrests to television cameras. Davis represented his extreme tactics as compensatory, because for years the LAPD had been "cowed," he said, into "being too lenient [by] the most powerful lobby in the city, the homosexual community."[77] Nevertheless, Peggy Stevenson, who chaired the council committee that had jurisdiction over the Police Commission's budget, succeeded in getting deducted from the LAPD's vice budget for the next year a sum equal to what the raid had cost.[78]

That was the year, 1976, that the mayor of Los Angeles, Tom Bradley, issued a proclamation signed by the city council, officially establishing a Gay Pride Week in Los Angeles.[79] The following year, 1977, when Mayor Bradley's office conducted a poll posing the statement, "Homosexuals who are qualified should be permitted to hold any Los Angeles City job for which they are qualified," only 21 percent disagreed, and more than 60 percent agreed.[80] Chief Davis's attack on the gays had backfired thunderously.

Continued gay political gains in Los Angeles were largely due to the Municipal Elections Committee of Los Angeles (MECLA), which became the most powerful gay political force ever seen in the city—or the nation. The group, which initially named itself Orion, developed from gay consciousness-raising sessions. Orion consisted originally of seven young, attractive, upper-middle-class men (of the type that Armistead Maupin has called "A-Gays").[81] Their sessions led them to the conviction that they must lend their clout to gay political concerns because it was important to change the public image of homosexuals from socially marginal individuals to a power with which politicians must reckon.[82]

Like the Gay Community Alliance, they were interested in creating gay-friendly politicians, but they operated on a much different scale. In a city that is so devoted to glamour and power, it would have been surprising if such a group had not emerged in the midst of the gay movement. Judge Steve Lachs, who was then an attorney and one of the founders of the Orion group, recalls that they made vehement distinctions between themselves and the "hippies," from whom they felt they needed to wrest the position of representing the gay community.[83] Peter Scott, who was also a successful attorney and had Marlboro-Man good looks, was a model of the A-Gays that the group hoped to attract in order to do its political work; thus he became the group's first president. What the group needed to do, they decided, was not to raise public consciousness through street demonstrations where scruffy Gay Liberation Front–types would take over, but rather to become a political action committee (the first openly gay PAC in the nation). Their PAC would raise large sums of money for gay-friendly political candidates through elegant and prestigious social gatherings.

The first challenge they undertook was with the advice of David Mixner, a hot-shot political consultant who was not yet out of the closet but was known for his tactical insights. Mixner was well connected both in Hollywood and in American politics' top circles (including the Clintons): He suggested that the Orion group try to influence the next municipal elections for the Los Angeles City Council. An overt homophobe, John Gibson, who had served on the city council since the 1950s and was its president, was running for another term and seemed destined to continue as president. No gay organization in the world had ever attempted to raise big money to influence a political campaign, and initially the group was at a loss for how to begin. (Someone actually suggested they hold a bake sale.) Steve Lachs, who had also been active in fund-raising for the Jewish community, proposed some tried-and-true techniques, as he remembers now: He suggested first of all that the group contact wealthy potential donors individually and explain, on a one-to-one basis, what they hoped to do: "Spend an hour with one wealthy person who's gay," Lachs said, "and you'll get far more than you'll make from a bake sale." He suggested, too, that they stage carefully planned events to which affluent gays would want to come and where they would be persuaded to make large contributions to the cause.

For its first event, the group rented the banquet room of the Carriage Trade, the popular gay bar and restaurant. Lachs recalls how they orchestrated that evening. First, he gave "the very emotional speech"; then another member, Rob Eichberg, made the pitch. Lachs had prearranged for a corporate attorney to raise his hand on cue and make the initial donation. "This sounds wonderful," the gay attorney said. "I pledge $1,000," a generous sum in 1976. Eichberg and Lachs played the room until $20,000 was pledged. Because it was necessary to deposit the funds into a bank account, the Orion group decided to give itself a new name, one that would reflect its political concerns but not reveal its sexual orientation lest timid donors fear to write "gay" or "homosexual" on a check.[84] They became the Municipal Elections Committee of Los Angeles (MECLA).

The organization was at that time all male, and the authors of *Out for Good,* a history of the national gay rights movement, have suggested that at this event (and in MECLA, generally) there had been "little ideology, other than the ideology of power and influence."[85] Be that as it may, for the very first time, a group of A-Gays had gotten together not simply to demonstrate power (or indulge their pleasure, which had already happened often in Los Angeles, for example, at the 1930s parties of George Cukor and Cole Porter). MECLA's end product was big bucks, raised specifically for the gay rights battle, which included the rights of those homosexuals who had no power. Monetary munificence on the scale that MECLA achieved that night at the Carriage Trade had been unprecedented in the community. Thus began serious gay fund-raising.

To help them spend the money it raised for best effect, MECLA was guided by David Mixner, whose savvy strategies brought L.A. politicians to believe that gay power and the gay vote were tremendous, that failure to get the gay vote could be fatal to a political career, and that MECLA, a chief power broker, could deliver it. Politicians were soon coveting invitations to "MECLA Breakfasts" at venues such as the Bel Age Hotel in West Hollywood, where candidates who had first been vetted by MECLA's board addressed potential donors over eggs Florentine. As an aide to a high-ranking elected official observed to a newspaper reporter at a MECLA event: "Powerful? You bet they're powerful. I have never seen anything like the gays [for raising money] from a minority group. . . . We pay attention, I can tell you that."[86]

In 1977, MECLA expanded its board from nine men to five women and ten men. The board's president, Peter Scott, claimed that feminist consciousness was behind the realization that women ought to be brought into MECLA: "Either you believe that women are equal or you don't. If you do, you have to recognize that they don't have equal opportunity, so it's your duty to bootstrap them up," he declared[87]—though he did not mean that MECLA's boardroom doors would be open to just any woman. Both men and women invited to serve on MECLA's board in the 1970s had to pledge to make contributions of at least $1,200 a year to MECLA.[88] Such a policy, which shut out gays and lesbians who were not affluent, soon set off smoldering resentments among some sectors of the community; they complained that "the people in the hills and the elitists" had commandeered gay politics, acting as though the movement were a commodity to be purchased. "MECLA Doesn't Speak For Us!" picketers proclaimed at one of the group's pow-wows. Such malcontents barely registered, however. MECLA aimed high and continued to recruit the wealthy.

Roberta Bennett and Diane Abbitt, a lesbian couple who became L.A. lawyers, were soon major players in MECLA. They had been leaders in both national and local NOW, heading its Lesbian Rights Task Force and organizing its lesbian "Alternative Lifestyles Conference." But they decided that "it was real crazy not to work with the gay male community"—against the advice of lesbian activists such as Jeanne Cordova, who told them, remembering her experiences at the Center, "What's wrong with you? Don't you know that anything lesbians do when they work with the boys gets co-opted by them and the women never get credit for anything?"[89] Bennett and Abbitt recall that the first time they attended a MECLA reception, they felt that finally they had found their movement home: "It was far more sophisticated than anything we had done with NOW. It was exciting, challenging, and it felt good.

These people were opening a new avenue of activism—the traditional political arena."[90]

MECLA men convinced the two women of the importance of raising money to give to political candidates who were supportive of gay rights. The lesbian community had never really been seriously tapped as *political* donors, but Bennett and Abbitt warmed to the challenge. The men had them listen to a tape of the first fund-raising event at the Carriage Trade "to see how it was done."[91] Then Bennett and Abbitt organized their own luncheon at the Carriage Trade Restaurant. They invited forty or fifty affluent lesbians who wore high heels and dresses (and whose class equivalents in the preceding generation would not have dreamed of setting foot in a semipublic lesbian gathering). Bennett and Abbitt told them, "We want you to hear about how the Municipal Elections Committee is working within the system in order to defeat discrimination in the gay community." They raised "big money," Bennett says. "The boys were very impressed."[92] She and Abbitt were each eventually elected co-chairs of MECLA.

Never before had upper-middle-class lesbians participated as a group in *any* homosexual cause. Eventually about one-third of the MECLA membership was female. As Esther, a Los Angeles physician, believes, the appeal of MECLA was twofold for women like her: She approved heartily of the organization's determination to "give the gay community a political voice in Sacramento and L.A., and Washington, too," but MECLA's "prosperous, grand fetes" also held a great attraction for her: "It was fun to get dressed up and see who else was dressed up."[93] Through MECLA's "fashionable" events, affluent lesbians became major donors in the movement for gay rights.

—

The greatest battle for MECLA and for the entire Los Angeles lesbian and gay community came in the wake of a disaster in liberal Dade County, Florida. An orange juice pitchwoman, Anita Bryant, had succeeded in getting the electorate to repeal an ordinance, very like one in Los Angeles, that forbade discrimination in jobs and housing on the basis of sexual orientation. The right-wing victory in Dade was soon followed by reversals of gay gains in three more cities. It did not take much prescience for the *Los Angeles Times* to understand—as it announced in an article titled "Gay Rights: Is a Backlash Forming?"—that next "the war [would] be waged in California."[94]

Gay Americans were shocked by Anita Bryant's victory. "No one thought she'd win," recalls David Mixner of an election day that, to homosexuals nationwide, became known, with gallows' wit, as "Horrible Tuesday."[95] But shock was not paralysis. All over America, in cities that had never had more than a dimly lit gay bar or two, gay organizations were formed to fight the right-wing attacks.[96] In Los Angeles, Troy Perry and Morris Kight organized the Coalition for Human Rights, and, days after the Florida vote, they were able to get 9,000 protesters to gather in the streets.[97]

The horror of Horrible Tuesday brought some immediate respite to the usual internecine lesbian and gay community battles. Kight, who had been a chief villain in the Gay Feminist 11 strike at the Gay Community Services Center, cleverly understood (as had gay male leaders since Magnus Hirschfeld in the nineteenth century) that the predominant negative stereotype that simplistically characterized homosexuals as wildly promiscuous men could be tempered and complicated by showing that women were also homosexuals. Kight declared that "co-sexual parity" must be a priority of the Coalition for Human Rights.[98] Class divisions were also tackled because the leaders realized that numbers counted. David Mixner, the most respected strategist among affluent gays, declared that gay people would win an upcoming war in California only if they fought in a single, united campaign, rather than one campaign of wealthy conservatives ("the Suits") and another of grassroots radicals ("the Streets"). To that end, Mixner approached Ivy Bottini, at that time the head of women's programming at the Gay Community Services Center. He told Bottini, who had not only impeccable lesbian credentials but also a working-class background, "We need the grassroots working on this campaign too. And if you come in, they'll come in."[99]

As the *Los Angeles Times* and gay activists predicted, war did come to California. It was brought by a Southern California state senator, John

Briggs, a right-wing Republican candidate for governor who believed he would bolster his odds by making gay people a scapegoat. Briggs hoped to replicate Bryant's success in Florida through a "California Save Our Children" ballot initiative. His supporters gathered half a million signatures, almost two hundred thousand more than what was required for the initiative to qualify for the 1978 California ballot. The chilling text of the initiative, which became Proposition 6, declared that "one of the most fundamental interests of the State is the establishment and preservation of the family unit"—and for that reason, public school administrators, counselors, teachers, and teachers' aides must be fired if it was discovered that they engaged in "the advocating, soliciting, imposing, encouraging, or promoting of private or public homosexual activity." That is, not only homosexuals would be fired but also all public school employees who indicated they were in any way supportive of the rights of gay people.[100]

Ivy Bottini had for years considered herself a lesbian separatist; but she realized that the right wing was now aiming for a far bigger victory than what they had achieved in one county in Florida: They were waging their antigay war statewide in the largest state in the nation. Their win would herald the end of homosexual progress. On the brink of such a war, Bottini recalls, separatism was a luxury that lesbians could not afford—though she admits that her first organizational meeting with gay men had been an emotional struggle for her: "I felt, 'I'm in enemy territory.' The men had been so separate from the lesbian community that I'd made my home." Yet she believed, as many in the lesbian and gay community came to believe, that she had no choice but to put aside differences.[101]

Once the Briggs initiative qualified for the ballot, lesbians and gays knew that the assault would not be limited to schoolteachers and school administrators (whose numbers are legion in the gay community): The Right, if they were not stopped, would ultimately attack all homosexuals. The 1950s would be repeated. Lesbians and gay men who had California licenses to practice a profession—physicians, lawyers, social workers, psychologists—felt that they had particular reason to worry: They would probably be next once Proposition 6 passed; the State of

California could well try to revoke their licenses, too. Thus even organizations that had been primarily social, such as Southern California Women for Understanding, realized that it was vital they join forces in the fight—that this was a witch-hunt that must be answered aggressively because closet doors would anyway be flung open by the enemy. Mere discretion, which middle-class lesbians such as those who belonged to SCWU had always tried to practice, could no longer be depended upon for protection. Southern California Women for Understanding now vowed to adopt "an aggressive stance with the media, asking for coverage and the opportunity to appear, in order to counter the vicious stereotyping" of homosexuals.[102]

One serious split remained in the lesbian and gay community as they waged war against Briggs. A faction believed that homosexuals could not win against the initiative without a heterosexual "twist." They hired an experienced strategist, Don Bradley, a straight man, who devised a campaign that deftly avoided explicitly gay issues, coining slogans such as "No on 6: Who Will Be Next?"[103] The No on 6 campaign was not alone in its strategy to be coy about *who* was leading the protest against Proposition 6 and *why.* The Coalition for Human Rights had been so named because it was hoped that people of color would agree that right-wing assaults were not gay-specific and thus would make common cause with homosexuals. MECLA, too, was circumspect: In keeping with the strategy to impress upon the electorate that Proposition 6 had implications beyond gay people, Peter Scott, representing the organization, characterized the Briggs initiative to the *Los Angeles Times* as "really a Jim Crow–type law."[104] But grassroots lesbians and gays hated the strategy. They feared that the real issue, right-wing homophobia, was being "washed down in the big morass of human rights."[105] They formed the Union for Lesbians and Gay Men, proclaiming that Bryant and others had made a categorical assault on homosexuals, and that to present it as an attack against all minorities was mendacity.

Ultimately, however, the fierce hostility of the external enemy made factionalism impractical. Radical groups such as the militant lesbian and gay Action Coalition to Defeat the Briggs Initiative realized that an effective strategy was vital, and they developed a slogan much like the one that Don Bradley had coined for No on 6: "Discrimination: Who's Next?"[106] Groups such as New Alliance for Gay Equality (better known by its acronym, New AGE), formed by MECLA members to fight Proposition 6, soon realized that MECLA's skillful fund-raising would be insufficient without grassroots workers who would register voters, make campaign signs, and help turn out the vote. Los Angeles lesbians and gays had work to do that required all of them.

To cover No on 6 campaign expenses, Troy Perry went on a much-publicized fast until he raised $100,000. No on 6 wanted to purchase media spots on television and radio, and for that, vast sums were needed. Even those who felt they had been burnt in the past by gay factionalism did their part. John Morgan Wilson, for example, threw a fund-raising party whose guests included Christopher Isherwood, Don Bachardy, Vito Russo, and the film star Bud Cort. "I gave [the No on 6 campaign] a pot full of money," he says, "but I didn't want to get near the leaders," whom he associated with past discord.[107] Money also came from those who had never given to a lesbian or gay cause before. Gayle Wilson, a wealthy Los Angeles realtor (Mixner calls her "the pioneer of Lipstick Lesbians")[108] put together the first fund-raiser for the campaign, a women's luncheon at the chic Beverly Hilton Hotel in Beverly Hills, to which she invited as guest speaker Midge Costanza, who had just left her position as President Carter's assistant. The 250 lesbians who were present donated $45,000 at the luncheon. The money was used to open an "Anti-Briggs Campaign" office.[109]

The diversity of lesbians and gays, which had been a huge source of conflict in the past, now worked to their benefit because they were able to produce results in diverse communities. When the Beverly Hills Chamber of Commerce made the mistake of endorsing Proposition 6, Gayle Wilson, along with her movie-star friend, Cher, launched a walkout and boycott of Beverly Hills businesses. (The Chamber of Commerce not only rescinded its endorsement of Proposition 6 within twenty-four hours but also came out publicly against it.)[110] The gay Los Angeles Stonewall Democratic Club mapped out an intensive, and successful, strategy to secure resolutions against Proposition 6 from the Democratic State Central Committee, the California Democratic Council, and the Democratic Committees from cities all over the state.[111] Lesbian and gay radicals such as Robin Podolsky, who had been a shop steward and a trade union organizer, joined the Action Coalition to Defeat the Briggs Initiative and focused on voter registration, fund-raising, and pamphleteering in working-class and people-of-color communities. Podolsky says that "one of [her] best memories" is the time she walked with other members of the coalition in the precincts of the African American community of Watts and talked about "discrimination and how anyone who suffered discrimination historically must understand that this was terrible trouble." The Action Coalition, Podolsky says, "raised incredible amounts of money" by throwing parties in bars, and then used it to take out ads in the *Los Angeles Times.* She is still pleased that her radical group "rivaled the rich organizations" in fund-raising, but the monies all went to a united cause.[112]

One source, however, could not be easily tapped: lesbians and gays in the entertainment industry. As David Mixner recalls, Rock Hudson wrote a check for $49, because campaign finance law required that any contribution of fifty dollars or more be reported. Celebrities and anyone else who felt the need to remain closeted feared to be thus exposed, and they contributed no more than the safe amount. Those celebrities who were straight-identified could afford to be less timid (the rumors about the homosexuality of some of them notwithstanding): Burt Lancaster, John Travolta, Donna Summer, Neil and Joyce Bogart (who were founders of Casablanca Records, the disco label that had signed The Village People as well as the gay icon Donna Summer)—all contributed large sums to the campaign.[113]

Republican celebrities helped through their endorsements, too. In the summer before the election, a closeted member of Ronald Reagan's entourage contacted New AGE, asking whether a statement against Proposition 6 from the former Hollywood actor/California governor would be helpful. Mixner and Peter Scott were invited to meet with Reagan in his West L.A. office, where he confirmed that he would support their fight, and he soon issued a public statement that Proposition 6 had "a potential for real mischief." Ivy Bottini says that Reagan's statement was "the kiss of death for Briggs."[114] Bob Hope, a fellow Republican who also wielded great power in the movie town and beyond, soon followed Reagan in opposing Briggs.[115] Before such well-known conservatives had expressed their opposition in public, potential-voter polls still showed 61 percent in favor of the Briggs initiative and 31 percent against. After a spate of announcements by the influential saying they opposed Proposition 6, polls moved to a virtual tie.[116] In the November election, Proposition 6 was defeated by 58 percent to 42 percent, with a margin of more than a million votes. "We even won [ultra-conservative] Orange County," Mixner, who had helped raise close to a million dollars for the campaign, delights in recalling.[117]

Ironically, Briggs' attack actually strengthened the gay community and healed many wounds. The combat against an external enemy made the community comprehend, as nothing ever had before, the adage "If we do not hang together, we shall surely hang separately." After the resounding defeat of the initiative, Ivy Bottini voiced the sentiments of many lesbians in declaring, "I loved working with those men! Let me tell you, I will NEVER AGAIN be a separatist!"[118] The war they fought together created a parity between Los Angeles lesbians and gay men. Finally, power (at least for political purposes) was genuinely shared, and lesbians were no longer merely token in mixed organizations. It could no longer seem to them that the men invariably co-opted everything for their own ends and ignored the women. Though there would be battles between them again in the future (such as the one spurred by the center's rejection of Del Martinez), during the Briggs campaign gay men and lesbians became closer than they'd been since their mid-century lavender tandems.

For the duration of the campaign, the community suppressed almost all the other bitterly cherished factions, too, even those of race, class, and political philosophy. As Jinx Beers declared in the *Lesbian News* right after the election: "What we now know is that all it takes is a strong central issue and we *can* pull together—even if most of the time we don't want to." Beers also thanked the enemies—Briggs and Bryant—"for giving us the opportunity and incentive to educate the general public." The widespread revelation of the shocking malice of homophobes and the innocence of gay people would, she predicted, go a long way toward helping lesbians and gays win future wars against their foes.[119]

The Briggs initiative had other salubrious effects as well. It pulled countless Los Angeles gay people out of the closet and got them used to supporting gay causes personally and financially. Its political results were measurable: MECLA credited the Briggs threat with 25,000 newly registered voters sympathetic to gay rights. The triumph was so total that in the words of the *Los Angeles Times,* the senator's "flamboyant campaign had provoked a pro-gay backlash."[120]

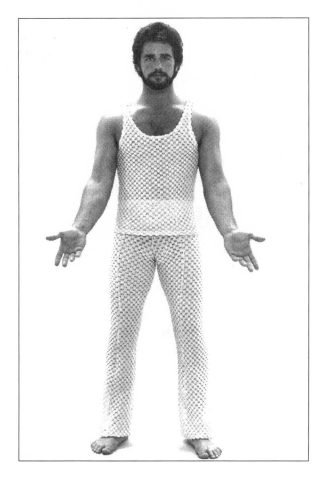

By marketing distinctive fashions, Ah Men brought a bit of
gay Hollywood to the provinces. *Courtesy of the ONE
National Gay and Lesbian Archives.*

CHAPTER 8

Glitz and Glam

GOLDEN BOYS

Admen are finding gold in marketing to upscale gays. . . . After all, if a silver-and-malachite saltcellar can be sold for $1,000 in the first hour of Los Angeles' recent Gay and Lesbian Lifestyle Expo, can Maseratis and Kieselstein-Cord belts be far behind?

—"But Will It Play in West Hollywood?"
Los Angeles Magazine, 1981[1]

West Hollywood by the mid-1970s had come to epitomize a new gay lifestyle, one that promoted a brotherhood of pleasure as a statement of gay liberation. Steve Schulte and his lover, who were part of still another great gay exodus from less-welcoming areas, moved to West Hollywood from Iowa. Schulte became—in very Hollywood fashion—both a male pinup model and an elected official: "I never would have imagined how many guys our age, like brothers and pals, were right there—open, attractive, and fun. Like ours, their lives had changed," he reminisces of those 1970s halcyon days. "There was euphoria and hopefulness in West Hollywood. . . . It was quite astonishing to find that, and to become part of it very quickly."[2]

West Hollywood—with its witty moniker "Boystown" (a reference to the 1948 Spencer Tracy film about a colony of orphaned newsboys)[3] and its double-entendre zip code, "90069"—had long been a gay male enclave. In the 1920s, the area, which bordered on Beverly Hills and was

231

part of Los Angeles County, had attracted speakeasies and bootleggers because it was not under the jurisdiction of the harsh Los Angeles (City) Police Department. It had drawn gay men for the same reason and continued to draw them through the years. It was a gay dreamland.

In the 1970s, the residents of West Hollywood became emboldened, expressing their gay freedom not just after dark, but brazenly in the sun: holding hands, flirting, and cruising all over the district. Boystown became even more of what it had been in earlier years; only now, gay-owned and gay-targeted businesses boomed there and glitzy consumption flourished. West Hollywood appeared to be not just a gay ghetto, but an entire gay town—though one with little class or racial diversity and, outside of a few nightclubs and bars such as Peanuts and the Palms, unreflective of the lesbian community.

On Santa Monica Boulevard, West Hollywood's main thoroughfare, one business advertised its services in pink neon cursive that resembled a beauty salon sign—but rather than "Perms and Hair-Tinting" the sign, which was on one of West Hollywood's first gyms, offered simply "Muscles." A few blocks up, the Big Weenie hot dog stand sign advertised its wares on a billboard with the slogan "Big Weenies Are Better!" All American Boy, a Boulevard boutique that sold casual clothes, was advertised most effectively by its young male customers who favored the form-fitting knit shirts that emblazoned the store's "All American Boy" logo—which read as a delicious irony on the pumped pectorals of America's outcasts.[4] The home décor industry virtually settled in West Hollywood, its panoply of costly shops displaying terra cotta, marble, wrought iron, fabrics, antiques, and all the other trappings of domestic elegance. In the mid-1970s, a surreal cobalt-colored glass high-rise that housed more than a hundred décor showrooms opened there.

It is ironic that, in L.A. as elsewhere, gay radicals, who prided themselves on their antimaterialism, were actually responsible for the inception of a new gay consumerism when they made the gay community widely visible. For a time, gay consumerism meant more than conspicuous consumption: It was also something of a political act. Any business owned by gay people might present itself as a "gay business," and to support it was to support the gay cause. But as the visible gay community

expanded, the businesses that qualified for community support proliferated: Even straight-owned companies began to vie for gay favor in a market economy where numbers are everything.

Gay men became the hot new demographic for corporate America
once it was announced by business researchers not only that there were
vast numbers of gays but also that the household income of gay males
far exceeded the average in America; and that, as Los Angeles–based
Walker-Struman Research announced, "eighty-three percent of gay men
order drinks by brand name, more than seventy-five percent prefer bot-
tled water, and about seventy percent are under forty years of age."[5] A
New Yorker cartoon summed up the effect such discoveries had on big
business: It depicted a pack of anxious-looking executives sitting in a
posh boardroom, the distinguished CEO peering at an intimidated un-
derling. The caption read, "I know the advertising department is gay,
Haskell, but are they gay enough?"[6]

Salivating thus over gay dollars even straight companies began buying ads in gay publications. And gay people responded, still at least
partly for political reasons: "Gay money," it was thought, demonstrated
and fostered "gay power" (though for some, silver-and-malachite salt-
cellars were not without charm). As *Los Angeles Magazine* suggested in
its article "But Will It Play in West Hollywood?" because gay L.A.—
youthful, affluent, and fashion-conscious—epitomized the demographics that impressed advertisers, it was thought to be an entrepreneurial
nirvana.

Many of the flourishing Los Angeles businesses based themselves on
a gay cultural myth that had been well promoted through the mid-century Athletic Model Guild, the *Advocate*'s Groovy Guy contests, and,
most of all, the movies: the fable that L.A. was a town chock-full of
golden-haired, surfer-bodied, actor-handsome youths. Gay-targeted
business often played on the fantasy that *you, too,* can look like those
Golden Boys if you wear . . . eat . . . do . . . whatever the business was selling. Ah Men, for example, a West Hollywood men's clothing boutique,
used the Golden Boy as their main advertising come-on—featuring gorgeous Hollywood models—to sell a fashion fantasy. Ah Men captured
the local gay market and, through its mail orders, brought a bit of gay

Hollywood to the provinces. It also made inroads among straight consumers, particularly men who worked in the entertainment industry.

Ah Men had already been popular with the West Hollywood crowd by the late 1950s. Don Cook, the founder, was selling see-through mesh pants, jumpsuits, low-rise slacks, and underwear styles that Macy's would never carry—"incredibly faggy" clothes, as even many gay men admitted. Nevertheless, Ah Men's styles eventually had great play: the *Los Angeles Times* published articles on Cook, his store, and his mail-order business; and Hollywood celebrities such as Richard Deacon, the acerbic gay actor who appeared on the *Dick Van Dyke Show,* posed for publicity photos with him.[7] Occasionally trading the Golden Boy image in for other kinds of prestige, Cook was even able, in the late 1970s, to persuade stars such as Sammy Davis, Jr. to let themselves be photographed in satin and leather for Ah Men catalogs.[8] Gay men as well as straight in small towns around the nation were able to "go Hollywood" by purchasing paisley bikinis and camouflage caftans modeled in the Ah Men catalogs by some of Hollywood's handsomest and sexiest. Cook's success paved the way for similar boutiques in West Hollywood, such as International Male, which earned millions in the 1970s by selling the gay look.[9]

GOLDEN BOYS DANCE, DANCE, DANCE

Hundreds of bodies writhe in the disco tempos of the latest hits. You can feel every bass note clear through every fiber of your body, and the pulsating rhythms make you want to dance, dance dance!

— *Data Boy,* on West Hollywood's Studio One[10]

Some Los Angeles businesses did not use sex to sell gay products—instead, sex itself was the product. Gay baths, bars, and that distinctly 1970s enterprise, discotheques, boomed and became money machines in Los Angeles. The biggest such business was West Hollywood's Studio One, conceived in 1972 when Scott Forbes, a Beverly Hills optometrist, asked Lee Glaze how he was able to draw an instant gay crowd when he revived Ciro's nightclub on the Sunset Strip. The ever-generous Glaze offered the use of his vast gay mailing list.[11] Two years later, Forbes opened Studio One (a name evocative of its Hollywood location) in a cavernous factory building that he outfitted with strobes and speakers in a hall of mirrors that became a temple of amplified sound and masculine vanity.

One thousand or more gay men gathered nightly at Studio One to "dance, dance, dance." Forbes' disco temple featured a deejay that a 1974 *Billboard* magazine named number one in Los Angeles. Studio One was also widely regarded as the number one dance spot, straight or gay. Music industry promoters vied to have their records played there;[12] it was featured on national television; and it was dubbed by many newspapers and magazines as one of the most exciting discos in the country. The cachet of Studio One was enhanced by its Back Lot Theater (another name chosen to evoke movie-studio proximity), which featured entertainers ranging from Joan Rivers to Wayland Flowers and his outrageous, foul-mouthed puppet, Madame.

Scott Forbes' disco became a legend; and its owner, the former optometrist who was now called the "disco king" by the press, became an overnight millionaire. His phenomenal prominence in promoting gay pleasure even rendered him a political power in the gay community. Forbes served on the boards of gay L.A.'s most important or prestigious organizations and agencies, such as the Gay Community Services Center and the Municipal Elections Committee of Los Angeles (MECLA).

To the media, Forbes often spoke of his business in tones of political pride: "Studio One was designed, planned, and conceived for gay people, gay male people," he announced to the *Los Angeles Times*. "Any straight people here are guests of the gay community."[13] Forbes insisted that his discothèque filled a vital community need: It celebrated sexual freedom for gay men. As he told the *Times* reporter, although many came to dance, just as many came primarily "for sexual purposes."[14] His admission elicited shocked letters to the editor: "What is this society coming to?" one reader lamented. "Don't people want any more out of another human being than their body for sexual pleasures?"[15] Apparently they did not: 1,600 invited guests packed the house for the disco's sixth anniversary. The crowd rarely thinned over the years.

The beauties of gay Hollywood could have the time of their lives at Studio One. But what to them was all the rage outraged others. Gay activists complained bitterly of Studio One–types who would rather dance than fight for gay rights, disparaging them as "disco bunnies—blond, built, and brainless."[16] Activists were also outraged at clubs that practiced hateful exclusionary policies, and Studio One was a prime target of their anger. Forbes' statement to the *Los Angeles Times* that his disco was simply "for . . . gay male people" was duplicitous by its omission of who counted in his definition of "gay male people." Studio One turned away almost everyone not meeting its Hollywood Golden Boy standard. Nonwhites were especially excluded: "to keep the club from getting too dark," as Mark Haile, a journalist for *BLK,* an African American gay magazine, says bitterly.[17] All but the most remarkably attractive blacks, Latinos, and Asian "gay male people" were generally asked for three pieces of picture identification—an effective ploy for weeding out the "undesirables." (Mark Haile observed a rite of passage for young gays of color: They would go to Studio One armed with three pieces of ID "so they could say they got in the door." But they didn't stay long: "It was too light.")[18] Dave Johnson, the activist son of actor Russell Johnson (of *Gilligan's Island* fame), reported in the *Los Angeles Free Press* that he had staked the place out and seen thirty-five instances in less than an hour in which people of color, and white females as well, were refused admission.[19]

Studio One was not alone among West Hollywood bars to practice exclusionary policies, which were an ironic by-product of the expansion of the gay community and the success of the gay movement. Tak Yamamoto recalls that in the 1960s, West Hollywood clubs "didn't have a policy of white-male dominance" because club owners needed all the customers they could get.[20] With the gay population explosion they could afford to turn away the "less desirable" since there were so many of the "more desirable" who were dying to get through their doors, bringing fame and fortune to the owner with their glamorous presence. Francesca Miller says that at one 1970s disco, where "the guys were really into flaunting muscles and male beauty," a guard at the door asked women for five pieces of identification. The presence of females, straight or gay, must have cramped the men's uninhibited sexual expression, she suggests. Miller also theorizes that lesbians were no longer needed as beards for gay men who "didn't want to be reminded of the past, like the 1950s, when gay men thought they had to have women around to protect them from the police."[21]

When the *Los Angeles Times* confronted Forbes in 1976 on allegations of racism and sexism at Studio One, he dug himself in deeper by claiming that he needed to keep out "the bad element."[22] Irate picketers, organized by the Gay Community Mobilization Committee, demonstrated in front of Studio One until they were granted a meeting with Forbes, who promised reform. When nothing changed at Studio One, the issue grew into a political crusade that revealed where the real power in the gay movement lay during those years. Because of Forbes' checkbook activism—his generous advertising in the gay press and his donations to gay causes—most community institutions did not support the boycott, and the media were reluctant even to write about the complaints against Studio One. The offensive door policy, as well as the protests, continued for years.

Other establishments that had excluded the non–Golden Boys reformed more quickly in response to the protest: Eddie Nash, who had earlier bowed to the Gay Liberation Front's pressure to allow same-sex dancing at the Farm, also owned Dude City in Hollywood, which banned women, and the Paradise Ballroom downtown, which banned blacks.[23] Troy Perry mobilized effective protests against Nash, and the bans were lifted right away. But Scott Forbes felt that he and Studio One could afford to be impervious to such pressure as long as the beauties kept flocking.

⸺

In earlier decades, gay men could find sex at bathhouses that were not explicitly gay, such as Brooks Baths on Beverly Boulevard, where the Orthodox Jewish clientele were oblivious to the patrons who were definitely not there for religious-ritual bathing. In the 1970s, however, "tubs" proliferated in Los Angeles. Some were consciously designed as gay sex clubs and usually required that a client become a member (and sign a waiver agreeing that no offense would be taken at the sight of homosexual activity). For many in that pre-AIDS era, gay L.A.'s new lifestyle meant that after the bars closed at 2:00 A.M. it was time to move on to the all-night and all-day baths. Some recall now that they lost entire weekends in such establishments.

The tubs often "specialized." The Corral Club in the Valley was reputed to have had a sling in every room for the leather crowd; Glen's Baths attracted young Latinos and their admirers.[24] Other baths were like Studio One, with a door policy that would ensure a "hot crowd" of the gorgeous and young. The 8709, a bathhouse nestled quietly just at the border of West Hollywood, was the most notable of the gorgeous-and-young tubs. One habitué recalls a night at the 8709 when almost every one of the five hundred or so "stunning" men there appeared to be under thirty.[25]

Gay activists may have objected to such discrimination, but pickets were not as feasible in front of a bathhouse as they might be in front of a disco, and exclusionary policies continued unabated in L.A. tubs. At Basic Plumbing on Fairfax, a "dry bath"[26] where men prowled dark corridors under red lights, customers were asked to lift their shirts before being allowed entry. Those with less-than-toned torsos were kept out. As Rick St. Dennis recalls, "pull-up-your-shirt places" became widespread in 1970s L.A.: "If you weren't built a certain way or you were too heavy, you'd get rejected."[27]

The 8709 became the most legendary of the Los Angeles bathhouses. Though located on an inconspicuous street corner, on the inside of the 8709 there was an elaborate maze, much black paint, and rooms large and small. According to legend, closeted actors entered through a secret door that led to an unlit, anonymous orgy room. The 8709 also attracted an endless stream of blond surfer types who migrated, erotically charged, from the disco down the street. One customer of the 8709 reminisces still about being "fortunate enough to go there" and recalls how he was "always amazed by the beautiful men."[28] Another remembers "walking through the large orgy room that was packed so tight with bodies you couldn't move." He says: "That was very much real fine!"[29] Because the ground floor backed onto a deli, 8709 customers could order food through a small window, precluding any need to leave.

By marketing a deliriously sybaritic sexuality, the 8709 became extraordinarily lucrative. Sheldon Andelson, the 8709's co-owner, made his appearances in the gay community dressed "casually in cashmere and hand-sewn shoes," accompanied often by a pair of elegant whippets who waited for him in his Jaguar.[30] Andelson was a successful lawyer; but he also had mainstream political ambitions, supported in part by revenues from the 8709. Paradoxically, it was his political ambitions that ultimately struck the death knell of his profitable bathhouse. In 1982, Governor Jerry Brown nominated Andelson to a seat on the University of California Board of Regents. Such a nomination had been unprecedented for an open homosexual, and Andelson felt elated and fulfilled. The bathhouse, however, became an albatross, threatening to break the neck of his nomination.

Andelson's co-ownership of a gay bathhouse was doubly problematic because the AIDS epidemic was under way by then, and the baths were considered by many to be among the most dangerous vectors for AIDS. He faced a huge dilemma. When, just before his nomination, the Municipal Elections Committee of Los Angeles (of which he had been a leading member since 1979) called for the closing of all bathhouses because they were hazardous to public health, Andelson was resentful. David Mixner writes that MECLA's position "threatened [his] economic base" and also "struck him as a personal betrayal."[31] However, a television reporter discovered his co-ownership of the 8709 just as his prestigious appointment was being debated in the California State Senate. Governor Brown had already made a huge leap forward by nominating a homosexual for the Board of Regents, but if it were known that the homosexual in question had a hand in L.A.'s premier gay orgy spot—in the midst of the AIDS epidemic, no less—the governor might be embarrassed to retraction. Andelson let himself be convinced by David Mixner and Peter Scott that he must not let that happen: He must procure for the community a phenomenal symbol of gay power and prestige by sacrificing the bathhouse. Andelson divested himself.

"SUCCESSFUL, ACHIEVING WOMEN"

Among lesbian feminists, there was a thing called downward mobil-
ity. Well, I've never heard of any revolution fighting for less. Women
already have less; we need to be fighting for more.

— Robin Tyler in the *Lesbian News*[32]

As many gay men pursued unrestrained sexual freedom in the 1970s, many gay women pursued professional success. Both groups sought what earlier eras had denied them most stringently and what the late 1970s finally made possible. Jeanne Cordova, who had been president of the Los Angeles chapter of Daughters of Bilitis, followed a trajectory in her development that was emblematic of the history of a sizable segment of the lesbian community. Attractive, young, and fiery, she quit the homophile Daughters because the organization seemed to her not at all attractive, young, and fiery. She then became a chief player among radical gays and was the editor of the *Lesbian Tide,* a magazine of the lesbian-feminist movement. Cordova says now that 1975 was "the last year of radicalism." In the second half of the decade, the gay movement "went civil rights, reformist, fund-raising."

This was a defensive move, she believes, necessitated by the war the community had to wage against homophobes such as Anita Bryant who were trying to destroy gay life. "We saw that the radical movement, where we'd wanted to create an egalitarian society and tried to use guerrilla tactics to that end, didn't do the job." The Dade County vote, Cordova claims, made gay people realize that they had to find more practical ways to survive. They understood that the point was no longer to get thousands of people into the streets, but rather to raise hundreds of thousands of dollars, which would enable them "to present television commercials to millions" and thereby to sway votes.[33]

The memory of the landslide defeat of Briggs, as well as flourishing gay economics, had made "survival" a moot point in the late 1970s. Cordova converted her magazine, the *Lesbian Tide,* which had been quite radical, to a "more middle-of-the-road publication."[34] The magazine was renamed *The Tide,* and Cordova became very concerned about its polish: "If we had continued to publish the same kind of shoddy pictures and stories like you'd find in some of the East Coast magazines, who would read it out here in L.A.?" she asks now. "We knew the audience we had to reach."

Cordova also learned about advertising and promotion, which cracked open new opportunities for her. The Los Angeles gay pride parade committee asked her to publish its parade booklet, which announced parade events and featured business ads that paid publication costs. She discovered then that the gay community included myriad real estate brokers, doctors, lawyers—all manner of business and professional people who had goods and services to offer and wanted to reach other gays and lesbians. In 1982, she began the *Community Yellow Pages,* a Los Angeles gay and lesbian directory. It was big business: "An incredible success. People loved it. I went from making $7,000 one year to $70,000 the next, and in a few years accumulated over $1 million."

Some of those who continued to be part of the radical community were bitterly critical of Cordova's transformation to a capitalist, and they lamented those leaders who, as they saw it, had abandoned responsibility to lead and teach in favor of "going mainstream for financial motives." Cordova, however, sees her metamorphosis as being consistent with a larger pattern: "It's an inevitable part of social change that grassroots radicalism should give way to middle-class assimilation. Though I have mixed feelings about it, I know that movements lose their sharp radical edge. No one can stop it." Movements dissipate like waves, she says, "and then another wave comes in."[35]

Southern California Women for Understanding came in with the next wave. It had been birthed through the Whitman-Radclyffe Foundation, a nonprofit, public-interest organization, formed first in Northern California in the early 1970s for the purpose of "enhanc[ing] the quality of life for gay people." Despite the nod to lesbians in the group's name ("Radclyffe," as in Radclyffe Hall; Walt Whitman was, of course, the group's other namesake), the foundation was made up largely of gay men, though Betty Berzon, the Los Angeles–based therapist and gay leader, served on its national board of directors and helped to establish a Southern California branch in 1974. Few women belonged to the Southern California branch, for the usual reasons: It was "too male-dominated and too male-oriented and [lesbians] were turned off to any deeper involvement."[36] But in 1976, Berzon called together two dozen lesbians who were in business and the professions and formed a "support group," the Southern California Women for the Whitman-Radclyffe Foundation. When the Whitman-Radclyffe Foundation announced, however, that its primary interest had become helping gay alcoholics, Southern California Women opted out. The members formed an independent organization, Southern California Women for Understanding.[37]

Betty Berzon had hoped to establish what had never yet existed—a political group made up exclusively of upper-middle-class lesbians. But when Myra Riddell, another Los Angeles psychotherapist, was elected Southern California Women's first president, the group's focus became at least as social as it was political. (However, even in its transformation it was revolutionary since a formally established social group made up exclusively of upper-middle-class lesbians had also never yet existed.) It did not take long for the most careful and closeted women to be drawn to SCWU events by the rumors that they were attracting A-list lesbians. Frieda, who had been a professor and an associate dean at a Los Angeles university, remembers:

> I was never an organizational person, but I was curious to see what they were concerned about . . . well . . . mostly to see what the people who went there were like. They had a dance in a beautiful old private house in Mt. Washington. They had a . . . ballroom . . . with a gallery above it. I went up to the gallery and looked down. And I saw a whole floor full of good-looking, elegantly dressed women. That was really nice. That really impressed me.[38]

Her partner, Marion, a retired psychiatrist, says that she had always been a "fag hag" because she loved the impeccable sophistication and refined tastes of the gay men she knew, but Southern California Women for Understanding attracted lesbians who were "just as polished."[39]

Though it was a vigorously social group, its steering committee members decided, in the midst of the Briggs battle, that SCWU could accomplish what they believed to be an important political goal: "to change the [public] image of lesbians by presenting our membership as successful, achieving women."[40] Fearing that such women might still be reluctant to participate in a gay women's group, the leadership penned a secret policy statement: Expressing concerns about appearance that were not much different from those that had been harbored by middle-class lesbians at mid-century, they wrote that the women they hoped to attract were no less repelled than were heterosexuals by lesbians who fit the "negative stereotype"—the old-style butches-and-femmes and the poorly dressed and ill-mannered lesbian-feminists. Southern California Women for Understanding planned to draw in more "successful, achieving women" by methods not unlike those that Delta Delta Delta might use to seduce prospective sorority members: They would demonstrate that the women who already belonged to SCWU were attractive and socially desirable, and they would provide "a non-threatening setting"[41]— poolside champagne brunches, golf tournaments, dance cruises, casino nights on board the *Queen Mary*[42]—all aimed at capturing the "successful, achieving" lesbian through snob appeal.

Cognizant that such elitism might lay them open to claims of racism, which would have been genuinely disturbing to many of these women,[43] SCWU made a special effort to place high-achieving lesbians of color in prominent positions, such as Joyce Gonzalez, a radio station manager, who was made a member of the first steering committee; and Estilita Grimaldo, the owner of an all-women's travel agency, who became the editor of the newsletter by its third issue.

The leaders worked hard to create "nonthreatening" social events, though many of the early attendees, who had never before set foot out of the closet, did not take their initial steps easily. SCWU's first party was held at the secluded hilltop home of Dr. Jane Patterson: The chances that neighbors or anyone else would see who was walking into the house were nil; everyone was invited by someone known to her; and yet, Myra Riddell recalls, "a lot of the women later told us that they drove around the hills for thirty or forty minutes before they could gather the courage to come in." But Southern California Women for Understanding's tactic of attracting women through social events before raising their "lesbian political consciousness" eventually worked well. Women who had found it difficult to attend a secluded lesbian party were before long taking giant steps, meeting at the Beverly Hilton Hotel with politicians and religious leaders to tell them what gay people needed and wanted.

SCWU became increasingly political. It formulated as a chief goal "to seek power and influence . . . in order to serve the community at large."[44] The organization not only worked on political campaigns, beginning with No on 6, but it was also interested in helping gays who needed help. For example, SCWU established scholarships for lesbian students and helped to fund Connexxus, the social service agency for lesbians. As early as the summer of 1983, SCWU began raising money and volunteers for the AIDS war.[45] SCWU membership burgeoned to more than 1,000, and chapters spread to Long Beach, Laguna, Orange, Garden Grove, Covina, North Hollywood, Altadena, Ventura, San Bernardino, Fullerton—all over Southern California. Southern California Women for Understanding was soon calling itself "the largest lesbian support group in the country."[46]

The leaders of SCWU who wanted to focus on the political aspects of the organization were ecstatic when they discovered a star for the cause in Jean O'Leary, an articulate, polished, handsome young woman with political know-how and surprising connections. O'Leary not only had been an executive director of the National Gay and Lesbian Task Force but had also spearheaded a campaign for the introduction of a Federal Gay Rights Bill into the House of Representatives. She was an openly gay delegate at the 1976 Democratic Convention, and she was also an intimate of Midge Costanza's, the special assistant to President Carter. It was O'Leary who convinced Costanza to arrange for lesbian and gay leaders to be invited in March 1977 to a meeting in the White House— the first such meeting in history. And in November 1977, O'Leary grabbed attention again when she was credited with leading the effort for the passage of a resolution supporting lesbian rights at the International Women's Year Conference in Houston.

Southern California Women for Understanding had discovered her even before those last victories. So delighted were they with their find— a famous lesbian who was determined to "work within the system and challenge it to broaden its scope"[47]—that in February 1977 they rented a huge hall that seated thousands at the Convention Center so that she might address the lesbians of Los Angeles. The delight was mutual. O'Leary decided to move to Los Angeles after appearing at SCWU events because she felt "a quiet power" there: "Things weren't radical, weren't out in the streets," she recalls. "People in L.A. moved things with money and influence. I knew this had to be the next level. L.A. was the place to be."[48]

GIRLS' NIGHT OUT

We were the "glam" lesbians. We set a lot of fashion trends. We weren't political at all.

— Heather Leavitt, of the women at
Peanuts in West Hollywood[49]

Not all L.A. lesbians were bent on power and influence, nor were they interested in radical lesbian feminism. Some just wanted to dance. Though their numbers were fewer than that of the "Golden Boys," Los Angeles was home to "Golden Girls," too. The gay historian John D'Emilio has suggested that throughout the 1970s gay men and lesbians were living lives that were diametrical opposites of one another: the men in "glitzy, high-tech, [urban] discos, . . . spending money, focused on themselves, and searching for sex"; the women "in self-sufficient, rural communities, . . . financially marginal, focused on group process, and nurturing loving relationships."[50] But D'Emilio had overlooked L.A.'s glam lesbians.

Lesbian bars proliferated and became big business during the late 1970s and into the 1980s. By 1983, there were more than forty lesbian bars in Los Angeles and its environs that aimed to be much more upscale than the old If Club or Open Door—as their names, such as "Executive

Suite" and "Cinema Lady," often announced.[51] The clientele for such bars had swelled for a variety of reasons: First of all, the Sexual Revolution had made women's undisguised pursuit of sex partners, even in public places, more permissible than it had been in earlier eras. Feminism, which helped to de-stigmatize love between women, encouraged more women to feel comfortable exploring lesbianism. Although lesbians generally continued to lag behind gay men in terms of income,[52] the feminist movement's battles for equal pay for equal work had succeeded in shrinking the gap, which meant that lesbians had more discretionary money to spend on entertainment. Finally, in an era of sexual revolution and rescinded antigay laws, more lesbians of middle-class background, whose earlier counterparts had socialized primarily in private homes, now dared to let their lesbianism show in semipublic settings.[53]

Lesbians who frequented the glamorous nightclubs had little in common with the radical lesbian feminists who sported T-shirts and jeans or SCWU types in business suits. The Palms, on Santa Monica Boulevard, attracted women who looked like the descendents of the ingénues that had frequented Tess's or Jane Jones' on the Sunset Strip two generations earlier. Marci says that the clients at the Palms "modeled themselves after Hollywood starlets." (Rather than emulating Dietrich or Garbo, as the women at Tess's used to, their ideal was Farrah Fawcett, the glamorous television star of the 1970s.) "The women who went to the Palms practically all had long blonde hair, though there were a few gorgeous black and Chicana lesbians there, too," Marci recalls. "Everyone was dressed like a movie star—lots of exotic jewelry, tight black dresses, high heels. And they always drank something sophisticated like cognac or martinis."[54]

Many of these women had found a niche in Hollywood production; they worked in behind-the-scenes jobs such as publicity, film editing, and script writing, professions that had become increasingly welcome to females. But lesbians who found employment in the movie industry in the late 1970s still feared that Hollywood had not yet recovered from the repressive mid-century, in which a Lizabeth Scott could be ruined if rumored to be gay. Marci speculates that the Palms lesbians dressed as they did because they were "still closeted at work and didn't want to look 'out' anywhere they went." The few women who dared to look "butchy" at the Palms, Marci says, were usually self-employed. She remembers a Palms habitué who owned her own insurance company: "She made over two million dollars a year. She could afford to look any way she pleased. But her style was tailored, polished, complete. More like Radclyffe Hall than a beer-hall butch."[55]

By the early 1980s, the style favored at the Palms had spread to other Los Angeles bars, such as Flamingo's in the Silver Lake district, where, Suzanne Gage remembers, "there was a lot of dressing to kill, a big lipstick lesbian crowd." The style eventually appeared in lesbian bars of the suburbs, too, such as Vermie's in Pasadena, where Melissa Etheridge, still an unknown, presented a new model for the "lesbian look," stunning the packed audiences with her long blonde mane and her raw sexual energy.[56]

Heather Leavitt, who frequented Peanuts as well as the Palms, recalls that the women at Peanuts were "light-years away" from some of their lesbian contemporaries: "All the crunchy Birkenstock lesbians were to the north" (in the Valley of North Hollywood, Studio City, Sherman Oaks, and Van Nuys). In West Hollywood, it was all about "the look." "The look" at Peanuts meant, she says, "beautiful": silk shirts ("polyester was a sin"), jeans by Calvin Klein or Jordache ("long before Jordache was popular in the straight community"), Gucci shoes, puka-shell necklaces, lots of gold. If the women at the Palms looked like starlets, some of those at Peanuts actually were—or they were the daughters of Hollywood stars. According to Heather, at the Palms the women spent their money freely; at Peanuts, they spent their parents' money freely. "These were very privileged girls; Peanuts was on the border of Beverly Hills, and the parking lot was full of Mercedes and Porches."

The Peanuts lesbians were not only as image-conscious as their male counterparts at Studio One; they were also as wildly uninhibited. The Sexual Revolution in which they'd grown up had demolished the manacles of restraint, as Heather recalls when she describes the night of a "wet T-shirt contest":

All the participants were under twenty-one. I wasn't even eighteen yet. We were all hot, young, tempestuous, and tempting. One gal—Frenchy, a blonde cutie—and I . . . we took our T-shirts off, and the audience's jaws dropped. I screamed, "Is this what you want?" They whistled and cheered. . . . We were so into pot and coke, and others kept pulling us into the bathroom for a snort. . . . It wasn't about relationships at Peanuts. It was about sex—everywhere, in the cars parked in the lot, in the bathrooms. We were young and dumb and full of come. But it was such a free and open time.

Even before West Hollywood was incorporated in the mid-1980s, Heather claims, gay people already felt that they owned that city. It never occurred to the lesbians at Peanuts to worry about a raid; the days when gay people feared they could get arrested for dancing together in public, or when police might hassle patrons merely for being in a lesbian bar, were ancient history. Though there were young lesbians and gay men who continued to be politically and historically aware, Heather says that those she ran with "believed that the big battles had all been won." She adds, "In their memory, they had never even existed."[57]

—

However, though the external struggles seemed to have been won, internal struggles, both old and new, continued to rage within the L.A. lesbian community. The lesbian sex wars, for instance, were essentially about the right to promulgate styles of lesbian sexuality condoned by neither Southern California Women for Understanding nor most lesbian feminists. Lesbian SM became a point of controversy in Los Angeles after a secret group, the Sado-Masochists Organization of Lesbians of Los Angeles (SMOLLA), expanded and morphed into Leather and Lace, and (after some resistance on the part of the newspaper) ran announcements of its meetings in the *Lesbian News*. Leather and Lace, established in 1982, featured SM theatricality—rituals, uniforms, dramatic trappings such as racks (as well as "warm, friendly rap groups, where the women could feel safe").[58] According to Leather and Lace's founder,

Sheree Rose, the group fell apart after three years, split over an issue that had been percolating in the L.A. lesbian community since the early 1970s.[59] Wendy, a beautiful, tall bottom, wanted to be allowed to join in the activities, to which some members objected because Wendy was a post-op male-to-female transsexual.

Other lesbian SM groups emerged in Los Angeles to take the place of Leather and Lace, such as Wild Women, Dominant Society (which men could join as submissives), Femmes and Butches ("an SM club for women who liked the old-fashioned way"), and LA RAWW (Los Angeles Radical and Wild Women). LA RAWW attracted to its parties "a hundred women going wild with SM sex, food, and a social place to talk," Rose says.[60] Eventually semipublic venues emerged as well, such as Cunt Club, Club Utero, and Ozone—all lesbian sex clubs.

But none of these sex clubs—private or semipublic—achieved great longevity, even in edgy, theatrical Hollywood. Vivian Escalante, who started Cunt Club, explains that there was great initial enthusiasm for such ventures (which sometimes included playful spoofs on bygone glamour, such as "gorgeous cigarette girls" carrying portable display trays from which they peddled lubricants and condoms instead of cigarettes). But unlike gay men, who have been able to support a multiplicity of such venues, lesbians, Escalante says, "are very shy."[61] Wet T-shirt contests and parking lot sex could be wildly successful at Peanuts, where one might indulge or not, but RAWW and the Cunt Club were too unambiguous to draw a large and steady lesbian clientele. Most of the lesbian sex clubs folded within a year or so, though others sometimes cropped up to replace them.

Nevertheless, the new open focus on lesbian sex and glamour did not go unnoticed or unlamented by committed old-school lesbian-feminists, such as Irene Weiss, a founder of Califia Community. Weiss, believing that the biggest battles with external enemies were still not won, sent out an impassioned plea to the "new lesbians" (whom she accused of preferring kinky sex to lesbian politics) to "rethink and reexamine" their priorities: "I call on you to pour your heart, soul, blood and guts, into *organizing.*"[62] Weiss' plea fell on young ears that were deaf. The L.A. radical lesbians of the early 1970s had not succeeded in birthing a large new generation in their own image. Much of the younger generation of lesbians lived in a different world—one in which the "sex, drugs, rock and roll," and, for some, edgy sexual experimentation seemed more compelling than antiquated politics.[63]

The "glam" lesbian trend, which started in Los Angeles, spread to big cities all over America by the end of the 1980s. Writing in *Out/Look Magazine* in 1989, Arlene Stein speculated that lipstick lesbians and other glam-lesbian types flourished not because there no longer were problems of homophobia or sexism that lesbians had to fight, but rather the phenomenon marked a triumph of "commercialization and popularization of feminist culture and the avant-garde art world," in which many lesbians participated.[64] But there were other reasons that new looks and lifestyles grew. The super-seriousness of radical lesbian feminism sounded too shrill and even gratuitous in the ears of the young. What were the radicals still fighting about so vehemently? The battles over freedom for women had been won, they insisted. The wage gap was closing, there were even affirmative action policies that helped women get into professional schools, and there were already women doctors and lawyers galore. In L.A., thanks to a tolerant cultural climate, lesbians could finally step out of the shadows and indulge openly in their pleasures. If problems of homophobia or sexism still existed, they believed, one had to look hard to find them.

"DISCO SUCKS"

Take off your watch, take off your rings.
You don't want to lose those things
When you fist-FUNK!
Won't you fist-funk with me?

— Lyrics by Craig Lee for Lotus Lame and the Lame Flames[65]

Though West Hollywood's relentless disco beat epitomized gay nightlife in the 1970s and early '80s, the very different subculture of punk rock, for which Los Angeles was a major center, also attracted young gay people. On the surface, disco (exuberantly bright and glitzy) and punk (darkly nihilistic) appeared to be diametrical opposites. Punkers mocked the West Hollywood lifestyle and coined the slogan "Disco Sucks."[66] But despite differences, the two subcultures surprisingly shared some attributes—particularly a gay sensibility (though in different guises) and a significant gay infrastructure.

Clubs such as Studio One usually excluded heterosexuals, but punk clubs played to a gay-straight mix and provided an avant garde haven for artists, actors, and musicians of all persuasions. Gay talent was not often identified as gay, but it infused L.A.'s dynamic punk scene with style and wit. Gay punks could be camouflaged in the sexual ambiguity and amorality of punk culture. Punks disdained the "straight" world, broadening the very word "straight" to signify "bourgeois conformity." They snubbed whatever smacked of the bourgeoisie and sometimes called themselves the "hip-eoisie." This blanket rejection of "normalcy" afforded refuge for homosexuality, though decidedly not of the West Hollywood variety.

Punks affected an alienated persona, but gay punks found West Hollywood alienating beyond endurance. Creative spirits burning to be different, descendants of bohemians, they were put off by what they saw as the glitzy pretensions and straightjacket conformity of West Hollywood. The punk clubs, located mostly in less-upscale areas, east of La Brea, were open to all races, classes, genders, and kinks; and for many gay men, the habitués of punk clubs were far more sexually thrilling than the predictable disco crowd. Those who felt like misfits in any world—straight or gay—could get happily lost in the camaraderie of the punk world, its live bands, and its edgy performance art.

But most punks who had gay sexual experiences did not identify as homosexual any more than they identified as heterosexual or even bisexual. Jack Marquette, who promoted punk nightclubs, recalls that many in that scene "thrived on sexual ambiguity,"[67] but they maintained a determined refusal to categorize their lifestyles. Their "orientation" (the very concept of which they would disdain) was best classified as "decline to state." John Callahan, who was openly gay, says that few in his crowd declared their homosexuality because "public sexual orientation was passé."[68]

Although sexual ambiguity may have been almost universal among them, however, the punk world was not always entirely accepting of males who were unambiguously homosexual. The punk persona, taking its roots in rock and roll to the extreme, gloried in crude and rude posturing. For men, punk sexual ambiguity alternated with punk machismo that could express itself in homophobia as hostile as a hardhat's. Craig Lee, a musician in several punk bands and the composer of "Fist Funk," was harassed for his homosexuality: The tires on his car were slashed; he was often taunted as a "fag," both by his audience and in print; and long before he fell ill, it was maliciously rumored that he had AIDS.[69] Such hassling caused many to hide the fact of their homosexual identity behind the more permissible "decline to state." Because of punk's macho affectations, the homosexual exploits of many male punkers had to be fueled by drugs and alcohol, and were seldom talked about. Some, like Darby Crash of the Germs, were revealed to be gay only posthumously.

Perhaps many of the punk musicians were encouraged to be discreet because they had big dreams of landing a lucrative contract from the nearby music industry. Nevertheless, there were some famous male punk rockers who appear to have been primarily or exclusively homosexual, including Gerardo Velasquez of Nervous Gender, Kid Congo of the Cramps, and Tomata du Plenty of the Screamers. A handful of punk icons flaunted gayness outrageously, such as the African American drag diva Vaginal Crème Davis, who created a band called Cholita: The Female Menudo (for which she performed as a Latina—swapping ethnic identity as well as gender).

Out or not, gays could easily conceal themselves in the fashions of punk. Though punks would have considered the gay male "clone look" (muscle-revealing pastel Izod shirts and 501 jeans) or the lipstick lesbian look (Gucci shoes and gold chains) as oppressively conformist as the businessman's three-piece suit, they created their own "look" that was as studied as the styles at Studio One or Peanuts, and one that young gays could love. Gay-boy punks were permitted to affect androgyny by dyeing their hair jet black and wearing eyeliner and face powder.[70] Gay girl punks could merge easily with other girl punks who were not lesbian-identified. Phranc, a Los Angeles–based musician who performed in Castration Squad and other punk bands such as Nervous Gender, recalls that the female-punk look could be very gender-bending: Even feminine punk rockers would wear "skinny ties and other boy things."[71]

Though homosexual practices were usually covert among male punks, among punk girls they were open and even signified a declaration of female sexual freedom, which punks resoundingly approved. Sheree Rose remembers her own early sojourns into the punk rock club scene: "There was an amorphous sexual energy," she says. "Who you slept with didn't have anything to do with gender. The men knew that the women were sleeping together. It was no problem."[72] According to Fran, who was also a punk rocker, everyone acknowledged that pansexuality was the female-punk "norm": "You'd go to a club, come back to the crash pad shit-faced, and end up sleeping with another girl as likely as with a guy, and you didn't have to hide it." In between visits to punk rock venues such as Florentine Gardens and Brave Dog, Fran would visit bars such as Peanuts, and, as she observes now, the distinctions were more apparent than real: "The girls [at Peanuts] were different from those at the punk clubs mostly because they had a gay identity. We punks did the same things in bed that they did. It was just that we never called ourselves 'gay.'"[73] Phranc, who was the public darling of sexually flexible punk rockers like Fran, agrees that although pansexuality was the punk female norm, a "lesbian identity" was rare in punk culture: "Everyone among the punk rocker girls was experimenting with sex, but I can think of only one other person besides me who actually called herself a dyke. The rest just did it."[74]

Punk females "were not at all political," Phranc says. "They were into 'anything goes.' It was all personal pleasure and fashion." Despite their sexual fluidity and gender ambiguity, the girl punks were nothing at all like the radical feminists of the decade before who had experimented with lesbian relationships as "the next important step" and wore "boy things" as a politically correct uniform. Like the lipstick lesbians, girl punks provided another model of style for young females who enjoyed sex with other females—one that was far more loose and light and trendy than anything lesbian feminists could be comfortable with.[75]

Lesbian feminists also disapproved of punk rock because of its trappings and symbols of violence (including swastikas, worn sometimes "just to piss people off").[76] But punk rock could be political in ways that even lesbian feminists would condone. Groups such as Age of Consent presented gay and feminist social critiques in rap songs such as "Missionary Position" and "Schizo Gay: Gay All Night and Straight All Day." Female punk rockers, disdaining conventional femininity, demanded what most women were still too timid to claim. Fran was a devotee of women's punk rock bands, including the Slits, Castration Squad, and Red Fear, which flaunted aggressive female pansexuality. She remembers that those performers "had so much strength, power, and presence," which was "really attractive and appealing to a girl like me who was looking for a way to be."[77]

Gay wit and imagination had a strong influence on the L.A. punk scene. Many of its prime venues, such as the Brave Dog, the long-lived Anti-Club on east Melrose, and a series of bohemian "events" called "Theoretical parties," were conceived and successfully run by gay men such as Jack Marquette and Jim Van Tyne. Alternating with the extreme of machismo, hints of gayness were sometimes provocative political statements because of their power to *épater le bourgeois*. Local punk rock bands called themselves by names such as Circle Jerks, the Weirdos, and the Dickies. L.A.'s first punk club, the Masque, featured Arthur J and the Gold Cups, a band name that referred (for those in the know) to two prime L.A. hangouts for gay hustlers. Gayness influenced punk culture and, in turn, exploited its outrageous challenges to convention. For instance, Craig Lee's lyrics for "Fist-Funk" lampooned gay sexual extremes and also introduced the shocking concept of fist fucking to heterosexual audiences. Under Lee's creative direction, the Lame Flames performed songs such as "Fist Funk" dressed in black SM caps and red jockstraps over black lace stockings and teddies, creating a defiantly queer effect.[78]

The gay and lesbian young who were rejected by the bouncers guarding the doors of West Hollywood's party temples—and many more who never even wanted to knock on those doors—found a temple of their own among the rejects and rejectors that defined the punk demimonde. Though it was a new frontier, it was also an old one: It was the latest incarnation of L.A.'s long-standing bohemian world, where lesbians, gays, and those who "decline to state" had always danced on the edge.

III: SMASH HITS, DEVASTATING BOMBS, STUNNING COMEBACKS

Hear
Rev.
Troy
D.
Perry

Every
Sunday
1:30pm

Metropolitan Community Church
Temporarily meeting at:
6205 Miles Ave., Huntington Park,
Phone: 581-9284   90255

The face that launched a worldwide church: Troy Perry, 1968. *Courtesy Aristide Laurent.*

CHAPTER 9

Building Worlds of Our Own

TEMPLES OF OUR OWN

Gay people came to our church out of the shadows, out of the clos-ets, out of the half-world.

—The Reverend Troy Perry, founder of
Metropolitan Community Church[1]

The early movement slogan—"Gay Liberation. Dig It. Do It."—that ex-horted gay people to claim their sexuality, the nightclubs such as Studio One and Peanuts that invited them to uninhibited release of sexual en-ergy, the panoply of erotic possibilities that were opening to gays in a city so large and diverse—all reflect a crucial part of the history of liberated gay L.A. But another crucial part concerns the ways that gay people built daytime lives in Los Angeles, how they formed vital institutions that compensated for those from which they had been barred, what they ul-timately did with the media savvy and money that has always been part of gay L.A., how they tended to the most vulnerable members of their community—the sick and old and young, and how they dealt with dev-astating setbacks.

One of the most remarkable of the daytime stories is about the birth of religious institutions in Los Angeles that went on to impact gay life all over America and beyond. Troy Perry and his Metropolitan Community Church are the central figures in that story. From its humble beginnings in 1968, when twelve men and women met in the living room of Perry's rented house in a Los Angeles suburb, the Metropolitan Community Church has grown to be the largest gay institution in the world. It has 275 congregations in twenty-three countries and houses of worship in all but four of the United States. It owns property worth about $100 million. In California, there are twenty-five MCC churches; in Texas there are fifteen. It is probably the world's largest employer of gays and lesbians.[2] Troy Perry's Metropolitan Community Church was, for a while, alone in providing the gay community with spiritual sustenance, but his success eventually led to the huge proliferation of MCCs as well as other gay and lesbian religious institutions. Steeped in the Bible and practiced in the rolling oratory of the fundamentalist South, Troy Perry became the major gay religious leader. Often described as "kinda hot," his strong features, penetrating hazel eyes, and towering six feet were a huge draw, as personal qualities often are with a charismatic preacher. It was inevitable that some gay male parishioners would fall in love with him, but Perry believed that a gay minister must be even more scrupulous than nongay religious leaders in delineating boundaries. When MCC eventually ordained more ministers, Perry used earthy humor to deliver a steadfast rule that would place the gay church above the scandals plaguing other denominations: "Don't fuck the flock."[3]

The flock continued to expand. By 1972, contributions were sufficient for MCC to purchase a former opera house in the depressed but architecturally-grand West Adams district. Perry, ever conscious of the rejection gay people had suffered in traditional religious institutions, was determined to create for them a bona fide and beautiful church. He had the walls papered with expensive silk and thick new carpets laid. It was not about style, Perry says: "It was about self-esteem. I wanted people to know that theirs was a 'real church.'" As one parishioner from the Hollywood Hills enthused, "It was one of the most elegant places to go. The choir all in robes; all these gay people in bright sunlight!"[4]

In his position as religious leader of an oppressed minority, Perry was determined to involve his congregants in committed social activism. Parishioner Lucia Chappelle recalls that in the 1970s, "someone would call a protest—against ABC television for supporting Anita Bryant, the *Los Angeles Times* for refusing to use the word 'gay' instead of 'homosexual," the Hollywood police for discriminatory policies—and then our telephone trees would be buzzing, and 80 percent of the people who showed up at the demonstration would be from the Metropolitan Community Church."[5] Perry says that his work to ensure that gays and lesbians would fight for their rights and "never take a backseat" was modeled on the goals of the black church in America in its historical struggles for civil rights.[6] (Gay wits, drawing on the parallel with another cleric who was a civil rights activist, called Perry "our Martin Luther Queen.")

Metropolitan Community Church also shared with black churches the terrible experience of noxious enemies. Frank Zerilli, who worked at MCC in its early years, recalls that hate mail came so frequently that it was "stacked a foot thick." In a mood of dark humor, MCC workers filed such mail under "Letters from Christians."[7] In January 1973, the "Christians" struck in person: The assistant pastor, Lee Carlton, returning at night from a funeral, found the church in flames. Zerilli, who arrived a few hours later, described the scene as "heart-wrenching," especially since MCC was "the first property ever owned by the gay community in America." Parishioners were convinced that the fire was an act of arson, and though official investigators claimed to find no evidence that the 1973 fire had been purposely set,[8] parishioners believed their theory was confirmed when other Metropolitan Community Churches were later torched.[9]

Nonetheless, the destruction of the edifice made the institution stronger. The following Sunday, so many people were intent on showing their support for the church and broadcasting the message that gays would not be intimidated that no building could be found to accommodate the crowd of more than 1,000 people. The Sunday service was held *en plein aire.* Councilman Bob Stevenson arranged to close 22nd Street to accommodate the horde of worshippers, who were accompanied by a horde of media. When the Metrochords, a gay singing group, expressed concern at this public exposure and asked for screens to sing behind, Perry was furious, as was MCC's music director Willie Smith, who told the complaining singers, "Sissy, the closet done burned down!"[10] That day, Perry says, "broke the back of people's worries about coming out of the closet." It also marked the beginning of an accelerated growth for the church, which was soon able to build far beyond the borders of Los Angeles, nationally and internationally, from South Africa to the Philippines to all over Europe and Latin America. The new Mother Church that was erected in the middle of Boystown is now valued at $9 million.[11]

—

From the beginning, Perry also earned the gratitude and respect of gays and lesbians who weren't Christian. "We can't bar other people the way we've been barred," he explained to his congregation in the early 1970s;[12] he opened the doors not only to all who wanted to come worship but also to those who wanted simply to use the church as a meeting place—even to the Wicca priestess Z. Budapest and the lesbian witches of the Susan B. Anthony Coven #1, which met in the church's social hall. At Perry's earliest Sunday services, Jewish gays were also part of the congregation, the men sitting wrapped in their prayer shawls as Perry preached in his Pentecostal style. Jewish lesbians attended MCC in its early years, too, and some even adapted Perry's example into viable models for their own women-centered institutions. Savina Teubal, a native of Argentina, came to Los Angeles to be a screenwriter, but instead became a feminist biblical scholar and the founder of Sarah's Tent, a Jewish women's religious group. Teubal said that she was inspired to establish Sarah's Tent, named for the Old Testament matriarch, after she attended MCC. "I was fervently interested in new movements that went against convention. The thought that Metropolitan Community Church could gather together so many people in a rebellious religious movement was inspiring to me. It reminded me of the Peronistas screaming against the Oligarchs, and the Communist rallies that I went to in Buenos Aires." It was the example of Perry's challenges to religious orthodoxy, she acknowledged, that helped her to rethink the meaning of women in the Bible and to invent feminist rituals and celebrations for Jewish women.[13]

Perry warmly welcomed gay Jews into Metropolitan Community Church, but he suggested in 1972 that perhaps they might want to form their own *minyan* (a prayer group of ten or more Jews). With Perry's encouragement, the Jewish congregants enlisted two Los Angeles rabbis,

Norman Eichberg and Erwin Herman, to help start a Metropolitan Community Temple within MCC.[14] Gay and lesbian religious Jews began going to Troy Perry's church because "Troy showed that religion is just as important to lesbian and gay people as it is to straight people," Mina Meyer, one of the first lesbians to be part of Metropolitan Community Temple, explains. "But we Jews didn't feel comfortable in straight synagogues. They didn't recognize our families as families." She recalls seeing at the earliest services "old Jewish gay men, in their fifties, sixties, and seventies. They hadn't been to a Jewish service since their bar mitzvah. They sat there crying. How much this meant to them!"[15] Harriet Perl, who was in her fifties when she joined the Temple, says, "When I first heard about it, I couldn't figure out why anyone would want to have a gay temple. I'd spent my whole adult life having nothing to do with Judaism. But this temple's traditions reminded me of being Jewish as a child. . . with my grandmother. . . . I felt like I could finally come back to that."[16]

On January 26, 1973, still housed at the Metropolitan Community Church, the Jews adopted for their group the Hebrew name Beth Chayim Chadashim, meaning House of New Life. It was that evening that MCC was mysteriously burned, though the Jewish arc, along with the Christian altar, was undamaged. The arc contained a newly acquired Torah[17] — one that had miraculously survived the Nazi invasion of Czechoslovakia and now miraculously survived the church fire. Homeless, with the Torah in tow, Beth Chayim Chadashim (BCC) was offered temporary space for services in the school building of the Leo Baeck Temple in West Los Angeles.[18] Among the traditionally observant, the existence of a gay temple became a point of hot debate. Even the Union of American Hebrew Congregations (later known as the Union for Reform Judaism) protested angrily when Rabbi John Sherwood proposed that Beth Chayim Chadashim be recognized.[19] The battle was quelled within months, however, and in 1974, the Union's national board gave its final approval for BCC's inclusion into the group of 1 million members.[20] This approval marked the first time that a gay congregation had been accepted by the governing body of an established religion.[21]

Beth Chayim Chadashim had been largely male to that point, though lesbians were welcome. Mina Meyer was BCC's first treasurer; Sharon

Raphael was the first social action chair. Mina Meyer was even invited to give the first sermon at the first BCC Yom Kippur service.[22] But for the most part, the Beth Chayim Chadashim patriarchy-quotient was no different from that of the straight world. Its members had backgrounds in various denominations—Orthodox, Conservative, and Reform—but its rituals were heavily Orthodox, which soon caused some lesbian feminists, such as Mina, to leave. The very traditional language of the prayers, "full of 'He's' and 'Him's'," as Harriet Perl says, "pricked our feminist sensibilities." Perl gathered the few remaining lesbian members, and together they challenged the men about the sexist liturgy. To make their point, Harriet read the Declaration of Independence, substituting "women" for "men." "That made the guys pretty uncomfortable," she recalls, "but they really listened, and there was never a need for a gender fight." Perl, a retired English teacher, was asked to sit with the men and figure out with them, each holding a prayer book, how they could "degenderize" its language. In 1974, BCC became the very first religious body with a de-androcentrized liturgy.[23]

Despite the nonsexist language of its liturgy, BCC had trouble attracting women in its early years. The BCC board of directors, appointing an Affirmative Action Committee that would be responsible for implementing a new policy, pledged that women would meticulously be given equal time and space in all functions of the temple: "For example, if men present sermons twice a month, then women shall present sermons twice a month." In 1975, the congregation also put out a call in lesbian periodicals and elsewhere for Jewish lesbians to "take their place in the temple . . . [and] help in creating a deeper involvement of women."[24] The congregation's sincerity about gender parity could hardly be questioned when Beth Chayim Chadashim, which had been served until 1983 only by rabbinical students, was finally in a position to hire an ordained rabbi: Janet Marder was their choice. Though Marder was a heterosexual woman, with the exception of two years, from 1992 to 1994, when Marc Blumenthal, a gay man, was the rabbi, all subsequent rabbis have been lesbians.

Metropolitan Community Church had similar gender issues to work through, and the unity of the institution was seriously threatened when lesbian congregants perceived the men to be insensitive to their needs.

The Christian liturgy included as many "He's" and "Him's" as the Jewish one. Taking Beth Chayim Chadashim as its model, a committee of MCC feminist men and women tried to get the church to adopt inclusive language, but the battles raged for years. Lucia Chappelle recalls that when a resolution for an inclusive language hymnal was proposed at the 1981 General Conference, one MCC clergyman cried out, "Father! Father! . . . Why do they want to take my Father away from me?"[25] When the resolution failed, committed feminists began De Colores, a women's outreach church within MCC, creating their own liturgy with prayers such as "We praise you, El Shaddai, breasted one, for giving us the courage to reach out to womyn."[26] However, the AIDS epidemic of the 1980s and '90s, which effectively destroyed a generation of male leaders, called on lesbians to make peace and assume leadership within the church. They became elders in MCC in unprecedented numbers. In 2005, when Troy Perry retired, the Reverend Elder Nancy Wilson, who had been a member of De Colores twenty years earlier, was named worldwide head of the Metropolitan Community Churches.

Some gay churches that had their roots in Los Angeles have grown branches elsewhere, as did their prototype, MCC. Carl Bean, a gay African American who had been an entertainer at Harlem's prestigious Apollo Theater and on Broadway, was drawn to Los Angeles in 1972 by its entertainment industry; but when he first walked into Metropolitan Community Church, he recalls, he was "so overcome by a sense of joy and community" that he cried. Bean sought ordination and in 1982 founded the Unity Fellowship of Christ Church, a church primarily for African American lesbians and gays. The church has grown to twelve congregations scattered around the United States, some of them, such as the New York congregation, with as many as 2,000 members on the rolls.[27]

Like MCC, BCC also inspired the founding of gay religious institutions elsewhere. There were no other gay Jewish institutions in the world when Beth Chayim Chadashim began in 1972, but several were soon created after the model of BCC: for example, in New York, Beth Simchat

Torah, established in 1973; in Philadelphia, Congregation Beth Ahavah, established in 1975; in Chicago, Congregation Or Chadesh, established in 1976; and in San Francisco, Congregation Sha'ar Zahav, established in 1977. The gay congregation of L.A. also grew. Members of Beth Chayim Chadashim were able to purchase a synagogue building in 1977. When Rabbi Denise Eger left her position at Beth Chayim Chadashim after a messy personal problem with the temple's board, she started another gay temple, the upscale Kol Ami in West Hollywood. That congregation too purchased its own building.

Both gay synagogues in L.A. now offer religious services that depart little from the Reform tradition and are in most ways like other Reform synagogues that attract young, middle-class Jewish families. Rabbi Eger remembers that when she became the rabbi at Beth Chayim Chadashim in the 1980s, in the midst of the AIDS epidemic, "my life was spent going from one hospital to another, one funeral to another."[28] Now, with the epidemic much more under control, Beth Chayim Chadashim is in the midst of the gay baby boom. Congregants have been so fertile or so active in adopting that the synagogue has started a religious school for five- and six-year-olds. "I officiated not only at the baby-naming ceremonies for most of the children," the current rabbi, Lisa Edwards, says, "but also at the weddings of most of their parents."[29] The Congregation Kol Ami membership, too, now includes about one hundred children under the age of sixteen, and the synagogue is becoming increasingly family-oriented. In fact, the gay and lesbian parents in Kol Ami have even deliberated about whether to opt out of the gay pride parade—where, they fear, proximity to contingents such as the leathermen may be troubling to young kids.[30]

The institutionalization of gay churches and synagogues has not satisfied many gay people who wish for something other than what they see as mere permutations of Judeo-Christianity, and who blame Western religion as the root and rod of homophobia. Some Los Angeles lesbians, led by witch Z. Budapest, turned to Wicca. Some gay men, led by the Mattachine Society's old founder, Harry Hay, and the Gay Liberation Front activist Don Kilhefner, fostered another branch of paganism. Hay and Kilhefner were convinced that the gay movement needed a radical spiritual culture to restore its meaning. Hay claimed that through years of research he had learned that gay people shared a unique consciousness, for which they had been honored rather than derided in non-Western societies.[31] Kilhefner and Hay, along with Mitch Walker, a psychologist, issued a call in 1979 for a "spiritual gathering of radical faeries," where gay men would enjoy "gay space" and goddess-worship (both influenced by tenets of lesbian separatism and spiritual feminism). That first gathering saw the beginning of numerous retreats that attracted thousands of gay men from all over the world and inspired the establishment of faerie households and rural communes.[32] Not only gay churches and synagogues, but also various sects have proliferated easily in Los Angeles because nonconventional spirituality has traditionally been freer there than anywhere in the country. Any and all spiritual bents can be satisfied.

MEDIA OF OUR OWN

When I realized that nobody would ever again produce me because they found out I was a lesbian, that's when I understood that I had to become a producer myself.

—Robin Tyler, comic and gay-and-lesbian event producer[33]

The rich and glamorous Hollywood entertainment industry has been essential to a large segment of the gay L.A. community, giving it employment and style. But the industry was slow to acknowledge to the outside world that "gay" existed, let alone that it was ubiquitous in Hollywood. In 1962, Hollywood's first post–Production Code forays into homosexuality on the screen, *The Children's Hour* and *Advise and Consent,* both concluded with the suicides of the "homosexually-inclined" characters. Throughout the decade, there was no such creature as a reasonably well-adjusted homosexual in the movies, and nary a gay character was permitted to escape death: For example, in *The Fox* (1967), the neurotic, hysterical lesbian is accidentally-on-purpose felled by a giant phallus in the form of a tree; in *The Sergeant* (1968), the gay male character (again) kills himself because it is so awful to be homosexual.

In the 1970s, when gay people were becoming increasingly visible throughout America, Hollywood was practically silent on the subject of homosexuality, though there were a few exceptions, such as *The Boys in the Band* (1970), which offered a host of gay stereotypes, each of them miserable. A movie made for television in 1971, *That Certain Summer,* finally dared to transcend stereotypes: The *New York Times* called it the first film "to take a mature and non-remonstrative approach to the subject of homosexuality." Ironically, it was around that sympathetic film that gays made an early organized attempt to put pressure on the industry. A media task force, formed by the new Gay Community Services Center when the movie was being filmed, demanded a meeting with the producers and script writers because they assumed *That Certain Summer* would contain the usual negative images of homosexuals. They were welcomed by the producer, Robert Wise, recalls Deni Ponty, a task force member: "He told us, 'I'm surprised you're here. I work with a lot of you boys.' I said, 'It's the 'you boys' we're here about.'" Ultimately, their conference was cordial. The task force was discouraged from further actions, however, when one of the writers privately scolded them, saying that he had been fighting effectively "behind the scenes" for gay progress, which such a meeting would endanger.[34] The task force did no more, and Hollywood was slow to improve.[35]

In the 1980s, several films finally attempted to feature sympathetic gay characters—for example, *Making Love* and *Personal Best* (both in 1982), and *Liana* (1983). But despite such projects, and despite the gayness of the town, Hollywood actors or their studios still remained as hypervigilant as their counterparts of the 1930s, '40s, and '50s had been in making sure that their heterosexual image remained beyond question in the world outside. The fiasco over the attempt to turn Patricia Nell Warren's best-selling gay novel, *The Front Runner,* into a Hollywood movie illustrated the point dramatically. Paul Newman had bought the rights to Warren's novel in the early 1980s and intended to play the role of the coach who falls in love with his champion runner. But Newman's studio would not permit it unless the script was rewritten to show him falling in love with a female teacher. Newman walked away from the project. In 1986, the producer Jerry Wheeler bought the rights and tried to find a star who would play the coach. According to Kim Garfield, Wheeler's publicist on the project, he solicited "every good-looking male star in Hollywood for the coach role." Tommy Lee Jones told him, "I ain't gonna play no fuckin' faggot." Burt Reynolds said, "I'd love to play the part, but if I do, everyone will think I'm gay (as they already do), and because I've lost weight they'll also think I have AIDS." Wheeler approached another star who said he was interested in the role, but he'd have to check with his agent. The next day, Wheeler found a newspaper-wrapped parcel at the door of his office. Inside the newspaper was a dead fish and a note: "Don't call any of my clients again or this will be your head."[36]

Time wrote bemusedly about Wheeler's casting frustrations in 1988: "Didn't anybody want to appear in his film? . . . What was the catch? Did he want someone to play a rapist, a child molester, or a drooling maniac? No. Those would have been easy parts to fill. Wheeler wanted a rugged star to play a college track coach who happens to be gay." Huge gay gains all over America notwithstanding, *Time* concluded, "Hollywood still feels that homosexual roles spell trouble."[37] Wheeler gave up the struggle to make the film in 1989; he died of AIDS in 1990.

If it was considered damaging for an actor simply to play the role of a homosexual, how much more damaging it was to be perceived as one, particularly if that perception threatened to spread beyond the relatively safe enclave of industry people. Sheila Kuehl, who played Zelda Gilroy on the television series, *The Many Loves of Dobie Gillis,* says that even in the uptight late 1950s, when she joined the industry, "everyone was thought to be bisexual" in Hollywood. "It was bohemian, an element of freedom," she notes. But many a promising Hollywood career came to an abrupt end if an industry executive believed that viewers, who lived in the world far from Hollywood, might suspect an actor of any kind of sexuality other than hetero. Sheila Kuehl's Zelda had been the most popular female character on the program, the only one to appear for four consecutive years. She was tapped to do a new series, a spin-off in which Zelda would be the main character. "But suddenly the pilot sank like a stone," Kuehl says. Her director told her that the president of CBS had watched her performance and opined that she came off as "too butch." That is, her homosexuality was discernible. The Zelda Gilroy project was killed.[38]

Michael Kearns, too, had a promising career as an actor. His big break came when he was cast in a wholesome, family-oriented television series, *The Waltons*. Kearns played John Boy's older brother in the close-knit rural family. He had leading-man good looks, talent, and youth (he was twenty-two when he landed the plum role in the series). His agent, who knew Kearns was gay, worried that if word got out beyond the industry, his promising career would be damaged. Kearns recalls that the agent admonished him "not to go to gay bars and not to go out without a woman!" Kearns played the Hollywood game, taking care to be absolutely closeted in public. But a friend who had ghost-written a gay book, *The Happy Hustler* (piggy-backing on the best-seller *The Happy Hooker*), asked him to pose for the cover picture, and he accepted the job. When Michael Kearns was revealed to be "the Happy Hustler," his Hollywood career came to a standstill and never fully recovered.[39]

Robin Tyler also had a Hollywood career that flashed and then expired. She had come to Hollywood with Patti Harrison, her lover and stage partner in what was the first feminist comedy act ever. They appeared on a midnight talk show, which Fred Silverman, the head of ABC, happened to see; the next day, their agent at the William Morris Agency called them to announce, "ABC is going to give you your own show, like *Laverne and Shirley!*" When Harrison and Tyler expressed reluctance about signing the contract that ABC offered them because of its morals clause, Silverman told them, "Look, I know you're lesbians. It's okay. Just don't act up publicly." They taped four episodes. ABC seemed pleased until one night they appeared at 10:00 P.M. on the Crofft Comedy Hour, and immediately after, Tyler appeared again—on the 11:00 P.M. news. There was a clip of her, speaking at a gay rally. The newscaster referred to her as "Robin Tyler, avowed lesbian." "Fred Silverman wouldn't see us anymore," Tyler remembers. Their contracts were dropped.[40]

But unlike Hollywood actors of an earlier era who were forced to sink into oblivion when rumors of their homosexuality got out, Kuehl, Kearns, and Tyler found the limelight again—because now there was an audience of fans made up of the large, openly gay community. Kuehl, who became a lawyer, ran for the State Assembly with the gay community solidly behind her, and she won—the first openly gay person even to have gotten through a California primary. When Kuehl ran for the California State Senate, again with the gay community's strong support, she won that race, too. Kearns found a successful career in Los Angeles gay theater. Robin Tyler became a producer of major lesbian and gay events, such as the 1979 and 1987 Marches on Washington and the Millennium March in 2000. She also became a leader in campaigns such as California's gay marriage struggle and the successful battle to derail a Paramount Television talk show that was to be hosted by arch homophobe Laura Schlesinger.

Los Angeles naturally draws a big population (a good part of it gay) that is gifted in media-making and distributing. Because producers of mainstream media continued to censor homosexuality even as the gay community grew stronger in the 1970s, L.A. gays developed their own media. Sometimes their efforts remained regional or countercultural, such as a gay-produced radio program, *IMRU*, which started in Los Angeles in 1971 and has continued uninterruptedly to the present. *IMRU* (the name refers to the ubiquitous gay graffiti, "IM1, R U12?") airs on KPFK, a progressive, listener-sponsored FM station, and brings gay and lesbian news and culture to the Southern California community. Outfest, L.A.'s gay and lesbian film festival, established in 1982 by the Lesbian and Gay Media Coalition, became the largest film festival (gay or otherwise) in Southern California, the film capital. Outfest has premiered such successful art house films as the transgender classic *Priscilla, Queen of the Desert,* and has grown to annual ticket sales of half a million dollars. Outfest also offers weekly screenings year-round and offshoots such as the Fusion Festival, billed as "the only multicultural gender inclusive film festival of its kind."

Other efforts have had a broader impact. The success of gay and lesbian bookstores such as those in Los Angeles not only encouraged the proliferation of lesbian and gay publishing houses nationally, but also showed the mainstream publishers and bookstores that there was a lucrative gay market. Simone Wallace, co-owner of Sisterhood Bookstore, says that during the store's first twenty years, from 1972 to 1992, the volume of sales increased dramatically every year. She recalls lines that ran down the street and around the block when popular lesbian authors, such as Lily Tomlin and Jane Wagner, who published *The Search for Signs of Intelligent Life,* came for signings.[41] A gay bookstore, A Different Light, was opened in the Silver Lake area in 1979, and its manager, Richard Labonte, brought in for signings major authors—Christopher Isherwood, Allan Ginsburg, William Burroughs, and Larry Kramer. A Different Light was packed with gay people from all over Los Angeles and quickly expanded to a chain of stores in West Hollywood, New York, and San Francisco. L.A.'s A Different Light succeeded in attracting the lesbian market, too, with an ambitious Lesbian Writers Series, beginning in 1984.[42]

Ironically, the remarkable success of stores such as Sisterhood and A Different Light mandated their eventual failure. As Ann Bradley, creator of the Lesbian Writers Series, points out, there were no "Gay and Lesbian" sections in mass-market chain bookstores at the time stores like Sisterhood and A Different Light began. The profitability of gay and lesbian books not only made New York publishers understand that there was money in the publication of such books, but also made Barnes and Noble and Borders understand that they had neglected a significant market. Soon the pioneers could not compete against the big chains. The owners of A Different Light were forced to close one of its L.A. stores, and then its New York branch and, finally, they sold the two other stores. Sisterhood shut its door in 1999. Nevertheless, such bookstores were responsible for what had been a great national boom in gay and lesbian publishing during the '80s and '90s.

—

Some L.A. gay productions, despite their humble origins, have "gone mainstream" themselves. Gay periodicals, born long ago into the L.A. counterculture as modest little magazines or mimeographed newsletters (for example, *Vice Versa* in the 1940s, *ONE* in the '50s, *The Advocate* in the '60s, *Lesbian News* in the '70s), grew in the 1980s to address a large national community and to reflect huge sociopolitical shifts among lesbians and gays. The most successful of the magazines capitalize on their proximity to Hollywood, promoting lesbian and gay glamour along with the news.

The Advocate, which started publishing in Los Angeles in 1967 as the newsletter of PRIDE, is today a glossy *"People"* magazine for America's "mainstream" gay population. In 1984, ten years after it had been taken off to the Bay Area by publisher David Goodstein, it returned to Southern California and settled in Hollywood. Under Goodstein, the ads and images of *The Advocate* had hyped gay male sexuality to the dwarfing of all else, and with the advent of AIDS, the magazine had gone into decline.[43] According to Mark Thompson, who was an *Advocate* editor, it was suffering from serious "moral confusion": How could a paper that ran ads for poppers and bathhouses (as *The Advocate* had under Goodstein) make its living off of a community that was now dying from a disease exacerbated by such marketed sexuality?[44]

In Hollywood, *The Advocate* was reinvented, and it became the top-circulating gay magazine in the country. The catalyst for its success was Richard Rouilard, who revamped the entire publication, including its design and content. Even the masthead was overhauled under Rouilard's direction: In an attempt to broaden the subscriber base (and compensate for the loss of readers who were succumbing to AIDS), *The Advocate,* for the first time, announced itself as "The National Gay *and Lesbian* Magazine."

Rouilard had been editor of the society pages of the *Los Angeles Herald Examiner.* With a penchant for flash that he had polished in his previous job, he aimed for *The Advocate* to become glossy and glamorous, a magazine that would be read by upwardly mobile gays everywhere. He often ran glitzy cover stories about the "beautiful people," especially the gay community's icons in Hollywood, such as Madonna, and handsome male stars (who in their interviews were usually very quick to make their sexual orientation clear: "I'm not gay . . . though I'm gay-friendly"). Rouilard managed to bring not only the magazine and Los Angeles gay culture to national attention, but himself as well. "I'm not just a homosexual," Rouilard quipped. "I'm a publici-sexual."[45] (*Time* magazine featured him in a November 1991 article as a "California trendsetter.")

But he also made *The Advocate* a widely respected publication. He hired new talent (including several lesbians) who produced professionally written and beautifully photographed stories on serious subjects such as gay bashing around the country. The mainstream press had generally been neglecting such incidents. But with the aid of a Manhattan publicist, Rouilard was able to bring *The Advocate* to the attention of editors such as those at the *Washington Post, USA Today,* and the Associated Press, who soon began following up on stories they had read about in Rouilard's magazine.[46]

The Advocate led the way for a whole spate of slick, national gay magazines, though none has ever achieved *The Advocate*'s prominence or longevity. In 2005, Planet Out, which owns Gay.com and other gay-specific internet interests, purchased all the assets of Los Angeles–based LPI Media (Liberation Publications Incorporated), of which *The Advocate* was a part, for a total of $31.1 million.[47]

The *Lesbian News,* like *The Advocate,* started out as a tiny, poorly produced newsletter. Its libertarian founder, Jinx Beers, says that she merely wanted to present an alternative voice to the hegemony of lesbian radicalism in 1975 Los Angeles.[48] Under Beers, the publication metamorphosed from the first issue of two 8.5 x 11-inch mimeographed sheets of typing paper to a multisectioned newspaper of up to one hundred pages, which included political columns, advice columns, horoscopes, lesbian news from around the world, and numerous ads addressed not only to Southern California lesbians but also to those all over America. In 1989, she sold the publication to Deborah Bergman, who had been a reporter for the *Los Angeles Times.*

Unlike Beers, Bergman had never been known as an activist of any stripe in the lesbian community. She undertook the paper as a business proposition. Under her ownership, the *Lesbian News* became the first publication in the country that promoted the image of lesbian glamour, featuring Hollywoodized lesbians—feminine, long-haired, voluptuous—in alluring ads for upscale cruises and trendy bars (usually described as "the hottest spot in town"). Bergman reversed, almost single-handedly, the print image of the lesbian as declassed and grim, which had been the most visible lesbian image of the 1970s. The *Lesbian News* was in good part responsible for popularizing the "lipstick lesbian," who had been born in L.A. and has more recently been made famous worldwide through the television series, *The L Word*.

Bergman, having changed the style of the paper, sold the *Lesbian News* for a hefty sum in 1994 to the L.A. entrepreneur Ella Matthes. Like Bergman, Matthes was not known for lesbian political activism: "I don't think I really know what 'politically correct' means," she still says;[49] but she tries to present the community's diversity in *Lesbian News,* hiring columnists who are African American, Latina, Asian, white, queer, lesbian, transgendered, baby dyke—the whole panoply.

Matthes' philosophy, however, is light-years away from the values of those lesbians of the 1970s who raised consciousness about the importance of such inclusion. She says she wants *Lesbian News* always to be "a Cadillac instead of a Ford," and almost every one of its glossy covers features a photo of a Hollywood-gorgeous woman. The more glamorous the cover, Matthes observes, the more popular the issue. "If there isn't a catchy cover, the magazines just sit there." The most popular issue to date had a cover picture of Gwen Stefani, in eye-popping décolletage, with the headline, "The Reigning Queen of Rock & Roll Talks to Us About Fame, Fashion, and her Lesbian Fans."[50]

As print pioneer of the glam image, *Lesbian News* has an estimated monthly readership of about 120,000 (counting the hand-to-hand circulation of issues, Matthes says) and is distributed in big cities everywhere—through mailed subscriptions, chains such as Barnes & Noble and Borders, and lesbian venues such as bars and centers. Matthes acknowledges the tremendous influence of Hollywood in *Lesbian News* since it was taken over from Jinx Beers in 1989. "It wouldn't still be around if we weren't in Hollywood. People love that. Hollywood sells." She says she hopes eventually to make *Lesbian News* an "all-glossy" magazine and wants to include even more articles on "the trends, how to dress, how to do your hair, how to buy great things for little dollars."[51]

The successes of *The Advocate* and *Lesbian News* encouraged numerous emulators in L.A. and elsewhere: By the end of the 1990s, there were ten lesbian and/or gay periodicals in Los Angeles alone; and advertisers, who now believed they had found a virtual gold mine in the gay consumer, were beating down the doors of the gay media. As the *Los Angeles Times* observed, though the rest of the publishing industry was barely holding its own, in gay periodicals advertising pages had swelled 35 percent in 1997 and another 20 percent in 1998. The gay L.A. newspaper *Frontiers* exceeded even those impressive figures, expanding over a period of four years from 100 pages to 180 pages, as its ads increased by 80 percent and its distribution spread to forty cities. Though the future of such publications is becoming somewhat unclear since more of the mainstream media are finding gay news to be "newsworthy,"[52] for that brief period, the gay print media, led by L.A., had become, as the *Los Angeles Times* wrote, "the biggest growth sector in publishing."[53]

A CITY OF OUR OWN

Together, this council and all of us can create the environment we need to feel safe and to prosper. We've made history together.

—Valerie Terrigno, newly elected lesbian mayor of the
newly incorporated City of West Hollywood, November 1984[54]

West Hollywood, a strip of 1.9 square miles that bridges Hollywood and Beverly Hills, was an unincorporated territory of Los Angeles County prior to 1984. For gay people, particularly men, it was certainly a party town, but it was also home: An estimated 40 percent of West Hollywood's 36,000 residents were gay. Another 30 percent of the population were seniors, primarily Jewish. The gays and the seniors had one clear common cause: Eighty-eight percent of West Hollywood residents were renters, and they hoped that if West Hollywood were incorporated, it would be possible to pass rent-control legislation, as the city of Santa Monica had done, and stem the runaway rent escalation occasioned by the rise in property values.[55] Gays and seniors in a friendly coalition agitated together for cityhood, wearing red, white, and blue "Vote for Cityhood" badges and packing the county's hearings on West Hollywood incorporation.[56]

Although rent control was the ostensible issue that ignited the drive for cityhood, gay residents wanted cityhood for a more emotional reason, too: West Hollywood had become a sort of "Israel" for some gays—a promised land, the best and only hope for "a city of our own." Of the thirty-five candidates vying for seats on the city council of the proposed city, seventeen were gay. As the *Los Angeles Times* observed: "Nowhere in the country have so many openly gay candidates run in one political race."[57] The coalition between the area's seniors and gays brought astounding victory: Not only was West Hollywood granted cityhood by a wide margin of voters in the November 1984 election, but also three gay people won their bids to sit on the five-member city council—Valerie Terrigno (who had been the director of Crossroads, a Hollywood Boulevard nonprofit job counseling agency that also provided emergency food and shelter for its largely gay clientele), Steve Schulte (who had been the executive director of the Gay Community Services Center), and John Heilman (an attorney). A gay judge, Rand Schraeder, who had been a Gay Liberation Front member, was selected to administer the oath of office to them all.

Thirty-one-year-old Valerie Terrigno, whom the media had described as "a blonde-haired, brown-eyed Golden Girl,"[58] had won the highest number of votes in the election, and she was chosen "by acclamation" of her fellow council members to be West Hollywood's first mayor.[59] Thus in quick order, West Hollywood had become the nation's first gay-majority government, and Terrigno had become the nation's first "out" lesbian mayor.[60] She also became the darling of the media everywhere, and for a time her celebrity vied with that of Hollywood's stars. A French television crew filmed her for three weeks. Reporters from *People* magazine followed her incessantly.[61] Requests for interviews numbered thirty a day. A delegation came to ask her to run for governor. She was invited to speak in South Africa, Japan, all over Europe. In Italy, she was called "the Virgin Madonna."[62]

Terrigno and the council were true to their campaign promises. The council's first significant action was to approve a rent rollback and a ban on evictions. The second significant action, at the start of 1985, was Mayor Terrigno's introduction of domestic partnership legislation, which meant that the partners of gay employees of the City of West Hollywood would receive medical insurance and other benefits. The passage of this legislation marked "the first legal recognition [by an American city] ever of same-sex relationships."[63]

Terrigno and the West Hollywood City Council went on a weekend retreat for an "encounter session." West Hollywood, they determined, was to be an unadulterated dream product of its Southern California heritage: a laid-back city of "a purer democracy, in which good intentions would not be smothered by the weight of bureaucracy."[64] The council passed other sweeping gay rights ordinances forbidding discrimination against homosexuals. The gay community cheered on Mayor Terrigno as she invaded Barney's Beanery with screwdriver in hand and, for the very last time, removed the offensive "FAGOTS STAY OUT" sign from its wall.

Among gay people worldwide, West Hollywood was soon seen as a "gay Camelot," as letters to Mayor Terrigno suggested: for example, from a French woman, "Felicitation on your victory. You are an escample [sic] for a French people homosescule [sic]"; from a Turkish man, "Homosexuality is completely forbidden [in Turkey]. Please, please, help me, take me near you—dear my friend, my sister."[65] Befitting gay aesthetic sensibility, the new city also underwent brightening and beautification as the mayor ordered that flowers be planted on the sad-looking median strip of traffic-heavy Santa Monica Boulevard.[66]

But the "victory" that Terrigno had declared for herself and the city soon turned to ashes. Shortly after her election, Terrigno recalls, she had been awakened at 3:00 A.M. when her dog started barking. Looking out the window, she saw men in brown polyester three-piece suits going through her trash. "The FBI," she says now.[67] Terrigno was under suspicion for embezzling federal funds—not in her role as mayor, but rather as director of Crossroads, the position she'd held before her election. Records reveal that Crossroads had been under investigation months before, when the Federal Emergency Management Agency, that had provided Crossroads with some its funding, began auditing its financial records because $24,000 of a $30,000 grant allocated to Crossroads in the winter of 1983–84 could not be accounted for. (Terrigno insists even now that when she took the job at Crossroads in 1983 she had inherited a financial mess that she had tried desperately and in vain to straighten out.) Morris Kight, eminence grise in the gay community by now and founder and first director of Crossroads, placed her under further suspicion by publicly accusing her of having mismanaged and possibly misappropriated funds given Crossroads by the Community Development Department.[68]

The investigation that ensued tore the gay community apart. Though a "Grassroots Justice for Valerie Terrigno Committee" denounced the charges against her as "a farce and a setup,"[69] little money was raised for her defense. Sheldon Andelson paid the entertainment mega-lawyer Howard Weitzman to be her attorney. Some, like Gene La Pietra, a West Hollywood power broker and the owner of a gay Latino disco palace, insist that Terrigno was crucified by the law and in the press because she was a lesbian mayor of a gay city: "They came after her like they were going after Mafioso," La Pietra says.[70] But many in West Hollywood were furious, believing that, because of her, "the reputation of the whole gay community will be smeared" and that "even if she is proven innocent, it will still be damaging [to the gay city] if she is shown to have been an incompetent administrator."[71]

In October 1985, less than a year after her remarkable victories, Valerie Terrigno was indicted on charges that she embezzled almost $11,000 in federal funds,[72] hardly a significant enough sum, her supporters pointed out, to warrant the prolonged government investigation of her, which the supporters called simply "a witch hunt." In May 1986, Terrigno was convicted of twelve counts against her. She was sentenced to sixty days in a halfway house and ordered to perform 1,000 hours of community service.[73] La Pietra says of Terrigno's ordeal, "It destroyed her." Although it did not destroy West Hollywood, the city found itself reeling from the tragic destabilization.

And at the same time, as the number of AIDS cases rose alarmingly, it had an even worse tragedy with which to deal.

A lesbian wedding party on the church steps. *Photo courtesy Jay Vega.*

CHAPTER 10

"Our Own"

Sometimes you need to be with your own and embrace who you are.

— Rita Gonzales, member of Lesbianas Unidas[1]

SEVERAL GAY people of color played key roles in ONE, the pioneering homophile organization of the 1950s and '60s.[2] In the early 1970s, groups such as the Gay Liberation Front were, according to Bruce Reifel, a GLF member, "the biggest ethnic mish-mash you ever did see."[3] Among the builders of L.A.'s gay institutions that were later perceived as "mainstream," people of color again played key roles: John Platania, who planned the Gay Center, grew up on the Akwasasne-Mohawk reservation; Greg Byrd, an African American, was the Gay Liberation Front's first president; Jeanne Cordova, a Latina, was a prime mover and shaker in lesbian and gay efforts throughout the 1970s and into the '80s. But more often in Los Angeles, gays of color and gay Euro Americans inhabited separate spaces.

Not only have gays of color had to struggle with battles that are particular to their parent communities but also they have felt that participation in white-dominated institutions and events was too much like "an excursion into whiteness." Los Angeles geography has exacerbated that problem. Gay institutions have tended to be located in areas where few people of color live. L.A.'s distinct ethnic neighborhoods, spread out over 450 square miles, and its clogged freeways and inefficient public transit system have created de facto segregation. When even "getting there" can be a major problem, how can gays of color believe they are welcome at gay film festivals, Women on a Roll dances, the Stonewall Democrats, the "Maybe Baby" groups?

Indeed, some gays of color have proclaimed, they should not even want to join activities that diminish the totality of who they are. The African American writer Alycee Lane admonished readers of *BLK,* the L.A.–based gay magazine, that it was pathetic for people of color to participate in a gay pride parade down the streets of white districts. A healthy integration of sexuality and ethnicity could be achieved only if people of color dared to "celebrate being lesbian and gay in our own neighborhoods":

> What is African-American gay and lesbian pride that is *only* articulated in the "safety" of white communities? It is not pride at all; *it is a bottomless self-hate,* for in those alien places we often subsume our blackness for the gay thing, and in our own neighborhoods, we subsume our gayness for the black thing. We divide ourselves into expendable parts. We *are* those expendable parts.[4]

In recent years, many gay people of color in Los Angeles have taken on the challenge to subsume neither ethnicity nor sexuality, while Euro American gays have been challenged to try harder to bring diversity into the larger community institutions.

COMING TO GAY L.A.

I knew other Guatemalan immigrants who became millionaires. But we didn't come for the money. We gay ones came for the freedom.
— Francisco Ico del Rio, immigrant from Guatemala City in 1962[5]

Gay men and women who were not born in the United States were long drawn to Los Angeles, often because they suffered harassment in their homelands and had heard of the city's legendary openness. Francisco Ico del Rio remembers the tone of romance and excitement in a letter that he received from a gay friend who had escaped the confines of Guatemala. The friend wrote about how from the moment he flew over L.A. it had seemed to him like a magical dream:

> He said it was like a field of black velvet covered with shimmering colored sequins. He talked about the endless wide freeways, about Hollywood Boulevard [where] everywhere were handsome hustlers showing their things through their pants. There was more freedom and more acceptance in Los Angeles. He urged us all to come.[6]

Del Rio and eight other Guatemalan men soon joined the lone gay explorer, who had succeeded in landing a job and an apartment in L.A. In Guatemala, del Rio complains, he'd been able to meet his boyfriend only in dark movie theaters because they could not risk being seen together. "If you said or did anything that looked too gay," he recalls, "your gay friends would warn you against the danger by whispering, 'You're throwing feathers!'" In Guatemala, another of the immigrants, Rudy Ruano, says, he had been beaten and threatened with death by his own brother because he was gay.[7]

In 1962, del Rio and the other men from Guatemala City shared a one-bedroom apartment on Franklin Avenue, splitting the $200 monthly rent. After paying his bills, del Rio purchased a new shirt every weekend so that he would "look sharp" in bars where Latinos mixed with Anglos—the Vieux Carré, the Gaslight, the Hideaway, and the Redwood Room. He was warned about the wiles of the Vice Squad, but he and his friends still marveled at the remarkable freedom their new home afforded. Rudy Ruano says he was astounded that by simply walking out the door of his Hollywood apartment he could "pick up four or five guys in a day."[8]

Gays in Mexico were drawn to L.A. for similar reasons. Andreas, who came in 1975, says that in Chihuahua "you are either a drag queen or a total closet case." There, too, family violence against homosexuals was not uncommon. "Brothers and fathers would think it was necessary to their honor to beat you up and drive you away or even kill you."

He went first to El Paso, where he met up with a circle of other Mexican immigrants and was befriended by Chino, "this fabulous queen [and] our real leader." Chino's brother, an actor, had secured a job at ABC Studios, and he helped Chino find work there as a wardrobe assistant on shows such as *Welcome Back Kotter*, where he dressed a young John Travolta. "One by one, we all decided that El Paso was too small and we moved to L.A.," says Andreas, recalling that he drove to Los Angeles with a lesbian couple, Lupe and Whiskey. Chino helped his friends get jobs, showed them gay clubs such as the Beer Can and Circus Disco, and most importantly, encouraged a sense of community among them. Andreas describes how for gay immigrants, who suffer from poverty, loneliness, and social limitations, such networks of compatriots were vital in holding at bay the alienation of a big city. "You *so* needed to be part of something."[9]

Other gay people of color came to Los Angeles not because they feared being beaten up or harassed back home, but because they could not let themselves be a part of anything gay under the eyes of their traditional families. Marcia Kawahara says that as long as she remained on Kawaii, in the presence of her "very heterosexual" Okinawan family and community, she had to deny her own sexuality because "I was afraid of sullying the family name." When she was a counselor for the Hawaiian police department, Kawahara had worked with juvenile female runaways. "The girls were considered 'status offenders,'" she says, "and I secretly felt that that's what I was too—a status offender." At the age of forty-eight, she realized that only if she ran away ("became a fugitive," as she characterizes it) could she let herself be gay. In L.A., she ultimately found what she could not even begin to look for back home—an entire community of Asian lesbians, many of them college students, who "took me in and treated me like a gray eminence."[10]

Some "immigrants" to gay L.A. had fewer miles to travel but felt nevertheless that they were crossing a border when they left their homes. Though covert same-sex sexual relations have been common in the barrios and ghettos of America,[11] to claim a homosexual identity has been problematic for people of color, and some have felt that to do it they must relocate to another part of the city, whether permanently or just for the evening. Jolino Beserra, who was born in East L.A. and raised in the San Gabriel Valley, recalls that "anyone that I knew who was gay was just beat up."[12] Jef Huereque says that though he had worked hard in the Chicano movement in East L.A., he found "little to no tolerance about homosexuality there," particularly for gay males.[13] If they wished to let their gayness show, it was safer to go elsewhere.

In the 1940s, '50s, and '60s, when semipublic meeting places for gay people were relatively scarce, it was not uncommon for blacks, Latinos, and whites to share bars,[14] such as the If Club, the Open Door, the Star Room, and the Sugar Shack for lesbians; the Piccadilly, the Waldorf, the Golden Carp, and the Vieux Carré for gay men. A lone bar opened for Chicana gay women in East L.A. in the 1960s and continues to this day, its name changing through the years from Redhead to Reds to Redz. But more often, Chicanas who lived outside of East L.A. mixed in bars with white women, as K.C. recalls of the lesbian bar she frequented in Gardena in the 1960s: "Sunday mornings we would all congregate there, a bunch of Mexicans and white girls. We'd usually gather up beers and sodas, go to a local park and play softball for a couple of hours, then end up back at the bar together."[15] Jeanne Cordova remembers a similar hangout, Tulley's in Pico Rivera, where she was a regular in the '60s. The working-class white and Latina patrons would meet over drinks there, play softball every weekend, and "sleep with each other."[16]

Even into the 1970s, the troubling attitudes toward homosexuality in their parent communities made some gay Latinos and Latinas continue to look to other parts of the city to claim a gay identity. JJ Vega, a Chicana who was a working-class woman in those years, says that it was access to places outside her barrio, such as North Hollywood, that changed her life. In predominantly white lesbian bars such as the Big Horn, she recalls, not only did she feel free as she never could in her own neighborhood but also she was able to meet women who would tell her about lesbian books and movement ideas, women who opened a new world to her.[17]

Joey Terrill remembers several gay venues in Hollywood that were ethnically mixed, such as the After Dark and the Paradise Ballroom; such
places permitted his "escape from the East Side, from a constricted,
Catholic upbringing; from the entrenched homophobia of the gangs and
the cholos." Terrill, who was raised by a single mother in East L.A., believes that any racism he may have encountered in Hollywood was balanced by a feeling, like JJ Vega's, that there he had "possibility" and could
be "a fish in a new ocean." Also like Vega, Terrill believes that the social
mobility that comes from cross-class relationships between gays, which
could be enjoyed outside the barrio, saved many Mexican American gays
from "economic dead-ends, jail, or getting killed in a drive-by."[18]

There was no gay male equivalent to Reds in an L.A. barrio until 1999,
when Chico, a men's gay bar, opened in Montebello. The clientele has not
always been comfortable with its proximity to home, though. One Chico
patron, interviewed by the *Los Angeles Times* in 2001, declined to give
his name because he did not dare let the men in his family know that he
is gay. He observed that still, even in the twenty-first century, "to have
something like this [a men's gay bar in the barrio] is so taboo."[19] It was
because the taboo was so powerful that closeted Chicano males, even
those who "passed" in barrio gangs, felt constrained to seek refuge in the
1970s in gay bars that were at least a few miles away from home, such as
Ken's River Club in East Hollywood.

The trek across the city did not always end in a welcome for people of
color, and positive experiences such as Vega's and Terrill's were by no
means universal. One white Hollywood man recalls that in the 1960s "we
were all closet bigots. It was considered real déclassé to go to bed with a
Mexican."[20] Others say that cross-racial relationships occurred often but
were rarely acknowledged. Gene La Pietra observes that it was "okay to
go into cubicles at the baths and sleep with every black and Mexican,
but not to be seen with them publicly," and that this hypocrisy "was tolerated at the highest levels of gay society."[21] Not all white gays would
"tolerate" such hypocrisy and discrimination, of course. When it became
known that the Canyon Club excluded African Americans, many white
patrons boycotted it in protest.[22] But often race relations among whites

and people of color in the gay community were not much different from those in the heterosexual community.

Racial discrimination in predominantly white venues encouraged the growth of clubs aimed specifically at gay people of color (though located usually outside the barrios and ghettos), such as Mugi's and Faces, whose clientele was mostly Asian gay men;[23] and the Silver Platter, which served recent gay Latino immigrants. The River Club hosted both Asian and Latino men. Catch One was opened by Jewel Williams in 1973 and was soon the city's premier disco palace for black gays. Now the longest-running gay black dance club in Los Angeles and the largest in the world, its cachet grew in the 1980s, when it was known to be a hangout for Madonna and other celebrities of her ilk. But at Catch One, whites were in the minority. There, the tables were turned. The African American journalist Mark Haile recalls that there was "some sense of tolerance" for the whites as long as the West Hollywood Madonna-groupies respected that it was "an African American space." (But, Haile adds, "there was almost a palpable sigh of relief" among black gays when the Catch One fad ended for whites.)

Some of these bars even served as community centers for gay people of color. Fund-raisers might be staged there for causes that were important to them. Fliers and periodicals might be distributed on the premises that would alert them to the existence of the gay ethnic community beyond the bar. A couple of these places became major community forces. At Catch One, Jewel Williams held Sunday afternoon tea dances to benefit the Carl Bean AIDS Hospice in South Central Los Angeles. She offered meeting space to organizations such as United Lesbians of African Heritage, Prime Plus (a group of older black lesbians), and "Sistah Session" raps. She invited Jesse Jackson to speak at Catch One in 1988, making him the first major presidential candidate to address a black gay audience anywhere.[24] Gene La Pietra's Circus Disco in Hollywood has had an equivalent significance for the Latino gay community. La Pietra's bar hosted numerous community fund-raisers, including an appearance by Cesar Chavez to encourage solidarity between gays and progressives. As Jewel Williams observes, many gays of color came to these dance palaces for pleasure on the night they turned twenty-one, but they were also ushered into a world of political activity and social support for their ethnicity as well as their sexuality.[25]

As these clubs became safe havens, gay people of color developed new cultures. Circus Disco was started by Gene La Pietra because his non-white friends had been barred from Studio One. Andreas recalls how the news that the Circus was to be a gay Latino disco was at first met with incredulity among his social set: "We couldn't quite imagine that." But when the doors opened, patrons found "good sound, great light systems, and the best music we'd ever heard." No one could have guessed how many gay Latinos were waiting for a dance palace of their own:[26] Circus Disco, which held more than 1,000, was packed every weekend. (It has now expanded to a venue that holds 3,000 and is still packed every week-end.) The habitués created styles of dancing that became vital to the gay Latino scene. An in-crowd formed. "If you didn't know the steps, you were dead," Andreas remembers.

—

Joey Terrill believes that not only the dancing but also the fashions had a profound purpose. "We were all making art and communicating with each other," he says. "I never thought of it per se as 'Latino.' It just so happened we all *were*. . . . We were all from the East Side and we were going into Hollywood." Before leaving his mother's home, Terrill would don platform shoes and baggy pants, stowing a woman's vintage beaded sweater in a plastic bag, and hop on the bus. Once he had crossed into Hollywood, he felt safe enough to complete his outfit by putting on the glittering sweater.[27]

Andreas believes that the sense of style at Circus Disco was dis-tinctly Latino. "It was a melding of the 1940s and the 1970s, somehow always with a Latin flavor. Imagine a Fred Astaire tux with jelly san-dals."[28] Andreas and his friends would transform an item, such as an apron that might be purchased for a dollar at a thrift shop, by making it into a tie, a vest, and a handkerchief. Outfits were often so fabulous that they set a trend and became a fine source of chauvinistic pride: "All dressed up, us Latin queens would go to Circus to perform. The look of West Hollywood was tame and lame. They tried to copycat us, but really couldn't."[29]

Gay Latinos also found other venues far from the barrios where they could be openly gay, such as Griffith Park, the great oasis dividing Hollywood from the San Fernando Valley. There, on Sunday afternoons, on a hill overlooking the city, a van with good speakers would become a mobile disco booth, and upwards of eight hundred gay Latino young people, male and female, would create a surreal social scene. "You'd see these beautifully dressed and coiffed people—the girls in stilettos, dancing in the dirt. You'd cruise; you'd get picked up—all the while looking at the fabulous city of Los Angeles."[30]

NEW HUNGERS

Our premise is simple. It is demoralizing ALWAYS to be in the minority, and we find that it is a refreshing change of pace for most [people] of color to be surrounded by [those] of similar interests and background.

— Founders of Debreta's, an L.A. African American lesbian group[31]

Clubs such as Catch One and Circus Disco tried to transcend their function as mere pleasure palaces, but most clubs, whether for gays of color, whites, or an ethnic mix, specialized in drinking and cruising. Horacio Roque Ramirez observes that the clubs "seem like heaven when you first go into them," but they have serious limits when it comes to sustaining community.[32] Terry Gock, a psychotherapist and the founder of Asian Pacific Lesbians and Gays, describes some gay clubs not only as "skuzzy" but also as places that foster competition and its concomitant, rejection: They can exacerbate a terrible feeling of isolation, despite their ostensibly social atmosphere.[33]

But alternatives to them appeared slim in other decades. Some people of color had tried to organize formally in the 1970s. Gay and lesbian Chicanos, concerned that there was "nothing, really, for Mexican Americans in the gay community,"[34] formed a group called Unidos in 1970. In 1974,

Estilita Grimaldo Smith, a Panamanian businesswoman (who ran Womantours out of the Woman's Building), started Latin American Lesbians of Los Angeles for women who had roots in Argentina, Chile, Columbia, El Salvador, Mexico, Nicaragua, Panama, and Peru.[35] But neither organization lasted long.

Informal social groups for people of color had more staying power. For example, Debreta's was started in 1977 by an African American lesbian couple, Bobreta Franklin and Deborah Johnson. When they'd first considered forming such a group, Franklin and Johnson acknowledged that they had white lesbian friends and had never encountered bigotry among them, yet something vital was lacking in those relationships. "We needed an atmosphere where we could see people like ourselves and know that we weren't the only ones, where we could talk about the oppression we had, both in the lesbian community and the African American community, and know that we'd really be understood on both fronts."[36] Debreta's sponsored cruises, theater parties, dances, picnics—but members could not ignore that by virtue of their being an organization of black lesbians their import went beyond the mere social. To "raise consciousness" in the outside world, for example, they rented the ballrooms of Hiltons or Marriotts as openly African American gay women; to raise their own consciousness, they conducted raps about the meaning and consequence of their dual identities. Though Debreta's may have started as a social group in 1977, it became part of what Johnson and Franklin called in 1981 "a growing group self-awareness among Third World gays" who were now "actively mobilizing and building coalitions."[37]

But even groups that had no such express awareness were important because they brought together gay people of color who felt they could not be comfortably ethnic in the white-dominated gay community. Gay politics of the 1970s and early '80s were often alienating to them. For example, lesbian-feminist separatism made little sense to black lesbians, who felt that they were more oppressed because of their race than their sexuality or gender, and that they needed to maintain alliances with their black brothers. Even the terms "lesbian" and "gay" felt odd to some people of color. Ayofemi Folayan, an African American women, explains:

"There were lots of black women who loved women in the 1970s, but 'gay' and 'lesbian' was a white thing."[38]

The declassed, radical, dress-down style of white lesbian feminists was also offensive to many people of color. Gayle, an office worker in the 1970s, remembers sartorial splendors at the elegant parties she attended with other black lesbians and gay men in Los Angeles:

> The air was always filled with perfume and cigarette smoke. The guys were in suits or silk shirts and slacks. Sometimes the ladies wore long gowns in pastel colors, or bell-bottoms with fancy tops. I used to wear these gorgeous Palazzo pants. And the hard-dresser butches—they liked tailored suits or jackets with contrasting slacks, pointy-collar shirts and French cuffs. One butch always wore plaid jackets that had pink that was boxed with blues or greens.

Even outside of private parties—for example, at the "Sunday cocktail hour" at Catch One, style prevailed, according to Gayle.[39] The fancy dress that would have scandalized most leftist lesbians and gays was seen by blacks who aspired to better their socioeconomic position as an important marker of respectability rather than something to eschew as "politically incorrect."

A major turning point for gays in African American communities occurred in the early 1980s, when gay-friendly institutions (that were not bars) began to be established in their own neighborhoods. "When Carl Bean started the Unity Fellowship of Christ Church, it tapped into a very below-the-surface crowd of people who didn't consider themselves activists, or involved, at all," says Mark Haile. He observes that the members of Unity Fellowship (which continues to this day) include those engaging in gay sex who are not gay-identified, people who do call themselves lesbian or gay, and often their straight families. Elegant fund-raisers are held by Gentlemen Concerned, Ladies Concerned, Sisters of Love—all groups within the church, to help support

Bean's Minority AIDS Project as well as Rue's House, which Jewel Williams founded for HIV-infected women and children of color. The garden parties and barbeques of these groups ("which do not face towards West Hollywood," Mark Haile says) include both working-class and middle-class black gay people.

"OUR PEOPLE, OUR PROBLEM, OUR SOLUTION"

Sure we supported our black brothers and were involved in fighting AIDS, and we even worked with some mostly-white groups. But we wanted to have something we could call our own, where black lesbians could connect just with each other—a black woman-space, where we could find each other as black women.

— Lisa Powell, a founder of United Lesbians of African Heritage[40]

Agencies such as the Gay and Lesbian Community Services Center and Connexxus hoped from the beginning, as GLF had before them, to provide a "healthy place" for the entire mix of the gay community. They continued to try to offer something for everyone: At the Center in 1988, for instance, the Black Lesbian Therapy Group met on Wednesdays, Gay and Lesbian Latinos Unidos (GLLU) met on Thursdays, Womyn of Color Rap met on Fridays, and so forth.[41] Leaders at the Center and other community institutions, wanting to integrate, also brought a few people of color into prominent positions. The logic was that others would then follow because they would understand they were welcome. But such attempts at inclusion could be awkward, as Lucia Chappelle, an African American lesbian, wryly points out: "The story of my life in the queer community has been, 'Oh, my God! A black lesbian! Grab her!'"[42] Those few lesbians and gays of color who were willing to work in predominantly white groups could be spread thin by being made token representatives on every gay L.A. institutional or organizational board in sight. Terry Gock says that in the 1980s he left the board of the Gay and Lesbian Center after a year because, although he admired the organization's work, he was weary of being the lone Asian board member. He also stopped attending the Stonewall Democratic Club because of the "extra work" required of the only Asian person at most meetings.

Resentments emerged when gay people of color felt they were being exhausted because the community wanted to rid themselves of perceived racism but did not know how. (Robin Podolsky, who was a founder of White Women Against Racism, says that her group began in the 1980s, when lesbians of color at Califia finally became exasperated and told the white lesbians: "All right, you guys have to do it for yourself. Do it like Alcoholics Anonymous. Unlearn your racist reflexes.")[43] Some who straddled the white and the people of color communities, such as Yolanda Retter, a longtime activist whose background is German and Peruvian, tried to serve as gadflies on the L.A. gay white-body-politic, urging it to look to its own racism and also telling gay people of color that they must find their own voice.

Suspicion continued even when predominantly white groups tried hard to bring in people of color, because mistrust had been built through the years. When Jim McDaniels, an African American raised in a white enclave in Orange County, became the facilitator of ACT UP's new People of Color Coalition, one member of the group remarked, "It's so great to have you here because you know how to navigate the white power structure of ACT UP." McDaniels was stunned to realize that some members of the People of Color Coalition saw ACT UP—which had prided itself on being an open populist alternative to an unresponsive power structure—as merely another part of the white power structure. "They just felt uncomfortable and unwelcome . . . completely disenfranchised from the one place you'd think they'd feel enfranchised. To them it was that 'white boys and girls club.' It might as well have been academia or a country club or the Republican Party."[44]

A number of groups for lesbians and/or gay men of color emerged in the 1980s, but most remained fairly small because potential members were often reluctant to join an organization in which they would be expected to espouse a gay political message in public and risk "outing" themselves to their parent community. Lisa Powell, director of United Lesbians of African Heritage (ULOAH), says that shortly after her group was formed, they tried to get a contingent of members to march in the Martin Luther King Day parade, which was held in an African American neighborhood, on Crenshaw Boulevard. "But," Powell recalls, "we could hardly get any of the women to agree to 'walk down Crenshaw,'" a phrase that has now become shorthand among black lesbians in L.A. for the test of being "out": "Would you walk down Crenshaw?"[45] Cleo Manago, the African American gay activist who organized the first gay contingent to march in the Martin Luther King Day parade, says he also had trouble mustering more than a skeleton crew to hold up the banner.[46]

Still, an inexorable momentum had begun in the 1980s, and such groups continued to form. Even organizations that started ostensibly as social groups came to realize that they were necessarily political because their members belonged to a dual minority, with inevitable issues that needed to be addressed. Rita Gonzales recalls that when she was invited to her first Lesbianas Unidas retreat she announced, "It's good to be with other Latinas, but I'm not very political." The response of Lydia Otero, president of Lesbianas Unidas, "scared the heck out of me," she says, but also made her understand a cogent concept: Otero shouted, "You're a lesbian? You're Latina? You're political!"[47]

The very act of forming a gay people of color group became in itself valuable because it helped members not only to define their identity but also to think of themselves as a community and cause others to think of them in the same way: The motto of the Black AIDS Institute, "Our people, our problem, our solution," expresses the empowering concept. Simply by its existence, the activist Mario Perez Ceballos insists, "Gay and Lesbian Latinos Unidos began to change the tone of how gay politics was conceived of . . . in L.A."[48]

Gay people of color groups in Los Angeles eventually proliferated, and the demographics of the city, with its abundant cornucopia of races, ethnicities, and sexualities, have made it possible to search out ever-closer matches to one's identity. There are not only enough lesbian and gay Latino artists to form an organization such as VIVA but also enough gay

Central American writers who rebel against the "dominant Chicano establishment in L.A." to form Equipo Y Vos, a separate group devoted only to people like them.[49] (Chicanos might laugh at their being considered an "establishment" by anyone; but Equipo's founder, Horacio Roque Ramirez, explains of his separate group that "it's calming to have that national identity, those national roots, to have history.")

One common pattern of division and multiplication in Los Angeles has been this: A few African American or Asian American or Latino gay men who felt alienated in gay organizations that were predominantly white formed a group. A few lesbians happily joined the group since it was concerned with issues of their race as well as of homosexuality. Their presence attracted more women, and eventually there was a critical mass of lesbians in the group. The communication among the lesbians led to their realization that their needs were not being met in an organization that addressed their race, and perhaps some aspects of their homosexuality, but not their gender. As their numbers grew, they demanded more voice, and gay men of color were not always open to granting their demands. The lesbians defected from the founding organization, and there were enough of them in populous and diverse L.A. to form a new group that shared not only the identities of race and sexuality, but even gender.[50]

The National Gay and Lesbian Black Leadership Forum, which was founded in Los Angeles by Phill Wilson in 1986, became one instance of such division and multiplication. As its name suggests, the organization was intended for both men and women, and it hoped to cultivate the concept of leadership within the black community. Up to a thousand African American gays were attracted each year to its national conference held in downtown L.A. hotels. But although the Black Leadership Forum had intended gender equality, it could not escape the same gender discontents that often troubled the larger lesbian and gay community. Saundra Tignor joined because it "fought on both the racial and sexual fronts." But its cogendered aspect, she says, "failed to meet women's needs."[51]

Tignor, along with other Black Leadership Forum members Lisa Powell and Yolanda Whittington, broke off in 1989. Powell recalls, "We wanted to prioritize for ourselves as women."[52] They founded their own organization, United Lesbians of African Heritage (ULOAH). Once they could claim an organization all their own, it became psychologically more appealing to participate as a group with other organizations that were cross-gender and cross-color, such as ACT UP and Queer Nation, in what Powell recalls as "those high and heady days of phone trees and taking it to the streets."[53] But the ULOAH activity that raised the most interest in its membership defines the group pointedly by its triple identity of race, sexual orientation, and gender. The annual Sistahfest, which attracts to Los Angeles women from everywhere in America as well as Africa, Europe, and the Caribbean, is an all-black-lesbian love fest, as Betty Smith glowingly describes it:

> Hundreds and hundreds of black women—being together, dancing together. We all sit by the campfire and people stand up and say things they'd never say anywhere. We wouldn't like it if it was racially or sexually mixed. It's so personal, like if you went to a psychiatrist and someone wanted to sit in. . . . None of us is a stranger at Sistahfest. It's family. It's one of the best things that ever happened to Black women. It's *our own,* created by *us.*[54]

The Sistahfest phenomenon fulfills those longings that make many gay people, nonwhite and white alike, search the huge city for the precise fit: It affirms identity; it provides a trusted group; it offers a place. While there, one is not a stranger.

Groups formed and split off in similar ways among the other gay L.A. people of color communities, too. For example, the women of Gay and Lesbian Latinos Unidos broke off to form Lesbianas Unidas; the women of Asian Pacific Lesbians and Gays broke off to form Los Angeles Asian/Pacific Islander Sisters (LAAPIS). Other divisions and proliferations also became possible in L.A. because the gay population continued to grow and to increase in diversity. Mark Haile has observed that ethnic gay groups in Los Angeles can be described as a series of "begats."[55] He uses the gay Asian community as an example, with Asian Pacfic Lesbians and Gays begatting not only the Gay Asian Pacific Support Network and LAAPIS but also the Gay Asian Rap Group. Those groups

begat Barangay—the gay Filipino group, as well as the L.A. chapter of
Trikone, the South Asian group. The begats continue: A former member
of LAAPIS explains that the latest proliferations are a result of burgeoning immigration into Los Angeles of non-English-speaking Asians:
"They want to be with lesbians who speak their own language."[56] But
even that division threatens to divide further. The Vietnamese lesbian
group, O-Moi, for example, has struggled with splits between those who
speak Vietnamese *well* and those who are losing the language because
they have become too Americanized.[57] The strength of Los Angeles as a
huge cornucopia also presents a huge challenge to unity since identity
can be defined more and more narrowly.

The abundance of L.A.'s diversity has fostered not only the splintering
of groups but also the founding of very specialized groups. Roland Palencia witnessed the loss of a generation of gay Latino artists to AIDS
and the attendant loss of cultural expression and record.[58] In response,
Palencia, who had been a founder of Gay and Lesbian Latinos Unidos,
now formed VIVA, a group of gay Latino artists. The group's task was
daunting because, as the playwright Luis Alfaro observed, "the Chicano
community was still holding on to the belief that Queer Latinos did not
exist," and gay Latinos were reluctant to expose themselves to their parent community.[59] The times were right for change, however. VIVA won
funding from the U.S. Conference of Mayors and produced a blitz of
readings, art openings, and other cultural events in L.A., including the
creation of Teatro VIVA, which used performance art and cross-dressing
to explore themes that were urgent or troubling for the gay Latino community, such as the importance of safe sex or how to disclose HIV status
to families. Though AIDS drove most of its programs, VIVA's leaders believed that lesbians' voices were crucial. (They made the point that "gay"
is not limited to male-male sex.) Lesbians were elected to the board and
hired on the staff. They launched an annual women's event, Chicks and
Salsa, which drew huge audiences of Latina lesbians. Some lesbian writers and artists of VIVA, such as Terri de la Peña, Cheri Moraga, and
Laura Aguilar, went on to win national reputations.

VIVA lasted for almost a decade, enough time, the artist Miguel Angel
Reyes says, to give gay Latino/Latina artists what they had never had: a

feeling not only that there was a critical mass to comprise an audience interested in what the gay Latino artist had to say or show but also that these artists "belonged somewhere." Knowing that there are both peers and an audience gets the artist started, Reyes suggests. And then "after awhile, you realize, you're fine now."[60]

—

Though Los Angeles is made up largely of areas that are segregated by ethnicity, class, or sexuality, Angelenos are occasionally brought together in surprising concord, as they have been in the Silver Lake area. A troubling gay/straight divide developed more than a generation ago between Silver Lake's working-class Latino families, who make up 40 percent of the population in the area, and gays (both white and people of color). Straddling Sunset Boulevard between Hollywood and downtown, Silver Lake had long served as a small, quiet gay enclave; but in the late 1970s, its cheap rents, Craftsman architecture, and bohemian ambiance drew larger numbers of gays into the district.[61] Gay realtors encouraged the trend, appealing especially to affluent homosexuals with the marketing slogan "West Hollywood Is Moving East."[62] Silver Lake's gay population was soon more than 20 percent.

The working-class community did not appear to welcome them. Gay people were deeply troubled by the blunt expressions of mistrust, such as that of a Salvadorean mother who admitted to a *Los Angeles Times* reporter, "I tell my children to be careful because they have to play in the street. I tell them to watch out for two things—cars and gays."[63] A series of muggings and several murders, as well as the firebombing of the Frog Pond, a Silver Lake gay restaurant, created serious tensions. Some gays were certain that local street youth were attacking gay people out of homophobic contempt. Others, however, pointed out that the attacks might be less hate crimes than the acts of poor residents who worried about the effects of gentrification. "Gays were moving in and fixing up the houses, and there was a perception that they would price Latinos out," said Michael McKinley, a Beverly Hills hairdresser who still lives in Silver Lake.[64]

An integrated lesbian and gay group, the Sunset Junction Neighborhood Alliance, decided to tackle the problem head-on.[65] Rejecting the idea of a demonstration, which could be regarded as hostile, they chose a quintessentially L.A. solution: They threw an outdoor party that evolved into a street fair (entertainment was provided by "guest" stars such as the Supremes). The Neighborhood Alliance also reached out to Latino community organizations, such as El Centro del Pueblo, a social service nonprofit, to broker a truce with the street gangs. Michael McKinley, a leader of the Neighborhood Alliance, was inspired to employ local gang members to work as security guards for the fair. Gang members were initially reluctant to be associated with what was perceived as a gay and lesbian event. But, McKinley says, they were won over because it gave them visibility and an unwonted respect from agencies such as the LAPD.[66] The first year, the LAPD, concerned with protecting the gays, warned the Neighborhood Alliance of a "bloodbath," but the fair proceeded without incident. Now, more than twenty-five years later, the annual Silver Lake Street Fair has grown from an initial crowd of 5,000 to more than 100,000, including gay cholos and yuppies, families and the elderly.[67] The fair's harmony, gay residents of Silver Lake report, laps over into everyday life—"like the Mexican restaurants . . . with the gay flag as part of their décor," the lesbian couple Lori Ball and Lisa Ginsburg say, "and the gay Salsa dancing at Rudolfo's Sunset Junction."[68]

Faces of AIDS activism: above Barry Diller, Steve Tisch, Barbra Streisand, and David Geffen. Below, Mark Kostopoulos. *Top photo: © 1992 Michael Jacobs/MJP/Courtesy APLA; lower photo: Chuck Stallard.*

CHAPTER 11

Devastation

A SUDDEN SIEGE

AIDS changed everything, literally overnight.

— Gene La Pietra[1]

IT HIT LIKE the bomb that kills people but lets buildings stand–except this bomb killed selectively, and the victims were mostly gay. The modern plague that would wipe out millions started killing just a few at a time: in private rooms at L.A.'s Cedars-Sinai Hospital; in crowded corners of County General; in hillside homes and in Skid Row alleys. Michael Gottlieb, a Los Angeles epidemiologist, was the man who "discovered" AIDS. He identified five male homosexuals with an unusual form of pneumonia at UCLA Medical Center during the summer of 1981 and made them the subject of the first article describing the mysterious new ailment.[2] Within weeks, the illness was noticed in New York and San Francisco, and gay ghettos began their long state of siege.

As the gay actor and activist Michael Kearns observes, "AIDS changed what it meant to be gay. We had to face the fact there was no going back, that what we called gay life was lost forever."[3] AIDS, Acquired Immune Deficiency Syndrome (named by the Los Angeles researcher Bruce Voeller),[4] wiped out a golden age of sexual freedom. It decimated a generation of gay men coming into their prime years of mature leadership as activists and political insiders. It killed choreographers, curators, artists, and designers, plundering the arts and entertainment industries of much of their best talent. It leveled closets and crippled communities. Its destructive ripple effect altered nearly every aspect of gay life.

For the straight world as well, AIDS wreaked havoc, evoking a dangerous level of public fear. The general population so dreaded contracting AIDS by the impossible transmission route of donating blood that the Red Cross had to declare a "blood emergency" in Los Angeles and Orange counties.[5] In the television industry, as *TV Guide* reported, "the comparative openness and liberalism of the '70s has disappeared. In their place is a climate of fear." Female stars began insisting that their leading men be straight.[6]

AIDS also wrought economic devastation on newly built businesses in the gay world. Before the epidemic, gay chic was beginning to draw straight clientele to gay discos, where straights and gays might mingle freely, much as their counterparts had in the Sunset Strip and Hollywood nightclubs of the 1930s. Gene La Pietra, owner of Circus Disco, recalls a news story that claimed that AIDS could be transmitted by casual contact. "The very next day," he says, "the whole club scene changed. It suddenly wasn't fashionable for straight people to have a gay friend."[7] Mixed nights ended in his club, as in most others. Heterosexuals continued to frequent those clubs only if the proprietors offered "straight dance nights." Within twenty-four months of Gottlieb's article, gay bars in the Hollywood/West Hollywood area reported a 20 percent drop in business, and the six bathhouses in the area suffered a revenue plunge of 50 percent.[8]

Public health concerns were sometimes confused with homophobic attacks, and vice versa. Some gay establishments angrily denied the danger of AIDS and tried to keep operating as usual. When *Frontiers* published its first cover story about the disease,[9] copies of the newspaper were thrown out of gay bars, whose owners thought it bad for business. A debate, not fully resolved to this day, began to call for the closing of the bathhouses—or, at the very least, for a regulation that would require the proprietors to hire monitors who would police the goings-on with flashlights to prevent unsafe sexual behavior. In an environment of scant information, the community was unmoored. No AIDS antibody test was available until 1985, and gay men lived in painful suspense, waiting in terror for the first symptom. One gay Hollywoodite who became sick early in the epidemic voiced the bewilderment and terrible sense of injustice that was common: "I don't think I overdid anything," he said. "I was just part of the flow."[10]

Gay life had indeed changed. The looming question now was whether AIDS had the power to revive closets, snuff out hard-won gains, and propel the gay community back to the 1950s.

—

For all its devastation, AIDS had the opposite effect. It triggered a resurgence of activism, as well as ingenuity and generosity the likes of which Los Angeles had never before seen. One of the first responses was archetypically "Southern California" in its New Age quality: Louise Hay, a former fashion model and motivational speaker, founded the "Hayride," a weekly support group. Hay offered spiritual encouragement, urged men to clutch teddy bears, and sold tapes with her message of positive thinking. Other responses addressed the effects of the epidemic more realistically. Gay bartenders, who witnessed countless gay men lose their health, jobs, and savings, set out coffee cans to collect change for a relief fund and threw benefit beer busts. A group of friends launched an organization called Aid for AIDS that focused on immediate cash relief for people with HIV living below the poverty line, where illness was propelling many. In 1982, the Gay Community Services Center called an emergency meeting to discuss the AIDS services they would need to provide.

The incidence of AIDS among lesbians has been low. Those few who have contracted the disease have usually gotten it through means other than same-sex sexual relations. (As *Time* quipped at the height of the epidemic, if you want to avoid AIDS, become a lesbian.) Nevertheless, L.A. lesbians were active in the earliest efforts to help when they saw that gay men were being felled by the disease. Ivy Bottini recalls that when her friend Ken Schnorr developed symptoms in 1982, doctors were still unsure of what his ailment was, and when she called the Centers for Disease Control for advice she was given only vague answers. Along with members of the politically sophisticated Municipal Elections Committee of Los Angeles (MECLA), she became a founding supporter of AIDS Project Los Angeles (APLA),[11] which, in the decade that followed, served more than 11,000 Angelenos.

From the beginning, AIDS Project Los Angeles was cochaired by a man and a woman, starting with Diane Abbitt and Joel Weisman. Lesbians were heavily involved in all aspects of the organization. Women's presence helped emphasize to the public that AIDS was a tragedy not just for gay men but for humanity—that although the disease targeted the gay male community, their friends outside were anguished for them and would fight by their side. Abbitt and her partner at the time, Roberta Bennett, also worked together with their old cohorts, David Mixner, Peter Scott, and Duke Comegys (a Los Angeles–based heir to Texas oil money), all of whom had already demonstrated in groups such as MECLA their ability to get the ear of elected officials.[12] Now their focus was on convincing those in power that AIDS drugs must be made available immediately. AZT was given early approval, Abbitt says, because she and her group were able to convince Henry Waxman—the congressman from Los Angeles who was head of the U.S. Congress' Health Committee—that the drug should be put on an expedited track.[13]

Lesbians also opened their purses to AIDS causes. Roberta Bennett, who served on the board of APLA for six years and was active in its money-raising drives, says she never had difficulty getting lesbians to donate and even to open a food bank that would serve people with AIDS.[14] Some lesbians, such as Sue Talbot and Liebe Gray, who were volunteers in APLA, say that they had been lesbian separatists before the epidemic called on them to help their brothers.[15] Just as the separate factions of L.A.'s gay community had banded together during the campaign against the Briggs initiative to fight an external enemy, so did they band now to fight a much more relentless internal enemy.

Their unified focus came with a price. Many gay women like Talbot and Gray turned their energies from lesbian concerns to the battle against AIDS—which accounts, in part, for the failure during the height of the epidemic of L.A. institutions that served lesbians, such as Connexxus and the Woman's Building. Other organizations within the community also found that their energies could no longer be focused on the old concerns, which seemed somewhat frivolous and self-indulgent in comparison to the cataclysmic disaster of AIDS. For instance, Gay and Lesbian Latinos Unidos (GLLU) had formed out of distrust for white-dominated groups; but at the height of the epidemic, members set aside their suspicions and worked closely with those groups. They translated into Spanish AIDS informational material that the Gay and Lesbian Community Services Center published, and they marched side by side with predominantly white organizations at AIDS demonstrations and protests: "'My group/your group' didn't seem right at that point," Rita Gonzales says.[16] AIDS became GLLU's main concern as its energies were put into founding Bienestar ("well-being" in Spanish), a Latino HIV-care nonprofit agency, which now has scores of employees and twelve locations in L.A. But Bienestar's establishment seriously shifted the focus of GLLU from an organization that dealt with all aspects of Latino gay and lesbian concerns to one that addressed the overwhelming problem of AIDS. Roland Palencia observes, "Ironically, we have the biggest [gay] Latino institution, and yet it's primarily around a disease; it's not around an entire community."[17]

Hollywood became a great asset in the fight against AIDS because movie stars were hugely effective in generating donations and spreading public awareness. One of the first actors to take an active role was Zelda Rubenstein, the diminutive star of the film *Poltergeist,* who donned a ruffled apron and admonished a series of bare-chested "sons" to "Play Safely" in ads that appeared on buses; Rubenstein also made videos that were shown between pop music numbers at gay bars.

Other Hollywood stars, such as Burt Lancaster, Angela Lansbury, and Joan Rivers, were quick to lend their clout. Elizabeth Taylor became the face of AIDS activism, as she continues to be. But the star whose impact was most powerful in these early efforts was Rock Hudson, whose AIDS diagnosis in 1985 shook the world. The closeted actor (who "came out" only in a posthumous memoir) lent his name to an AIDS Project Los Angeles event that year. As he languished in the hospital, a dinner featuring tributes to him from Elizabeth Taylor, Betty Ford, Burt Reynolds, and even a polite letter from Ronald and Nancy Reagan raised $1.1 million.[18] When ruggedly handsome and big-screen-familiar Rock Hudson made his famous Hollywood face the face of AIDS, Americans began to view the crisis differently.

AIDS Project Los Angeles, continuing to use its proximity to the entertainment industry to brilliant advantage, began an annual Commitment to Life event. The first, a dinner at which Elizabeth Taylor was the star attraction, raised $1.3 million.[19] Subsequent fund-raisers featured luminaries such as Barbra Streisand, Bruce Springsteen, and Whitney Houston. They filled L.A.'s Shrine Auditorium and the Universal Amphitheater. At 1998's Commitment to Life event, the recently outed industry executive Barry Diller wryly announced: "My money-grubbing, money-raising friends and cochairs have just delivered $3.2 million."[20]

But APLA did not rely on Hollywood alone to bring in money for AIDS causes. The Los Angeles AIDS Walk it sponsored was expected in its first year to raise a few hundred thousand dollars. It attracted a broad swath of the public and brought in more than $1 million. Since its inception, it has raised a total of more than $50 million. The event became a model for AIDS Walks all over the country. AIDS Project Los Angeles and other AIDS groups also organized candlelight marches for the growing numbers of grieving, angry survivors. With tearstained faces and dripping candles, thousands flooded the streets annually, from Pasadena to West Hollywood, honoring the dead and calling for a cure.[21]

But even as marches, agencies, and public awareness increased, so did death. By 1987, more than 71,000 cases of AIDS had been diagnosed nationally, and AIDS-related deaths had exceeded 41,000. *San Diego Update*, which covered the Los Angeles beat, carried an obituary section illustrated with photos, mostly of AIDS casualties in their thirties and forties. As one reader recalls, "It got to the point where you opened the paper with a knot in your stomach because you didn't know who was dead."[22]

Death was as visible on the streets as in the papers. John Morgan Wilson remembers how, walking down Santa Monica Boulevard in the 1980s, "you would see homeless men dying of AIDS on the sidewalk. They couldn't pay their rent and got evicted." But AIDS did not distinguish between the rich and the poor. Within a few years, many of the most prominent, powerful, wealthy, and talented of the gay L.A. community were also dead or dying: the pillars of MECLA and the board of directors of the Gay and Lesbian Community Center—Sheldon Andelson, Rob Eichberg, Peter Scott, Judge Rand Schrader, Duke Comegys; Scott Forbes, the Disco King; Paul Monette, a National Book Award winner; the up-and-coming writers Gil Cuadros and Steven Corbin; the artist Mundo Meza. A whole generation of leaders of gay L.A., as well as their presumed inheritors, were disappearing.

The pain and pang of it all were especially apparent at a Hollywood performance of *The Normal Heart,* Larry Kramer's play about AIDS. John Morgan Wilson says that when he turned around in his seat in the theater and looked back, he saw, in the glimmer of the stage lights, dozens of I.V. poles holding bags of intravenous medicine that dripped into the veins of patients who were sitting in the audience. "They came to see this play pulling their I.V. units on wheels," he recalls. "It was about them."[23]

AN ARMY TO FIGHT AGAINST AIDS

We were loud and rude. . . . We didn't fit the MECLA mold at all.

—Bruce Mirken, AIDS activist and journalist[24]

Even in the war against AIDS, internal struggles arose. The government response to AIDS seemed hopelessly inadequate in the face of the mounting toll of suffering, and some gay people insisted that what was required now was not simply fund-raising and grieving but grassroots militancy. They feared that the nonprofit power structure—dominated by MECLA types who hoped to work within the system—was not angry enough and not effective enough in the battle. In 1986, an external threat in the form of a hostile ballot proposition crystallized for them the conviction that "loud and rude" was a more appropriate response to the enemy than the "MECLA mold's" well-modulated tones.[25]

Right-wing politicians had hoped that AIDS, which they imagined as a "gay plague," would be a wedge to help them turn back gay rights once and for all. In California, the furthest extremist among them, Lyndon La Rouche, introduced a 1986 ballot measure that made John Briggs' initiative look downright gay-friendly. La Rouche's Proposition 64 called for mandatory HIV testing, barred exposed Californians from working with children or food, and, most terrifying, raised the specter of quarantine relocation camps for those found to be HIV-infected. (An Orange County congressman who endorsed the initiative vowed to expand on La Rouche's idea by making it a federal crime for infected persons to kiss.)[26] Despite the efforts of Hollywood celebrities such as Elizabeth Taylor, early polls indicated that La Rouche could win by a wide margin. Torie Osborn (the young lesbian who was to become executive director of the Gay and Lesbian Community Services Center two years later) was hired to run a Southern California "No on 64" office and, with David Mixner, to plan a media campaign against the proposition. Affluent L.A. gays donated $3 million to the campaign.[27]

But, as the journalist Bruce Mirken recalls, other gay people whose approach was very different from that of the No on 64 campaign office now decided that it was "time to wake up and get involved." They formed a coalition that distributed 60,000 fliers in gay bars and neighborhoods across L.A. calling for a protest at La Rouche's headquarters. More than 4,000 people joined their march, invading the streets of L.A.'s quiet Atwater Village. (La Rouche, who promoted the slogan "Spread panic, not AIDS," denounced the march itself as a "public health threat.")[28] The combined efforts of the No on 64 campaign and those who took to the streets of Atwater helped to defeat the proposition by a huge margin: 71 percent to 29 percent. The street-fight against La Rouche provided the momentum and model for a new style in the AIDS war.

Following the victory over La Rouche, the Stop AIDS Quarantine Committee, a group that had been formed by Michael Weinstein and Chris Brownlie as part of the March-on-Atwater coalition, turned to other compelling AIDS problems. Weinstein and Brownlie, old comrades from the Lavender and Red Union, called a public hearing that addressed the County's failure to provide decent AIDS health care. More than a third of L.A.'s HIV-infected population relied on the Los Angeles County–USC Hospital, where the grim clinic was known only as "5P21" for its room number. Patients were forced to wait up to six weeks for an appointment at County. In the interim, they went untreated; some died.[29]

At the Stop AIDS Quarantine Committee hearing, hundreds of people got up to speak, and the meeting, which started in the morning, lasted well into evening. In the midst of their testimonies, Chris Brownlie was suddenly flattened by an attack of pneumonia and was rushed to the hospital. For three days, he lay on a gurney in a hallway because no room was available. Only a plea from Michael Weinstein to Supervisor Edelman finally got Brownlie into a hospital room. Weinstein had grown from a youthful radical to an admirer of Sheldon Andelson's expert politicking. Now, however, he realized that gay political circumstances had changed yet again. He saw clearly that "AIDS was so horrifying, and the treatment of AIDS patients was so horrifying, that rubbing elbows wasn't going to cut it."[30]

What would cut it—he and many others came to believe—was a response that was tailored to the times and the dire crisis of the epidemic. AIDS activism required a high-impact form of organized protest, backed by complex political strategy: It had to be forceful, intelligent, and most of all it had to convey the urgency of the situation. Such massive, enraged, and organized civil disobedience was on display in 1987 at the March on Washington, a national protest with a sizable Los Angeles contingent. The march included a same-sex wedding of hundreds of couples on the steps of the U.S. Supreme Court, followed by a group arrest of dozens protesting federal homophobia. But it was the blunt signs and rude day-glo stickers of an organization recently formed in New York, the AIDS Coalition to Unleash Power, that provided a new blueprint for the grief-stricken and the angry. "The Government Has Blood on Its Hands!" the stickers read. "You Say Don't Fuck. We Say Fuck You!" And next to a picture of President Reagan, "He Kills Me." John Fall recalls seeing the New Yorkers' signs and thinking instantly, "Oh, how obvious. That's what we're going to do!"[31] He was not alone in that epiphany. Another Angeleno who was present at the march, Mark Kostopoulos, of the gay socialist group Lavender Left, began organizing ACT UP/LA the minute he returned to Los Angeles.

Like the Gay Liberation Front nearly twenty years earlier, ACT UP spread to dozens of cities. Los Angeles formed the second-largest group of this decentralized and autonomous movement. In contrast to AIDS Project Los Angeles, ACT UP/LA had no interest in quiet political diplomacy. Instead, with playful media mastery it promoted open expressions of fury about AIDS and how little was being done to end it.

Kostopoulos and the Lavender Left notified local gay groups that they would be holding a "Town Hall Meeting to Beat AIDS."[32] Hundreds of people braved a torrential downpour to attend.[33] The group's tone was emphatically angry, and its thrust was emphatically activist. Michael Weinstein demanded "an army to fight against AIDS." From the outset, the group based its strategy on a firmly progressive analysis of the epidemic: For example, the organization proclaimed that AIDS disproportionately affects poor men and women of color, and they called for a free, nationalized health care system.[34] Kostopoulos charged that the government was "prolonging and creating the AIDS crisis."[35] ACT UP/LA would attack not only the medical and drug industry profiteering, which it derisively called "AIDS, Inc.," but also every level of government for its "inadequate and harmful" response.[36] Though the members were nearly all gay, ACT UP/LA was *not* to be a gay activist group. John Fall remembers that the distinction was clear: "Our focus was on AIDS–and we were gay."

ACT UP/LA stopped traffic on the streets and ambushed bureaucrats in spectacular actions. The group seemed to operate by raw passion. As one veteran described the experience of working in ACT UP/LA, it was "an adrenaline rush that lasted for nearly four years."[37] But passion was balanced by strategic discipline and a fine ability to coolly negotiate complex budgets with government bureaucracies. ACT UP was a movement of *organized* outrage, deliberately nonviolent. Guile and cheekiness were among its methods. For example, gay men and lesbians in ACT UP/LA dressed up as heterosexual couples and infiltrated a Catholic prayer breakfast. At the right moment—when Archbishop Roger Mahoney, who had been denouncing safe sex, stepped up to the microphone—the ACT UPers shouted "Hypocrite!" and "Murderer!" and kept shouting until they were dragged out of the dining room by aging Knights of Columbus.

The cheek had great charm for the participants. But Craig Collins recalls that "anger was at all times seething below the surface."[38] "We all knew people who were simply dying," says John Fall. "The sense was, because we're gay, they're gonna let us all die." Those in ACT UP could not fail to be mindful that every minute counted. The doctrinaire aspects of Lavender Left dissolved quickly. When meetings stretched into four-hour debates and those attending were "held hostage by these ideological discussions about socialism, we just wouldn't tolerate it," John Fall remembers. Frustrated with the cautious bureaucratese of AIDS agencies, they chose a course of direct action. "The organization would not be what it said, but what it did," says Peter Cashman, who termed the group "a new beast" in activism.

The impatience of ACT UP/LA members, many of whom were HIV positive, drove them to master the most effective methods to get their message out. "We got professional very quickly," says Fall, who wrote the group's press releases. Entertainment industry professionals aided their efforts. For instance, for eight months after his diagnosis, Steven Kolzak, the casting agent responsible for the hit television show *Cheers,* had kept silent about his medical condition, but after the death of a producer friend who never mentioned that he had AIDS, Kolzak became part of ACT UP and went public, even to speaking out in middle-America's *TV Guide.*[39] ACT UPers also learned that the drama of civil disobedience was very effective in helping the organization attract desired media attention, and that arrests practically guaranteed a spot on television news. They also learned that cameras provided protection from police abuse.

Initially, some had feared being arrested at ACT UP protests because of the stigma of a police record and the trauma they associated with incarceration. But when they learned that a bail fund and volunteer attorneys would help ACT UP members get quick release, more and more members began to volunteer to be carted off to the station. When John Fall was merely cited rather than arrested, "everyone's reaction was, 'Oh, you just got a citation?'"[40] Many ACT UPers let themselves be arrested because they felt they had nothing to lose. "We all thought we were dead men anyway. That makes it very easy for you to risk your life in front of a policeman," recalls Gunther Freehill.[41]

ACT UP members developed a distinct sartorial aesthetic: leather jackets, Doc Marten boots, black jeans, and among the most daring, the new fad of piercings. Their tough-guy style sometimes had an amusing effect: During one jailhouse stay, ACT UPers were asked by other inmates, "When did you join the Silent Death gang?" It took a few moments for them to understand that, because they were all wearing "Silence = Death" T-shirts of pink and black, they'd been perceived as a new Los Angeles gang, complete with colors.

Many in ACT UP were suffering from various stages of the disease; some had never been tested or were asymptomatic. Nevertheless, they all shared a wordless sense of destiny. Those who were uninfected often claimed, when they were arrested in actions, to be HIV positive in solidarity with the infected. If they felt dispossessed by their government, they felt all the more connected to one another. When comrades were released from jail, ACT UPers threw parties. When comrades died, ACT UPers stopped traffic with political funerals, holding signs that read "Murdered by Government Indifference." They exhorted one another to bravery and wrote of their battles in heroic terms, as did the male-to-female transgender "AIDS diva" Connie Norman, who was dying of AIDS.

She urged her fellow warriors:

Someday this plague will be over and we will survive as a people to tell the tales. Don't forget to tell how much we honored life. Don't forget to tell how hard many of us have fought for it. Life is and has always been precious to us and our community's response to this plague proves it. . . . Remember our heroes and heroines.[42]

GETTING HEARD

It was a branded presence. You knew something very different was going on here; a very different notion of what political activism can be.

— Craig Collins on ACT UP's Coffee Pot
Brigade in the Gay Pride Parade[43]

Christopher Street West, the organization sponsoring L.A.'s gay pride parade, did not know what hit it. After contingents of lesbian and gay business and professional groups, politicians waving from convertibles, sound trucks pulsating with dance music, and oiled boys grinding in swimsuits, a new contingent marched. Its message was neither bland nor sexy, and it was causing a huge stir at the 1989 parade. "The reactions," recalls one marcher, "ranged from drunken disco queens being completely flabbergasted to people jumping in to join us."[44] Contrary to Christopher Street West rules, ACT UP had simply attached itself to an accommodating group. It had not registered or submitted its controversial message for approval. Among the palms framing Santa Monica Boulevard, two men bore a smartly painted black banner shaped like a giant funeral ribbon; its shocking pink inscription read, "Wake Up and Smell the Coffee!" Directly behind that, an eight-foot white Chippendale coffee pot danced like a surreal Disney character, its own banner announcing, "Homophobia Is Brewing!" Behind these heralds, from out of mammoth coffee cups, loomed huge portraits. One, of L.A. Sheriff Sherman Block, carried the slogan "Arrested Equals Tested," which reflected the proposed legislation he was backing. Over the portrait of a known homophobe, Pete Schabarum, the L.A. County supervisor, was stenciled the word "GUILTY!" Holding chrome percolators and wearing their "Silence = Death" T-shirts, the ACT UP contingent marched. Each expertly crafted prop was the labor of movie- and television-studio professionals: graphic designers, lighting designers, costumers, artists. ACT UP roared like a flood down the main drag of Boystown.

The media strategy and artistry that was the daily bread of many local activists became one of the most powerful weapons in ACT UP/L.A.'s arsenal. The subversive artists who created the "Coffee Pot Brigade" knew well how to make statements that would grab the attention of the media. They even sang—as when responding to Archbishop Roger Mahony's proclamation in 1989 that young people should avoid "being trapped into the 'safe-sex' myth," which, he said, "is both a lie and a fraud."[45] On the same December day that ACT UP/New York made headlines by disrupting a mass in St. Patrick's Cathedral, ACT UP/LA unleashed an action titled "Slice Mahony's Baloney." Dressed in red-and-white cassocks, their cheeks rouged, tinseled halos wobbling over their heads, they visited five cathedrals in Los Angeles. They gleefully mocked Catholic demands for lifelong celibacy among homosexuals by dubbing themselves "the Altered Boys." They waited for parishioners to enter or leave the cathedrals, then burst into parodies of hymns and carols, such as one sung to the tune of "We Three Kings":

We Gay Queens of Hollywood are
Bearing condoms, O yes we are.
Vine and Fountain, Magic Mountain,
Schlepping from bar to bar.

The action proceeded peacefully, except for a parishioner at Good Shepherd Cathedral in Beverly Hills who punched a protestor. News coverage was substantial. It was also, as Craig Collins, who coordinated the media, recalls, "the first positive treatment of anything ACT UP." He explained to one reporter, who was puzzled about the group's stridency, "These people are going to die." Collins says that he still remembers "the look on her face as she got that." And, he adds, "it showed up in her story."[46]

Not everything that AIDS activists promoted, however, was tinsel and carols, though to protect ACT UP, individuals who inflicted property damage to make a symbolic point claimed to be representing "independent affinity groups." Days before the "Mahony's Baloney" action, four L.A. Roman Catholic churches were splattered with red paint and plastered with posters labeling the archbishop a murderer. "Greater Religious Responsibility" took credit for the action. Religious officials and authorities immediately denounced the vandalism, which ACT UP denied having a hand in—while also voicing sympathy with the vandals via its spokesperson Helene Schpak, who told the *Los Angeles Times,* "We believe any [action] is appropriate to protest a policy of death."[47]

Another "affinity group" briefly halted the 1990 Rose Parade when activists brandished a banner that read "Emergency—Stop the Parade—70,000 Dead from AIDS," which was flashed on television worldwide. Though such actions were never officially connected to ACT UP, they potently embodied one of the group's infamous day-glo sticker philosophies: "We're ACT UP. Fuck you."

ACT UP/LA achieved a significant victory in getting the County to take seriously the need to put energy and dollars into improving public health care for AIDS patients. This did not happen overnight. With the growing number of newly diagnosed AIDS cases, many of them nonwhite and uninsured, a gruesome health care apartheid developed. In a *Los Angeles Times* editorial, activists had denounced the shockingly inadequate facilities at County Hospital for people with AIDS:

> People with temperatures of 103 or higher sit for hours on hard wooden benches waiting for help. Some receive chemotherapy in crowded hallways, vomiting in bags. Others in the same hallways, stripped to the waist, have IVs hooked to their arms.[48]

Duly shamed, the L.A. County Board of Supervisors voted to improve AIDS care at County Hospital, but progress was glacial.[49] To goad them into action, activists held a weeklong vigil, setting up a tent city where protestors slept overnight and demonstrated during the day. They constructed an ongoing mock AIDS ward outside the hospital gates: Some activists dressed as doctors; others, many genuinely ill, lay on cots, and they acted out the horror of the disease. Demanding a fifty-bed AIDS ward and treatment that would be equal to what was available for the affluent, activists braved cold and rain. Connie Norman, the earthy, opinionated male-to-female transsexual, finagled the donation of a trailer in which she heated gallons of soup to keep protestors warm and fed. At one of the daily rallies, Chris Brownlie, the man who three years earlier had languished on a gurney in a hallway inside the nearby building, stepped up to the podium. Bruce Mirken recalls Brownlie as a powerful speaker who built to an electrifying crescendo: "'It's not about the T cells, the fevers, the day-to-day struggles,' Chris said. Then he burst into this scream. 'It's about caring! And the policy of the County is not to care!'"[50]

Near the end of the vigil, Supervisor Ed Edelman appeared before the crowd and offered cautious encouragement. It had been Edelman who steered millions of public dollars toward gay health care for nearly two decades, but his past helpfulness could not stand him in good stead among this outraged crowd. To these impatient activists, his speech was "pathetically wishy-washy." They booed him offstage. Edelman appeared shocked;[51] he had not understood that with this generation of activists, old alliances carried little weight. (Despite the crowd's hostility, Edelman continued his support. He arranged for County funding that would help Weinstein's new AIDS Hospice Foundation; its first facility was named the Chris Brownlie Hospice.)

Because of ACT UP's rowdy persona and insistence on action over talk, it found itself largely shunned by L.A.'s gay political elite. "MECLA, which set the agenda in the L.A. gay community, was opposed to ACT UP,"[52] recalls Peter Cashman. So was *Frontiers,* the largest local gay publication, which refused to cover the activities of ACT UP. But by 1989, the epidemic had become so bad that diverse groups within the gay community finally realized that, as Rita Gonzales says, "my group/your group didn't seem right." Rank-and-file activists and leaders of the gay establishment finally converged in a demonstration at the Federal Building. The huge mob was fiercely determined to send a message to the feds, who had been dragging their feet on issues such as safe-sex education and compassionate early approval of drugs. They created a cacophony of drumming and banging, ear-splitting whistles, and the incessant shouting of "Shut it down!" "No business as usual!" Eighty activists volunteered to be arrested: Among them were the Reverend Troy Perry, a veteran of many arrests; Torie Osborn, now director of the Gay and Lesbian Community Services Center; Gil Gerard, director of the Minority AIDS Project; and the *Frontiers* publisher, Bob Craig.

Federal officers wore latex gloves, plastic shields over their faces, and panicked expressions. Terrified, they roughly dragged the eighty activists into custody. Perry said that in twenty years of activism, he'd never experienced such brutal treatment. But the protestors could not be daunted. One told a reporter, "I'm about to get arrested, and I'm a little afraid. But I'm willing to get arrested because I'm more afraid of doing nothing."[53] While the officers, wearing their protective latex gloves, manhandled them, the arrestees kept chanting, "Your gloves don't match your shoes!"[54]

NOT JUST WHITE GAY MEN

It's the radicals who change history, like the suffragette who was killed by the racehorse. I want to live my life that way. The exhilaration of it. That's the kind of life I had in ACT UP.

— Cyndy Crogan, lesbian member of ACT UP[55]

West Hollywood became one of the most AIDS-proactive cities in the nation because its local government and its large gay population were willing to support services. But West Hollywood remained Boystown, which helped fueled perceptions that AIDS was a gay white male disease. The medical truth was far different, but it was slow to be widely recognized. It was not until 1991, when Magic Johnson declared he would retire from the Los Angeles Lakers basketball team because he was infected with HIV, that the myth of AIDS as a gay white disease substantially eroded. Johnson's revelation reverberated—as the *Los Angeles Times* observed—everywhere: "in playgrounds, health clinics, the offices of activists, and [to] government figures in Washington, D.C." The telephones at AIDS clinics all over Southern California were flooded with calls from people suddenly wanting an HIV test.[56]

The need for AIDS care facilities was great in L.A.'s vast communities of color, located primarily east of La Brea and south of Olympic, in areas where the populations were poor and less likely to have private health insurance. By 1992, almost 40 percent of all the AIDS cases that were reported countywide were Latinos or African Americans. And that official statistic did not reflect the large number of infected people who would not reveal their illness because of cultural stigma or the fear of deportation if they were undocumented immigrants.[57] Over time, as infection rates soared among people of color, AIDS service institutions were opened in their communities. But there was no established model of care specific to them; as the founder of the AIDS clinic in Watts concluded: "What's good for West Hollywood doesn't necessarily work for South-Central" (an African American district). Gay activists of color organized to serve their specific communities. The Minority AIDS Project, the first and largest community-based black gay AIDS organization, was founded by the Reverend Carl Bean of Unity Fellowship of Christ Church. Bienestar, the HIV service agency for Latinos, soon spread to locations in such diverse areas as El Monte, Van Nuys, Wilmington, Hollywood, San Bernardino, and Boyle Heights. In response to the high incidence of the disease among L.A.'s nonwhite plurality, ACT UP began publishing its newsletter in Spanish and established the People of Color Caucus.

About 10 percent of ACT UP/LA activists were lesbians.[58] Almost none were infected, but they came to the organization for the same reasons that lesbians had joined AIDS Project Los Angeles and other AIDs groups—because of a sense of "the unfairness of genocide,"[59] because "you begin to appreciate people when you might lose them,"[60] because of a desire to be helpful amidst the devastation. Many had been caregivers for gay male friends with AIDS or had worked professionally with AIDS patients. (As Torie Osborn observes, the number of lesbians in health care has always been astronomical: "When straight nurses didn't want to work in AIDS wards, lesbian nurses did it," she says. "They *wanted* to do it.")[61]

Robin Podolsky, a performance artist and writer, had been active in the mainstream feminist movement, but with the advent of the epidemic, her perspective changed: "I took the straight world's response to AIDS personally, their terrible indifference and smugness," she explains. "I knew if it were lesbians who had AIDS, straight women [in the feminist movement] would feel indifferent, too. My allegiance shifted." She was among the ACT UP/LA members who participated in the huge vigil and campout at County Hospital to protest that one of the biggest hospitals in the world couldn't give adequate AIDS care to the poor; with other ACT UP members she took over the Federal Building and was one of the eighty dragged off to jail; and she devoted her writing and art to AIDS causes.[62] Much rarer in ACT UP was a lesbian member such as Mary Lucey, who says she came to ACT UP because she had been diagnosed as HIV positive and her doctor told her that she had only thirteen months to live. Lucey recalls that when the facilitator asked at the first meeting she attended who had the disease, she was the only woman in the room to raise her hand.[63]

Other lesbians became active in ACT UP not only because they wished to help gay men with AIDS but also because they had been won over by ACT UP's willingness to make coalitions with other progressive causes and protest groups, such as abortion clinic defense.[64] The lesbians admired ACT UP's style and believed they could learn important methods from the passionate ACT UPers. Cyndy Crogan, who was an activist with Fired Up For Choice, a predominantly lesbian organization that fought against right-wingers who were blockading access to abortion clinics, says she first learned of ACT UP when she worked by the side of ACT UP members. "That's my tribe over there," she thought as she watched ACT UP's "radical approach at clinic hits."

Among the ACT UP men, Crogan observed a haughty "sense of entitlement," a "male characteristic" about which lesbian feminists had been bitterly critical. But Crogan says that the ACT UP men's feeling of entitlement soon empowered her, too: "I was swept up with it. I became part of their power. I learned how to claim power myself." She liked it, also, she says, that ACT UPers merged playfulness with serious structure. "I learned from ACT UP the incredible planning that needs to go into anything that comes off well. It's so organized, like a corporation." Crogan says that her years in ACT UP taught her that a group cannot be effective without a sense of urgency, and she has applied it to her lesbian political work, such as organizing a Los Angeles Dyke March: "From ACT UP men I learned to oppose having 'crowd control' in the Dyke March. It's too engraved in women to be nice. Until women get angry, they won't be free. That's what the men taught me."[65]

Women assumed leadership roles in ACT UP through their own initiative, but also through the inexorable loss of men. Mark Kostopoulos, the founding member who became so identified with ACT UP, chose Helene Schpak to be his successor, and it was she who ultimately facilitated more than half the meetings. The women had learned from the examples of ACT UPers, and they were as brash as the boys—for instance, burning Bibles in a portable barbecue near a clinic to distract and taunt Operation Rescue volunteers.[66] ACT UP women also had their own muscle and could be fearless hand-to-hand combatants. At one abortion clinic action, Helene Schpak recalls, Mary Lucey and her partner Nancy McNiel had just entered an elevator with two men from Operation Rescue who began to push the women belligerently just as the doors were closing. Schpak, witnessing that bit of the scene, raced upstairs to help Lucey and McNiel. When the doors opened, she says, "the guys were on the floor. Those two women had beat the crap out of them!"[67]

Despite the horrors of the plague, gay progress did not cease. L.A. saw a mass exit from the closet of those who were infected ("mainly because they had nothing to lose," the writer David Ehrenstein noted).[68] Widespread homophobia was much less possible once it became clear to heterosexuals that beloved friends and relatives were gay and needed help in their fight against AIDS. Los Angeles did eventually rise to the terrible challenge of the epidemic, thanks in good part to the work of groups such as AIDS Project Los Angeles and ACT UP/LA. Dave Johnson, who had been active in the Studio One boycott and was openly HIV positive, was appointed the city's first AIDS coordinator. Michael Weinstein's group, which had begun as the Stop AIDS Quarantine Committee and became the AIDS Healthcare Foundation, received monetary support from the City of Los Angeles and Los Angeles County, as well as from the federal government; this support helped the foundation evolve into a huge provider of AIDS care services, with clinics not only in the West but also in Africa and Mexico.

Some ACT UP/LA activists became "suits," getting jobs with non-profits or government AIDS organizations. They carried over a sense of urgency into the realm of bureaucracy. Occasional old associates worried that as "suits" they would sell out to "AIDS, Inc"; but those like Gunther Freehill, who became an administrator with the Los Angeles County Office of AIDS Programs and Policy, say their past activism in fiercely radical groups such as ACT UP gave them a militant resolve that will forever inform everything they do on behalf of people with AIDS.[69]

Former T.V. star Sheila Kuehl became the first openly gay state legislator in California. Kuehl pioneered a law to protect gay students. *Courtesy Sheila Kuehl.*

CHAPTER 12

Stunning Comebacks

If there is a place that seems like home and heart, it's San Fran-cisco. New York is mind. And Los Angeles is power and politics.

—National gay movement historian, John D'Emilio, 1993[1]

G AY ANGELENOS had become expert in waging massive protests over AIDS issues, and their honed skills were put to spectacular use in subsequent political battles. In September 1991, Pete Wilson, the Republican governor of California, vetoed Assembly Bill 101, which would have outlawed job discrimination against homosexuals. "We were betrayed," Laurie McBride, a gay rights lobbyist in Sacramento, complained. "Before he was elected, Pete Wilson looked me right in the eye and said he would help craft a bill that he would sign. He's reneged."[2] The governor claimed that AB101 would be burdensome to small businesses because it would impose excessive regulation. Gay L.A., after years of weathering the brutal AIDS war, was in no mood to be put off by such an absurd excuse. The dramatic fury of the gay community became, according to Wilson's aide, Dan Schnur, "one of the single biggest frustrations of the first two years [of Wilson's governorship]."[3]

The flashpoint for the fury was Rob Roberts of Queer Nation, who had been fasting until AB101 would be made law. He had set up a camp he called "Queer Village" in a West Hollywood park, and other activists joined him nightly. When news of Wilson's veto broke, the crowd that had already been building at Queer Village took to the streets. Within hours, word had spread all over Los Angeles, and, despite the city's handicap of its vast sprawl, massive demonstrations began. Hoards of protestors eventually descended not only on West Hollywood, Beverly Hills, and Silver Lake, but also on the San Fernando Valley, Anaheim, and at the Los Angeles International Airport, where they took over a runway. For seventeen days, night after night, gay men and women congregated to stage protests throughout the Los Angeles Basin. Protests also broke out in cities up and down the state, but the L.A. response was described as "the most massive and sustained civil unrest in California since the 1960s."[4]

As many as 50,000 gay people came out of their various exclusionary niches of class, gender, race, political affiliation[5]—and again banded together against an external enemy. "We hit the streets, leaderless. It was one of those times when the situation catalyzes everyone. People showed up that we'd never seen before," the veteran lesbian activist Robin Podolsky recalls.[6] Members of the Log Cabin Republicans shouted their protests alongside the pierced radicals of Queer Nation and the United Lesbians of African Heritage and the Stonewall Democratic Club. "I remember us chanting on Santa Monica Boulevard, 'Out of the gyms and into the streets,'" recalls Michael du Plessis of Queer Nation. To the astonished delight of the protestors, gay people did pour out the gyms, and even out of the bars.[7]

In Boystown, gays burned Governor Wilson in effigy. In the Silver Lake district, people emerged from their houses and cheered the demonstrators on. On the fourth night of the demonstrations, they brought their protests downtown to the Ronald Reagan State Building, where a protestor shattered a heavy glass door and the LAPD SWAT Team was called out. When in the midst of the nightly demonstrations the foolhardy governor appeared in Los Angeles for a Republican fundraiser at the County Art Museum, thousands of demonstrators surrounded the building, chanting "Pete Wilson, you fucking weasel! Come out and face the people!" They sat on the street, intoning "Aaaahhh," an eerie mantra and war cry right in the middle of traffic-heavy Wilshire Boulevard. They followed the governor to the Plaza Hotel in Century

City, where the police in full riot gear were called in and, clubs in hand, moved down on them.

Many were beaten and arrested. (The police actions at the Century Plaza Hotel led to the largest gay-and-lesbian class action suit ever against the police department.)[8] But the L.A. gay community had already experienced beatings and arrests in AIDS protests, and they were less flappable than virgin demonstrators might have been. They had both passion and sangfroid, as Cyndy Crogan, who participated in AIDS demonstrations as well as the AB 101 protests, suggests: "I thought then, 'If my life ends right here, in this action, what better way to die. That's when life means the most.'"[9]

They had also learned methods from militant AIDS campaigns, and the seeming disorder of the protestors had its own logic. For instance, Jehan Agrama, who was president of the media watch organization, Gay & Lesbian Alliance Against Defamation (GLAAD), explains that groups worked in tandem: "Queer Nation would be invasive and rude. GLAAD would just stand quietly handing out fliers. The effect was great."[10] Though the protests were ostensibly leaderless, they were far from disorganized. The switchboard of the Gay and Lesbian Community Services Center spread the word daily about the changing locations of the nightly demonstrations.[11] The Center also provided a truck and an amp system from which speakers would rally the community. ACT UP sent trained legal observers out to note instances of police brutality.[12] The protestors knew well how to use the media. As the police were descending aggressively on them at the Century Plaza Hotel, Jehan Agrama grabbed a microphone and sang, "We are a gay and gentle people, singing, singing for our lives." Television cameras zoomed in, the police were confused and fell back, and the demonstrators took the opportunity to regroup.[13]

The AB 101 demonstrations became a symbol of some pride to L.A. gay activists, who, as Torie Osborn observes, had been irritated because Los Angeles had not been given the respect it merited as a political force among gays nationally. But with the 1991 L.A. protests, she says, "the baton moved." Gays in Los Angeles such as Osborn credit their seventeen days of protest with persuading Governor Wilson to look again at the problem of job discrimination.[14] The following year, Wilson reconsidered his veto, signing into law a similar version of a gay rights bill. "The gay community is an extremely potent force politically and is taken extremely seriously," Dan Schnur, the governor's aide, conceded.[15]

MAKING THE MEDIA BEHAVE

We're here to tell you how to do it better. This is how we prefer to be called: not "avowed homosexual," but "gay" or "lesbian"; not "AIDS victim" but "person with AIDS."

—Jehan Agrama, co-chair of GLAAD,
in 1990s meetings with the news media[16]

From the beginning, the entertainment industry, fueled by gay talent and surrounded by a gay culture, kept its truths secret and promulgated lies in films when it mentioned homosexuality at all. It was rarely challenged. In 1980, the Alliance of Gay and Lesbian Artists (AGLA) was founded as a support group for actors struggling to be part of the gay movement while employed in the industry. They became early media watchdogs, issuing criticism for negative portrayals of gays and publicly offering awards for positive ones—to Cher who played a lesbian in *Silkwood,* to *Hill Street Blues* for addressing the plight of a gay policeman, to Phil Donahue for his sympathetic discussions about homosexuality. Julie Harris and Alan Bates presented awards at AGLA's annual gala, which filled the Huntington-Hartford Theater.[17] The group's watchdog role, however, conflicted with the members' careers as workers in the industry. Chris Uszler, who had been the executive director of the organization, recalls that AGLA fell apart because many members were reluctant to be confrontational with Hollywood executives from whom they might be seeking employment.[18] But in the next years a variety of gay L.A. groups began to tackle Hollywood. Their agitation finally succeeded in raising consciousness and conscience in the industry.

The worst fears of members of the Alliance of Gay and Lesbian Artists—that producers and directors would not hire them if they openly agitated for homosexual concerns—were somewhat eased when producers and directors themselves became founding members of Hollywood Supports, an organization dedicated to reversing discrimination against gays in the entertainment industry. Established in 1992 by the former Fox chairman, Barry Diller, and the MCA president, Sidney Sheinberg, Hollywood Supports attracted prominent Hollywood power brokers such as David Geffen.[19] With such clout on their side, a network of gay and lesbian industry employees could finally persuade Hollywood to declare support aloud. All the major guilds, agencies, and studios (including the conservative Fox as well as Disney, which suffered a three-year Southern Baptist boycott for its new policies) were soon offering domestic partner benefits for gay and lesbian employees.

Other groups also formed in the late 1980s and early '90s to call Hollywood to conscience. The usual gay L.A. split between fiery radicals who wanted to take it to the streets and the A-Gays who wanted to play power politics emerged again in the Hollywood battle. But, as Jehan Agrama observes, both sides understood the global impact of what the industry wrought, and both sides had the same goal—to make Hollywood change. Their difference in approach became a kind of strength: Together they played good cop/bad cop.

Jehan Agrama, a lesbian producer, and Richard Jennings, a gay attorney for Paramount Studios, both quit their jobs and devoted their energies to the Los Angeles Gay & Lesbian Alliance Against Defamation, founded in 1989.[20] Agrama and Jennings demanded meetings with Hollywood executives and media representatives, presented their impressive credentials as members of the entertainment industry, and said that GLAAD was willing to "educate." Had the times not been right, they might not have gotten past the door to begin with. But years of gay movement progress had made the times right.

Agrama says the news media began calling GLAAD to discuss coverage of stories about gay people. Jay Leno told Barbara Walters on a television special that he would not do humor that was offensive to gays and lesbians, and he consulted with GLAAD about whether certain jokes were "appropriate."[21] GLAAD also took out ads in the *Hollywood Reporter* and *Variety* in the form of "open letters" that called Hollywood to task. When *Basic Instinct*, a movie about a lesbian serial killer, was being filmed in 1991,

GLAAD protested that "while none of us supports censorship, we are tired of having the diversity of our lives censored by the media." The organization demanded that Hollywood portray real-life lesbian and gay images rather than noxious sensationalism.[22] Their protest did not stop the filming, but it garnered GLAAD international support and, as its star Sharon Stone told Barbara Walters, as much publicity as the film itself got.[23]

The Los Angeles Queer Nation's approach was very different from that of GLAAD. Queer Nation prided itself on being, as one member, Judy Sisneros, described it, a "small, broke, rowdy group of queer activists."[24] They had learned through the examples of AIDS activism how to use the media to call attention to their cause and get their message out. They, too, felt provoked in the early 1990s when "the stuff coming out of Hollywood was really indefensible," Queer National Michael du Plessis recalls.[25] In 1992, they invaded the 6:00 A.M. Oscar nominations press conference and handed out fliers with their blunt messages. The press leapt at the chance to talk to radical queer activists, hoping for sensationalistic stories about which movie stars were hiding in the closet.[26] "Gay Groups Plan an Oscar 'Outing,'" *New York Newsday* proclaimed, explaining in terms calculated to titillate, "Shouting 'FIRE' in a crowded theater may not be protected free speech, but some radical gay activists believe shouting 'dyke' and 'queer' at actors reputed to be gay during next Monday's Oscar telecast is."[27] Queer Nation threatened that as part of its "Stop Hollywood Homophobia" action they would storm the stage at the Dorothy Chandler Pavilion, where the Academy Awards were being held. Even major newspapers delightedly ran front-page stories with headlines such as "Angry Gay and Lesbian Activists Plan to Upstage Oscar Tonight."[28]

As the stars strolled down the red carpet the evening of the awards, Queer Nation members sat down on the street outside the Dorothy Chandler Pavilion and chanted: "We're not here to educate. / We're here to ruin your date."[29] Mounted police immediately surrounded them. Queer Nation hoped to gain worldwide attention for the cause by disrupting Hollywood's most glittering event, and they succeeded. Several were arrested, and the incident was covered by the media all over the planet.

That same year, the joint efforts of GLAAD and Queer Nation nipped in the bud plans for a Rush Limbaugh television talk show on CBS. Limbaugh's nationally syndicated radio programs were a thorn to gay people, who perceived him not only as a bigot but also a fomenter of violence against them. When Limbaugh was invited to L.A. to stand in for the television host Pat Sajak as a trial run for his own CBS talk show, GLAAD and Queer Nation, along with ACT UP, were ready for him. Dozens of members of the organizations managed to get seats in his audience. Queer Nation and ACT UP were planning to shout Limbaugh down. Before that could happen, Sylvia Rhue, a GLAAD board member who had planned just "to sit there and scowl and offer quiet passive resistance," found herself on national television when she uttered an objection to one of Limbaugh's antiwomen diatribes. "He came up and stuck a microphone in my face," she says. A shouting match ensued between them, the audience, packed by the three gay organizations, cheering Rhue on. "He couldn't handle me; he couldn't handle the crowd who was on my side. Limbaugh totally lost it." And he lost his television program because the gay groups had made him betray his inability to deal with a live and hostile audience.[30]

Like GLAAD, Queer Nation takes credit for helping to change Hollywood. "A lot happened as a result of our Oscar action and other protests," Judy Sisneros says. "Look at what the movies have produced over the last decade."[31] But the two groups were vital complements to one another. When the comic Andrew Dice Clay's gay-bashing concert film *Dice Rules* (distributed by Carolco Pictures, the same company that produced *Basic Instinct*) was being marketed, Queer Nation gathered on the Sunset Strip at 3:00 A.M. and defaced the Andrew Dice Clay billboard by throwing Christmas tree ornaments filled with enamel paint on it, scrawling the word "HOMOPHOBIA" over it, and disconnecting the electric lights that illuminated it.[32] GLAAD, in contrast, met with theater executives and explained their objections to the film.

But because the militants acted out in rowdy ways, Jehan Agrama says, it was easier for GLAAD, with its button-down style, to approach executives: "Would you rather do business with those guys or with us?" GLAAD representatives could imply. The desired end was achieved through double-barreled pressure. In this instance, GLAAD convinced the Loews Theaters chain, most of the United Artists chain, Cinemark, and the American Multi-Cinema chain to refuse to screen the Andrew Dice Clay film. They succeeded in part because the radicals once again moved the center to the left: Queer Nation's unruly Sunset Strip action made GLAAD's polite demands that the theater chains boycott the film appear reasonable by contrast.

The metamorphosis in Hollywood that resulted from gay pressure was reflected throughout the 1990s in the GLAAD awards dinners. In 1991, Universal studio heads despaired when GLAAD announced that *Fried Green Tomatoes,* a movie that hinted at a lesbian love story, would be given the GLAAD Award for Best Film at the annual awards dinner. "They freaked out about it. This was one award they didn't want," Agrama says, since they thought that the film would lose revenue at the box office if it were widely acknowledged to be lesbian. But as the decade progressed, not only did the nominees show up for GLAAD's annual awards dinners but the studios began to buy out entire tables. The dinner has become a mini–Academy Awards, attracting celebrities such as Elizabeth Taylor, Carrie Fisher, Whoopie Goldberg, Sharon Stone, and Roseanne, and it raises more than $1 million for the organization.[33] It is produced by some of the best talent in the industry and held at places such as the Century Plaza Hotel (of AB 101–protest fame) and the Kodak Theater (which also hosts the maxi–Academy Awards). For an extra $1,000 donation to GLAAD, a dinner guest can share the cocktail hour with celebs.[34]

GIRLS RULE

Republican leader in the California Legislature Jim Brulte: *"Sheila, one question. If you're a lesbian, how come all my guys like you so much?"*

Assemblywoman from Los Angeles Sheila Kuehl: *"Discrimination demonizes the truly fabulous."*

—First California State Assembly session of 1995.[35]

By the 1990s, many L.A. lesbians, whose predecessors had been silent in the 1950s and separatist in the 1970s, had taken a place at the larger gay community table. In part because the AIDS epidemic decimated so much of the gay male leadership, lesbians even sat often at the table's head. They ran many of the major L.A. gay institutions, from the Gay and Lesbian Community Services Center,[36] where they served as executive directors as well as chairs of the board, to both of the gay synagogues, where they served as rabbis. Lesbian ascendancy is not peculiar to Los Angeles, of course, but since that city's population is so immense, there are probably more lesbians in prominent positions there than anywhere in the world.[37]

Their leadership has not been limited to the gay community. The women's movement too opened the door to high places, and the decrease in homophobia has meant that "out" lesbians might step in. They've represented Southern California in the legislature, and they've been appointed or elected judges and mayors and directors of city offices. Some of those who found themselves in prominent positions in the 1990s had been lesbian-feminist separatists twenty years earlier. A new era permitted them to carry what had once been radical feminist values into the Southern California "establishment"—where they no longer seemed so radical.

Renee Cowhig came to Los Angeles from Boston in 1973 to escape her rigid Irish Catholic working-class family. "I grew up in Boston," she says, "where the cops chip your teeth in the gay bars and toughs chase you around." In L.A., she joined the Women's Center and worked on the radical feminist newspaper *Sister*. With another lesbian feminist, Ariana Manov, she devised a program for women, including herself, to learn building-trade skills, and they received federal CETA funds to run the program. Their ambition was born out of the lesbian-feminist polemic arguing that gender should not be tied to career opportunities and that nontraditional jobs should be open to women. Cowhig made her reputation as a building and safety manager following the Northridge earthquake. Santa Monica hired her in 1994 to be the head of the Division of Maintenance and Management for the entire city, where she supervises 120 workers, mostly male, and is out as a lesbian. At Maintenance headquarters, she also runs an annual summer program, Rosie's Girls (the reference is to Rosie the Riveter), that is funded by the City of Los Angeles and incarnates her 1970s utopian dreams: to teach hundreds of adolescent females carpentry, welding, and electrician skills.[38]

Judy Abdo, an out lesbian who was elected to the Santa Monica City Council and then became mayor for two terms in the 1990s, believes that her successes were possible in Santa Monica because that town has long been "home to beatniks, hippies, Jane Fonda and Tom Hayden"; it was also "neighbor to the Church in Ocean Park, where at Sunday night dances in the '70s gays and straights would share the dance floor." Abdo's explanation for the liberality of the area is that "people who live life on the edge go for the edges of places. Santa Monica is the edge of the city, county, country. You go west and there's no place else to go." During her first term as mayor, Santa Monica even paid for her to attend the National Lesbian Conference in Atlanta. "It's that kind of city," she says.[39]

But neighboring L.A. has also become "that kind of city." The 1980s rise to judgeships of out gay men, such as Rand Schrader and Steve Lachs, was followed by the 1990s rise to judgeships of out lesbians. Stephanie Sautner, a former New York City police detective, came to Los Angeles to study law, joined the L.A. Gay and Lesbian Bar Association, and stayed, first becoming deputy city attorney and then, after Governor Wilson's veto of AB 101, deciding in outrage to run for judge as an openly lesbian candidate. She won her municipal court judicial bid in 1992 and later became a judge in the superior court. Rita Baird, who had also been a member of the Gay and Lesbian Bar Association, says that Judge Rand Schrader served as a mentor and model for her. Like him, she determined to be out in her legal career. Baird says that in Southern California it has been a "nonissue" in her advancement. Governor Gray Davis appointed her to the superior court, and her fellow judges elected her a court commissioner. The only way in which being an out gay woman has had significance, Baird says, is that "it is probably important for young lawyers' growth and development to know that the judge before them is a lesbian, and that she will do a good job and they will get a fair hearing."[40]

Since the 1990s, L.A. has also been represented in the California State Legislature by out lesbians. In 1994, Sheila Kuehl, a.k.a. Zelda Gilroy, one of the "loves of Dobie Gillis," became the first openly gay state assemblyperson. She had come out publicly in 1991 on *Good Morning, America; Entertainment Today;* and *Geraldo;* but when she announced her intention to run, three years later, *People* magazine headlined the "scoop": "Zelda Jumps Out of the Closet and into a State Government Race." The sensationalism could not hurt her race in Southern California, even among her constituents who were not especially pro-gay, as she wryly tells:

> During the time of that campaign I was sitting in a Santa Monica restaurant and this big, burly guy comes barreling up to my table and bangs on it. He says, "Sheila, I hate all politicians, because they lie. I hate them all, except for you—because you've already told us the worst thing about yourself, so why would you lie about anything else?"[41]

Kuehl ran her first assembly race against six men, but her credentials as a law professor and the head attorney at the California Women's Law Center made the voters in her district, the west end of Los Angeles and the San Fernando Valley, pay attention. (That she had once been Zelda also helped in starstruck Southern California.) When one of her opponents suggested that she was not fit for office because she was a lesbian, his smear campaign backfired on him. "People find it distasteful if you're not talking about the issues," she says. She herself brought up her homosexuality whenever she thought it relevant to make a point: for example, "It's like the experience of my gay-and-lesbian community . . . talents being wasted, people being treated like outsiders." Polls showed that she won because the issues on which she ran—education, the environment, and public safety—mattered most to her constituency. In other districts, it is possible that she would not have done so well in 1994, despite her focus on the issues; but in her district, with its affluent and well-educated population, she received 20 percent more of the vote than her closest contender.

Kuehl says that although her sexual orientation was of no interest to her constituents, she feared that it might make a difference to her colleagues. On her first day in the legislature, a newly elected Christian conservative announced on the assembly floor, "I don't want to make a mistake. What do I call you, Ms. or Mr.?" But his hostile voice was in the minority. At lunch that day, she was approached by John Vasconcellas, Antonio Villaraigosa, Kevin Murray (an African American), and a half dozen other assemblymen, who told her, "We don't want you to eat lunch by yourself, so we're gonna be the 'gay-and-lesbian caucus.'" She was voted the first-ever freshman chair of the California Assembly's judiciary committee, and, before her successful bid for the state senate in 2000, she became Speaker Pro Tem in the assembly.

Beginning with her second year in office, Kuehl had been introducing a bill to protect gay, lesbian, and transgendered students from harassment in California schools. It passed in 1999 as Assembly Bill 537, after the African American assemblyman, Herb Wesson, made "the most eloquent speech," Kuehl says. Publicly proclaiming to her and Carole Migden, a lesbian from Northern California who by then had joined Kuehl in the assembly, "Ms. Kuehl, Ms. Migden, this is not just your fight," Wesson demonstrated that Kuehl did indeed have a "caucus."

The following year she ran for the state senate on issues such as gun control and education. She won handily in an area that includes Hollywood, West Hollywood, Beverly Hills, Universal City, Malibu, Pacific Palisades, Brentwood, and Sherman Oaks—the richest district in the state, which is also socially liberal and well-populated by industry people.[42]

As Kuehl was contemplating her senate run, she encouraged another out lesbian politician from Los Angeles to run for the assembly. Jackie Goldberg had been president of the school board and in 1992 was elected to the Los Angeles City Council, representing Echo Park, an ethnically diverse, working-class district near downtown Los Angeles—an area with a population very different from the ones that put Sheila Kuehl in office. Goldberg had not been out when she ran for the city council because, she says, she and her partner, Sharon Stricker, were raising an adopted son and they feared he would be harassed by his classmates if it were known that he had lesbian mothers. But by the 1990s, L.A. gays would not tolerate what they saw as the hypocrisy of the closet. Goldberg admits that even close friends were angry when she did not come out during her city council campaign. The Stonewall Democratic Club, resenting her silence, outed her in the *Los Angeles Times*. (When she expressed concern to her son, then a high school senior and a basketball player, his response was, "Oh, Mom, no big deal. Jocks don't read the paper.")[43] Once outed, Goldberg actively targeted the gay voter. "I'd start out at midnight, go to all the gay bars. I'd stand on a bar stool and make my speech." Goldberg says now that her outing actually helped her race because many gay people who might not have voted, did; and since they made up at least 15 percent of her district, she won easily.

As a councilwoman she was sensitive to that strong constituency. As early as 1985, inspired by the neighboring city of West Hollywood, a task force had been appointed by the L.A. city government to study the issue of domestic partnership legislation. They recommended that the City of Los Angeles offer a full package of benefits for the domestic partners of all its employees. This was the first time in history that a *major* city had even considered the issue, though the recommendation was not adopted until 1993, when Goldberg drafted legislation to put those recommendations into effect. Thirteen of the fifteen council members voted in favor of it. As a result of its adoption, even businesses vying for city contracts are now informed: "If you do business with the City of Los Angeles, you must provide domestic partner benefits to all your employees."[44]

By the time Jackie Goldberg ran for the California State Assembly, in 1999, being openly lesbian in L.A. was clearly no hindrance. She received almost 75 percent of the vote and was even endorsed by *L'Opinion,* the major citywide Spanish paper, because, she explains, on the city council she'd fought to make Los Angeles the first major city with a living-wage ordinance, and the working-class Latinos in her district were grateful. That she was a lesbian, Goldberg says, was entirely irrelevant to them.[45]

In 2000, gay Angelenos, who had had good reasons in recent years to believe that their fellow citizens were behind them, received a shocking blow: Sixty-one percent of the California electorate, under right-wing-fomented hysteria, voted to approve Proposition 22, the Knight initiative that stated: "Only marriage between a man and a woman is valid or recognized in California." The proposition not only blocked gay marriage for Californians, but also preempted the possibility that a gay marriage that was valid in another state would be recognized in California. In 2003, Goldberg authored Assembly Bill 205 to cushion the worst effects of Proposition 22, which denied any legal recognition to gay commitments. The bill, which was approved by the California legislature, gave gay and lesbian domestic partners a panoply of rights, including community property protections, housing protections, and surviving-partner benefits.

Many California gays refuse still to relinquish their aspirations for the full spectrum of federal rights and the recognition that only marriage can provide, but with the exception that domestic partners cannot file a joint tax return, the bill completely mirrors California's marriage laws. It was signed by Governor Gray Davis and went into effect in 2005.[46]

The 2004 California elections brought six openly gay people to the state legislature: four out lesbians—Goldberg in the assemby; Kuehl, Migden, and Chris Kehoe in the senate; and two out gay men—Mark Leno and John Laird in the assembly, making the California State Legislature the only one in the union to have now a true gay-and-lesbian caucus.[47]

TAKING CARE OF OUR OWN

The Society for Senior Gay and Lesbian Citizens [will] help relieve the suffering of less fortunate Gay and Lesbian Senior Citizens who are forced to stare down the double-barreled gun of POVERTY and LONELY ISOLATION. . . . [Our] primary emphasis will be on COMMUNITY LIVING. . . . It is very cruel to expect a person to retreat back into the closet once they reach retirement age.

—Fund-raising appeal for a proposed L.A. "residence for needy older Gay and Lesbian Citizens," 1980[48]

Since homophobia has abated over the last couple of generations, fewer gays have felt compelled to marry someone of the opposite sex and leave the gay world—which means that they live in the gay community longer; and because people are also living longer, there are more elderly among L.A. gays than ever before. The community is expanding at the other end, too. More young people are becoming part of the gay world because in the current social milieu the young, including gays, have been discovering their sexuality earlier. Thus the gay population is not only larger than ever but also younger and older.

Attempts to address the special needs of the elderly in the gay community were frustrated in the past because money went to what appeared to be more pressing needs—for example, providing mental health services to a community that had been wounded; getting gay-friendly politicians elected; addressing the AIDS crisis. In 1980, Robert Arthur, a popular movie actor of the 1930s and '40s, established a non-profit public-benefit corporation, the Society for Senior Gay and Lesbian Citizens (SSGLC), its purpose being, as its logo announced, "Taking Care of Our Own." The main goal was to provide the first residential facility of its kind in the world, giving "food, shelter, and a place of acceptance and understanding to those Gay and Lesbian Citizens who find themselves alone and without adequate financial support in their senior years."[49]

SSCLC could not raise sufficient money for such a utopian facility, but in 1982, as an intermediate step, it was able to procure a "Project Rainbow" office at the Angelus Plaza, a 1,093-unit apartment complex for the elderly on Bunker Hill, which had once been a gay area. It was now estimated that from 4 to 10 percent of the residents were homosexual. Project Rainbow hoped to offer to them social gatherings, legal aid, field trips, and "mobile volunteer visiting." In an article headlined "Antidote to Loneliness," the *Los Angeles Times* announced that the city council's president, Joel Wachs, and an L.A. resident, Christine Jorgensen (who, in 1952, became the world's most famous transsexual), were on hand, along with hundreds of gay activists, to celebrate the official opening of the Project Rainbow Center at Angelus Plaza. A proclamation from Mayor Tom Bradley declaring a Gay/Lesbian Senior Citizens Week in Los Angeles hung in the Project Rainbow office.[50]

But not all the elderly residents of Angelus Plaza were thrilled to have openly gay people in their midst. A retired naval officer who had just moved in to Angelus Plaza when the Project Rainbow office opened protested that he had spent "thirty years keeping such people out of the navy [and] the first notice that caught [my] eye was an announcement of a lesbian women's meeting." A ninety-three-year-old resident complained of the gay and lesbian seniors who now openly shared the complex with him: "They're not natural. They belong with dogs and monkeys. . . . They ought to build a little island and send them all there."[51] What the lesbian and gay seniors needed was a residential facility of their own. But the AIDS crisis was already hitting the gay community. Charitable giving as well as government monies would soon be diverted to AIDS.[52] Young men were dying as in a holocaust, and a project for the elderly had to be put on the back burner.

Ivy Bottini, the veteran activist and leader in L.A.'s gay community, says that for twenty years she kept trying to raise the issue of housing for indigent lesbian and gay senior citizens, but it was "never the right time." Finally, she and John Fournier, who was head of Senior Services at the Gay and Lesbian Community Services Center, brought together representatives from various gay groups that dealt with the elderly. As they testified, it was not only indigent gays who needed special housing: "Even if we do have some money when we're old, we go into retirement homes and there we have to go back into the closet," they said. "If we have a partner, we have to take two rooms. That's horrible, too!" The group decided it would establish a nonprofit corporation, Gay and Lesbian Elder Housing, that would work to provide residential space for a socioeconomic spectrum of gay and lesbian elderly, including those who needed affordable housing.[53]

Unlike a generation earlier, when such a project was unfeasible, now L.A. gay money and political clout finally came together to serve what had been the most neglected gay population.[54] Eric Garcetti, a city council member, helped the group procure a piece of land in Hollywood, on Ivar Street and Selma Avenue. The Los Angeles City Council voted unanimously to transfer $6 million to the project. Plans got under way to build Encore Hall (appropriately named for its entertainment-industry site), which would be a complex of 104 one- and two-bedroom apartments for lesbian and gay seniors. An L.A. lesbian heiress donated $1.5 million to the project because she "wanted to make sure that more lesbians would be involved." Another woman donor instituted the "1,000 Women Campaign," pledging to give $100,000 if 1,000 other women would each give $100.[55] Gay and Lesbian Elder Housing finally raised $20 million to complete the project. In July 2005, officials and advocates for lesbian and gay seniors held a groundbreaking ceremony at Encore Hall's construction site for "the nation's first affordable housing facility aimed at older GLBT adults."[56] Thirty percent of the apartments have been set aside for people with AIDS or gay seniors "who are in immediate danger of being homeless." In the "Gayle Wilson Pool" (named for the deceased lesbian activist and real estate millionaire), senior aerobics will be taught. A large community center on the site will offer classes, plays, and musical entertainment.[57]

—

Since the 1920s, Hollywood has been a seductive magnet for attractive young people who have arrived from all over the country, suitcase in hand, at the Greyhound bus station, or by train at Union Station, hoping, often naïvely, to find a career in the movie industry. Gays, especially young gay men with artistic bent and dreams, were disproportionately represented among them. For many of those who did not make it, the choices could be grim: They could go home again; they could find menial jobs to keep themselves fed; they could hustle in the sex industry. Because existing social agencies had little interest in their particular problems, one of the reasons for the establishment of the Gay Community Services Center in 1972 was to help just such a population by providing shelter and food, so they would not feel forced to prostitute themselves. The center was soon being contacted regularly by the Los Angeles Probation Department to help deal with "displaced" gay youth, especially in the Hollywood area. In 1982, Los Angeles City Council members who had long political ties to the gay community, including Zev Yaroslavsky, Peggy Stevenson, and Joel Wachs, helped the Gay Community Services Center in securing a block grant to purchase property in Hollywood for a facility for homeless lesbian and gay teenagers. Martel House, as it was called, was professionally staffed and provided counseling, education, and social services in a supportive "home" environment.

Los Angeles is still the number one destination for homeless youth in the country, and it is estimated that 30 percent of them are gay, lesbian, bisexual, or transgendered (GLBT).[58] The Gay and Lesbian Center (the present name of the Gay and Lesbian Community Services Center) has expanded its services for them over the years. Its Jeffrey Griffith Youth Center is a drop-in facility on Santa Monica Boulevard. The site was chosen because gay boys often work that district, known as Hustlers' Row, for food and a place to stay.[59] The youth center now serves about 7,000

GLBT young people each year with counseling, free meals, showers, and clothing. The Gay and Lesbian Center also has a residential program, Kruks/Tilsner, which houses young people whose ages range from eighteen to twenty-four (about 60 percent are male, 30 percent female, 8 percent transgendered, and 2 percent undeclared) for up to eighteen months.[60] Most of the youths are "rescued off the streets" where they, too, have been engaging in survival prostitution. The Center has vans that travel the area so that program personnel can spot likely candidates and offer to take them to the shelter.[61]

Such resources proliferate in Los Angeles. The existence of one inspires others. Several other programs to serve youth were born at the Gay and Lesbian Center or have been influenced—sometimes in unlikely ways—by the center. A Los Angeles high school teacher, Virginia Uribe, wandered into the center's Lesbian Central office around 1982. She was close to fifty years old, had long been a lesbian, but had been too scared to seek out gay events; this was her first excursion into a large group of homosexuals. "I found a great cross-section of people, just like in the rest of the world (except the men I saw around the Center were a lot better looking than guys in the rest of the world). They welcomed me in. I finally felt like I was a part of something," she says. The experience made her especially sensitive to a student at her school, an effeminate young man. "The other kids spat at him," she remembers. "They threw eggs at him. He was never given a chance to be 'a part of something.'" When he fought back, he was expelled from school.

Remembering her happy experiences of inclusion and her student's wretched exclusion, Uribe put up a sign in her class announcing that she would conduct a "Gay Support Group" during lunch hours.

The group came to be called "Project 10" (with reference to the statistic that about 10 percent of the population is gay). Within a month, twenty-five students were attending Project 10 meetings. Books on gay subjects were ordered for the high school library, and a bulletin board announced gay news such as the celebration of National Coming Out Day. Uribe's goal was to keep gay youth in school and to keep them from despair. It was, she says, the first such program in the country to address the needs of gay kids in mainstream schools.[62] Once teachers elsewhere began hearing about Project 10, they would call the very supportive principal at Fairfax High School, Warren Steinberg, to say, "We need a Project 10 at our school. How do we do it?" Project 10 became the inspiration for "Gay-Straight Alliance" groups, which now exist in almost all the secondary schools in Los Angeles and in many schools all over America. Uribe suggests that Project 10 even triggered the impulse behind the "Dignity for All Students" bill, sponsored by Sheila Kuehl, which added protection from harassment on account of "sexual orientation and gender" to the California State Education Code.[63]

But Uribe's Project did encounter opposition. Lou Sheldon of the Traditional Values Coalition wrote to state legislators saying, "Did you know they are teaching a sodomy class at Fairfax High School? They are teaching the kids how to get AIDS." He attacked Uribe directly as a lesbian, calling her "a fox guarding the henhouse." U.S. Senator Jesse Helms ordered an investigation into whether Project 10 was receiving federal funds. (It was not.) In 1988, Sheldon convinced a right-wing assemblywoman on the Education Committee to introduce a resolution to suspend all state money coming into Los Angeles schools until Project 10 was stopped.

The City of Los Angeles and the L.A. media came to Uribe's defense. All the members of the Los Angeles Board of Education not only signed a "big scroll" honoring Uribe,[64] but also expressed the board's strong commitment to diversity and reiterated that commitment in a 1990 document that established guidelines for dealing with diversity throughout the school district. An entire page of supportive letters appeared in the *Los Angeles Times,* along with a powerful editorial defending her and the program. City council members castigated Sheldon and his followers directly for opposing a program that had been established for the purpose of "keeping kids from killing themselves."

Another major program for youth that was inspired by L.A.'s Gay and Lesbian Center is Terry DeCrescenzo's Gay and Lesbian Adolescent Social Services (GLASS). DeCrescenzo was president of the Center's board of directors when Martel House was being established. Through her own experience working at the Los Angeles County Probation Department she had seen that gay and lesbian adolescents, sometimes only twelve years old, desperately needed even more than Martel House (aimed at teens and young adults) could offer. In existing agencies, gay kids were abused, treated as though they were mentally ill, and held up to ridicule. She decided she would focus her career on helping such children. Again, L.A. money made it possible. In 1984, she obtained a large unsecured personal loan from the gay activist-millionaire Sheldon Andelson, who had just started his own bank, and with that money DeCrescenzo opened GLASS's first group home to address the needs of L.A.'s huge population of GLBT throwaway children. Eventually, seven group homes were opened, and GLASS became a model for gay adolescent residential programs "from Indiana to Israel."[65]

For a time, however, GLASS' survival was in question. DeCrescenzo says that in the early 1990s, her program was constantly being harassed by the Department of Social Services (DSS). GLASS was attacked with allegations such as had always been the nightmare of gay adults who work with youth:

> DSS didn't even want to know from gay kids. When I started talking about transgendered kids, they were really unhappy. They went on a fishing expedition. They got one of our kids and said, "We heard you're having sex with one of the staff." He said, "No!" They said, "We know you're lying." The investigation went on for two years. They even had people go to the Gay Pride Festival and find our kids and say, "We hear you're having sex with the staff." They terrorized the staff and the kids.

Finally, seven men on the staff were accused of sexual malfeasance. The children were removed from the group homes—those on probation as juvenile delinquents were led away in shackles. DeCrescenzo was served with a "lifetime exclusion order," forbidding her from working ever again in social services in California, or even from being in the presence of a minor. Sensationalistic media accused her of "pimping the boys off to major donors," DeCresenzo says. She fought the charges in court, and ultimately not one of them could be upheld. GLASS was, nevertheless, put on a five-year probationary period. "For a long time, the staff members were afraid to be alone with a kid, even for a minute," she says.

Those difficult years came to an end, and GLASS now continues to flourish, serving 1,500 adolescents a year on a $10 million budget. The adolescents, most from poor Latino and African American families, are referred to GLASS from the Los Angeles Department of Mental Health, the Department of Children and Family Services, and the Probation Department. Many of them had been street kids who supported themselves by drug dealing and prostitution. Many had grown up "in the system," moving from one foster home to another because their parents were incarcerated, abusive, drug addicts, or otherwise dysfunctional. Michael Marchand, the director of GLASS's day treatment program, says the children wind up at GLASS, generally, because their gender behavior had been an uncomfortable issue in their other placements. He gives the example of one very effeminate boy who was constantly being beaten up by the other children in his previous group home and was told by the staff, "If you didn't act like such a sissy, they wouldn't pick on you." The only way he knew to prevent a beating was to smear his feces all over himself.[66]

Although the children in GLASS are not always kind to one another, no one ever gets harassed because they are not "appropriately" masculine or feminine. Sexuality appears to be of less concern to GLASS adolescents than gender expression. Many of the girls are "studs" or wear boys' clothes exclusively. A few of the boys wear makeup and feminine clothes. Some say they will have a sex-change operation when they are older. "Lucy" has been in GLASS for three years. He was raped by a seventeen-year-old boy when he was six or seven, taken from his drug-addicted mother by Child Protective Services, and placed in Five Acres and then Vista del Mar group homes for children. There, he says, the kids would call him faggot and "give me shit everyday because I always loved to do girl's things." He sees himself as a lesbian—that is, he prefers girls and feels that he, too, is a girl. At GLASS, he met another transgendered male-to-female adolescent who "showed me how to walk and talk like a girl should"; now his GLASS counselor "tells me how to carry myself like a lady. She says, 'Don't put your makeup on in class. Don't curse. Don't burp.' She gives me tips about lipstick and eye shadow and blush, and we talk about ladies clothing, like what you should buy." Lucy remembers that "Before, I used to be a demon. I'd bite people. I'd go AWOL from my placement." Now, he says, "everyone tells me I'm a beautiful spirit."[67]

"Jessica," who has been at GLASS for two years, "likes boys" and feels "like a woman," but he has never had a "serious relationship." When his mother could not take care of him, he went to live with his aunt, and at thirteen he was raped by her husband's cousin. Jessica was sent to group homes and foster care where he was beaten up so often that he began to cut himself on his arms—"to get some of the pain out," he says. Jessica was in a mental hospital for six months before winding up at GLASS. He goes to Oasis, a continuation school for gay and lesbian youth during the day, and lives in a GLASS group home. His GLASS counselor, he says, "buys me teddy bears every time I get an A at school."[68]

Many of the children at GLASS suffer insurmountable depression because of past trauma. Some are suicidal; several, like Jessica, are "cutters." But others are clearly making it. "Mary," who had run away from her mother's house "because of all the men raping girls, and all the drugs and gang-banging going on," met up with a pimp who put her on the streets. She was sent to GLASS after she was arrested and told a probation worker she was bisexual. She has a girlfriend now—"a stud," Mary says, "who looks like a guy"—who is also in the GLASS residency program. Mary has been at GLASS for eighteen months. She is on the honor roll in high school and is taking a class at West Los Angeles Junior College. She also has a job working with elementary school children in an after-school enrichment program. "I put my past in a box and threw it away," she says. "I'm never going to look for that box again." But, she observes, not all the kids she knows in GLASS have such happy stories. "A lot of them, maybe 60 percent of them, just have to step out on the street and they can get in trouble again. They [go] AWOL, do drugs. They don't take things seriously here anymore than they did anywhere else."[69]

Still, her success story is not unique. "Junior," who is seventeen years old, has been at GLASS for a year. She calls herself a "stud" and says she knew she was gay from the time she was twelve, when she lived with her mother and five brothers in a barrio in Wilmington. Her mother was a cocaine addict, and Junior started selling drugs before she was in her teens. Junior's life has been violent. She was raped by one of her mother's husbands, her mother's boyfriends, her uncles. She was a cutter and attempted suicide repeatedly. She was living in foster homes, juvenile hall, and a mental hospital more than she was living with her mother, who was incarcerated when Junior was fourteen. Junior seldom went to school. Now, she says, she has 144 high school units, her grades are high, and she is president of the Activities Board at GLASS, which she sees as a great honor—"I never would have thought it could happen." Her therapist and her girlfriend at GLASS have made all the difference, she claims. Now she knows what she wants to do. "The big thing," she says, "is I don't want to be like my mom." She hopes to go to college when she graduates from SEA Girls Academy, the charter school to which GLASS sends her. "I want to become a psychotherapist. I knew a lot of therapists, at the mental hospital and places, who don't know how to do it because they haven't been through what their clients have. I've been there. I'll know how to do it."[70]

GLASS not only runs group homes but also subsidizes foster parents (75 percent of whom are lesbian or gay), offers services such as job-skill training, and supports a doctor's office on wheels that provides health care to street kids. Some of GLASS's money comes from public agencies, but the gay and lesbian community in Los Angeles has also supported GLASS well. There are donors' brunches, for instance, where a GLASS resident, seventeen-year-old "Leticia," reads her poems; they have titles such as "Look—Do You See Me or Just a Placement Child?" and "Where I've Been and Where I'm Going," the latter being an autobiographical piece about being molested and having to grow up too fast.[71]

Terry DeCrescenzo says that it helps that GLASS is based in Los Angeles, a city of celebrities and wealth. "We had a fund-raiser for Gay and Lesbian Adolescent Social Services to which we invited ten donors, at $5,000 a plate, to have dinner with Ellen DeGeneres and her mother. We sold half the tickets the first day. Nobody batted an eye at the cost."[72] Gay L.A.'s legendary obsession with power and glamour can be turned to good use, as she observes, in the service of the most vulnerable members of the community.

One of the community ads placed by Asian Pacific Islanders for Human Rights. *Courtesy
APIHR.*

The Twenty-first Century

As with most social trends, especially the ones involving tomorrow, what is true of the world is doubly true of America, and what is doubly true of America is quadruply true of Los Angeles.

—Pico Iyer, "Where Worlds Collide"[1]

THE CHANGES in gay life over the past half-century have been astonishing. They have surpassed by far the fantasies that Wally Jordan spun in his 1943 letters to Jim Kepner about the Sons of Hamidy, the marvelous (nonexistent) organization of socially and politically prominent homosexuals. In 2002, a blue ribbon committee was appointed to select a new chief of police for Los Angeles, and a seat on it was reserved for the openly lesbian executive director of the Gay and Lesbian Center, Lorri Jean. In 2004, during the L.A. mayoral race, Antonio Villaraigosa, campaigning energetically in the gay community, chided the incumbent for making only ten gay appointments out of 364 slots. "That's offensive!" Villaraigosa said.[2] He won the election.

That gay people would not only cease to be persecuted by police and politicians but would also be wooed by them under official policy; that they would not only have public faces but those faces would be of all races and ethnicities; that transgender people (who had been even more despised than the homosexuals with whom they were associated) should come out in the daylight and organize; that unbiased portrayals of gays should someday be beamed from L.A. into the world's living rooms and be shown on the big screen everywhere—these were beyond Jordan's wildest dreams.

CORNUCOPIA

I was already an ethnic minority there. That was hard enough. I didn't want to stick out as a sexual minority, too. In Los Angeles I don't feel like I stick out that much.

— Kim Swindle-Bautista, a Korean who
was adopted and raised in Indiana[3]

Los Angeles, always a magnet for the adventurer, the disaffected, the haven-seeker, continues to be a Promised Land for gay people from everywhere. It is a global village to which gay immigrants continue to be drawn because life back home can be immeasurably more difficult. Ewa, a Polish chess champion, was first sent to the United States for an international tournament. She says she immediately longed to stay, though it was "very stressful" for her to learn to speak English. She fought to remain in Los Angeles because she "hated how closed" Poland was for gay people. "*Lesbijka* has a very negative connotation there," she says. "I had to always keep secret who I was." In L.A. she easily found an open lesbian culture: "For a person who had to hide all the time, coming into a roomful of women who could sit in a circle and talk openly about their women lovers . . . well, it was so amazing."[4]

In recent years, there has been an enormous flowering in and around L.A. of gay organizations for immigrants, as well as for people of color, who are increasingly willing to be out. For example, there is now a Russian and Eastern European Gay and Lesbian Group that meets on the border of West Hollywood. There is GALAS, the Gay and Lesbian Armenian Society of Los Angeles. There is ELAD for "Ebony Lesbians of Afrikaan Descent." Not only is there O-Moi for Vietnamese lesbians,[5] but also an organization of gay and lesbian Asian Pacific Islanders has designed services and programs for twenty-seven Asian ethnicities in Los Angeles. The proliferation of gay Latino organizations has been especially impressive (though not unexpected because Los Angeles now includes more same-sex Latino households than any other place in America);[6] there is Latinas Understanding the Need for Action (LUNA) for Latina lesbians and bisexuals, Sabores for "Gay, Lesbian, Transgender and Bisexual Youth," Latinas and Friends for Latina lesbians and those who love them, a reconstructed Gay and Lesbian Latinos Unidos, Que Onda Queers, "Groupo de Apoyo Para Lesbianas Latinas," Gay Latinos/Latinas Bible Study, Tu for Spanish-speaking transgenders, and Vida for Spanish-speaking HIV+ transgenders.[7]

Though many groups meet a quick demise after the initial burst of enthusiasm, others invariably crop up to take their place. The tenor of these organizations keeps evolving. For example, Luis Lopez, a policy analyst, who says he was "amazed at the lack of civic engagement from the largest concentration of gay Latinos in the country,"[8] founded "Honor PAC," a political action committee for LGBT Latinos. ("Honor" translates as "pride" in Spanish). Lopez, thirty-two, had never heard of MECLA (Municipal Elections Committee of Los Angeles), which flourished almost thirty years earlier, but he understands the political potential of gay Latinos who are now coming into the middle class in large numbers. His goals are similar to those MECLA had, except that he hopes to work specifically with Latinos to raise money and support candidates that "serve the unique needs and interests of Latina/o/LGBT communities."[9]

L.A.'s abundance makes possible a profusion of alternatives for a profusion of gay populations. For gay Latinos who are not politically active, for example, bars and clubs continue to proliferate: Red's, Circus Disco, the Plaza, and Chico now have competition from such venues as Club Bravo, Coco Bongo, Fuego, Club Infierno, El Maguey, El Calor, Olé Olé, OZZ, Club Tomboys, Club Tempo, Club Temptations, and Club Papi.[10] Those who see themselves outside the common working-class affinity of gays of color can also find limitless new affinities in Los Angeles. Julia Salazar says that though her parents speak Spanish, she never learned the language, and professionally and socially she has blended in with an upper-middle-class gay community whose ethnicity is not a major factor in their lives.[11] Monserrat Fontes, a lesbian writer whose family is from Mexico, points out that Mexicans have been "the working backbone of this state," and she is involved in registering Latina women to vote; but, she says, "I don't even know where the Chicana lesbian groups are. I'm doing more than I can handle now. Call me and I'll send money, but that's about it."[12] Both Salazar and Fontes have been in long-term relationships with women who are not Latina. Davi Cheng, whose family came to Los Angeles via China and Hong Kong, says she "never felt comfortable in an Asian lesbian group." She converted to Judaism in 1997 and organized a klezmer band at the gay and lesbian synagogue, Beth Chayim Chadishm, where she also became president of the congregation.[13]

As more gays of color have been willing to take a proverbial "walk down Crenshaw"—Lisa Powell's phrase for being out anywhere, even in one's parent community—they have altered the previously monochromatic public face of gay L.A. Charlene Nguon, for example, a suburban Los Angeles high school student from an Asian family, has become the poster girl for a minor's right to privacy regarding sexual orientation. Nguon, who refused to stop "hugging, kissing, and holding hands with her girlfriend," brought a lawsuit against the school district when her principal informed her parents of her homosexual behavior. Her suit, supported by the American Civil Liberties Union of Southern California as well as her family, argues that "a student has a right not to have her sexual orientation disclosed to her parents, even if she is out of the closet at school." Nguon also seeks to create a district-wide policy that would not treat gay students differently from their straight counterparts when they express affection.[14] Such visibility speaks eloquently to parent communities of color that have often in the past dismissed homosexuality as a "white disease," to the pain of their gay children.

Gay people of color in Los Angeles have also been waging campaigns that tackle directly the homophobia of their parent communities, such as the Asian Pacific Islanders for Human Rights ads in numerous Asian language newspapers that are published in Los Angeles: Each ad features the image of an attractive Asian lesbian, gay, or transgendered young person, stating, for example, "I am your daughter/cousin/sister/friend/ neighbor/co-worker. I am also a lesbian. . . . I ask for your tolerance and acceptance of me as part of our community."[15]

There is some evidence that such efforts by gays of color have been working—that the parent communities are beginning to acknowledge the gay sexuality of some of its members and to understand gays as another legitimate minority group. In January 2006, the Asian Pacific American Legal Center of Southern California, along with 250 other civil rights and church groups, including the NAACP, the Mexican-American Legal Defense and Education Fund, and the National Black Justice Coalition, filed a joint amicus brief asking the California Court of Appeals to apply a 1948 California Supreme Court decision, Perez v. Sharp—which struck down laws banning interracial marriage—to gay marriage. Karen Wang, vice president of the Asian Pacific American Legal Center, declared, "People of color in California are sadly familiar with marriage discrimination, as many of our communities were targets of racially restrictive marriage rules in the past [and must] stand together in support of marriage equality [for gays]."[16] The connection she draws between racism and homophobia represents a moving victory for gay people of color. Their parent communities have begun to come to their defense. Although support is certainly not universal in communities of color,[17] that it should be so publicly and well articulated would have been unimaginable in earlier eras.

It is also a moving victory for gay people in general. L.A.'s Mattachine Society first voiced in the 1950s the revolutionary concept that gays were a "cultural minority." Discrimination against homosexuals, they said, is no different from discrimination against other minorities. Both prejudices are rooted in the dominant society's unjust and irrational impulse to demonize the "other." Wang's assertion that "the civil rights of all communities are inseparably linked" is what gay people have tried to argue all along.

TRANS LOS ANGELES

Many mixed race people are saying that race, as a means of cate-gorizing people, no longer works. Transgender people are showing us that gender, as a similar construct, has no meaning either.

—"Era of the Gender Crosser," *Los Angeles Times*, 2001 [18]

Transgender people have always been drawn to L.A. where they could find community or pass far more easily than they could in smaller towns; and historically, performing a gender other than the one into which they were born may have felt more comfortable in a city of performers than it would have been elsewhere. It is not surprising that George Jorgensen, an ex-G.I. who grabbed headlines in 1952 when Danish doctors helped him become "Christine Jorgensen," decided to settle in Los Angeles. She aspired to the profession of "Hollywood photographer or actress," she announced, and was soon "deluged [with] fabulous contract offers." She lived as a celebrity in L.A.[19] It was also in L.A., in 1970, that "Virginia Prince," the male publisher of the magazine *Transvestia* (1960–1976), coined the word "transgender," which became an umbrella term to describe both those who were transsexuals such as Jorgensen, and those who were transvestites, as Prince was.[20]

But Christine Jorgensen and the performativity of Hollywood culture notwithstanding, for much of L.A.'s history, transgenders had a difficult time with the police, and, as the mid-twentieth-century drag queen Miss Destiny observed, they were "outcast among outcasts."[21] For years, transgender activists agitated for more sensitivity among law enforcement officers, and Los Angeles has witnessed important changes in official attitudes.[22] The captain of West Hollywood's Sheriff's Station, Richard Odenthal, worked with transgender support groups at the end of the twentieth century to create a "briefing program" for his deputies when he realized that some officers were "having trouble dealing with the growing transgender population in the city." West Hollywood became officially supportive of transgenders. Odenthal observed that although some deputies were sympathetic to begin with, others "needed a bit more time, and some still did not like the idea." But, he added, their prejudices would not be tolerated: "They know that they are expected to behave professionally." A seven-member task force was appointed by city officials "to study the needs" of the transgender population.[23]

As in other big American cities, the transgender community in L.A. is organizing seriously, sponsoring "Transgender Days of Remembrance" to memorialize those who were killed in the past by hate crimes; Transgender Leadership Summits to help groups all over California strategize methods for local organizing; and annual Transunity Conferences, which are "pride" events for "transsexual, transgender, gender-queer, and cross-dressing individuals and those who love and care for them," and have been drawing more than 1,000 people each year.[24] As the *Los Angeles Times* suggested in a two-part article on transgenders in 2001, the community has "found a voice" because it has been "buoyed by the successes of gay liberation and freed by medical advances."[25]

The first attempt to bring transgenders together in Los Angeles was in 1980, but the secretive group remained small and wound down after a few years.[26] Bamby Salcedo, an MTF from Mexico, migrated to L.A. in 1986, at the age of eighteen, when a friend wrote her that in Hollywood "there was a lot of 'family,'" that is, other male-to-female transsexuals. "I did what many of us do," says Salcedo, who was unable to speak English. "I came to Santa Monica Boulevard and started doing sex work." Salcedo, who had been sexually abused as a child and started sniffing glue by age nine, found that drugs were easily available on the streets of Hollywood. After years of taking heroin, meth, and crack, she concedes, she was "pretty much a garbage can."[27] She complains that there was little by way of community services in L.A. to pull transwomen like her back from the edge.[28]

But in more recent years, Salcedo says, AIDS programs have been helping L.A. transwomen. She believes her life took a turn when she was invited to a party of trans "girls" sponsored by the Latino AIDS service, Bienestar. "The other girls I knew before were either from the street or in prison. I'd never seen such a party of girls . . . like a fun, clean party." Salcedo signed up as a client with Bienestar and completed an addiction treatment program. She was offered employment as a Bienestar case manager and works in an office on Sunset Boulevard, decorated with posters by Frida Kahlo, whose bright palette is reflected in the makeup of the "girls" who are employed there. Salcedo's job is to refer transwomen to clinics and other services. But she hopes also to expand transgender organizing, observing that the few MTFs she knows who have been politically active have worked mostly for AIDS groups. "For transgenders there's so many other issues that our community [largely working-class, people of color MTFs] needs to address. Drug abuse. Incarceration. Homelessness. Prostitution." Because there is no organization for transwomen, Salcedo has joined the board of the FTM Alliance.

Much of the transgender leadership in Los Angeles has come from transmen—female-to-male transgenders—though they have needed to overcome barriers in order to organize. As might be expected, female-to-male transgenders (FTM) have been less flamboyant in their life styles than many male-to-female transgenders. Masen Davis, a founder of the FTM Alliance, points out that one of their biggest obstacles to organizing has been that many FTMs hope only to get on with their lives in their chosen gender, and in vast Los Angeles, where one can don a new identity as easily as a costume, that hope is not unrealistic. But the increasing visibility of transgenders (including their big-screen visibility in the successful 2005 Hollywood film *Transamerica*) has stimulated the growth of the FTM Alliance. Transman Daniel Gould, a staff person for the Alliance, says the group is reaching a broader population also because biological females are now identifying as FTM at a young age and have more family support than their counterparts did in the past. A Significant Others group, which the Alliance had intended originally for partners of transpeople, is now serving many parents of minors who are transgender. Most of the children range in age from eleven to fourteen, but the youngest, Gould says, is five.[29]

The issues of gender and identity have become increasingly complex and increasingly conceptualized in big cities such as Los Angeles. It has long been recognized that not all transvestites are gay: "Virginia Prince," for example, insisted that transvestites were generally heterosexual, married, and fathers—as he himself was.[30] It is now also recognized that not all transsexuals, pre- or post-op, become "straight." Many prefer bisexuality or homosexuality. A *Los Angeles Times* article on L.A. transsexuals, "Fitting into Their Own Skin," featured one couple, Boe Randal, an FTM who was born Karen Ann, and his spouse, Mona Rios, an MTF who was born William John.[31] The possible permutations of sexual identity among transsexuals are copious.

The possible permutations of gender identity are also copious. Transsexualism is merely one choice among many. Raquel Gutierrez, a founder of Butchlalis de Panochtitlan, a Los Angeles performance group of "butch stars of pussylandia . . . for gender muthaphukkin," explains the vast array of options for those who do not accept the usual roles. She points out the subtle gradations between numerous gender concepts, such as "butch," "stud," boi," and "baby daddy." For instance, "butch," in the historical sense, she says, is reliant on its binary opposite, "femme." Gutierrez rejects the term "butch" for herself because it is too limited and she does not need a femme to be who she is. She calls herself a "boi," and at twenty-nine says she looks like a fifteen-year-old boy. She believes the "boi" concept "relates to a sophisticated understanding of gender presentation," permitting her, Peter Pan–like, to "play with gender maturity or the lack of it." Gutierrez is not interested in becoming a transman "because the surgery is too big, and anyway I'm content as I am. I don't feel that much of a man." She finds gradations not only in gender and sexual identities but in all aspects of identity. She says she "exhausted [her] identity as a 'lesbian of color'" when that community was critical of her dating a white woman. But, as she affirms, there is a panoply of identities from which to chose in expansive gay L.A.[32]

HOLLYWOOD IN THE TWENTY-FIRST CENTURY

Everything I had hoped would be true when I was eighteen years old mostly is in Hollywood.

— David Taylor, the executive director of Out at Warner Brothers[33]

For most of Hollywood's history, the strong gay and lesbian presence there, which has always helped fashion American culture, was kept more or less secret from the outside world. Gay Hollywood today, if not precisely rushing from the closet, is coming out gradually. The ubiquitous presence of gays in various parts of the industry has ceased to be a Hollywood secret. Working openly now—as producers, directors, programming heads, screenwriters—gays bring increasingly complex gay themes and characters into movies and television, and they have even established new television networks that speak directly to a national gay audience. Though most gay actors still share the fear of their earlier counterparts that their onscreen credibility in heterosexual roles would be compromised if they declared themselves, straight actors are no longer as panicked (as Tommy Lee Jones was when offered the lead in *The Frontrunner* in the 1980s) about playing gay. Some gay actors are coming out—women while they are working and men after they stop working: for example, Ellen DeGeneres, Rosie O'Donnell, Lily Tomlin, Tab Hunter, Richard Chamberlaine, and George Takei.

The distance Hollywood movies have been able to travel with regard to the subject of homosexuality is particularly impressive if one compares, for example, the 1946 film about Cole Porter's life, *Night and Day,* which totally suppressed his homosexuality, with the twenty-first-century version: In *De-Lovely* (2004), the Cole Porter character is shown kissing his virtually naked male lover, hosting one of his famous Hollywood parties where the guests are a bevy of obviously gay male beauties, and staring seductively into the eyes of a singer and future trick as he coaches the young man on the vocal intricacies of "Night and Day." Though the movie industry still has a way to go before gay and lesbian audiences can feel they are being depicted in all their diversity and complexity, films of the early twenty-first century have shown Asian American lesbians living happily ever after *(Saving Face);* African American lesbians and white lesbians happily giving male chauvinist pigs their comeuppance *(She Hate Me* and *Broken Flowers);* male homosexuals who are supermacho and those who are effete *(Alexander* and *Capote);* lesbian cheerleaders who double as secret agents *(D.E.B.S.);* and gay men who are the only sane beings in a dysfunctional world *(The Family Stone).*

The phenomenon of *Brokeback Mountain,* the gay cowboy love story, heralds even more remarkable change. It opened to the highest per-screen attendance average of any movie of its year (2005). Its success at the box of-fice—earning about $150 million worldwide in its first two months—indi-cated that its appeal went far beyond the "gay niche."[34] Multiplex theaters in such unlikely places as Tulsa, Oklahoma, had to add extra screens to satisfy audience demands for showings.[35] It swept the major critics' awards (voted best picture by the New York Film Critics Circle, the Los Angeles Film Crit-ics Association, the San Francisco Film Critics, the Boston Society of Film Critics, the Dallas-Fort Worth Film Critics Association, the Utah Film Crit-ics, the Iowa Film Critics, the St. Louis Film Critics Association, etc.).[36] It swept the Golden Globes awards.[37] It had more Oscar nominations than any film that year and received three Academy Awards, including one for the best adapted screenplay and one for the best director.[38]

By 2005, gay men and lesbians had also become a staple on network television. If, as culture critic Larry Gross has suggested, television is the greatest source of "common information and images that create and maintain a world view and a value system,"[39] the old view and system that had long worked against gay people appears to be under deadly attack. Hollywood now brings a profusion of images of likable and human gay characters to the general populace.[40] Stories about lesbian parenting, un-conventional gender identity, and coping with HIV infection are common fare on mainstream legal and medical shows. The multiseason runs of broadcast and cable programs in which gay characters or personalities are prominent—such as *Will and Grace,* the *Ellen* talk show, *Six Feet Under, ER, Queer Eye for the Straight Guy,* and *The L Word*—have given birth to yet a new surge of broadcast programs that includes major gay episodes or features gays regularly.[41] Some gay media pundits have worried that this rapid proliferation merely indicates a transitory "gay craze," and that the fickle medium will retreat to its old malign neglect. Time will, of course, tell, but as of the first half-dozen years of the new century gay characters have been presented in ways that are increasingly daring. In the first scene of the ABC weekly comedy series, *Crumbs,* for example, the very sympa-thetic main character wakes up in bed next to another man. The pro-gram's out writer-producer, Marco Pennette, says that when he shared this idea for an opening scene with executives at ABC they "didn't blink": "We can show this on TV in 2005. The world will keep spinning."[42]

Perhaps the growing inclusion of gay people on broadcast television was nudged by the sudden appearance of three gay television networks, which threatened to siphon off what was perceived as an affluent gay audience. The first, Here! TV, began in 2003 and soon had competition from Logo, a network backed by MTV and Viacom. Logo, established in 2005, became the first-ever basic cable channel to devote itself exclusively to programs with LGBT content. (Q Television Network began in 2004, with satellite and digital cable subscribers in urban areas across the country, but met its demise within two years. The broadband channel OutzoneTV.com soon sprang up to take its place.

Whether gay networks will be able to sustain a place in a competitive market also remains to be seen, but their birth is a quintessential example of the current risk taking and stretching in the industry. Meredith Kadlec, vice president of original programming at Here! TV, observes of the innovative concept of gay networks: "In Hollywood, the old adage is, 'Everything has been done before.' But not in this realm!" What can be done that is new in soap opera?—Here! TV's *Dante's Cove,* a soap opera about Kevin and his gay pals battling supernatural forces in their town. What can be done in a comedy-drama serial that is original?—Logo's *Noah's Arc,* about a screenwriter in Los Angeles who is an African American gay man. Action films?— Here! TV's produced-for-television movie about a lesbian hero who "kicks ass and gets the girl."[43]

Onscreen gay ubiquity has been greatly aided by the growing number of "out" gay people in high places in the industry. Since the 1992 founding of Hollywood Supports by the former Fox chair, Barry Diller, and the MCA president, Sidney Sheinberg, the Hollywood closet, whose door had been soldered shut in mid-century, opens wider and wider, at least for those who work behind the camera. The president of entertainment at Showtime is out, for example, as is the president of entertainment at the WB television network.[44] They acknowledge their responsibility to the larger world. As the WB president of entertainment observed shortly after his appointment: "It would be really remiss of me if I didn't try to find shows on this network that accurately reflect gay life."[45] At the major studios, David Taylor, who is an executive assistant to a vice president at Warner Home Videos, observes, "There's no tolerance for prejudice. It's explicit. Diversity is encouraged." Since 2002, Warner Brothers has been sponsoring Out at Warner Brothers, an industry affinity group of gays and lesbians, which now has hundreds of members and is a major presence at gay events such as the Outfest Film Festival.[46]

Lesbians have not yet had the same degree of prominence and success as have gay men in behind-the-camera Hollywood (reflecting perhaps the male-female success ratio in much of the outside world). But young lesbians in the industry are reassured in their ambitions by the out lesbians who have made it, and the current milieu encourages them to be out, too. Ashley Kaplan, the twenty-four-year-old manager of development for Evolution, a reality television production firm, says that her role model is Caroline Strauss, the out president for original programming at HBO, who has been responsible for shows such as *Six Feet Under*, which regularly presents gay characters.[47] Meredith Kadlec says that since joining the industry in 1994 (two years after the founding of Hollywood Supports) she has never been closeted: "If there are people at some industry meeting who don't know, I find a way to drop it into the conversation." She believes that homosexuality is even a "plus" in Hollywood: "There's a 'hip' factor in being a lesbian."[48] (Joe Libonati, a thirty-year-old publicist for NBC, says that for men, too, "in this city and industry, being gay helps tremendously.")[49]

Young lesbians in the industry have also organized in order to encourage one another. POWER UP (Professional Organization of Women in Entertainment Reaching Up) was founded in 2000 "to promote the integration and visibility of gay women in all areas of the industry." The 1,500-member group finances short films made by its members, and Stacy Codikow, POWER UP's founder, proudly points to its various successes—such as the production of a short movie of *D.E.B.S.* (by the African American filmmaker Angela Robinson), which was then bought by Screen Gems and made into a successful full-length feature film.[50]

Among the most encouraging developments for lesbians in the industry has been the comedy-drama series, *The L Word,* which the television executive and producer Ilene Chaiken pitched to Showtime after witnessing the triumphs of *Will & Grace* and *Queer as Folk.*[51] Chaiken's project was an instant success in its first year, and Showtime "renewed it faster than any series in its history."[52] *The L Word,* about a group of lipstick lesbians in West Hollywood, affects lesbian life in the real world, too. GirlBar, a West Hollywood venue, packs in hundreds of *L Word* lookalikes, who also gather at places such as the Falcon, an upscale West Hollywood restaurant, for huge *L Word* viewing parties.[53] But the series' impact goes further: Just as groups of lesbians in the 1950s used to gather on Sundays in living rooms around the country to hear the weekly radio programs of Tallulah Bankhead (whom they knew was a lesbian by her enchanting whiskey voice and their own gaydar), so have they been gathering, in greater numbers now, around television sets or DVDs everywhere to watch *The L Word.* Hollywood lipstick-lesbian style thus spreads across America.

The gay styles that Hollywood promotes spread across America for men, too, as they have since the 1920s when Rudolph Valentino influenced the look of the American male.[54] Cowboy wear had been long out of fashion, but—as the *New York Times* observed in 2006—though *Brokeback Mountain* failed to win as best picture at the Academy Awards, the movie's representation of "two plain cowboys who fell in love in plain old Western wear" conquered in another way: It "hit the fashion bull's-eye." The fashion writer David Colman suggested on the front page of the *New York Times* "Styles" section that the film brought cowboy clothes "striding back into style," evidenced by nationwide interest in the fashion right after the film was released: Ralph Lauren opened two New York stores devoted to "a vintage Western feel"; a "venerable Denver retailer" reported sales of Western shirts up 25 percent; and just before the Academy Awards, "on eBay, Western hats, belt buckles, and shirts were up 25 percent in the last month alone."[55]

What transpires in L.A. sooner or later affects the rest of the world— at the least because of the city's position as the center of entertainment that speaks to the masses. Frank Rich's rhetorical question in a *New York*

Times review of *Brokeback Mountain*—"What if they held a culture war and no one fired a shot?"—defines a vital aspect L.A.'s power: A Hollywood film's tremendously moving depiction of homosexual love, which is being seen everywhere, may bloodlessly win a culture war.[56]

―

Social trends that point to the future have always been "quadruply" more pronounced in Los Angeles, as Pico Iyer has suggested. Its location at the edge of the continent, far from "back home," has sharpened its cutting edge and sanctioned experimentation such as would have been impossible elsewhere. From its beginnings as a frontier town, it has permitted, or has seemed to permit, what was unconventional, creative, daring. Michael Weinstein, who created the international AIDS Healthcare Foundation, explains that it was easier to do that from Los Angeles than it would have been elsewhere because the city is still something of the "Wild West," without a long-established power structure in place "that you have to be part of or pay homage to, such as exists in New York or San Francisco."[57] Terry Wolverton says that she left Grand Rapids, Michigan, so that she could develop her lesbian art and writing: "The Midwest operates on a philosophy of limitations. In L.A., no matter how unusual an idea is, there are enough people who'll tell you, 'Yeah, let's give it a try.' In L.A., you can invent new institutions in which you can be yourself."[58]

That ethos helps to explain why it was Los Angeles that gave birth to the country's first gay organizations, churches, synagogues, magazines, community centers. L.A.'s growth to gargantuan magnitude and its vast diversity also help to explain why gay men and women flocked there: In Los Angeles, they knew, they could find both anonymity and community, which have been vital to gays' survival and development. During the last half-century, gay life has been transformed in cities all over America. But in Los Angeles these transformations have occurred on a huge scale; and the gay consciousness and lifestyles that have developed there have had tremendous influence on how gay life is lived everywhere.

NOTES

INTRODUCTION

1. Frank Fenton, *A Place in the Sun* (New York: Random House, 1942).

2. ST interview with John Rechy, 71, August 29, 2005.

3. Michael Datcher, "Blue Spirits Rising: The Re-emergence of the L.A. Jazz Scene," *American Visions* 8, no. 2 (April–May 1993): 42.

4. Item S–001–368 120, Shades of Los Angeles Collection, Los Angeles Public Library.

5. In Jim Heimann, *Sins of the City: The Real Los Angeles Noir* (San Francisco: Chronicle Books, 1999), 154.

6. Steven L. Isoardi, "Central Avenue Sounds, oral history transcript, 1990," Clora Bryant interviewed by Steven L. Isoardi, Los Angeles: Oral History Program, University of California, Los Angeles, 1994, 105–107.

7. ST interview with Mark Haile, December 13, 2005; and Mark Haile, *The BLK Guide to Southern California for Black People in the Life* (Los Angeles: BLK Publishing Company, 1997), 11.

8. Bryant interview.

9. Ibid. See also Clora Bryant et al., eds., *Central Avenue Sounds: Jazz in Los Angeles*. (Berkeley, CA: University of California Press, 1998), 352.

CHAPTER 1

1. In George Devereux, "Institutionalized Homosexuality of the Mohave Indians," *Human Biology* 9 (1937): 501.

2. Cary McWilliams, *Southern California Country: An Island on the Land* (New York: Duell, Sloan, and Pierce, 1943), 44.

3. Herbert Ingram Priestly, ed. and trans., *A Historical, Political, and Natural Description of California by Pedro Fages* (1937; rpt. Ramona, Calif.: Ballena Press, 1972), 48, 33.

4. Geronimo Boscana, "Chinigchinich: A Historical Account of the Origins, Customs, and Traditions of the Indians at the Missionary Establishment of San Juan Capistrano, Alta California: Called Acagchemem Nation," trans. Alfred Robinson, in Alfred Robinson, *Life in California During a Residence of Several Years in That Territory . . . to Which Is Annexed a Historical Account of the Origins and Customs of the Indians of Alta California* (New York: Wiley and Putnam, 1846), 283–284.

5. Herbert E. Bolton, ed. and trans., *Font's Complete Diary: A Chronicle of the Founding of San Francisco* (Berkeley: University of California Press, 1931), 105.

6. Albert L. Hurtado, *Intimate Frontiers: Sex, Gender, and Culture in Old California* (Albuquerque: University of New Mexico Press, 1999), 5. See also Albert L. Hurtado, "Sexuality in

California's Franciscan Missions: Cultural Perceptions and Sad Realities," *California History* 71, no. 3 (Fall 1992): 370–385, 451–453.

7. See Lillian Faderman, *Surpassing the Love of Men: Romantic Friendship and Love Between Women from the Renaissance to the Present* (New York: William Morrow, 1981).

8. Garci Rodriguez de Montalvo, *The Labors of the Very Brave Knight Esplandian,* trans. William Thomas Little (Binghamton, N.Y.: Medieval and Renaissance Texts and Studies, 1992), 456–458.

9. Will Roscoe identifies honored roles and spiritual sanction for "third and fourth genders" among Native Americans throughout North America: See *Changing Ones: Third and Fourth Genders in Native North America* (New York: St. Martin's Press, 1998). See also Walter Williams, *The Spirit and the Flesh: Sexual Diversity in American Indian Culture* (Boston: Beacon Press, 1986).

10. A. L. Kroeber, *Handbook of the Indians of California* (1925; rpt. Berkeley: California Book Company), 46, 180, 647, 748–749.

11. See Sue-Ellen Jacobs, Wesley Thomas, and Sabine Lang, eds., *Two-Spirit People: Native American Gender Identity, Sexuality, and Spirituality* (Urbana: University of Illinois Press, 1997).

12. Boscana, "Chinigchinich," 283–284.

13. Francisco Palou, *Palou's Life of Fray Junipero Serra,* ed. and trans. Maynard J. Geiger (Washington, D.C.: Academy of American Franciscan History, 1955), 198–199.

14. John P. Harrington, "Cultural Element Distributions 19: Central California Coast," *University of California Anthropological Records* 7, no. 1 (1942): 32, 45. The contemporary Gabrielino playwright Cindi Alvitri says that to this day homosexuality is kept highly secret among the Tongva (Gabrielino): ST interview with Alvitri, April 7, 2005.

15. Of the Chumash, whose territory extended to Malibu Beach, A. L. Kroeber reported in 1925 that males were observed "in the dress, clothing, and character of women." Kroeber, *Handbook,* 497.

16. Ibid., 517.

17. Jack D. Forbes, *Warriors of the Colorado: The Yumas of the Quechan Nation and Their Neighbors* (Norman: University of Oklahoma Press, 1960), 57.

18. Devereux, "Institutionalized Homosexuality," 508.

19. Ramona Ford lists several West Coast (California and Oregon) tribes in which there were "female cross-gender roles": see "Native American Women: Changing Status, Changing Interpretations," in *Writing the Range: Race, Class and Culture in the Women's West,* ed. Elizabeth Jameson and Susan Armitage (Norman: University of Oklahoma Press, 1997), 52. See also Sue-Ellen Jacobs, "Berdache: A Brief Review of the Literature," *Colorado Anthropologist* 1 (1968); Evelyn Blackwood, "Sexuality and Gender in Certain Native American Tribes: The Case of Cross-Gender Females," *Signs: Journal of Women in Culture and Society* 10, no. 1 (1984): 27–42; Harriet Whitehead, "The Bow and the Burden Strap: A New Look at Institutionalized Homosexuality in Native North America," in *Sexual Meanings: The Cultural Construction of Gender and Sexuality,* ed. Sherry Ortner and Harriet Whitehead (Cambridge: Cambridge University Press, 1981), 80–115.

20. E. W. Gifford, "The Kamia of the Imperial Valley," *Bureau of American Ethnology Bulletin* 97 (Washington, D.C.: U.S. Government Printing Office, 1931), 6, 12.

21. Devereux, "Institutionalized Homosexuality," 503.

22. Ibid., 504.

23. Ibid., 511.

24. Boscana, "Chinigchinich," 330–332.

25. Devereux, "Institutionalized Homosexuality," 514.

26. "Los Angeles Disgraced," *California Argus,* May 9, 1896, in La Fiesta Scrapbook, Braun Research Library, Southwest Museum, Los Angeles (MS 207S1).

27. *Tarnished Angels: Paradisiacal Turpitude in Los Angeles,* ed. W. W. Robinson from an 1897 Los Angeles "Souvenir Sporting Guide" (Los Angeles: Ward Ritchie Press, 1964), 13.

28. Harris Newmark, *Sixty Years in Southern California, 1853–1913* (1916; rpt. Boston: Houghton Mifflin, 1930), 29–31, 266–267.

29. "Along El Camino Real," *Los Angeles Times,* January 31, 1939, 14.

30. Christine Fischer, "Women in California in the Early 1850s," in *Women in the Life of Southern California,* ed. Doyce B. Nunis, Jr. (Los Angeles: Historical Society of Southern California, 1996), 48.

31. For women who passed as men in other parts of the West, see, for example, "Little Jo Monoghan," in James Horan, *Desperate Women* (New York: G. P. Putnam's Sons, 1952); Mrs. E. J. Guerin, *Mountain Charley; or the Adventures of Mrs. E. J. Guerin, Who Was Thirteen Years in Male Attire* (rpt. Norman: University of Oklahoma Press, 1968); Mabel Rowe Curtis, *The Coachman Was a Lady: The Story of the Life of Charley Parkhurst* (Watsonville, Calif.: Pajaro Valley Historical Association, 1959). Albert Richardson, writing in 1867, said that it was so common for women to dress as men and go West that "help wanted" ads in mining country had to state: "No young women in disguise need apply," Albert D. Richardson, *Beyond the Mississippi: From the Great River to the Great Ocean, 1857–1867* (Hartford, Conn.: American Publishing Company, 1867), 200. Richardson also described the women in drag whom he had met in the West as all belonging to "the wretched class against which society shuts its iron doors."

32. Newmark, *Sixty Years,* 278.

33. Evelyn A. Schlatter, "Drag's a Life: Women, Gender, and Cross-Dressing in the Nineteenth Century West," in *Writing the Range: Race, Class and Culture in the Women's West,* ed. Elizabeth Jameson and Susan Armitage (Norman: University of Oklahoma Press, 1997), 338.

34. "Scenes on the Streets," April 18, 1895, unsourced clipping, item 1178, Max Meyburg, La Fiesta de Los Angeles Scrapbook, 1894–1931, Seaver Center, Los Angeles.

35. "Down with the Queen," *Los Angeles Record,* April 11, 1896, in La Fiesta Scrapbook, Braun Research Library, Southwest Museum, Los Angeles (MS 207 S1).

36. "Methodist Preachers Inveigh Against a Feature of the Fiesta," *Los Angeles Express,* March 16, 1896, in La Fiesta Scrapbook, Southwest Museum; and "Hell Turned Loose on Los Angeles," *Los Angeles Independent,* May 9, 1896, in Scrapbook, Braun Research Library, Southwest Museum.

37. "Hell Turned Loose on Los Angeles," Scrapbook, Braun Research Library, Southwest Museum (MS 207S1).

38. Ibid.

39. Los Angeles City Council Minutes, April 4, 1898: City of Los Angeles Records, vol. 25, February 21, 1898, to June 24, 1898, 248–249, in Los Angeles City Archives.

40. Los Angeles City Council Meeting reported in *Los Angeles Times,* March 26, 1895, 8.

41. City Council minutes, April 4, 1898: City of Los Angeles Records, vol. 25, Feb. 21, 1898, to June 24, 1898, 248–249, Los Angeles City Archives.

42. Impersonation acts were popular in nineteenth-century theater all over America. See Laurence Senelick, "The Evolution of the Male Impersonator on the Popular Stage," *Essays in Theater* 1, no. 1 (1982): 31–44; Laurence Senelick, "Boys and Girls Together: Sub-cultural Origins of Glamour Drag and Male Impersonation on the Nineteenth-Century Stage," 80–95; and Elizabeth Drorbaugh, "Sliding Scales: Notes on Storme DeLarverie and the Jewel Box Production Review," 120–143, in *Crossing the Stage: Controversies on Cross Dressing,* ed. Lesley Ferris (New York: Routledge, 1993); Gillian M. Rodger, "Male Impersonation on the North American Variety and Vaudeville Stage" (PhD diss., University of Pittsburgh, 1998), 66–69. For a discussion of the popularity of vaudeville in early-twentieth-century Los Angeles see Stan Steiner, "Vaudeville in Los Angeles, 1910–1926: Theaters, Management, and the Orpheum," *Pacific Historical Review* 61, no. 1 (February 1992): 103–113.

43. Rodger, "Male Impersonation," 66. (Rodger is quoting an August 6, 1870, newspaper, the *Clipper.*)

44. Ibid., 96.

45. Ibid., 72.

46. *Los Angeles Times,* September 1, 1924, A7.

47. Marshall L. Wright, *Before There Was a Hollywood: An Early History of Entertainment in Los Angeles, 1830–1930* (Los Angeles: self-published, 1998); in the Los Angeles Public Library Reference Collection.

48. "The Stage," *Los Angeles Times,* March 18, 1894, 19; also "Amusements," *Los Angeles Times,* February 2, 1893, 4.

49. "The Stage," *Los Angeles Times,* July 6, 1891, 4.

50. "Ko Vert, Female Impersonator, Wants Divorce," *Los Angeles Times,* September 30, 1922, II, 8. Ko Vert's one-day marriage was described as "a surprise to the film world."

51. Eltinge postured as a homophobe, but historians have documented his homosexuality: See, for example, Daniel Loftman Hurewitz, "Made in Edendale: Bohemian Los Angeles and the Politics of Identity, 1918–1953" (PhD diss., University of California, Los Angeles, 2001); Sharon Ullman, *Sex Seen: The Emergence of Modern Sexuality in America* (Berkeley: University of California Press, 1997); and Stan Steiner, "The Orpheum Theater of Los Angeles: An Overview," *Southern California Quarterly* 72, no. 4 (Winter 1990): 339–372.

52. Senelick, "Boys and Girls Together," 93.

53. The new ordinance regulated both masquerading and the issuance of permits to masqueraders. It was passed June 14, 1922, and given the number 43939, sections 1 and 2: See City of Los Angeles Records, vol. 128: 805, and vol. 129: 132–133. In 1936 this ordinance became 52.51 and 52.52 of the Los Angeles Municipal Code.

54. "Boy Role Easy for Her," *Los Angeles Times,* February 20, 1924, A10, and "Looking Through the Lens at Bits of Life," ibid.

55. "Billie's Way Is Feminine: Man-Milliner of El Monte 'a Perfect Lady,'" *Los Angeles Times,* January 13, 1907, II, 3.

56. "Flirtatious Willies Kept Upon the Run," *Los Angeles Times,* September 10, 1911, II, 9.

57. "Feminine Togs Not for Him; 'Lady Cook' Must Return to His Own Attire," *Los Angeles Times,* February 27, 1912, II, 14.

58. Eliza W. Farnham, *California, In-Doors and Out; or, How We Farm, Mine, and Live Generally in the Golden State* (New York: Dix, Edwards, and Company, 1856), 28.

59. Mary E. Blake, *On the Wing: Rambling Notes of a Trip to the Pacific* (Boston: Lee and Shepard, 1883), 2.

60. Farnham, *California, In-Doors and Out,* 27, 106.

61. Ibid., 188–189, 177–178.

62. Caroline M. Churchill, *Over the Purple Hills, or Sketches of Travel in California* (Denver: C. M. Churchill, 1876), 255–256.

63. The names of numerous women physicians who practiced medicine in turn-of-the-century Los Angeles are included in George H. Kress, *History of the Medical Profession in Southern California* (Los Angeles: Times-Mirror, 1910).

64. Emma H. Adams, *To and Fro, Up and Down: Southern California, Oregon, and Washington Territory* (Chicago: Cranston and Stowe, 1888), 67, 229.

65. Ibid., 229–230.

66. See Faderman, *Surpassing the Love of Men,* 239–253, for a discussion of how the nineteenth-century sexologists "morbidified" love between women.

67. Mary Casal, *The Stone Wall: An Autobiography* (Chicago: Eyncourt Press, 1930), 183.

68. In Eugene Fisher report on Los Angeles "degenerates," Sacramento City Archives, folder CD1 002 060.

69. "Man by Nature Really Woman," *Los Angeles Times,* September 30, 1917, V, 12.

70. "Science Aids Masquerader," *Los Angeles Times,* November 19, 1938, A3.

71. "Girl 'Husband' Gets Liberty," *Los Angeles Times,* January 15, 1929, A14.

72. See chap. 2.

73. "What We May Expect When the New Shirtwaist for Men Is 'In Flower,'" *Los Angeles Times,* August 15, 1900, I, 1.

74. Delegate to the California Constitutional Convention, Charles Botts, quoted in Donald Hargis, "Women's Rights in California, 1849," *Historical Society of Southern California Newsletter,* December 1955, 320–334.

75. "Uncle Walt," *Los Angeles Times,* May 11, 1911, I, 14.

76. Quoted in Jane Apostol, "Why Women Should Not Have the Vote: Anti-Suffrage Views in the Southland in 1911," in *Women in the Life of Southern California,* ed. Doyce B. Nunis, Jr. (Los Angeles: Historical Society of Southern California, 1996), 267–281.

77. Ibid.

78. Ibid.

79. In his dissertation on Bohemian Los Angeles and the politics of sexual identity, Daniel Hurewitz speculates that gay men and lesbians were attracted early to Los Angeles because it was a haven in which nontraditional behavior would be tolerated: Hurewitz, "Made in Edendale." Already at the beginning of the twentieth century, Los Angeles prided itself on being something of an art colony: "Los Angeles, always aspiring to be at the head of every procession, can exhibit a group of such as artists as is unknown to any other community of the same size and years," a 1901 newspaper article declared, observing the "artistic temperament" of those artists who lived in L.A.'s "Little Bohemia": "Los Angeles Becoming a Recognized Art Center," *Los Angeles Times,* June 23, 1901, C1.

80. *Sisters of the Road: The Autobiography of Box-Car Bertha,* as told to Dr. Ben L. Reitman (1937; rpt. New York: Harper and Row, 1975), 39, 60, 283, 290.

81. "'Mr.' Beach Held Romeo," *Los Angeles Times,* December 18, 1924, A1. See also the "Peter Stratford" case, "Grave Hides Strange Tale," (obit. of "Peter Stratford") *Los Angeles Times,* May 4, 1929, A2.

82. "Faint Reveals 'He's' a Woman," *Los Angeles Times,* September 28, 1932, 11.

83. The *Sacramento Bee* had hired Eugene Fisher to investigate a 1914 Long Beach scandal, discussed below. A folder of his field notes and correspondence is preserved at the Sacramento City Archives (folder CD1 002 060). Fisher's most detailed account of the episode consists of nineteen pages, hereafter referred to as the "Fisher Report." For another discussion of the Long Beach scandal see Ullman, *Sex Seen.*

84. "Some Phases of the Woman Question," *Los Angeles Times,* September 29, 1895, 15. By 1911, "effeminate undesirables" were said to be found on "any corner of the principal streets of Los Angeles"; "Flirtatious Willies."

85. "Says He Was Robbed," *Los Angeles Times,* February 2, 1896, 34.

86. Earl Lind [Ralph Werther], *The Female Impersonators* (1922; rpt. New York, Arno Press, 1975), 123.

87. "An Infamy; Vile Orgies at a Dance in a Public Hall," *Los Angeles Times,* June 3, 1887, 5.

88. Ibid. See also "End of the Carnival," *San Francisco Examiner,* April 14 [undated (1894?), in Seaver Center Scrapbook, 1894–1931, Seaver Center, Los Angeles], which refers to the Turnverein's young male athletes appearing in a Los Angeles parade "wearing little more than a feather."

89. See "By Laudanum," *Los Angeles Times,* November 24, 1887, 2. See also "Is Jailed in Turkish Bath," *Los Angeles Times,* January 22, 1913, II, 1.

90. Purssord's record as a "degenerate" is discussed in the Fisher Report. His career as an electrical therapist is discussed in "Adam's Garb Is Doctor's," *Los Angeles Times,* November 2, 1906, I, 13. "He is the most indecent man . . . ," ibid. Fisher describes Purssord as French; the U.S Census for 1900 lists him as British.

91. Purssord's suicide is discussed in the Fisher Report.

92. For a detailed account of this topic, see George Painter's Web-published "The Sensibilities of Our Forefathers: The History of Sodomy Laws in the United States–California," http://www.sodomylaws.org/sensibilities/california.htm.

93. *People v. Ed Wilson,* CR 2218, December 11, 1896, Judge J. W. McKinley, Los Angeles Hall of Records.

94. "Vile Criminals," *Los Angeles Times,* March 26, 1888, 8.

95. *People v. Charles Murphy,* CR 243, April 4, 1888, Los Angeles Hall of Records.

96. Los Angeles County Jail Register, April 1888–January 1897, Seaver Center, Los Angeles.

97. "Terrible Revenge; Two Brothers Take the Law Into Their Own Hands," *Los Angeles Times,* March 17, 1896, 3.

98. Ibid.

99. Sweeping vagrancy ordinances were common in the nineteenth century and after (see chap. 3) to run "undesirables," including homosexuals, out of town at the discretion of the police.

100. Fisher Report.

101. See, for example, "Wanted: Free Baths," *Los Angeles Times,* July 31, 1898, B4, in which the editors urged the city council to subsidize public baths.

102. Anecdotal information suggests that fellatio continued to be the preferred sexual activity of Los Angeles gay men through the mid-twentieth century: for example, ST interview with Harry Hay, May 17, 1987; ST interview with Oreste Pucciani, October 3, 1982. Also, a gay *male* publication, *Gay Girls* [sic] *Guide to the M.S. and the Modern World, 3rd Edition* (Fall 1957), notes on p. 19: "With the great increase in universal bathing facilities and personal hygiene in the 20th Century, oral techniques occupy a more prominent place than at any time in previous history." Pamphlet collection, ONE National Gay and Lesbian Archives, University of Southern California, Los Angeles.

103. The new law was enacted June 1, 1915. See *Statutes and Amendments to the Codes of California,* 1915, chap. 586, p. 1022. See also Painter, "The Sensibilities of Our Forefathers: The History of Sodomy Laws in the United States–California."

104. Letter from Eugene Fisher to C. K. McClatchy (owner of the *Sacramento Bee*), December 5, 1914. Sacramento City Archives (folder CD1 002 060).

105. "Takes His Life Through Shame: Note Asserts Innocence, but Unprovable," *Los Angeles Times,* November 15, 1914, I, 8.

106. "Are They Insane? A Woman's Query," *Los Angeles Times,* November 18, 1914, II, 5.

107. Fisher Report.

108. "Revival at Long Beach," *Los Angeles Times,* December 14, 1914, II, 1.

109. "Long Beach Morality Argument Ends in Fight" and "Long Beach, California—The Home of 'Social Vagrants.' Oh You 'Holy' City!" *Venice Daily Vanguard,* November 16, 1914, 1, 2. A *Los Angeles Times* article concluded, "What a Holy City Long Beach is!" in "Long Beach Uncovers Social Vagrant Clan," November 14, 1914, II, 8. See Mark Twain's *The Man That Corrupted Hadleyburg and Other Stories* (New York: Harper Brothers, 1900).

110. Eugene Fisher to C. K. McClatchy, November 20, 1914, Sacramento City Archives.

111. "Recital of Shameless Men," *Los Angeles Times,* November 19, 1914, p. 1.

112. Undated handwritten notes of Fisher, Sacramento City Archives.

113. Eugene Fisher to C. K. McClatchy, November 20, 1914.

114. "Long Beach Uncovers Social Vagrant Clan," *Los Angeles Times,* November 14, 1914, II, 8.

115. "Attorney Aims Blow at Detective Witness," *Los Angeles Times,* December 11, 1914.

116. "Publicity Is Needed and Then More Publicity," *Los Angeles Times,* November 26, 1914, II, 8.

117. "Long Beach Recital of Shameless Men," *Los Angeles Times,* Novemebr 14, 1914, II, 1.

118. "Jury Acquits in Six-O-Six," *Los Angeles Times,* December 12, 1914, II, 9.

119. Eugene Fisher to C. K. McClatchy, November 23, 1914, and Eugene Fisher to C. K. McClatchy (undated). Sacramento City Archives.

120. Fisher Report.

121. "Vast Scandal in Los Angeles Is Reported as Suppressed," *Sacramento Bee,* November 18, 1914, 1.

122. The *Bee*'s substantial file on this scandal contains no evidence for five hundred arrests. The Fisher Report does state that Warren and Brown made "fifty or more arrests . . . in the decency campaign which was carried on in Los Angeles."

123. Fisher Report.

124. Eugene Fisher to C. K. McClatchy, December 5, 1914, ibid.

125. Ibid.

126. Wright quoted in Cary McWilliams, *Southern California Country*, 158.

CHAPTER 2

1. "Hollywood Lowdown," *Broadway Brevities*, April 11, 1932, 10. "Hollywood Lowdown" was a regular column in *Broadway Brevities*, a New York City tabloid of the 1920s and '30s; its frequent gay references, though often scathing, contained verifiable details.

2. Frances Marion, *Off with Their Heads: A Serio-Comic Tale of Hollywood* (New York: Macmillan, 1972), 2–4.

3. Mary Winship, "Oh, Hollywood," *Photoplay*, May 1921, 112.

4. Merry Ovick, *Los Angeles: The End of the Rainbow* (Los Angeles: Balcony, 1994), 168.

5. Cal Yorke, "Plays and Players," *Photoplay*, January 1922, 95.

6. "Julian Eltinge," *Photo-Play Journal*, October 1917, 27.

7. Gavin Lambert, *Nazimova* (New York: Knopf, 1997), 201, 248.

8. Anthony Slide, "The Silent Closet," *Film Quarterly* (Summer 1979): 27.

9. To forestall government censorship, the Hays Office was established within the Motion Picture Producers and Distributors of America as a mechanism for self-censorship. Toward the top of the list of what Hollywood pledged not to show in films was references to homosexuality.

10. Mildred Adams, "The City of Angels Enters Heaven," *New York Times*, August 3, 1930, 5.

11. William Mann, *Behind the Screen: How Gays and Lesbians Shaped Hollywood* (New York: Viking, 2001), 84. See also Toto le Grand, "The Golden Age of Queens," part 4, *Bay Area Reporter* 4, no. 21 (October 1974).

12. Sheila Donisthorpe, *Loveliest of Friends* (New York: Charles Kendall, 1931).

13. Salka Viertel, *The Kindness of Strangers* (New York: Holt, Rinehart, and Winston, 1969), 175.

14. Josef von Sternberg, *Fun in a Chinese Laundry* (New York: MacMillan, 1965), 247.

15. "Tsk, Tsk, Such Goings On," *Variety*, February 28, 1933, 2.

16. In Barry Paris, *Louise Brooks: A Biography* (New York: Alfred A. Knopf, 1989), 400.

17. "Rambling Reporter," *Hollywood Reporter*, September 29, 1932, 2.

18. Ibid., October 20, 1932, 2.

19. Louise Brooks, *Lulu in Hollywood* (New York: Alfred A. Knopf, 1982), 96–97. See also Mel Gordon, *Voluptuous Panic: The Erotic World of Weimar Berlin* (Los Angeles: Feral House, 2006).

20. David King Dunaway, *Huxley in Hollywood* (New York: Harper and Row, 1989), 72.

21. As George Chauncey points out in *Gay New York: Gender, Urban Culture, and the Making of the Gay Male World, 1890–1940* (New York: Basic Books, 1994), New York, too, had its areas of gay sophistication in the early decades of the twentieth century, including Greenwich Village and Harlem. See also Lillian Faderman, *Odd Girls and Twilight Lovers: A History of Lesbian Life in Twentieth-Century America* (New York: Columbia University Press, 1991), especially chap. 3, "Lesbian Chic: Experimentation and Repression in the '20s."

22. Mercedes de Acosta, "Here Lies the Heart," manuscript version 02:04, chap. 32, 336, in Rosenbach Museum and Library, Philadelphia. We thank Dr. Kathleen Hall for providing us with this material.

23. By the 1920s, dance halls, cabarets, and speakeasies had sprung up all over Hollywood: Jim Heimann, *Out with the Stars: Hollywood Nightlife in the Golden Era* (New York: Abbeville

Press, 1985), 23–24. According to Axel Madsen, there were already several all-lesbian bars in Los Angeles by the 1920s. He cites The Big House on Hollywood Boulevard and the Lakeshore Bar near Westlake Park: *The Sewing Circle: Hollywood's Greatest Secret: Female Stars Who Loved Other Women* (New York: Birch Lane Press, 1995), 96–97. However, Madsen sometimes errs on dating: For example, he presents the Open Door, a bar that was established in the 1950s, in his discussion of lesbian bars of the 1920s and '30s.

24. For a discussion of New York's "pansy craze," see Chauncey, *Gay New York,* 314–321.

25. Jack Lord and Lloyd Huff, *How to Sin in Hollywood* (Hollywood: Jack Lord, 1940), 39.

26. Richard Barrios, *Screened Out: Playing Gay in Hollywood from Edison to Stonewall* (New York: Routledge, 2003), 103.

27. *Los Angeles Times,* December 21, 1932, A5.

28. Fletcher is the subject of Tyler Alpern's extensive biographical Web site, http://www.tyler-alpern.com/bruz.html. Fletcher rated more than one hundred mentions in the *Los Angeles Times* between 1935 and 1939.

29. "B.B.B.'s Cellar," *Variety,* October 4, 1932, 53.

30. "Coast Raid on Panze Joints," *Variety,* October 4, 1932, 52.

31. Gavin Lambert, *Nazimova* (New York: Alfred A. Knopf, 1997), 210.

32. ST interview with Mark Bortles, September 6, 2004. Cukor and Cole Porter vied for preeminence as partygivers and were jealous of one another's success, as their guests understood. "I had lunch at Cole's and dinner at George's," one partygoer recalled, "but you never told one about the other," Patrick McGilligan, *George Cukor: A Double Life* (New York: St. Martin's Press, 1991).

33. McGilligan, *George Cukor,* 120–126.

34. Donald Bogle, *Bright Boulevards, Bold Dreams: The Story of Black Hollywood* (New York: Ballantine Books, 2005). Bogle also discusses other African American gay and bisexual actors of the period such as Hattie McDaniel.

35. April 2, 1937, Howard Greer to James Broughton, p. 4, box 2, folder 101, James Broughton Papers, Collection 1, Special Collections, Kent State Library, Ohio. "Belle" is mid-century gay slang for an attractive young gay man. We thank Tyler Alpert for providing us with this material.

36. Ibid.

37. Heimann, *Out with the Stars,* 72–73.

38. "Hollywood Goes Beer Quaffing," *Variety,* November 21, 1933, 59.

39. See also Daniel Loftman Hurewitz's discussion of Hollywood nightclubs in the 1930s in "Made in Edendale: Bohemian Los Angeles and the Politics of Sexual Identity" (PhD diss., University of California, Los Angeles, 2001), 112–117.

40. Jack Lord and Lloyd Huff, *How to Sin in Hollywood* (Hollywood: Jack Lord, 1940), 39.

41. ST interview with Duncan Donovan, April 1, 2004. "Fegaleh," meaning a little bird, is Yiddish slang for "fairy."

42. LF interview with Beverly Alber, 78, February 15, 2004. See also Lester Strong and David Hanna, "Hollywood Watering Holes '30s Style," *Harvard Gay and Lesbian Review,* July 31, 1996.

43. W. K. Martin uses this term in *Marlene Dietrich* (New York: Chelsea House, 1995).

44. Kenneth Tynan regarding Marlene Dietrich in *The Sound of Two Hands Clapping* (New York: Holt, Rinehart, and Winston, 1975), 58.

45. Of the books included in these notes, we have found the most useful with regard to establishing actresses' sexuality are Anthony Slide's *The Silent Players;* William Mann's *Behind the Screen;* Gavin Lambert's *Nazimova;* Barry Paris' *Louise Brooks;* Steven Bach's *Marlene Dietrich;* Maria Riva's *Marlene Dietrich;* Lawrence Quirk and William Schoell's *Joan Crawford;* Brendan Gill's *Tallulah;* Karen Swenson's *Greta Garbo;* Barry Paris' *Garbo: A Biography;* Hugo Vickers' *Loving Garbo;* Robert Schanke's *That Furious Lesbian;* and Judith Mayne's *Directed by Dorothy Arzner.* See also Graham Russell Gao Hodges, *Anna May Wong: From Laundryman's Daughter to Hollywood Legend* (New York: Palgrave, 2004), and the Mercedes de Acosta Collection at the

Rosenbach Museum and Library, especially letters from Greta Garbo, Marlene Dietrich, Ona Munson, Polly Kirk, and Eva LeGalliene.

46. For a discussion of pioneering professional women who were "unstraight," see Lillian Faderman, *To Believe in Women* (New York: Houghton Mifflin, 1999).

47. Havelock Ellis, *Studies in the Psychology of Sex: Sexual Inversion in Women* (1897; rpt. New York: Random House, 1942), 230.

48. Christopher Anderson, *Young Kate* (New York: Henry Holt, 1988), 140.

49. A. Scott Berg, *Kate Remembered* (New York: G. P. Putnam and Sons, 2003), 45.

50. Raymond Daum, *Walking with Garbo* (New York: HarperCollins, 1991), 22.

51. Jack Grant, *Screen Book*, excerpted in *Hollywood and the Great Fan Magazines*, ed. Martin Levin (New York: Arbor House, 1970), 47+.

52. Steven Bach, *Marlene Dietrich: Life and Legend* (New York: William Morrow, 1992), 19.

53. Lawrence J. Quirk and William Schoell, *Joan Crawford: The Essential Biography* (Lexington: University Press of Kentucky, 2002), 2.

54. Adele Whitley Fletcher, "They Weren't Born Beautiful," *Modern Screen*, September 1930, 40–41.

55. Maria Riva, *Marlene Dietrich, by Her Daughter* (New York: Alfred A. Knopf, 1993), 87.

56. Mercedes de Acosta in Lambert, *Nazimova*, 178.

57. Robert A. Schanke, "Alla Nazimova: The Witch of Makeup," in Robert A. Schanke and Kim Marra, eds., *Passing Performances: Queer Readings of Leading Players in American Theater History* (Ann Arbor: University of Michigan Press, 1998), 133.

58. The sexuality of Nita Naldi and Pola Negri is discussed in Anthony Slide, "The Silent Closet," *Film Quarterly* (Summer 1999): 24–32.

59. Vamp image described in "Garbo Is Still Queen," *Motion Picture*, August 1936, 37+.

60. Bach, *Marlene Dietrich*, 74, 245–246.

61. Brendan Gill, *Tallulah* (New York: Holt, Rinehart, Winston, 1972), 51–52.

62. Martin, *Marlene Dietrich*, 91. Maria Riva claims that Bankhead never actually succeeded in that desire: Riva, who was briefly an actress and toured in a play with Bankhead, recalls that Bankhead, "completely naked, liked chasing me down hotel corridors. Poor Tallulah, she hadn't managed to get 'into Dietrich's pants' at Paramount, [and] now figured she'd get into the daughter's," Riva, *Marlene Dietrich, by Her Daughter*, 554.

63. Berg, *Kate Remembered*, 4–5. Other biographers, too, who knew the two women personally offer evidence that suggests that Phyllis was more than an employee to Katherine: See, for example, James Prideaux, *Knowing Hepburn and Other Curious Experiences* (Winchester, Mass.: Faber and Faber, 1996), 62.

64. Quoted in Lambert, *Nazimova*, 315. Wilbourn had played a similar role for the actress Constance Collier until Collier's death. There is some indication that Greta Garbo was once interested in Wilbourn. Garbo's friend and correspondent, Cecil Beaton, teased Garbo in a 1948 letter: "There's not much point in trying to find out if you've been seeing Constance Collier's companion." In Hugo Vickers, *Loving Garbo: The Story of Greta Garbo, Cecil Beaton, and Mercedes de Acosta* (New York: Random House, 1994), 145.

65. Patrick McGilligan, *George Cukor: A Double Life* (New York: St. Martin's Press, 1991), 82, 85.

66. Berg, *Kate Remembered*, 350.

67. Ibid., 83.

68. Katharine Hepburn, *Me: Stories of My Life* (New York: Alfred A. Knopf, 1991), 131–132.

69. Ibid., 400.

70. Selznick is quoted in Berg, *Kate Remembered*, 266–267.

71. Ibid., 81.

72. James Robert Parish, *Katherine Hepburn: The Untold Story* (New York: Advocate Books, 2005), 66, 121. Parish characterizes their relationship as "a marriage of convenience" (96).

73. Don Camp, "Hepburn Goes in for Hobbies in a Great Big Way," *Motion Picture*, February 1937, 40+.

74. Quoted in Homer Dickens, *The Films of Katharine Hepburn* (1971; rev. ed. New York: Carol Publishing, 1990), 43.

75. Joel Ryan, *Katharine Hepburn: A Stylish Life* (New York: Byron Preiss Visual Publications, 1999), 83.

76. Gully and Edwards quoted in Parish, *Katherine Hepburn*, 208.

77. Sternberg, *Fun in a Chinese Laundry*, 246.

78. "I'm One of the Boys," in *The Hollywood Party* (1933), quoted in Brett L. Adams, "Latitude in Mass-Produced Culture's Capitol: The New Woman and Other Players in Hollywood, 1920–1941," *Frontiers: A Journal of Women's Studies* 25, no. 2 (June 2004): 65–96.

79. *Hollywood Reporter*, June 18, 1934, 1–2.

80. "Cardinal Raps Public Filth," *Los Angeles Times*, April 28, 1938, 9.

81. Herbert Blumer, *Movies and Conduct* (New York: Macmillan, 1933), 45, 71. See Jack Lait and Lee Mortimer, who attributed the "epidemic of homosexuality" among young women almost twenty years later to "knowledge that many of the movie set prefer it that way," in *U.S.A. Confidential* (New York: Crown, 1952), 42–43.

82. Caroline Sheldon, "Lesbians in Film: Some Thoughts," in *Gays in Film*, ed. Richard Dyer (New York: Zoetrope, 1984), 5–26. For the influence of the 1930s' lesbian images on lesbians today, see also Andrea Weiss, *Vampires and Violets: Lesbians in Film* (New York: Penguin, 1992), especially "A Queer Feeling When I Look at You," chap. 2, and Patricia White, *UnInvited: Classical Hollywood Cinema and Lesbian Representability* (Bloomington: Indiana University Press, 1999).

83. Gore Vidal, *The City and the Pillar* (New York: Dutton, 1948), 109.

84. Donald Spoto, *Blue Angel: The Life of Marlene Dietrich* (1992; rpt. New York: Cooper Square Press, 2000), 124.

85. Historically, passionate relationships between women were often seen by the uninitiated as merely "romantic friendships" rather than lesbian love, perhaps because in a more puritanical era people preferred not to entertain the notion of autonomous female sexuality such as lesbianism required: See Lillian Faderman, *Surpassing the Love of Men: Romantic Friendship and Love Between Women from the Renaissance to the Present* (New York: William Morrow, 1981).

86. We have found the most useful with regard to establishing male actors' sexuality: Mann, *Behind the Screen* and *Wisecracker: The Life and Times of William Haines* (New York: Viking, 1998); Slide, "The Silent Closet"; McGillian, *George Cukor*; Anthony Slide, *Silent Players: A Biographical and Autobiographical Study of 100 Silent Film Actors and Actresses*, (Lexington: University Press of Kentucky, 2002); Joseph Morella and George Mazzei, *Genius and Lust: The Creative and Sexual Lives of Cole Porter and Noel Coward* (New York: Carroll and Graf, 1995); Hector Arce, *The Secret Life of Tyrone Power: The Drama of a Bisexual in the Spotlight* (New York: William Morrow, 1979); Larry Swindell, *The Last Hero: A Biography of Gary Cooper* (New York: Doubleday, 1980); Allan R. Ellenberger, *Ramon Novarro* (Jefferson, N.C: McFarland, 1999); and Arthur Laurents, *Original Story By: A Memoir of Broadway and Hollywood* (New York: Alfred A. Knopf, 2000).

87. Mann's focus, as his subtitle suggests, is "How Gays and Lesbians Shaped Hollywood: 1910–1969."

88. Morella and Mazzei, *Genius and Lust*, 103.

89. ST interview with Malcolm Boyd, 80, September 3, 2004.

90. Leonard Spigelgass quoted in David Grafton, *Red, Hot, and Rich: An Oral History of Cole Porter* (New York: Stein and Day, 1987).

91. Sidney D. Kirkpatrick, *A Cast of Killers* (New York: E. P. Dutton, 1986), 229.

92. Ibid.

93. Edward Doherty, *Denver Post*, March 3, 1922.

94. *New York Herald,* February 6, 1922.

95. *New York News,* February 6, 1922.

96. Ibid.

97. Joe Domanick, *To Protect And Serve: The LAPD's Century of War in the City of Dreams* (New York: Pocket Books, 1994), 121. See also Charles Higham and Roy Moseley, *Cary Grant: The Lonely Heart* (New York: Harcourt Brace Jovanovich, 1989), 147, for an example of the police covering up the gay arrest of a star.

98. "Rambling Reporter," *Hollywood Reporter,* July 3, 1934, 2.

99. William J. Mann, *Wisecracker: The Life and Times of William Haines* (New York: Viking, 1998), 260.

100. ST interview with Duncan Donovan, 84, April 1, 2004.

101. "Hollywood Lowdown," *Broadway Brevities,* April 11, 1932, 10.

102. ST interview with Harry Hay, 76, January 3, 1988.

103. Slide, *Silent Players,* 159.

104. Arce, *The Secret Life of Tyrone Power,* 69.

105. Swindell, *The Last Hero,* 104–105.

106. Dagmar Godowska, *First Person Plural: The Lives of Dagmar Godowska* (New York: Viking Press, 1958), 71.

107. "Thank God for Five-Yard McCarty," *Chicago Tribune,* November 10, 1925.

108. "Pink Powder Puffs," *Chicago Tribune,* July 18, 1926.

109. "Rudy's So Sore, It's Just Awful," *Los Angeles Times,* July 21, 1926, 2.

110. Ellenberger, *Ramon Novarro,* 15, and David Brett, *Valentino: A Dream of Desire* (London: Robson Books, 1998).

111. Lambert, *Nazimova,* 223.

112. Ibid., 223–224. See also Emily W. Leider, *Dark Lover: The Life and Death of Rudolph Valentino* (New York: Farrar, Strauss and Giroux, 2003), 99–101.

113. On Negri see William Mann, *Wisecracker,* 109; John Baxter, *The Hollywood Exiles* (New York: Taplinger, 1976), 46–47; and Pola Negri, *Memoirs of a Star* (Garden City, N.Y.: Doubleday, 1970).

114. See Leider, *Dark Lover,* passim.

115. In Lambert, *Nazimova,* 397–400.

116. Quoted in Cal Yorke, "Plays and Players," *Photoplay,* December 1921, 80.

117. Aspirants to stardom also went along with the game, not only to bolster their images but sometimes, too, for the sake of glamour and a good meal: Tab Hunter recounts that before he became a star, he was willing to do publicity dating with actresses: "Having ourselves described as 'an item' or 'deeply involved' was a small price to pay for access to lavish parties overflowing with delicacies otherwise unavailable to actors living on saltines, sardines, and soda pop." Tab Hunter with Eddie Muller, *Tab Hunter Confidential: The Making of a Movie Star* (Chapel Hill, N.C.: Algonquin Books of Chapel Hill, 2005), 73–74.

118. Lesley Ferris, "Kit and Guth," in Schanke and Marra, *Passing Performances,* 197–220. The practice of lavender marriage in Hollywood extended even to those who were not in front of the camera, according to the actor Rex Evans and his partner Jim Weatherford. As they recall, decorator Jimmy Pendleton, who was "as gay as could be," married "a Texas rich woman who was the ugliest thing." Weatherford says that Pendleton's wife "gave him one night out a week to be with his gay friends." ST interview with Jim Weatherford, June 29, 2004.

119. Charles Higham and Roy Moseley, *Cary Grant: The Lonely Heart* (New York: Harcourt Brace Jovanovich, 1989).

120. Arce, *Tyrone Power,* 113.

121. Val Holley, *Mike Connolly and the Manly Art of Hollywood Gossip* (Jefferson, N.C.: McFarland, 2003), 103.

122. Ramona Bergere, "She Does as She Pleases," *Modern Screen,* March 1937, 18.

123. Gladys Hall, "'Tis the Likes of Kelly," *Motion Picture*, January 1937, 32+.

124. "A Woman's Touch," *Motion Picture Studio Insider*, July 1937, 20.

125. Judith Mayne's *Directed by Dorothy Arzner* (Bloomington: Indiana University Press, 1994) discusses Arzner's career as well as her lesbian relationships. See also Weiss, *Vampires and Violets*.

126. Charles Higham, *Lucy: The Real Life of Lucille Ball* (New York: St. Martin's Press, 1984), 52.

127. Quoted in Barry Paris, *Louise Brooks* (New York: Alfred A. Knopf, 1989), 419.

128. Lambert, *Nazimova*, 162.

129. *Hollywood Reporter*, July 31, 1935.

130. For example, McGilligan, *George Cukor*; Barry Paris, *Garbo: A Biography* (London: Pan Books, 1996); Mann, *Behind the Screen*; Lambert, *Nazimova*.

131. "How To Hold a Husband/Wife in Hollywood," *Photoplay*, June 1929, 106.

132. Gladys Hall, "Lil's Baby!" August 25, 1931, typescript in the Gladys Hall file, Academy of Motion Picture Arts and Sciences.

133. Mann, *Behind the Screen*, 115.

134. Huxley quoted in Basil Rathbone, *In and Out of Character* (Garden City, N.Y.: Doubleday, 1956), 143.

135. "Rambling Reporter," *Hollywood Reporter*, November 21, 1931, 2.

136. "Ambidextrous" and "new love" quoted in Karen Swenson, *Greta Garbo: A Life Apart* (New York: Scribner, 1997), 259–260. "Lavender" speakeasy in "Rambling Reporter," *Hollywood Reporter*, January 7, 1932, 2.

137. "The Lowdown," *Hollywood Reporter*, January 27, 1932, 2. Mercedes de Acosta writes of her romances with Garbo, Dietrich, and other famous actresses in *Here Lies the Heart* (1960; rpt. New York: Arno Press, 1975). In the various drafts of this autobiography, now at the Rosenbach Museum in Philadelphia, she was even more explicit about these love relationships than she was in the published version. Among Mercedes de Acosta's papers at the Rosenbach are also letters sent to her by Dietrich and Garbo regarding their relationship. See also Robert A. Schanke, *"That Furious Lesbian": The Story of Mercedes de Acosta* (Carbondale: Southern Illinois University Press, 2003), and Hugo Vickers, *Loving Garbo: The Story of Greta Garbo, Cecil Beaton, and Mercedes de Acosta* (New York: Random House, 1994).

138. Greta Garbo to Mercedes de Acosta, April 29, 1950, box 23, file 30, Rosenbach Museum and Library.

139. Quoted in Weiss, *Vampires and Violets*, 32.

140. "Hedda Hopper's Hollywood," *Los Angeles Times*, January 15, 1941, 12.

141. Stiller's homosexuality is discussed in Swenson, *Greta Garbo: A Life Apart*, 56.

142. Marcella Burke, "Why Garbo Has Never Married," in *Hollywood and the Great Fan Magazines*, ed. Martin Levin (New York: Arbor House, 1970), 74+.

143. Gary Carey, *All the Stars in Heaven: Louis B. Mayer's M-G-M* (New York: E. P. Dutton, 1981), 215.

144. Don Camp, "Hepburn Goes in for Hobbies in a Great Big Way," *Motion Picture*, February 1937, 40+.

145. Romano Tozzi, *Films in Review*, December 1957, 484.

146. ST interviews with Jim Weatherford, June 29, 2004, and Michael Kearns, September 21, 2004.

147. Robert S. Sennett, *Hollywood Hoopla: Creating Stars and Selling Movies in the Golden Age of Hollywood* (New York: Billboard Books, 1998), 61.

148. Rock Hudson and Sara Davidson, *Rock Hudson: His Story* (New York: William Morrow, 1986), 74.

149. Robert Hofler, *The Man Who Invented Rock Hudson: The Pretty Boys and Dirty Deals of Henry Willson* (New York: Carroll & Graf, 2006). It was Willson who arranged a front marriage

between Hudson and Phyllis Gates: Trudy Ring, "Behind the Screen," *Advocate*, February 28, 2006, 47, and Robert Hofler, "Outing Mrs. Rock Hudson," ibid., 46–47.

150. Hofler, *The Man Who Invented Rock Hudson*.

151. Hunter with Muller, *Tab Hunter Confidential*, 51–52.

152. Steve Govoni, "Now It Can Be Told," *American Film*, February 1990, 28–33+.

153. Quoted in Max Pierce, "In Search of Lizabeth Scott, the Sphinx from Scranton," *Films of the Golden Age*, Summer 2002, 21.

154. Hedda Hopper, "Star By-passes Romance for Career," *Los Angeles Times*, October 14, 1951, E1.

155. Pierce, "In Search of Lizabeth Scott," 24.

156. Hopper, "Star By-passes Romance."

CHAPTER 3

1. Raymond Chandler, *The Big Sleep* and *Farewell, My Lovely* (New York: The Modern Library, 1995), 279–280.

2. Kevin Starr, *Embattled Dreams* (New York: Oxford University Press, 2002), 36. Total blackouts followed the immediate attack on December 7, 1941, and partial blackouts continued.

3. "Facts of Japanese Inquiry Released," *Los Angeles Times*, March 20, 1942, 9.

4. Starr, *Embattled Dreams*, on LAPD treatment of Latinos: "For years, in fact, the LAPD and the sheriff's department had been making war on young men of Mexican descent. . . . The sheer presence of young Mexicans on street corners in the barrio . . . was seen by patrolling police or sheriff's deputies as de facto proof of a crime in process or about to happen. . . . Beatings were frequent, as were frame-ups" (98).

5. LF interview with Stella Rush, 79, November 10, 2004.

6. Edith Eyde [a.k.a. Lisa Ben] made such observations firsthand in her Los Angeles–based lesbian magazine, *Vice Versa*: "Here to Stay," September 1947, 4–5.

7. Kenneth Marlowe, *The Male Homosexual* (Los Angeles: Sherbourne Press, 1965), 46. Also, ST interview with Norman Stanley, 78, September 17, 2004.

8. Alan Berube, *Coming Out Under Fire: The History of Gay Men and Women in World War Two* (New York: Free Press, 1990), 114.

9. Ibid., 123.

10. Carey McWilliams, *California, the Great Exception* (New York: Current Books, 1949), 13–14.

11. LF interview with Beverly Hickok, 85, September 17, 2004.

12. Jim Kepner, "The Loves of a Longtime Activist: An Autobiography and Gay Movement History, Sort Of, in 181 Vignettes" (unpublished ms., 1993). LF interview with Laura Sherman, 77, July 26, 2004. Beverly Hickok, *Against the Grain: Coming Out in the 1940s* (Philadelphia: Xlibris, 2003), 50–51.

13. Stanley interview.

14. *The Complete Reprint of Physique Pictorial, 1951–1964*, vol. 1 (Cologne, Germany: Taschen, 1997), 6–17.

15. Tom of Finland Foundation, *Tom of Finland: Retrospective* (North Hollywood: London Press, 1988), 5.

16. Michael Duncan, "Bob Mizer at Western Projects," *Art in America* 93, no. 3 (March 2005): 146. See also Stuart Timmons, "Wanted: Athletic Models," *The Advocate*, July 30, 1992, 56–60.

17. Joe Domanick, *To Protect and to Serve: The LAPD's Century of War in the City of Dreams* (New York: Pocket Books), 12. The philosophy established by Parker was continued by his protégé, Daryl Gates, LAPD Chief from 1979 to 1992.

18. Correspondence from Norman Stanley to Sallie Fiske, March 15, 1961, private collection.

19. According to LAPD statistics, in 1947, the police made 1,656 arrests for "sex perversion." Three years later, when Parker became chief, arrests increased 86.5 percent: Los Angeles Police Department, *Annual Report*, 1947 and 1950. Even admired public figures who were gay, such as the tennis star Bill Tilden and the civil rights organizer Bayard Rustin, suffered career-wrecking lewd conduct arrests by the zealous LAPD.

20. Eugene D. Williams, introduction to *The Sexual Criminal: A Psychoanalytic Study*, by Paul de River, 2nd ed. (1949; rpt. Springfield, Ill.: Charles C. Thomas, 1956).

21. De River, *The Sexual Criminal: A Psychoanalytic Study*, 276–277.

22. "Increase in Sex Crimes Laid to War Influence," *Los Angeles Times*, November 11, 1948, A6.

23. "Closing of Eight Bars Urged by Assembly Group," *Los Angeles Times*, February 6, 1948, 1. These sanctions also targeted prostitution.

24. "Degenerate Ban Voted," *Los Angeles Times*, March 12, 1949, A1.

25. *Stoumen v. Reilly* (California 1951), in *Lesbians, Gay Men and the Law*, ed. William B. Rubenstein (New York: The New Press, 1993), 205–206. See also Nan Boyd, *Wide Open Town: A History of Queer San Francisco to 1965* (Berkeley: University of California Press, 2003).

26. Rubenstein, *Lesbians, Gay Men and the Law*, 206.

27. *People v. Guynn*, 1950, CR A 2551; *People v. Granato*, 1950, CR A, 2552: *Los Angeles Municipal Code*, 1956, vol. 2, 28 (52.51).

28. The 1958 LAPD Annual Report reveals that the police felt embattled by judicial decrees which, the department said, had "hamstrung" officers and "hoodwinked an apathetic public." Nevertheless, the report said, the LAPD would not be daunted in "its resolve to keep the city free from corruption": VICE section, 14.

29. Helen Branson, *Gay Bar* (San Francisco: Pan Graphic Press, 1957),42.

30. ST interviews with Jim Weatherford, 84, June 29, 2004; William Joseph Bryan, 78, March 16, 2004; and Malcolm Boyd, 81, June 27, 2004.

31. ST interview with Marvin Edwards, 73, June 7, 2004.

32. Mike Rothmiller, *L.A. Secret Police: Inside the LAPD Elite Spy Network* (New York: Pocketbooks, 1992), 73.

33. The term "Hollywood reject" became so widespread it rated inclusion in a national gay lexicon: Bruce Rodgers, *Gay Talk: A Sometimes Outrageous Dictionary of Gay Slang* (New York: Paragon Books, 1972).

34. ST interview with Stanley Markowitz, 75, June 7, 2004.

35. ST interview with Tom Gibbon, 78, June 12, 2004.

36. Markowitz interview.

37. ST interview with Rudy Ruano, 60, September 16, 2004.

38. Donovan interview.

39. ST interview with Jack (pseud.), 79, June 4, 2004.

40. ST interview with John Rechy, August 29, 2005.

41. Ed Jackson, "647: The Catch-All That Catches All," *Los Angeles Advocate*, June 1968, 9.

42. Quoted in William Mann, *Behind the Screen: How Gays and Lesbians Shaped Hollywood, 1910–1969* (New York: Viking: 2001), 87.

43. Kenneth Marlow, *The Male Homosexual* (Los Angeles: Sherbourne Press, 1965), 46.

44. Ibid.

45. Rechy interview, 71, August 29, 2005.

46. A number of our narrators recounted stories of a flashing red-light signal at the Canyon Club. However, one woman who went often to the Canyon Club says, "The guy who owned it was a cop, and the police never showed up"; she speculates, "Maybe he flashed the lights to add atmosphere. Maybe it was just a game." LF interview with Myra Riddell, 77, November 9, 2004.

47. Rothmiller, *L.A. Secret Police*, 73.

48. ST interview with Steve Hodel, 65, September 14, 2005.

49. Kevin Brownlow recalls that from its first days, Hollywood proved "a paradise" for blackmailers: *The Parade's Gone By* (New York: Alfred A, Knopf, 1968), 39. Organized crime used to target homosexuals for a blackmail scheme they referred to as "fruitshakes."

50. Gibbon interview; ST interview with James Miller, July 5, 2004.

51. ST interview with Bill Regan, 73, July 1, 2004.

52. ST interview with Aristide Laurent, 63, August 25, 2004.

53. ST interviews with Guy Richards, 73, June 21 and July 1, 2004.

54. Donovan interview. See also Cy Rice, *Defender of the Damned: Gladys Towels Root* (New York: The Citadel Press, 1964).

55. Weatherford interview.

56. Donovan interview. The attorney Bill Stephens, who defended men against entrapment charges, corroborated Donovan's obvservation. ST interview with Bill Stephens, 64, August 27, 2004.

57. Lisa Ben, taped interview with Paul Cain. We are indebted to Mr. Cain for sharing his transcription with us.

58. Jane Jones' bar is described in Lester Strong and David Hanna, "Hollywood Watering Holes, 30's Style," *Harvard Gay and Lesbian Review,* July 31, 1996.

59. Tess's various venues and names are described in Jack Lord and Lloyd Hoff, *How to Sin in Hollywood* (Hollywood: self-published, 1940), 38–39; in a taped interview with Rikki Streicher, July 1981, June Mazer Lesbian Archives, West Hollywood, California; in Beverly Hickok, *Against the Current: Coming Out in the 1940s* (Philadelphia: Xlibris, 2003); in Hickok interview; and in Hanna, "Hollywood Watering Holes."

60. LF interview with Dottie, 77, February 14, 2004.

61. Eileen Leaffer makes a similar distinction between lesbian nightclubs and bars in "Gay Life: An Ethnography of Lesbian Society" (unpublished paper, Occidental College, Department of Sociology, 1967), 1, June Mazer Lesbian Archives.

62. LF interview with Terry DeCrescenzo, April 4, 2004.

63. LF interview with Min, 80, and Marion, 76, February 12, 2004.

64. Streicher taped interview, June Mazer Lesbian Archives.

65. LF interview with Nancy Valverde, 73, October 5, 2004.

66. See, for example, Betty Friedan's *The Feminine Mystique* (New York: Penguin, 1963), for a discussion of how American women were encouraged after World War II to limit their pursuits exclusively to domestic life.

67. Though there is little evidence that lesbians were prosecuted under the 1915 California law against oral sex, because the law was part of the Penal Code, they knew they could be. See "The History of Sodomy Laws in the United States: California," http://www.sodomylaws.org/sensibilities/california.htm: The author identifies only four published cases that dealt with "consensual relations between women" in the United States.

68. LF interview with Maggie (pseud.), 76, February 13, 2004.

69. Liz quoted in Janise Gravlin, "Old Trees with White Blossoms: An Ethnography of Aging Lesbians" (master's thesis, University of California, Los Angeles, 1998), 57–58.

70. LF interview with K.C. (pseud.), 61, April 22, 2004. Softball attracted many young gay women in Los Angeles, and not all teams were generated in the bars. Elena Martinez (pseud.), who played with corporate-sponsored Buena Park and Huntington Park teams in the 1950s and '60s, says that those teams were largely lesbian, but she and her friends seldom hung out at the lesbian bars because they wanted to play well and they feared that drinking would interfere with their ability (LF interview, April 19, 2004). Softball games provided some social outlet where working-class and young gay women could meet other women. However, because softball was widely associated with lesbianism by mid-century and was played in public, many feared to participate, believing (ironically) that the bars, which were hidden from public view, were a safer venue.

71. LF interview with Sharon A, Lilly, 58, April 8, 2004. Elizabeth Lapovsky Kennedy and Madeline D. Davis have also observed, in their study of mid-century working-class lesbians in Buffalo, New York, that lesbian bars served as centers of community: *Boots of Leather, Slippers of Gold: The History of a Lesbian Community* (New York: Routledge, 1993). See also Joan Nestle, *A Restricted Country* (Ithaca, N.Y.: Firebrand Books, 1987), regarding community in lesbian bars in New York City.

72. Hearing before the Alcoholic Beverage Control Appeals Board of the State of California, December 16, 1959, "In the Matter of the Accusation Against William Ford and Ernestina D. Jones," proprietors of The Party Pad in Los Angeles, folder #404, file 50897, "Proceedings," 56.

73. "Proposed Decision," 8, 2, ibid.

74. Strong and Hanna, "Hollywood Watering Holes, 30's Style," 30. Allan Berube's narrators also observed that bars during World War II attempted to cater to mixed crowds in order to camouflage the character of the establishments and thus avoid police harassment: *Coming Out Under Fire,* 113–114.

75. LF interviews with Violet, 71, February 14, 2004, and Saundra Tignor, 67, August 20, 2004.

76. Raids on lesbian bars were also frequent in other big cities during those years: See, for example, Maxine Wolfe, "Invisible Women in Invisible Places: The Production of Social Space in Lesbian Bars," in *Queers in Space: Communities, Public Spaces, Sites of Resistance,* ed. Gordon Brent Ingram, Anne-Marie Bouthillette, and Yolanda Retter (Seattle: Bay Press, 1997), 301–324; Nestle, *A Restricted Country*; "The Gay Bar—Whose Problem Is It?" *The Ladder,* December 1959, 4–13+; and *Improper Bostonians,* comp. The History Project (Boston: Beacon Press, 1998).

77. LF interview with Stella Rush, 79, November 10, 2004.

78. LF interview with Eileen Cusimano, 67, October 6, 2004.

79. Leaffer, "Gay Life."

80. LF interview with Meko, 64, July 23, 2004.

81. LF interview with Sally (pseud.), 69, February 18, 2004.

82. "Mayor Fletcher Bowron Against Slacks for Women at City Hall," *Los Angeles Times,* April 22, 1942, 1.

83. "Woman Barber Wins Leniency," *Los Angeles Times,* May 1, 1940, A2.

84. LF interview with Nancy Valverde, November 5, 2004.

85. Valverde interviews.

86. Ibid.

87. LF interview with Frankie Hucklenbroich, 65, March 20, 2004. See also Frankie Hucklenbroich, *A Crystal Diary* (Ithaca, N.Y.: Firebrand, 1997), and Lillian Faderman, *Naked in the Promised Land* (New York: Houghton Mifflin, 2003).

88. LF interview with Flo Fleischman, 74, April 7, 2004.

89. Cross-dressing lesbians everywhere sought means—whether creative, silly, or demeaning—to evade masquerading laws by wearing three articles of women's clothing. A New Orleans woman, for example, remembers that in addition to wearing panties and bra, she sewed lace on all her socks so that the police would believe they were indeed an article of women's clothing: in Maxine Wolfe, "Invisible Women in Invisible Places."

90. Lou, in Gravlin, "Old Trees with White Blossoms," 40.

91. Violet interview.

92. LF interview with Betsy, 78, July 25, 2004.

93. LF interview with Harriet Perl, 83, February 14, 2004.

94. LF interview with Donna, 70, January 11, 2004.

95. Perl interview.

96. In Gravlin, "Old Trees with White Blossoms," 79.

97. LF interview with Myra Riddell, 77, November 9, 2004.

98. LF interview with Dr. Mandy (pseud.), 74, February 15, 2004.

99. Lesbians and gay men fronted for one another elsewhere as well in mid-century: See, for example, David K. Johnson, *The Lavender Scare: The Cold War Persecution of Gays and Lesbians in the Federal Government* (Chicago: University of Chicago Press, 2004), 150–154.

100. LF interview with Millie, 79, October 7, 2004.

101. Hickok interview.

102. Stanley interview.

103. LF interview with Jo Duffy, 78, July 27, 2004.

104. Millie interview.

105. LF interview with Saundra Tignor, 67, August 20, 2004.

106. LF interview with Mynun, 63, and Gayle, 64, April 5, 2004.

107. ST interview with Tom Gibbon, 82, and Bob Clark, 80, June 21, 2004.

CHAPTER 4

1. *The Ladder,* May 1957, 28. Under the name Lorraine Hansberry, the author went on to write the groundbreaking play *Raisin in the Sun* in 1959.

2. Mina Robinson (a.k.a. Mina Meyer), "The Older Lesbian" (master's thesis, California State University, Dominguez Hills, 1979).

3. Numerous interviews with "Lisa Ben" have been published in recent years. See, especially, Leland Moss, "An Interview with Lisa Ben," *Gaysweek,* January 23, 1978, 14–16; Eric Marcus, *Making History: The Struggle for Gay and Lesbian Equal Rights, 1945–1990* (New York: Harper-Collins, 1992); Zsa Zsa Gershick, *Gay Old Girls* (Los Angeles: Alyson, 1998); Rodger Streitmatter, *Unspeakable: The Rise of the Gay and Lesbian Press in America* (Winchester, Mass.: Faber and Faber, 1995); Vern Bullough, ed., *Before Stonewall: Activists for Gay and Lesbian Rights in a Historical Context* (interview with Lisa Ben by Florence Fleischman) (New York: Harrington Press, 2002); Paul D. Cain, *Leading the Parade: Conversations with America's Most Influential Lesbians and Gay Men* (Lanham, Md.: Scarecrow Press, 2002). We are grateful to Paul Cain for permitting us to see his unedited interview transcript. Eyde has given various reasons for changing her name to Lisa Ben ("lesbian"). In some interviews, she says she became Lisa Ben when the editors of the *Ladder* refused to let her publish a piece under the name "Ima Spinster." In others, she says she took the name Lisa Ben when invited to record a song for a Capitol Records album.

4. Marcus, *Making History,* 6.

5. Ibid., 8.

6. Beginning in the late nineteenth century in Europe, there were also several journals and magazines directed at "sexual inverts" (primarily men), including, in Germany, *Der Eigene* and *Jahrbuch für sexuelle Zwischenstufen* (the journal of Magnus Hirschfeld's Scientific-Humanitarian Committee); in Switzerland, *Der Kreis;* in France, *Le Cercle;* in Denmark, *Vennen.*

7. Gershick, *Gay Old Girls,* 49–50.

8. Cain transcript.

9. Gershick, *Gay Old Girls,* 49.

10. Film review of *Children of Loneliness, Vice Versa* 1, no. 1 (June 1947): 9–13.

11. "Here to Stay," *Vice Versa* 1, no. 4 (September 1947): 4–5.

12. Cain transcript. Jim Kepner, who was also a member of that group, cautiously discussed gay rights as a utopian "fantasy" with science fiction/fantasy fans that he suspected were gay.

13. Gershick, *Gay Old Girls,* 62.

14. Cain transcript.

15. Kepner Papers, ONE National Gay and Lesbian Archives, University of Southern California, Los Angeles.

16. George to James Kepner, July 1945, Kepner Papers. The phrase "bisexual" is clearly a euphemism for "homosexual."

17. Wally Jordan to James Kepner, May 14, 1943, Kepner Papers.

18. Harmodius, with his lover, fellow Athenian Aristogeitan, killed the tyrant Peisistratus in 514 B.C. Statues and a song immortalized the lovers; in 1827, Edgar Allen Poe translated the hymn, lauding "Harmodious the gallant and good" and Aristogeitan as "deliverers of Athens from shame."

19. Jordan to Kepner, May 14, 1943, Kepner Papers.

20. Marcus, *Making History*, 29.

21. Henry Gerber, "The Society for Human Rights," *ONE Magazine*, September 1962, 5–10.

22. Ibid.

23. On the Veteran's Benevolent Association, see Jonathan Katz, *Gay American History: Lesbians and Gay Men in the U.S.A.* (New York: Harper and Row, 1976), 635, and John D'Emilio, *Sexual Politics, Sexual Communities: The Making of a Homosexual Minority in the U.S., 1940–1970* (Chicago: University of Chicago Press, 1983), 32.

24. Joseph Hansen, *A Few Doors West of Hope: The Life and Times of Dauntless Don Slater* (Los Angeles: Homosexual Information Center, 1998).

25. See Stuart Timmons, *The Trouble with Harry Hay: Founder of the Modern Gay Movement* (Boston: Alyson, 1990), 136–137, and David K. Johnson, *The Lavender Scare: The Cold War Persecution of Gays and Lesbians in the Federal Government* (Chicago: University of Chicago Press, 2004), 170–171.

26. Harry Hay's life is discussed in Timmons, *The Trouble with Harry Hay*; Harry Hay and Will Roscoe, *Radically Gay: Gay Liberation in the Words of Its Founder* (Boston: Beacon Press, 1996); and Vern Bullough's entry in *Before Stonewall: Activists for Gay and Lesbian Rights in Historical Context,* ed. Vern Bullough (New York: Harrington Park Press, 2002).

27. Jordan to Kepner, March 19, 1943, Kepner Papers: "A silver ring . . . will be all you'll need to recognize them."

28. The founding date of the Mattachine Society has been variously set: See Timmons, *The Trouble with Harry Hay*, 132–138, 140, 143–145.

29. Cf. "the closet," a mid-twentieth-century term that refers to being secretive about one's homosexuality.

30. There are parallels between Gerber's fledgling movement and that of the L.A. homophiles. Each conceptualized an educational component, aimed both at building the awareness of gay men and at external law reform. "I realized at once that homosexuals themselves needed nearly as much attention as the laws pertaining to their acts." Gerber, "The Society for Human Rights," 5–10.

31. Though Mattachine's cell structure paralleled that of the Communist Party, it was, in fact, more closely based on such secret organizations as the Masons: See Timmons, *The Trouble with Harry Hay*, 156.

32. The organization was also called Knights of the Clocks: Jim Kepner, undated memo, Knights of the Clock folder, ONE National Gay and Lesbian Archives; also, Wayne R. Dynes, "W. Dorr Legg," in *Before Stonewall: Activists for Gay and Lesbian Rights in a Historical Context,* ed. Vern Bullough (New York: Harrington Park Press, 2002), 98.

33. "Installation Procedure," Knights of the Clock folder, subject file, ONE National Gay and Lesbian Archives.

34. ST interview with Harry Hay, 76, October 10, 1988.

35. Marvin Cutler [Dorr Legg], ed., *Homosexuals Today* (Los Angeles: ONE Press, 1956), 93.

36. ST interview with John Gruber, 77, June 23, 2005.

37. ST interview with Jim Kepner, August 22, 1986.

38. "Well, Medium and Rare," Paul Coates, *Los Angeles Daily Mirror*, March 12, 1953. See also Kenneth Frank, "Homosexuals, Inc.," 1950s file, undated clipping, ONE National Gay and Lesbian Archives. Frank, who proclaims, "Don't sell the twisted twerps short!" fancifully describes Mattachine as having 9,000 members and branches in "principal cities across the country"; he also comments on Hay's Communist ties and calls the organization "decidedly pinko."

39. Marcus, *Making History*, 59.

40. ST interview with Jamie Green, 71, March 11, 2006.

41. ST interview with John Gruber, 77, June 23, 2005. In interviews with Stuart Timmons, neither Hay nor the other Mattachine founders ever mentioned—and likely regretted—this political compromise. See Timmons, *The Trouble with Harry Hay*.

42. "The Fabulous Miss Destiny," *ONE Magazine*, September 1964, 6–12.

43. Jim Kepner, "The Loves of a Long-Time Activist: An Autobiography and Gay Movement History, Sort of" (unpublished manuscript, Los Angeles, 1993), 93, collection of ST. Kepner reports that "[when] Mexican doctors began performing sex-change operations, Carioca died on a Calexico butcher's table."

44. Denise D'Anne (Tony Albanese) as told to Cathy Cade, "Going the Distance: The Life of Denise D'Anne" (unpublished manuscript, 2003), 34.

45. Ibid.

46. Ibid, 45.

47. "The Fabulous Miss Destiny."

48. Ken Burns, quoted in Jim Kepner, "My First Sixty-five Years in Gay Liberation: Myself and Our Movement" (unpublished ms., c. 1980), 12, 1956 section, ONE National Gay and Lesbian Archives. The title of Kepner's ongoing manuscript shifted as he aged (see also chap. 6, note 9).

49. Five thousand is the figure cited by Streitmatter in *Unspeakable*, 28. Martin Block cites 3,400 copies in 1955, *ONE's* "peak year": in Marcus, *Making History*, 41. See also Craig Loftin, "Passionate Anxieties: McCarthyism and American Sexual Identity, 1945–1965" (PhD diss., University of Southern California, 2005).

50. J. B. Berkvam to ONE, Inc., received July 5, 1957: ONE, Inc., Social Service file, 1957, ONE National Gay and Lesbian Archives.

51. ST interview with Skip Foster, June 27, 2005.

52. Kepner, "My First Sixty-five Years," 24.

53. Joyce Murdock and Deb Price, *Courting Justice: Gay Men and Lesbians v. the Supreme Court* (New York: Basic Books, 2001), 27.

54. LF interview with Stella Rush (Sten Russell), 79, November 10, 2004.

55. ST interview with Eric Julber, 80, June 24, 2005.

56. Julber recalls a *Los Angeles Daily News* headline "Police Brutality Victim Acquitted."

57. By ONE's Legal Counsel (Eric Julber), "The Law of Mailable Material," *ONE Magazine*, October 1954, 5.

58. Julber interview.

59. (Julber), "The Law of Mailable Material," 6.

60. Julber interview.

61. Clarke quoted in "The Post Office Case," *ONE Confidential*, March 1956, 17.

62. Kepner, "My First Sixty-five Years," 19.

63. Murdoch and Price discuss the Supreme Court decision at length in *Courting Justice*, 27ff.

64. Interview with Dorr Legg in Cain, *Leading the Parade*, 5.

65. Don Slater, *ONE Magazine*, February 1958, 17.

66. "A Milestone in Education," *ONE Confidential*, December 1956, 3.

67. Merritt Thompson was closeted and used the pseudonym Tom Merritt.

68. Kepner, "My First Sixty-five Years," 24. See also Dorr Legg, *Homophile Studies in Theory and Practice* (Los Angeles: ONE Institute Press, 1994).

69. Legg, *Homophile Studies*.

70. "Milestone," 3.

71. Kepner, "My First Sixty-five Years," 34.

72. Cutler, *Homosexuals Today*, 81.

73. ONE case form (unnumbered), Social Service file, 1957, ONE National Gay and Lesbian Archives.

74. "You and the Law," *ONE Confidential,* August 1956, 12.

75. "Crackpots in Our Hair," *ONE Confidential,* December 1956, 2.

76. Dale Jennings, "Address to the Mattachine Society Banquet," November 14, 1953, Homosexual Information Center Archives.

77. Kepner, "My First Sixty-five Years," 4.

78. "Kwack, Kwack," *ONE Confidential,* 1956.

79. ST interview with Bob Mitchell, 90, June 19, 2005: Mitchell referred to himself as a "cardboard president" of ONE, Inc.'s board.

80. See Timmons, *The Trouble with Harry Hay,* 215–218, and Cain, *Leading the Parade,* 7–8.

81. Holly Devor, "How One Transsexual Man Supported ONE," 383–392, and Dynes, "W. Dorr Legg," 94–102, in *Before Stonewall.*

82. Laud Humphreys, "An Interview with Evelyn Hooker," *Alternative Lifestyles* 1, no. 2 (May 1978): 194. Isherwood later became her tenant.

83. Ibid., 195.

84. ST interview with John Gruber, 77, July 2, 2004.

85. Bruce Shenitz, "The Grand Dame of Gay Liberation," *Los Angeles Times Magazine,* June 10, 1990, 25.

86. Evelyn Hooker, "A Preliminary Analysis of Group Behavior of Homosexuals," *Journal of Psychology* 42 (1956): 217–225.

87. Gruber interview, July 2, 2004.

88. ST Interview with Skip Foster, June 27, 2005.

89. In Shenitz, "The Grand Dame," 20.

90. *The Ladder,* 1957, 15–16.

91. Some scholars have argued that working-class lesbians created their own protopolitical movements through the communities they formed in lesbian bars: See, for example, Joan Nestle, *A Restricted Country* (Ithaca, N.Y.: Firebrand, 1987), and Elizabeth Kennedy and Madeline Davis, *Boots of Leather, Slippers of Gold* (New York: Routledge, 1993), on lesbians in New York City and Buffalo.

92. ST interview with Herb Selwyn, 80, January 16, 2005. Similarly, Flo Fleischman complains of ONE Institute, which she visited in the late 1950s: "There was nothing to interest women, no women's values. Nothing but talk about restroom sex and entrapment": LF interview with Flo Fleischman, 74, April 7, 2004.

93. For example, Magnus Hirschfeld's Scientific Humanitarian Committee, established in Germany in 1897 to fight Paragraph 175 (which penalized male homosexuality), actively recruited women. Hirschfeld's 1896 book, *Sappho und Sokrates,* also emphasized that homosexuality was a "natural" phenomenon, common to both sexes.

94. Timmons, *The Trouble with Harry Hay,* 149.

95. On Bernhard's participation in early Mattachine, see ibid., 154. On Bernhard's career, see Tee Corinne, "Ruth Bernhard," in *The Queer Encyclopedia of the Visual Arts,* ed. Claude J. Summers (San Francisco: Cleis Press, 2004), 52–53.

96. Marilyn (Boopsie) Reiger played a crucial role in changing Mattachine from a secret society to a more transparent organization: See Martin Meeker, "Behind the Mask of Respectability: Reconsidering the Mattachine Society and Male Homophile Practice, 1950s and 1960s," *Journal of the History of Sexuality* 10, no. 1 (2001): 78–16; D'Emilio, *Sexual Politics,* 76–79; and Timmons, *The Trouble with Harry Hay,* 176–177.

97. Del Martin and Phyllis Lyon, *Lesbian/Woman* (1972; rpt. New York: Bantam, 1983), 210–211.

98. Inez Wagner, "Café Saturday Night," *ONE Magazine,* February 1954, 24.

99. Doug McAdam, *Political Process and the Development of Black Insurgency, 1930–1970* (Chicago: University of Chicago Press, 1982), 36–38.

100. See p. 99.

101. LF interview with Myra Ridell, 77, November 9, 2004.

102. For a discussion of NOW, Southern California Women for Understanding, and Connexxus, see chaps. 7 and 8.

103. Though the founders of Daughters of Bilities were not aware in 1955 of Mattachine's existence, by the following year, the two organizations had discovered one another. Del Martin acknowledged commonality between the all-lesbian Daughters and the primarily male Mattachine Society, and in the first issue of *The Ladder*, the Daughters' newsletter, she made sure to credit Mattachine as being the pioneer in "a nationwide movement to bring understanding to and about the homosexual minority." But at the same time, she observed crucial differences between the primary political interests of lesbians and gay men that explained why an all-lesbian organization was necessary. Lesbian concerns centered not on "difficulty with law enforcement," Martin wrote, but on issues of status—on the bigotry, intolerance, and discrimination they suffered merely by *being* lesbian: Del Martin, "President's Message," *Ladder* 1, no. 1 (October 1956): 6. John D'Emilio also discusses the influence of Mattachine on Daughters of Bilitis in its formative stages: *Sexual Politics*, see esp. 103–104. However, despite Martin's recognition of the pioneering role that the men's homophile organization played, serious conflicts developed between Daughters and the men's groups, culminating in 1961 when the ONE Institute composed a "Homosexual Bill of Rights" and Daughters opposed it, arguing that to announce such a bill would "set the homophile movement back into oblivion . . . and would leave us wide open as a target of ridicule from those who already dislike us": Del Martin, "How Far Out Can We Go," *The Ladder*, January 1961, 4–5.

104. In 1956 and '57, Del Martin appealed to Ann Carll Reid (Corky), then a writer for *ONE Magazine*, and Alison Hunter (Vicki), who was briefly the women's editor at *ONE Magazine*, to help her establish a Los Angeles chapter of Daughter of Bilitis. (Alison Hunter was a "floating name" used by several people who wrote for *ONE*.) Reid responded (April 2, 1956) that she would help in any way she could, DOB file, ONE National Gay and Lesbian Archives. An organizing meeting was held in Los Angeles in January 1957 ("Daughters Hold Brunch in L.A.—Plans for Chapter Underway," *The Ladder*, February 1957, 10), but the chapter was not established until 1958.

105. Rush interview.

106. LF interview with Ann Bannon, April 3, 2004.

107. Jonathan Katz interview with Barbara Gittings, in *Gay American History* (New York: Harper and Row, 1976), 425–426.

108. Kristen Esterberg suggests that Daughters of Bilitis went through three distinct phases of development, moving from an "integrationist" organization which took the position that lesbians were just like heterosexual women except for what they did in bed, to an organization allied with the militant segment of the homophile movement, to a feminist organization: "From Accommodation to Liberation: A Social Movement Analysis of Lesbians in the Homophile Movement," *Gender and Society* 8, no. 3 (1994): 424–443. However, the various Daughters chapters, which were organized eventually in other Southern and Northern California towns as well as in New York, Chicago, and Rhode Island, retained some autonomy in their direction. Regardless of the position the chapters took, the organization struggled always for membership.

109. Rush interview; also, Stella Rush's essay on Helen Sandoz in *Before Stonewall* (see note 32).

110. Rush interview.

111. Dorr Legg correspondence, in Daughters of Bilitis file, ONE Institute Papers, ONE National Gay and Lesbian Archives, and *ONE Magazine*, October–November, 1956, 37. Despite Legg's "nonsexist" efforts, lesbian leaders were often suspicious of him: See Martin, "How Far Can We Go?" Flo Fleischman recalls Legg as "a sexist": Fleischman interview.

112. "The Feminine Viewpoint," *ONE Magazine*, February 1956, 26–27.

113. Jane Dahr (James Barr Fugate), "Sappho Remembered," *ONE Magazine*, October 1954, 12–15. Stella Rush resigned from *ONE* in anger because, she complained, *ONE* men felt "justified in writing the most drastic opinions under a feminine pseudonym if a feminine [writer] happens to be lacking at the moment": Letter to ONE board, July 26, 1961, Tangentgroup, online, http://www.tangentgroup.org/history/RusgResig.html. Jim Kepner, in his essay "The Women of ONE" (ONE National Gay and Lesbian Archives), mentions several other women who played fairly minor roles on the magazine and in ONE, Inc.

114. Cutler, *Homosexuals Today*, 91. Edythe Eyde remembers Reid and Elloree as being among the readers of *Vice Versa* that she knew personally: Cain transcript.

115. Cain transcript.

116. Kepner, "My First Sixty-five Years," 8.

117. Ibid., 45.

118. Tee Corinne's telephone interview with Joan Corbin, December 10, 2000, in "Queer Caucus for Art," http://www.artcataloging.net/. (This article is no longer posted online.)

119. E-mail communication to ST from Craig Loftin, May 3, 2006.

120. Letter from Miss O. E. Fisher, October 12, 1957, ONE, Inc., Social Services file, 1957, ONE National Gay and Lesbian Archives.

121. Letter from Elizabeth Mellikant, January 23, 1956, ONE, Inc. Social Services file, 1956, ONE National Gay and Lesbian Archives.

122. Letter addressed to "Miss D'Ann Carroll [Ann Carll Reid], Feminine Editor," from Margot Robert, July 11, 1956, *ONE Magazine* letters, ONE National Gay and Lesbian Archives.

123. Letter addressed to "Dear Editor," from Clare Robertson, August 13, 1955, ONE National Gay and Lesbian Archives.

124. Ann Carll Reid to Miss Toni Lyon, July 5, 1954, ONE National Gay and Lesbian Archives. (ONE also received countless such requests from men for gay contacts, especially in rural areas.)

125. Letter from Ann Carll Reid to Clare Robertson, October 3, 1955, ONE National Gay and Lesbian Archives.

126. Letter from William Lambert (Dorr Legg) to Miss R. A. Tolmie, Augusta, Georgia, August 17, 1955, ONE, Inc., Social Services file, 1955, ONE National Gay and Lesbian Archives.

127. See Lillian Faderman, *To Believe in Women: What Lesbians Have Done for America* (New York: Houghton Mifflin, 1999).

128. Gene Damon (Barbara Grier), "The Year of the Chapter," *The Ladder*, December 1969–January 1970.

129. L.A. DOB Center announcement in *Lesbian Tide*, December 1971, 16–17, and inside cover.

130. Paul Welch, "Homosexuality in America: A Secret World Grows Open and Bolder," *Life*, July 27, 1964.

CHAPTER 5

1. Myron Roberts, "Our Changing Morality," *Los Angeles Magazine*, December 1963, 1960s file, ONE National Gay and Lesbian Archives.

2. The Brown Berets were among the chief organizers of the Chicano Moratorium in 1970, a protest that attracted 25,000 and was the largest North American Latino demonstration until the 2006 protests over immigration policies.

3. Social historian Andrew Kopkind writes that it took a few years after the Watts riots before "white radicals began to speak of 'revolution' or 'Revolution'": Arthur Kopkind, "Looking Backward: The Sixties and the Movement," *Ramparts*, February 1963. Perhaps Kopkind was thinking of the "Siege of Chicago" and Tom Hayden's threat during the 1968 Democratic Convention that "the period of organized, peaceful, and orderly demonstrations is coming to an end." "WE WILL BECOME WARRIORS," Hayden roared after pointing out that for blacks, peace-

ful tactics such as the 1963 March on Washington for Jobs and Freedom had less effect than the militant tactics of the Watts riots: Hayden's speech reported in *Los Angeles Free Press,* September 13, 1968. In Los Angeles, however, young people became "warriors" by 1966.

4. Art Seidenbaum, "Spectator, 1967," *Los Angeles Times,* January 10, 1967, DI.

5. ST interviews with David Crittendon, 59, October 12, 2004, and Lee Mentley, 56, August 19, 2005.

6. Mentley interview.

7. Art Berman, "Shutdown of Teenage Clubs Demanded by Businessmen," *Los Angeles Times,* November 15, 1966, 1.

8. Los Angeles in the mid- and late 1960s had an ongoing hippie "summer of love," both before and after the 1967 Haight-Ashberry "Summer of Love."

9. Ridgely Cummings, "Pershing Square Is Defoliated: City Says 'Get Out' to Eccentrics, Pensioners, Non-Conformists," *Los Angeles Free Press,* September 3, 1964, 1.

10. William T. Margolis, "A Plot to Overthrow the Overground," *Los Angeles Free Press,* March 10, 1967, 10–11.

11. Ibid.

12. Reported in "Obscenity Ordinance Ruling," *The Ladder,* January 1960, 20.

13. Quoted in Larry Gross and James D. Woods, *The Columbia Reader on Lesbians and Gay Men in Media, Society, and Politics* (New York: Columbia University Press, 1999), 292.

14. Sam Winston (Sam Allen), "The Bead Reader," *Los Angeles Advocate,* July 1968, 8.

15. "Cancer-Like Vice Spreads in Los Angeles," *Los Angeles Times,* January 29, 1961, G1, an article about prostitution, pornography, and narcotics, which mentions homosexuals in relation to a leap in the incidence of venereal disease.

16. ST interview with Milton, 62, June 15, 2004.

17. L. Jay Barrow, *Hollywood, Gay Capitol of the World: The Homosexual and How He Lives* (Van Nuys, Calif.: Triumph News Company, 1968), 14.

18. "Are You a Man?" (flier), Paul Lamport file, ONE National Gay and Lesbian Archives.

19. Robin Rauzi, "Lesbians Have Been Drawn to Area's Suburban Lifestyle Since Long Before 'Ellen,'" *Los Angeles Times,* April 27, 1997, B4 (Valley section); and LF interview with Jo Duffy, 78, July 27, 2004.

20. LF interview with Del Martinez, 71, August 12, 2005.

21. Carol Collins, "Sex Deviates Menace L.A.; Southland's VD Rises 1,000 Pct!" *Hollywood Citizen-News,* February 4, 1963, 1.

22. Carol Collins, "Parker Hits SD Coddling: Jail Terms Urged by City Officers," *Hollywood Citizen-News,* February 6, 1963, 1.

23. Paul Coates, "The Sick, Sick, Sick Young Men," undated clipping, c. February 1963, 1963 clippings file, ONE National Gay and Lesbian Archives. Coates' title parodies the 1959 "Ballad of the Sad Young Men."

24. Jon J. Gallo et al., "The Consenting Adult Homosexual and the Law: An Empirical Study of Enforcement and Administration in Los Angeles County," *UCLA Law Review* 13, no. 3 (March 1966): 643–832.

25. ST interview with Jon Gallo, 63, August 18, 2005.

26. Stephens interview.

27. LF interview with Connie Eddy, 62, July 23, 2004.

28. About a dozen of those bars were exclusively lesbian; another dozen were frequented by both lesbians and gay men: *The Address Book,* comp. Bob Damron, mid-1966, ONE National Gay and Lesbian Archives.

29. *Bob Damron's Address Book,* 1969, ONE National Gay and Lesbian Archives.

30. LF interview with Sharon A. Lilly, 58, April 8, 2004.

31. LF interview with Francesca Miller, 57, July 24, 2004.

32. Personal recollections of LF. See also John Rechy, "The City of Lost Angels," in *Beneath the Skin: The Collected Essays of John Rechy* (New York: Caroll and Graf, 2004), 30.

33. Don Noyes-More, *California Boomer: Keeper of the Story* (Plymouth, Vt.: Five Corners Publications, 2000), 61.

34. Stephens interview. Stephens noted that gay teens also enjoyed a circuit of house parties in the same era, where hundreds paid a dollar admission to an "old man" of twenty-five.

35. ST interview with Aristide Laurent, 63, June 30, 2004.

36. ST interview with L.N., June 18, 1997.

37. Barrow, *Hollywood, Gay Capitol,* 89.

38. Ibid., 67.

39. Ibid., 109. Owner Lee Glaze renamed Ciro's The Patch II.

40. Robert Gregory, editorial, *ONE Magazine,* August 1961, 4–5.

41. LF interview with Jeanne Cordova, 56, August 21, 2004. The magazine's confrontational tone was not immediately apparent: The first issue of the *Lesbian Tide* betrayed its roots in a 1950s organization, declaring that Los Angeles Daughters of Bilitis was "nonpolitical," that it staged "PEACEFUL" events, and that feminists were objectionable in their "I hate men" rhetoric: *Lesbian Tide,* July–August 1971, 1–3.

42. Erickson Educational Foundation brochure, Reed Erickson Collection, box 2, ONE National Gay and Lesbian Archives.

43. Institute for the Study of Human Resources brochure, Reed Erickson Collection, box 18, ONE National Gay and Lesbian Archives. See also Holly Devor, "How One Transsexual Man Supported ONE," 383–392, and Wayne Dynes, "W. Dorr Legg," 94–102, in *Before Stonewall: Activists for Gay and Lesbian Rights in a Historical Context,* ed. Vern Bullough (New York: Harrington Press, 2002). ONE offered a master's degree and doctorate in "Homophile Studies." Soon after ONE received the coup of accreditation, Erickson, who was addicted to drugs, claimed that his putative "wife," Evangelina, was suing him for 50 percent of his fortune, his sister and former wife were blackmailing him for money, and he could no longer afford to support the Institute. Beginning in 1984 to his death, Erickson tried unsuccessfully to evict ONE from the Milbank estate. (See correspondence between Reed Erickson and Dorr Legg, especially 1/3/83 and 1/14/83, box 18.) The Institute ceased offering degrees in 1986, but after Erickson's death, ONE was granted half interest in the estate by the courts. In 1997, ONE sold its share of the property; its library was moved to the ONE National Gay and Lesbian Archives at USC.

44. Brochure, "Society of Anubis, Inc.," Anubis file, ONE National Gay and Lesbian Archives.

45. *Anubis Bulletin,* March 1969, Anubis file, ONE National Gay and Lesbian Archives.

46. The Anubis raid is discussed in the *Los Angeles Free Press,* January 2, 1970, 2; and in *The Ladder,* April–May 1970, 31.

47. For example, letter to Anubis membership from Voter Registration chairman, January 21, 1970, Anubis file, ONE National Gay and Lesbian Archives.

48. Don Slater, "Protest on Wheels," *Tangents,* May 1966.

49. Stuart Timmons, *The Trouble with Harry Hay: Founder of the Modern Gay Movement* (Boston: Alyson, 1990), 220–222.

50. After his departure from ONE in 1965, Slater set up the Homosexual Information Center on Cahuenga Boulevard. Because he called his new magazine *Tangents,* the Center was alternately known as "the Tangents Group."

51. Slater, "Protest on Wheels."

52. Ibid.

53. Ibid.

54. "Patch Fights Three-Way Battle," *Los Angeles Advocate,* August 1968, 3+.

55. Kepner, who became an activist in the 1940s, remained so until his death in 1997. He joined Mattachine, ONE, the Council on Religion and the Homophile, and virtually every Los

Angeles–based gay organization throughout the 1960s and '70s, often serving on their boards and producing their newsletters.

56. Vernon Mitchell (obituary), *Los Angeles Times,* December 26, 1991; "Can Homosexuals Trust the Health Dept.? Two Views of the VD Danger: Mike Kinghorn says 'No!' 'We Must!' says Jim Kepner," *PRIDE Newsletter,* September 9, 1966, 2.

57. Other cities also showed signs of incipient gay radicalism in the 1960s. For example, Marc Stein points out that in Philadelphia, in 1965, three teenagers held "the first gay sit-in" in protest over the refusal of Dewey's Restaurant to serve homosexuals and people wearing "nonconformist clothing." See "The First Gay Sit-In," http://www.hnn.us/aritcles/116522.html. The New York City Mattachine Society staged a "Sip-In" in 1966 to protest a bar's refusal to serve avowed homosexuals: See John D'Emilio, *Sexual Politics, Sexual Community: The Making of a Homosexual Minority in the United States, 1940–1970* (Chicago: University of Chicago Press, 1983), 207–208. Susan Stryker's documentary, *Screaming Queens* (2005), concerns another early protest, in San Francisco in 1966, of transgender people. Columbia University chartered the first gay student organization in 1967.

58. Steve Ginsberg, "Pride Organizes Homophiles: New Group Wants Militant Civil Rights Drive," *Los Angeles Free Press,* 1966 (clipping), PRIDE file, ONE National Gay and Lesbian Archives.

59. *PRIDE Newsletter,* September 9, 1966, 4.

60. Ginsberg, "PRIDE Organizes Homophiles."

61. Ibid.

62. Jim Highland, "Raid!" *Tangents,* January 1967, 5. The Black Cat in Los Angeles was not related to the San Francisco Black Cat.

63. "Bushwhacker Declared Historic Site," undated memo (circa 1980), signed by Jim Kepner, Black Cat file, ONE National Gay and Lesbian Archives.

64. "Guilty As Charged," unsigned, undated manuscript, Black Cat file, ONE National Gay and Lesbian Archives.

65. Untitled clipping, *Open City,* October 11, 1967, Black Cat file, ONE National Gay and Lesbian Archives.

66. The gay protesters were joined by a Leftist nongay group, the Right of Assembly and Movement Committee. See also John Bryan, "Police Outrages Help Create Los Angeles Homosexual Rights Drive," *Los Angeles Free Press,* March 10, 1967, 5.

67. "Bushwhacker Declared Historic Site," ONE National Gay and Lesbian Archives.

68. Two San Francisco groups, the Council on Religion and the Homosexual and the Tavern Guild, supported the L.A. demonstration: "Monster of a Protest Set for Saturday," *Los Angeles Free Press,* February 10, 1967, 1. Jim Kepner appealed to the Manhattan chapter of the Daughters of Bilitis for support: Jim Kepner to DOB, New York City, March 2, 1967.

69. Joyce Murdoch and Deb Price, *Courting Justice: Gay Men and Lesbians v. the Supreme Court* (New York: Basic Books, 2001), 143–146.

70. "Gay-In in Griffith Park" (photo essay), *Los Angeles Advocate,* July 1968, 18. See also Moira Rachel Kenny, *Mapping Gay L.A.: The Intersection of Place and Politics* (Philadelphia: Temple University Press, 2001), 170–171.

71. "Patch Fights Three-Way Battle," *Los Angeles Advocate,* August 1968, 3+.

72. ST interview with Lee Glaze, 66, September 19, 2004.

73. Dick Michaels, "Patch Raids Police Station," *Los Angeles Advocate,* September 1968, 6–7.

74. Ibid.

75. Glaze interview.

76. ST interview with Aristide Laurent, 63, August 25, 2004.

77. Dudley Clendenin and Adam Nagourney, *Out For Good: The Struggle to Build a Gay Rights Movement In America* (New York: Simon and Schuster, 1999), chap. 18, "Citizen Goodstein."

78. Laurent interview.

79. "U.S. Capitol Turns on to Gay Power," *Los Angeles Advocate,* September 1967, 1.

80. Minutes, PRIDE, March 27, 1968, PRIDE file, ONE National Gay and Lesbian Archives. See also Mark Thompson, ed., *The Long Road to Freedom: The Advocate History of the Gay and Lesbian Movement* (New York: St. Martin's Press, 1992), xix.

81. Bill Rau, Dick Michaels' partner, became Bill Rand. Sam Allen wrote for the *Los Angeles Advocate* under the name Sam Winston.

82. P. Nutz [Aristide Laurent], "First L.A. Gay-In: Ultra High Camp," *Los Angeles Advocate,* April 1968, 3–4.

83. Laurent interview.

84. ST interview with Rob Cole, 75, July 25, 2005.

85. Jim Kepner, "The Posthumous Trial of Ramon Novarro, *Los Angeles Advocate,* October 1969, 5+; "Brothers Convicted of Novarro Murder Face Life," *Los Angeles Advocate,* November 1969, 1; "Paul Ferguson's Story: 'Tom Did It!'" *Los Angeles Advocate,* December 1969, 5+; "Tom Ferguson Blames Paul, then Confesses," *Los Angeles Advocate,* January 1970, 5+.

86. Notes from ST interview with Jim Kepner, May 25, 1990.

87. Cole interview.

88. For more on Goodstein's regime at the *Los Angeles Advocate,* see Clendenin and Nagourney, *Out for Good,* "Citizen Goodstein," 245–260.

89. Cole interview.

90. Written communication, Jeanne Barney to ST, July 11, 2005.

91. Laurent interview.

92. "What Is The C.R.H.?" *Concern: Newsletter of the Southern California Council on Religion and the Homophile,* February 1967, 1.

93. LF interview with Stella Rush, 79, November 10, 2004. As progressive as the Unitarian Church was, however, when Harry Hay approached its famous Rev. Steve Fritchman in 1952 with the request that he lend his support to the Mattachine Society, he was rebuffed: as discussed in Timmons, *The Trouble with Harry Hay,* 147.

94. Rev. Ted McIlvenna, quoted in *Concern* 5 (February 1967): 2.

95. LF interview with JJ (Jay) Vega, 50, September 18, 2004.

96. Troy Perry, *Don't Be Afraid Any More: The Story of Reverend Troy Perry and the Metropolitan Community Churches* (New York: St. Martin's Press, 1990), 34; and *Out for Good,* 179–180.

97. Perry, *Don't Be Afraid,* 36.

98. ST interview with Troy Perry, 65, August 30, 2005.

99. *God, Gays, and the Gospel: This Is Our Story,* documentary video (Los Angeles: Universal Fellowship of Metropolitan Community Churches, 1984).

100. ST interview with Lucia Chappelle, 53, August 3, 2005.

101. Perry interview.

102. John Dart, "A Church for Homosexuals," *Los Angeles Times,* December 8, 1969, C1.

103. ST interview with Joey Terrill, 49, July 31, 2004.

104. LF interview with Flo Fleischman, 74, April 7, 2004.

105. ST interview with Frank Zerelli, 60, July 8, 2004.

106. Display advertisement, *Los Angeles Times,* January 17, 1970, A3.

107. Chappell interview.

108. "Ex-Councilman Paul H. Lamport Dies," *Los Angeles Daily News,* April 3, 1984.

109. "Lamport Raps Stand of Two Newspapers," *Hollywood Citizen-News,* May 16, 1969.

110. Jim Kepner reported this suspicion to subscribers of his newsletter, *Pursuit Letter* no. 1, April 28, 1969, Paul Lamport file, ONE National Gay and Lesbian Archives.

111. Ibid.

112. "Lamport Raps Stand of Two Newspapers."

113. Ibid.

114. Quoted in "Cross Currents," *The Ladder,* October–November 1969, 32–33.

115. "Tiger Changing Stripes: Lamport Tours the Bars," *Los Angeles Advocate,* March 28, 1973.

116. ST interview with John (Jon) Platania, 65, July 28, 2005.

CHAPTER 6

1. LF interview with Jeanne Cordova, 56, August 21, 2004.

2. Karla Jay, *Tales of the Lavender Menace: A Memoir of Liberation* (New York: Basic Books, 1999), 168–171,

3. ST interview with Troy Perry, 65, August 30, 2005.

4. LF interview with Ariana Manov, 57, May 2, 2004.

5. Manov interview.

6. Sharon Raphael, "Coming Out: The Emergence of the Movement Lesbian" (PhD diss., Case Western Reserve University, 1974), 53.

7. The Gay Women's Service Center is described in Raphael, "Coming Out," 53–55; LF interview with Mina Meyer, 64, and Sharon Raphael, 62, April 5, 2004; and LF interview with Del Whan, 65, July 14, 2005.

8. E-mail correspondence to LF from Sharon A. Lilly, July 13, 2005.

9. Jim Kepner, "My First Sixty-six Years," in "Gay Liberation: Myself and Our Movement" (1989), 1969 section: "Praising Morris and Righting the Record" (unpublished ms.), ONE National Gay and Lesbian Archives, University of Southern California, Los Angeles. The title of Kepner's ongoing manuscript shifted as he aged (see also chap. 4, note 48).

10. Eighty chapters of the GLF formed after Stonewall. See http://www.angelfire.com/on2/glf2000/Page2.html.

11. Flier, "Gay Liberation Front," GLF-LA file, ONE National Gay and Lesbian Archives.

12. Morris Kight, "Where We've Been; Where We Are Going," *Front Lines* 1, no. 1 (December 1970): 2, 7–8.

13. ST interview with Gary Hundertmark, 57, September 14, 2004.

14. Wilson interview.

15. LF interview with Sharon A. Lilly, 58, April 8, 2004.

16. LF interview with Simone Wallace, 58, July 25, 2004.

17. LF interview with Sue Talbot, 57, and Liebe Gray, 58, October 4, 2004.

18. Marsha Salisbury et al., at the Lesbian Feminist Reunion, held at the ONE National Gay and Lesbian Archives, July 25, 2004.

19. LF interview with Donna Cassyd, 64, July 28, 2004.

20. Eric Marcus, *Making History: The Struggle for Gay and Lesbian Equal Rights, 1945–1990* (New York: HarperCollins, 1992), 32.

21. Lynn Lilliston, "The Woman Homosexual," *Los Angeles Times,* June 21–25, 1970.

22. It was resurrected three times before its permanent removal by Valerie Terrigno, first mayor of West Hollywood.

23. Letter dated January 8, 1971, from Bob Wright, associate producer, *Carol Burnett Show,* to John Bexter, GLF file, ONE National Gay and Lesbian Archives.

24. Letter from Troy Perry to Don Kilhefner (GLF), October 3, 1970, GLF file, ONE National Gay and Lesbian Archives.

25. See also "Eddie Nash Convicted on Seven Drug Counts," *Los Angeles Times,* October 6, 1982, B1, and "Murder Probe Figure Faces New Charges," *Los Angeles Times,* December 2, 1981, B11.

26. Written communication to ST from Jack Willis (pseud.).

27. "Down on the Farm," undated GLF flier, Gay Liberation Front L.A. Demonstrations file, ONE National Gay and Lesbian Archives.

28. "Why Can't We Hold Hands in Our Own Bars?" GLF flier, c. September, 1970, Gay Liberation Front L.A. Demonstrations file, ONE National Gay and Lesbian Archives.

29. ST interview with Jaime Green, 72, June 24, 2004.

30. Gay-In organizers claimed their purpose to be "to get our gay brothers and sisters out of their closets and to show society again that we intend to claim full participatory rights." *Front Lines* 1, no. 1 (December 1970): 6.

31. Mark Thompson, ed., *Long Road to Freedom: The Advocate History of the Lesbian and Gay Movement* (New York: St. Martin's Press, 1994), 36.

32. Complaint for Violation of Civil Rights, *Gay Liberation Front v. Edward M. Davis et al.*, August 7, 1970, U.S. District Court, Central District of California.

33. "Homosexuals Receive ACLU Aid in Parade Permit Fight," *Los Angeles Times*, June 13, 1970, B4. A detailed history of the Los Angeles gay pride parade, which is called "Christopher Street West" (a name chosen to obfuscate the parade's purpose to hostile Angelenos while communicating clearly to gays, who would have heard of the Stonewall Rebellion on Christopher Street) may be found at http://www.lapride.org/pages/cswhistory.html.

34. E-mail correspondence from Carolyn Weathers to LF, April 23, 2004; and other informants at the Lesbian Feminists reunion, July 25, 2004, at ONE National Gay and Lesbian Archives. San Francisco gays and feminists protested a similar meeting in May 1970.

35. Weathers and Lilly interviews.

36. "Alpine Co., Here We Come!" *Front Lines* 1, no. 1 (December 1970): 1+.

37. Proposals for "Master Planning the Alpine County Project" were submitted by Ladd & Kelsey and Architects and Economic Research Associates ($15,000 and $35,000 respectively), both dated December 2, 1970, GLF-LA file, ONE National Gay and Lesbian Archives.

38. "Alpine Co. Here We Come!"

39. "Homosexuals Weigh Move to Alpine County," *Los Angeles Times*, October 19, 1970.

40. "Alpine Co., Here We Come!"

41. Morris Kight interview, "Gay Liberation Front: 20th Anniversary," CD produced by Bob Dallmeyer, June 1989.

42. Weathers and Lilly interviews.

43. In one case, *People v. Manicap*, 1953, a heterosexual couple and another woman were charged and convicted of consensual oral sex on the testimony of LAPD officers, who had spied in their windows. That the three were African American may have encouraged this rare prosecution: CA Crim. 4992.

44. ST interview with Tom Coleman, 57, August 16, 2005; and e-mail correspondence to LF from Jeanne Cordova, January 19, 2006. Cordova and Troy Perry were among the Felons 6.

45. Gudron Fonfa, "Most Wanton Women," *The Lesbian Tide: A Feminist Lesbian Publication Written by and for the Rising Tide of Women Today*, July 1974, 8+.

46. California Statutes, 1975, chs. 71 and 877, pp. 131 and 1957.

47. Brenda Weathers interview.

48. Sharon Zecha, March 25, 1971 speech, rpt. in *Everywoman* 2, no. 10 (July 9, 1971).

49. LF interview with Jeanne Cordova, 56, October 3, 2004.

50. Michele Ross, "Gay Women's Lib Center," *Los Angeles Free Press*, October 23, 1970.

51. Brenda Weathers, *Front Lines* 1, no. 1 (December 1970): 6.

52. E-mail correspondence to ST from Stanley Williams, August 7, 2005.

53. "New Gay Women's Liberation Office at the Women's Center," *Women's Liberation Newsletter*, October 1970.

54. Michelle Moravec, "In Their Own Time: Voices from the Los Angeles Women's Movement, 1967–1976" (bachelor's thesis, University of California, Los Angeles, 1991), and Adele Wallace, "The Los Angeles Women's Movement: A Research Guide," Library and Information Science Special Project, San Jose State University, 1999.

55. LF interview with Ivy Bottini, 78, August 19, 2004. Bottini, who became a resident of Los Angeles, recalls that at the 1971 national NOW conference in L.A., "Word had just gotten out about what happened to me. I was a hero. It was so different from what I'd left in New York."

56. Personal recollection of LF.

57. Nancy Robinson at the Lesbian Feminist Reunion, held at the ONE National Gay and Lesbian Archives, July 25, 2004.

58. Lesbian Feminist Reunion.

59. Bottini interview.

60. Personal recollection of LF.

61. "Victory at Los Angeles," a headline in *The Ladder* blared, December 1971–January 1972, 14–16.

62. Whan interview.

63. Lesbian Feminist Reunion.

64. Formal groups such as most lesbians feared to join in earlier eras now boomed in L.A. In 1971, the three major lesbian groups, Daughters of Bilitis, the Gay Women's Services Center, and the Lesbian Feminists, were so active that women had to make hard choices about which of a plethora of interesting events to attend on any given night. The groups decided it was essential to form an "Intergroup Council" of lesbians/gay women so that they might coordinate calendars, discuss common problems, air differences, and plan joint events, such as the Gay Women's West Coast Conference, which they cosponsored in June of that year. By the next year the council had become so large, representing so many lesbian groups from Los Angeles and nearby cities such as Orange County and San Diego, that it was renamed the Southern California Coalition of Lesbian Organizations. The times were a far cry from a generation earlier, when lesbians were hiding out in bars or secret little enclaves and L.A. Daughters of Bilitis was starved for members.

65. Terry Wolverton reveals a meaning of the term "crackpot" that, she suggests, is apt for much of the L.A. lesbian experimentation of the 1970s: "During the process of alchemical transformation, as one substance is transmuted into another, the pot cracks. The old container is insufficient to house the new substance. Thus a 'crackpot' may be someone undergoing just such a transformation of the self." *Insurgent Muse: Life and Art at the Women's Building* (San Francisco: City Lights Books, 2002), 60.

66. The founders of Califia had been to Sagaris, a radical feminist institute in Vermont, and thought that California women "could do it better." ST interview with Josy Cattogio, 54, August 2005. About 20 percent of the Califia participants were heterosexual. See Marilyn Murphy, "Califia Community," in *Learning Our Way: Essays in Feminist Education,* ed. Charlotte Bunch and Sandra Pollack (New York: Crossing Pressing, 1983), 138–153; and Betty Brooks, "All the Teachers Are the Taught and All the Taught Are the Teachers," in Califia Community file, ONE National Gay and Lesbian Archives.

67. The Feminist Women's Health Center also specialized in safe abortions once they became legal in 1973. LF interview with Suzanne Gage, 52, September 10, 2004. Gage, who worked at the Feminist Women's Health Center, also founded in 1980 the Lesbian Well-Women's Clinic.

68. Lesbian life in 1970s Los Angeles is also discussed in Yolanda Retter, "Lesbian Spaces in L.A., 1970–90," in *Queers in Space: Communities, Public Places, Sites of Resistance,* ed. Gordon Ingram, Anne-Marie Bouthillette, and Yolanda Retter (Seattle: Bay Press, 1997).

69. LF interview with Sue Maberry, 55, and Cheri Gaulke, 56, July 27, 2004.

70. Gaulke interview.

71. LF interview with Ann Giagni, 55, July 27, 2004.

72. LF interview with Terry Wolverton, 50, August 19, 2004. See also Wolverton, *Insurgent Muse.*

73. Wolverton interview.

74. Maberry and Gaulke interview.

75. Gray interview.

76. Wallace interview.

77. McKay quoted in Jeanne Cordova, "When We Were Outlaws: A Memoir of the '70s" (unpublished ms., 2004 version).

78. Gray interview.

79. Cordova, "When We Were Outlaws."

80. Berson interview. If Olivia Records profited by its L.A. connection, the L.A. lesbian-feminist community also profited: Olivia's artists lent their talents to fund-raisers for the Woman's Building as well as to L.A. lesbian-feminist theater, such as Liebe Gray's 1976 play, *To See the Elephant*, about six nineteenth-century women who travel across America in hot pursuit of Calamity Jane (played by the Olivia Records star Cris Williamson), who is their passion: LF interview with Liebe Gray, 58, October 4, 2004.

81. LF interview (telephone) with Ginny Berson, August 3, 2005.

82. Wallace interview.

83. LF interview with Donna Cassyd, 64, July 28, 2004.

84. Several periodicals were published in 1970s Los Angeles that were either lesbian or lesbian-friendly, including *The Lesbian Tide*, started by Jeanne Cordova as the newsletter of the Los Angeles chapter of Daughters of Bilitis. For nine years *The Lesbian Tide* enjoyed the largest circulation of any lesbian magazine of the era. The *Lesbian News*, which began in 1975, is still in production. Lesbian-friendly periodicals included *Sister*, published by a collective at the Westside Women's Center and produced largely by lesbians, as well as *Everywoman* and *Chrysalis*.

85. "Joan," "The Gay Women's West Coast Conference," *Everywoman* 2, no. 10 (July 9, 1971), and Cordova interview, August 21, 2004.

86. E-mail correspondence from Carolyn Weathers to LF, January 15, 2006.

87. Raphael, "Coming Out," 77, and Cordova interview, August 21, 2004. Sheila Kuehl, then associate dean of students, virtually sneaked the conference onto campus one weekend in the spring, arranging to have rooms and auditoriums opened, but never indicating to UCLA authorities the nature of the group that would be using them: LF interview with Sheila Kuehl, July 24, 2004. In 1960, the Daughters of Bilitis held what was billed as the first "National Lesbian Conference" in San Francisco with approximately two hundred participants.

88. E-mail correspondence to LF from Jeanne Cordova, January 19, 2006.

89. Cordova interview, August 21, 2004.

90. Quoted in Joanne Meyerowitz, *How Sex Changed: A History of Transsexualism in the United States* (Cambridge, Mass.: Harvard University Press, 2002), 260.

91. Recollection of Kate Kauffman, quoted in "Changing the World, Building New Lives," http://www.CathyCade.com. Despite the various conflicts, the UCLA conference also inspired the Lesbian Rights Task Force of Los Angeles NOW to undertake an annual lesbian conference at USC, beginning in 1975. The NOW lesbian conference was coyly called "Women and Alternate Lifestyles."

92. LF interview with Mary Margaret Smith, 55, April 7, 2004.

93. Cassyd interview.

94. ST interview with John (Jon) Platania, 65, July 28, 2005.

95. Kight quoted in Thompson, *Long Road to Freedom*, 55.

96. ST interview with Joey Terrill, 49, July 31, 2005.

97. John [*sic*] Platania, "The Gay Community Services Center: A proposal directed toward the planning, programming, funding, and implementation of a multiple human services center open to homosexual women and men of the Greater Los Angeles Area," July 1971, collection of ST, courtesy Jon Platania.

98. Richard Nash, "Power to Gay People: A Los Angeles Experiment in Community Action," *After You're Out: Personal Experiences of Gay Men and Lesbian Women*, ed. Karla Jay and Allen Young (New York: Pyramid Books, 1975), 248–255.

99. E-mail correspondence to LF from Terry DeCrescenzo, January 17, 2006.

100. Don Kilhefner to James Griffith (IRS), May 14, 1973, ONE National Gay and Lesbian Archives.

101. John Kyper, "Gay Community Centers," Los Angeles, box 104-106, ONE National Gay and Lesbian Archives.

102. Terrill interview.

103. Dudley Clendinen and Adam Nagourney, *Out for Good: The Struggle to Build a Gay Rights Movement in America* (New York: Simon and Schuster, 1999), 84.

104. Lachs interview.

105. Remarks by Don Kilhefner and Morris Kight, "Speaking the Vision," Plummer Park, November 7, 1986.

106. ST interview with Steve Schulte, 59, September 8, 2005.

107. Lynn Lilliston, "Help Center for the Gay Community," *Los Angeles Times,* July 6, 1973, B1.

108. Wilson interview.

109. ST interview with Ben Teller, 64, September 2, 2005.

110. Ibid.

111. ST interview with Ed Edelman, 74, September 5, 2005.

112. "Gay Clients," developed by Don Clark and Betty Berzon, box 104-106, ONE National Gay and Lesbian Archives.

113. Wilson interview.

114. ST Interview with Ken Bartmess, 80, June 27, 2005.

CHAPTER 7

1. ST interview with Steve Lachs, 60, July 21, 2004.

2. Robin Stevens, "Eating Our Own," *The Advocate,* August 13, 1992, 32.

3. February 27, 1955, Homosexual Information Center Library, California State University, Northridge.

4. See chap. 4.

5. ST interview with Rick St. Dennis, 56, August 27, 2005.

6. ST interview with John (Jon) Platania, August 17, 2005.

7. ST interviews with Deni Ponty, 57, July 15, 2005; Josy Cattogio, 54, September 1, 2005; and Cosmo Bua, 53, September 6, 2005.

8. ST interview with Rob Wray, 49, September 7, 2005.

9. *Southern California Women Newsletter,* November–December 1978, 4. (The name of the newsletter was altered throughout the years as the group changed affiliation; see references below to Southern California Women for the Whitman-Radclyffe Foundation, Southern California Women for Understanding, etc.)

10. ST interview with Mike Manning, 57, August 28, 2005.

11. John Rechy, eulogy, "Tribute to Morris Kight," January 29, 2000, ST's personal collection.

12. E-mail correspondence from Robin Tyler to LF, September 15, 2005.

13. Loraine Hutchins, "Festival," *Off Our Backs* 11, no. 10 (November 1981): 1+.

14. LF interview with Mina Meyer, 64, April 5, 2004. The strike had essentially destroyed the women's clinic. When Josy Catoggio joined the Center in 1978, Sheldon Andelson, head of the board, discussed with her the idea of establishing another women's health clinic, but Catoggio felt that by then the Feminist Health Center had sufficiently filled the gap and the Gay Community Services Center's efforts would be redundant: ST interview with Josy Catoggio, 54, August 1, 2005.

15. LF interview with Sylvia Rhue, 56, October 7, 2004.

16. ST interview with Michael Weinstein, 53, September 20, 2005.

17. ST interview with Jaime Green, 72, June 24, 2004.

18. Carolyn Weathers, "An Early History of the Alcoholism Center for Women" (unpublished document), LF's personal collection.

19. Letter from Don Kilhefner to Dr. Gilbert Shaw, chief administrator of the federal granting agency (NIAAA), proposing that "APW be enabled to establish its autonomy and operate independently of GCSC," May 8, 1975. We are grateful to Terry DeCrescenzo for drawing this correspondence to our attention.

20. LF interview with Brenda Weathers, 67, April 5, 2004.

21. "Gay Center May Drop One Million Dollar Program," *NewsWest,* May 30, 1975.

22. LF interview with Robin Podolsky, 48, April 6, 2004.

23. "Chronology of Recent Events at the Gay Community Services Center," April 29, 1975, in GCSC file, June Mazer Lesbian Archives, West Hollywood, California.

24. Weinstein interview.

25. ST interview with Bruce Reifle, 63, September 29, 2005.

26. Jeanne Cordova, "The Strike," in "When We Were Outlaws: A Memoir" (unpublished ms., 2004 version).

27. LF interview with Lillene Fifield, 62, July 28, 2004.

28. "Doctors Say 'No' to GSCS Clinic," *Lesbian News,* October 1975, 2.

29. LF interview with Mary Margaret Smith, 55, April 7, 2004.

30. "Women Speak Out About GCSC," ONE National Gay and Lesbian Archives, University of Southern California, Los Angeles.

31. "'Gunfight' at the L.A. Saloon," *Lesbian News,* September 1975, 1; and LF interview with Jinx Beers, 72, August 27, 2005.

32. Fifield interview.

33. LF interview with Josy Catoggio, 53, July 26, 2004.

34. "GCSC Dispute Settled," *Lesbian News,* September 1978, 1, and e-mail correspondence to LF from Jeanne Cordova, January 19, 2006.

35. LF interview with Carol Nottley, 65, October 10, 2005.

36. LF telephone interview with Beth Nottley, 48, October 21, 2005.

37. Carol Nottley interview.

38. Bua interview.

39. ST interview with Ben Teller, 64, September 2, 2005.

40. Carol Nottley interview. The Los Angeles Gay Community Services Center took a leap toward professionalization in 1977, when Carol Nottley was recruited from a Beverly Hills certified public accounting firm to become the Center's chief financial officer. During her tenure, Nottley says, she often had to struggle with the staff who were left over from the more radical early years. "They didn't like structure. They just wanted a place that was theirs."

41. Schulte interview.

42. Bua interview. See also the *Los Angeles Times* article reporting critics' complaints that Schulte, "in his zest to legitimize and sanitize the center, turned his back on people who depended on it for basic services like food and legal aide": Alan Citron, "Homosexual Quits Job to Run for Office," *Los Angeles Times,* December 22, 1983, WS1.

43. Memo dated 2/15/78, Gay Community Services Center, box 103-118, ONE National Gay and Lesbian Archives.

44. Schulte interview. Gay Community Services Center services to the needy did expand with the influx of money and they continue to this day, but the name has been changed to the "Gay and Lesbian Center" to reflect a broader purpose. In the 1990s, the Center began a fund-raising campaign (with a lead donation of $1 million) to establish the Village, a separate lesbian/gay venue, which offered programs that were not "crisis oriented." The Lily Tomlin/Jane Wagner Cultural Arts Program at the Village includes theatrical productions and art exhibits, as well as book discussion groups, courses such as "Taking the Mystery Out of Remodeling Your Home," and a comprehensive program for lesbian and gay seniors: LF interviews with Lorri Jean (CEO of

the Gay and Lesbian Center), 47, April 30, 2004, and Julia Salazar (Director of Community Outreach and Education), 47, August 19, 2004.

45. LF interview with JJ (Jay) Vega, September 18, 2004.

46. LF interview with Terry DeCrescenzo, April 4, 2004.

47. "Annual Summer Lawn Party Set for August 27," *The Center News,* Summer 1989, 1.

48. Information from LF interview with Rita Baird, 58, July 25, 2004: Los Angeles Gay Community Services Center board member from 1983 to 1986.

49. DeCrescenzo interview.

50. LF interview with Del Martinez, 71, August 12, 2005.

51. Ibid.

52. Ibid.

53. *Connexxus Newsletter,* January 10, 1985.

54. Martinez interview. See also fund-raising flier, "The Vision Connects Us: So Far It's Working," 1988, Connexxus Papers, June Mazer Lesbian Archives, West Hollywood, California.

55. Garland Richard Kyle, "Connexxus May Well Be the Most Cost-Effective Human Service Organization in All of Los Angeles County," *Frontiers* 6, no. 23 (March 9–March 23, 1988): 70–71.

56. Moira Rachel Kenney, *Mapping Gay L.A.: The Intersection of Place and Politics* (Philadelphia: Temple University Press, 2001), 136.

57. Martinez interview. The Gay and Lesbian Community Services Center's Lesbian Central had been disbanded by then. Julia Salazar (who worked at the Center from 1982 to 1995) says, "There were several really integral women on the board, such as Gwen Baba, a philanthropist, and they felt lesbians shouldn't want to be shuffled into that little space. We met as a group and said, 'What if we made the entire center a place for women, not just this room?'" In 1988, Salazar was asked to create more women's programming, including courses such as "Dating Skills for Women," "Effective Public Speaking," "Astrology for Women," "Buying Your First House," and creative writing classes: Salazar interview.

58. LF interview with Torie Osborn, April 30, 2004. Also, Torie Osborn, *Coming Home to America: A Roadmap to Gay and Lesbian Empowerment* (New York: St. Martin's Press, 1996).

59. Wilson quoted in "Gayle Wilson—Elitist," *Southern California Women Newsletter,* November–December 1978, 1.

60. ST interview with Bob Geoghegan, 61, September 5, 2005.

61. Manning interview, and "Gay Community Alliance," subject file, ONE National Gay and Lesbian Archives.

62. Gay political activists, including Dave Glascock, volunteered for Pines' campaign, sensitizing Pines to the injustice of certain city policies and practices. The gay philanthropist Lloyd Wrigler was Pines' most generous contributor. District Attorney Vince Bugliosi campaigned in gay bars a year before Pines did so.

63. ST interview with Burt Pines, 66, September 22, 2005.

64. Frank del Olmo, "Pines to Curb 'Gay Bar' Prosecutions," *Los Angeles Times,* April 23, 1974, A1.

65. "'No Legal Bars to Homosexuals as Officers'—Pines," *Los Angeles Times,* May 10, 1975, A1. See also, "Thank You, Burt," *NewsWest,* May 30, 1975, in which the new L.A. gay paper acknowledged gay Angelenos' debt to Burt Pines. Pines remained gay-friendly and in 1981 was appointed by Governor Jerry Brown to head a California State commission studying discrimination against homosexuals, the elderly, and the handicapped.

66. ST interview with Ed Edelman, 74, September 5, 2005.

67. "Edelman Says He Knew of Gay Aide's Past Conviction," *Los Angeles Times,* January, 14, 1975, B3.

68. ST interview with Troy Perry, 65, September 16, 2005, and ST interview with Mark Haile, 49, December 13, 2005.

69. Edelman interview.

70. ST interview with Mark Thompson, 53, October 29, 2005.

71. "Chief Davis Cancels His Subscription," letter to the editor, *Los Angeles Times,* August 20, 1975, A12.

72. ST interview with Jeanne Barney, July 19, 2005.

73. "Southland," *Los Angeles Times,* June 29, 1976, B2.

74. Barney interview.

75. ST interview with Aristide Laurent, 63, August 25, 2004.

76. Barney interview.

77. "LAPD Has Been Cowed by Gays, Davis Charges," *Los Angeles Times,* May 21, 1976, E1.

78. Perry interview. Peggy Stevenson understood that she was reelected to her council seat in good part because of the gay vote, and she was the Los Angeles City Council's most important ally of the gay community in those years.

79. "The Los Angeles Gay and Lesbian History Map," "Los Angeles Lesbians" file, ONE National Gay and Lesbian Archives.

80. "Results of Poll Conducted by Mayor Bradley's Pollsters, 1977," Gay Press file, ONE National Gay and Lesbian Archives.

81. The term was coined in 1976 in Maupin's *Tales of the City.*

82. Orion's purpose and membership described in LF interview with Diane Abbitt, 62, October 17, 2005.

83. Lachs interview.

84. Ibid.

85. Dudley Clendenin and Adam Nagourney, *Out for Good: The Struggle to Build a Gay Rights Movement in America* (New York: Simon and Schuster, 1999), 357.

86. Doyle McManus, "Gay Rights Group Displays Power," *Los Angeles Times,* March 18, 1979, C5.

87. As told to LF in Abbitt interview. It is perhaps significant that MECLA decided to add women to its board the month after the June 1977 success of Anita Bryant's vicious Dade County, Florida, campaign to repeal gay rights. Bryant's campaign argued that the gay movement was really about increasing opportunities for gay men to have sex with impunity. As even the homophiles recognized thirty years earlier, the presence of lesbians in the organization would show that its purpose was more serious.

88. Abbitt interview.

89. LF interview with Roberta Bennett, 63, December 18, 2004, and Robbi Simon, "herstories/theirstories" (an interview with Roberta Bennett and Diane Abbitt), *Southern California Women for Understanding Newsletter,* December 1982–January 1983, 10–11.

90. Simon, "herstories/theirstories," and Bennett and Abbitt interviews.

91. Bennett and Abbitt interviews.

92. Bennett interview.

93. LF interview with Esther (pseud.), 74, December 19, 2004.

94. "Gay Rights: Is a Backlash Forming?" *Los Angeles Times,* July 29, 1978, F1. See also the discussion of Anita Bryant's and John Briggs' campaigns against gay rights in Clendenin and Nagourney, *Out for Good.*

95. ST interview with David Mixner, 59, September 4, 2005.

96. Jim Kepner, "Becoming a People: A 4,000-Year Chronology of Gay and Lesbian History" (Los Angeles: self-published, 1995), 110, ST collection.

97. "New Group Already at Work: March Its First Success," *NewsWest,* June 23, 1977, 7.

98. Ibid.

99. LF interview with Ivy Bottini, 78, August 19, 2004.

100. Initiative text from *Southern California Women Newsletter,* 1978.

101. Bottini interview.

102. Myra Riddell, "Notes from the Chair," *Southern California Women/Whitman-Radclyffe Foundation News,* 1977.

103. Clendenin and Nagourney, *Out for Good,* 382–383. Despite the straight shield and obfuscating ploys, gay talent really ran the campaign. For example, Sally Fiske, a television anchor, came out as a lesbian on the local "Evening News" because she was outraged by Briggs. When she was fired from her job, she became the public relations director of No on 6.

104. Doug Shuit, "Bitter Fight Expected on Gay Teacher Issue," *Los Angeles Times,* June 2, 1978, B3.

105. LF interview with Suzanne Gage, 52, September 10, 2004.

106. LF interview with Robin Podolsky, 48, April 6, 2004.

107. ST interview with John Morgan Wilson, 60, July 18, 2005.

108. Mixner interview.

109. Bottini interview. See also: "Gayle Wilson—Elitist," *Southern California Women Newsletter,* November–December 1978, 1.

110. Mixner interview.

111. Stonewall Democratic Club Announcement of Its Agenda for Summer and Fall of 1978, Stonewall Democratic Club files, ONE National Gay and Lesbian Archives.

112. Podolsky interview.

113. Mixner interview.

114. Bottini interview.

115. Mixner interview.

116. Jinx Beers, editorial, *Lesbian News,* November 1978, 1.

117. Mixner interview.

118. Quoted in "One Hell of a Campaign—And We Won!" *Southern California Women Newsletter,* November–December 1978, 1.

119. Jinx Beers, editorial, *Lesbian News,* December 1978, 10–11.

120. "Gay Rights Group Displays Power," *Los Angeles Times,* March 18, 1979.

CHAPTER 8

1. Lucinda Pennington, "But Will It Play in West Hollywood?" *Los Angeles Magazine,* May 1981, 117–118.

2. ST interview with Steve Schulte, 59, September 8, 2005.

3. The real Boystown had been started by Father Flanagan in 1917 to care for orphaned newsboys.

4. Jim Morris, a retired African American bodybuilder who had won the title of Mr. America in 1973, owned the gym and pioneered personal training. "Big Weenies" T-shirts were popular among gay and even straight Angelenos. Following every fad of his day, the owner, Charles Roberts, even organized the Big Weenie jogging team.

5. Quoted in Pennington, "But Will It Play in West Hollywood?" Assertions about gay affluence have been highly controversial in the community. See John W. Stiles, "The Myth of Gay Affluence: Why Does the World Think We're So Well Off? And How Is It Hurting Us That They Do?" *OutSmart,* June 2004; and M. V. Lee Badgett, "Income Inflation: The Myth of Affluence Among Gay, Lesbian and Bisexual Americans," *Income Inflation* (joint publication of the Policy Institute of the National Gay and Lesbian Task Force and the Institute for Gay and Lesbian Strategic Studies, Washington, D.C., 2000), http://www.thetaskforce.org/downloads/income.pdf.

6. "But Will It Play in West Hollywood?" ("Gay" in this *New Yorker* cartoon referred, of course, to men and did not include lesbians, who were perceived by big business as barely better off financially than their straight female counterparts.)

7. Photos in the Ah Men file, ONE National Gay and Lesbian Archives, University of Southern California, Los Angeles.

8. "Listen," *Los Angeles Times,* December 7, 1979, K6.

9. Doug Edwards, "Business: Gene Burkard, the Man Behind International's Mail Male," *The Advocate,* June 28, 1979. Burkard began his business in San Diego before opening a West Hollywood shop.

10. "Studio One a Big Hit!" clipping, *Data Boy Southern California* (July 1977), Studio One file, ONE National Gay and Lesbian Archives.

11. ST interview with Lee Glaze, 66, September 19, 2004.

12. Dennis Hunt, "Disco DJ: Producer of the Beat," *Los Angeles Times,* Jan 12, 1979, F14.

13. Jack Slater, "Discotheques Dance to Another Tune," *Los Angeles Times,* August 11, 1976, G1.

14. Ibid.

15. Jan Lang, "A Higher Goal," letters to the editor, *Los Angeles Times,* August 29, 1976, E18.

16. Personal recollections of ST.

17. ST interview with Mark Haile, 49, December 13, 2005. Ironically, Manny Slali, an Arab Mexican, was the *Billboard*-anointed deejay who made the club's reputation in its early years: "Disco DJ: Producer of the Beat," *Los Angeles Times,* January 12, 1979, F14.

18. Haile interview.

19. Dave Johnson, "Studio One Hit with Charges of Racism, Sexist Discrimination," *Los Angeles Free Press,* June 13, 1975. See also Eric Wat, "Three Pieces of ID," in *The Making of a Gay Asian Community: An Oral History of Pre-AIDS Los Angeles* (Lanham, Md.: Rowman and Littlefield, 2002), 55–58.

20. Wat, "Three Pieces of ID," 56. Asians, blacks, and Latinos, who compose large segments of L.A.'s gay population, were eventually welcomed by enterprising gay businessmen who built vast dance clubs catering to them.

21. LF interview with Francesca Miller, 57, July 24, 2004.

22. "Discotheques Dance," *Los Angeles Times,* August 11, 1976.

23. ST interview with Troy Perry, 65, August 30, 2005. Perry recalls that Hal Gitman, the manager of Dude City, told him that "gay men don't want women in the bar." Perry replied, "Nonsense. I've never met a gay man yet who'll let a woman get in the way of his cruising."

24. For more on the history of L.A.'s baths, see Eddie Coronado's extensive Web site, http://www.gaytubs.com/losangels.htm.

25. E-mail correspondence, "Jack" (age unknown) to Eddie Coronado, October 10, 1999.

26. Clubs exclusively for sex, with no pretense of bath facilities, were known as "dry baths." The phenomenon grew in the 1970s.

27. ST interview with Rick St. Dennis, 56, August 27, 2005. A gay businessman, Marty Benson, opened several bathhouses catering to older and heavier men; he became extremely rich in the process.

28. "Jack" to Eddie Coronado, October 10, 1999; and "Richard" (age unknown), September 27, 1999.

29. E-mail correspondence, "Raul" (age unknown) to Eddie Coronado, September 20, 1999.

30. "Today," biography and excerpts of award acceptance speeches, p. 1 (c. 1993), Andelson file, ONE National Gay and Lesbian Archives.

31. David Mixner, *Stranger Among Friends* (New York: Bantam Books, 1996), 163.

32. Lauren Hanson, "The Life and Times of Robin Tyler," *Lesbian News,* July 1991, 50.

33. LF interview with Jeanne Cordova, 56, October 3, 2004.

34. Scott Anderson, "The Gay Press," *The Advocate,* December 13, 1979, 22. Cordova points out that even the great radical media icon, the *Los Angeles Free Press,* had become "much less political and more sexual" before its demise in 1977: Cordova interview, October 3, 2004.

35. Cordova interview, October 3, 2004.

36. *Southern California Women for Understanding Newsletter,* Summer 1976.

37. SCWU Steering Committee minutes, June 8, 1978, SCWU Papers, June Mazer Lesbian Archives, West Hollywood, California.

38. LF interview with Frieda (pseud.), 74, August 20, 2004.

39. LF interview with Marion (pseud.), 78, August 20, 2004.

40. SCWU Steering Committee minutes, January 5, 1978.

41. "Surprise Information," policy statement, SCWU Activities Committee file, June Mazer Lesbian Archives.

42. SCWU Activities Committee file, June Mazer Lesbian Archives.

43. Such complaints were leveled against SCWU even by its own members. In the February 1977 newsletter, for example, Dr. Shevvy Healy complained that because SCWU charged an admission of $7.50 for Jean O'Leary's speech at the Convention Center, black and Chicana women had been unable to attend (p. 5). See also Irene Robertson's impassioned defense in the following newsletter, March 1977, in which she says that SCWU works to combat the stereotype that there are no affluent black and Chicana lesbians (p. 2).

44. Board of Directors Minutes: SCWU Goals, August 23, 1984, SCWU Papers, June Mazer Lesbian Archives.

45. Executive Committee minutes, July 21, 1983, SCWU Papers; Agenda, Board of Directors, August 25, 1983, SCWU Papers, June Mazer Lesbian Archives.

46. *Lesbian News,* August 1982, 3.

47. Flier announcing O'Leary's speech in SCWU Activities Committee file, SCWU Papers, June Mazer Lesbian Archives.

48. LF interview with Jean O'Leary, February 16, 2004.

49. LF interview with Heather Leavitt, 40, July 20, 2004.

50. John D'Emilio, *Making Trouble* (New York: Routledge, 1992), 258.

51. See Southern California Women for Understanding's list of lesbian bars in which they intended to distribute their newsletter: "SCWU Board Decides to Bar None," *SCWU Newsletter,* February–March 1983.

52. In 1981, annual gay-male-household incomes averaged $30,000 and lesbian incomes averaged less than $20,000: Lucinda Pennington, "But Will It Play in West Hollywood?" *Los Angeles Magazine,* May 1981, 118.

53. Seventy-five percent of the members of the upscale Southern California Women for Understanding admitted in the organization's survey that they "liked" lesbian bars: "SCWU Board Decides to Bar None."

54. LF interview with Marci (pseud.), 55, July 25, 2004.

55. Marci interview. Styles changed from year to year in lesbian bars of the 1970s. Suzanne Gage says that when she arrived at the Palms in the early 1970s, the women had "an androgynous, studied look—leotards or spaghetti straps, tight jeans, belts with studs. Country Western was big." But even then, "going to the Palms was like making an appearance," Gage notes. "Everyone is checking you out. This is Hollywood, after all." LF interview with Suzanne Gage, 52, September 10, 2004.

56. Gage interview.

57. Leavitt interview.

58. LF interview with Sheree Rose, August 30, 2004.

59. See chap. 7 for the transsexual conflict at the West Coast Lesbian Conference in 1973.

60. Rose interview.

61. LF interview with Vivian Escalante, 51, December 3, 2005.

62. Irene Weiss, letter to the editor, *Lesbian News,* August 1982, 28.

63. Some SM lesbians, including Sheree Rose, have been active in both radical feminist politics and SM and say that they are not mutually exclusive.

64. Arlene Stein, "All Dressed Up and No Place to Go: Style Wars and the New Lesbianism," *Out/Look,* Winter 1989, 36.

65. Performed by Lotus Lame and the Lame Flames, a girl-punk band masterminded by Lee.

66. "Disco Sucks" was a movement that spanned British and U.S. cities starting in 1979; some felt it was clearly antigay, despite the gay leadership in punk rock: See Peter Braunstein, "The Last Days of Gay Disco," *Village Voice,* June 24–30, 1998.

67. ST interview with Jack Marquette, 54, September 18, 2005.

68. ST interview with John Callahan, 61, September 23, 2005.

69. Brendan Mullen, Stuart Timmons and Geza X, "Craig Lee, 1956–1991," *LA Weekly,* October 18, 1991.

70. Personal observation of ST, c. 1983.

71. LF interview with Phranc, 47, August 18, 2004.

72. Rose interview.

73. LF interview with Fran (pseud.), 40, August 1, 2004. Bisexuality among the female punk rockers in Hollywood during the early 1980s is also described in Aimee Cooper, *Coloring Outside the Lines: A Punk Rock Memoir* (Elgin, TX.: Rowdy's Press, 2003).

74. Phranc interview.

75. Fran interview.

76. Phranc interview. In an effort to address this issue, the Dead Kennedys performed a song called "Nazi Punks Fuck Off!"

77. Fran interview.

78. Another of Lee's songs, "Bad Sex," thrilled straight hedonists with gay wisdom: "I feel like my life is under a hex / All I wanted was love, all I got was bad sex."

CHAPTER 9

1. ST interview with Troy Perry, 65, September 16, 2005.

2. Statistics: e-mail correspondence to LF from the Rev. Nancy Wilson, November 16, 2005; MCC press advisory, October 29, 2005; John Dart, "Gay-Oriented Church Joins Ecumenical Group," *Los Angeles Times,* February 21, 1997, B1; *Our Facts: 2004 Annual Report, MCC Metropolitan Community Churches,* May 16, 2005.

3. Perry interview, September 16, 2005.

4. Ibid.

5. LF interview with Lucia Chappelle, 52, August 27, 2005.

6. Perry interview, September 16, 2005.

7. ST interview with Frank Zerilli, 60, July 8, 2004.

8. "Probers Say Church Blaze Was Not Arson," *Los Angeles Times,* February 24, 1973, A27.

9. Dudley Clendenin and Adam Nagourney discuss arson at other Metropolitan Community Churches in *Out for Good: The Struggle to Build a Gay Rights Movement in America* (New York: Simon and Schuster, 1999), chap. 12.

10. ST interview with Lucia Chappelle, 52, September 1, 2005.

11. Wilson communication.

12. LF interview with Chappelle. Chappelle was a congregation member beginning in 1971.

13. LF interview with Savina Teubal, 77, February 17, 2004. See also Teubal's books, *Sarah, The Priestess: The First Matriarch of Genesis* (Athens, OH: Swallow Press, 1984), and *Hagar the Egyptian: The Lost Tradition of the Matriarchs* (New York: HarperCollins, 1990).

14. ST interview Troy Perry, August 30, 2005. Rabbi Eichberg was the father of MECLA's Rob Eichberg.

15. LF interview with Mina Meyer, 64, April 5, 2004.

16. LF interview with Harriet Perl, 83, February 14, 2004.

17. Perry interview, August 30, 2005.

18. "New Life for Jewish Temple," typescript, Beth Chayim Chadashim file, ONE National Gay and Lesbian Archives, University of Southern California, Los Angeles.

19. http://www.mljewish.org, vol. 9, no. 14. This article is no longer available online, but see John Sherwood, "Reform Judaism and Homosexuality," http://www.mljewish.org/cgi-bin/retrieve.cgi?VOLUME=10&NUMBER=63&FORMAT=html.

20. "Hebrew Group Okays Beth Chayim Temple," *Los Angeles Times,* July 20, 1974, 26.

21. See Jeannette Vance, "The Impact of HIV/AIDS on Queer Spiritual Communities: Metropolitian Community Church and Beth Chayim Chadashim" (master's thesis, Claremont Graduate School, 2000); see also Gary David Comstock, *Unrepentant, Self-Affirming, Practicing: Lesbian/Gay/Bisexual People Within Organized Religion* (New York: Continuum, 1996).

22. Meyer interview, and LF interview with Sharon Raphael, 62, April 5, 2004.

23. Perl interview.

24. "Women Take Their Place in the Temple," *Lesbian News,* September 1975, 2.

25. LF interview with Chappelle.

26. Paula Schoenwether, "Celebration of Our Birth," in "Worship Resources from the Women of De Colores M.C.C. and Friends" (Los Angeles: self-published by De Colores, undated), 1.

27. Lynn Simross, "The 'Rev.' Responds to Calling," *Los Angeles Times,* August 15, 1985; and Darryl Fears, "Gay Blacks Feeling Strained Church Ties," *Washington Post,* November 2, 2004, A3.

28. LF interview with Rabbi Denise Eger, 45, October 18, 2005.

29. LF interview with Rabbi Lisa Edwards, 53, October 16, 2005.

30. Eger interview.

31. Hay had been researching the Native American *berdache* tradition since the 1950s. Walter Williams' *The Spirit and the Flesh: Sexual Diversity in American Indian Culture* (Boston: Beacon Press, 1986) and Will Roscoe's *The Zuni Man-Woman* (Albuquerque: University of New Mexico Press, 1991) both acknowledge his studies in this area.

32. See also Stuart Timmons, *The Trouble with Harry Hay: Founder of the Modern Gay Movement* (Boston: Alyson, 1990); Mark Thompson, *Gay Spirit: Myth and Meaning* (New York: St. Martin's Press, 1987); and Arthur Evans, *Witchcraft and the Gay Counterculture: A Radical View of Western Civilization and Some of the People It Has Tried to Destroy* (Boston: Fag Rag Books, 1978).

33. LF interview with Robin Tyler, 62, August 22, 2004.

34. ST interview with Deni Ponty, 57, July 15, 2005.

35. During the 1979 filming in Greenwich Village of *Cruising,* a movie portraying homosexuality and SM as ending in murder, gays staged a protest, which, the film historian Vito Russo claimed, "was the beginning of a heightened sensitivity around Hollywood." Interview with Vito Russo in Eric Marcus, *Making History: The Struggle for Gay and Lesbian Equal Rights, 1945–1990* (New York: HarperCollins, 1992), 393. *That Certain Summer* may have been dismissed by Russo because it was a film made for television.

36. LF interview with Kim Garfield, 71, October 13, 2005.

37. "A Reluctance to Play Gay," *Time,* July 4, 1988, 61.

38. LF interview with Sheila Kuehl, 63, July 24, 2004.

39. ST interview with Michael Kearns, 54, June 18, 2004.

40. Tyler interview, August 22, 2004, and LF interview with Robin Tyler, August 28, 2005; LF interview with Patti Harrison, 70, August 28, 2005; Lauren Hanson, "The Life and Times of Robin Tyler," *Lesbian News,* July 1991, 32+.

41. LF interview with Simone Wallace, 58, July 25, 2004.

42. LF interview with Ann Bradley, 50, April 6, 2004.

43. Mark Thompson, ed., *The Long Road to Freedom: The Advocate History of the Gay and Lesbian Movement* (New York: St. Martin's Press, 1994), xxvi.

44. ST interview with Mark Thompson, 53, October 29, 2005.

45. Elizabeth Venant, "Richard Rouilard Is Proud, Outrageous and . . . in Your Face," *Los Angeles Times,* January 2, 1992, E1. Rouilard's transformation of *The Advocate* caused a huge jump in subscriptions, though his lavish spending cut his tenure short. However, his innovations left a lasting mark on the nation's leading gay publication.

46. Ibid.

47. *The Advocate,* January 17, 2006, 26.

48. LF interview with Jinx Beers, 72, August 28, 2005.

49. LF interview with Ella Matthes, August 27, 2005.

50. Ibid. The Gwen Stefani cover was dated May 2005. Similarly, editors of *The Advocate* and *Frontiers* have complained that their publications did not sell unless the cover featured an alluring male. The magazines have also been criticized by various segments of the community for the lack of diversity on their covers.

51. Matthes interview.

52. In 2005, for example, the Los Angeles gay pride parade received coverage in 120 broadcast media (Lorri Jean, "Pride and Paris," *Lesbian News,* August 2005, 10), and gay marriage as well as the groundbreaking Western film, *Brokeback Mountain,* became a topic of focus in all major newspapers.

53. *Los Angeles Times,* November 12, 1999, C1.

54. Quoted in Kevin Roderick, "New City Debuts in Rousing Old-Time Meeting," *Los Angeles Times,* November 30, 1984, C3.

55. Stephen Braun, "West Hollywood Decision Delayed," *Los Angeles Times,* July 29, 1984, WS1.

56. Stephen Braun, "West Hollywood: Vote May Make It First Gay-Run City," *Los Angeles Times,* October 14, 1984, C1.

57. Ibid.

58. "The Friends of Valerie Terrigno," *Los Angeles Reader,* November 22, 1985, 1.

59. Roderick, "New City Debuts."

60. Stephen Braun, "The Trouble With Terrigno," *Los Angeles Times Magazine,* June 1, 1986, 17; Dorit Phyllis Gary, "Mayor Terrigno," *L.A. Weekly,* July 5–11, 1985.

61. Braun, "The Trouble with Terrigno," 19.

62. ST and LF interview with Valerie Terrigno, 51, October 16, 2005.

63. West Hollywood lobbyist Helene Myshar. The city council of Berkeley, California, also proposed domestic partnership legislation that year, but West Hollywood preceded Berkeley in enacting such legislation.

64. Chris Woodyard and Deborah Anderluh, "West Hollywood's First Mayor Indicted," *Los Angeles Herald Examiner,* October 24, 1985, A1, and Braun, "The Trouble with Terrigno," 17.

65. Braun, "The Trouble with Terrigno," 19.

66. Terrrigno interview.

67. Ibid.

68. Gary, "Mayor Terrigno," 24.

69. "Terrigno Supporters Demonstrate," *The News,* April 4, 1986, 20.

70. ST interview with Gene La Pietra, 57, October 21, 2005.

71. Gary, "Mayor Terrigno," 24.

72. George Ramos and Stephen Braun, "Probers Accuse Terrigno of Embezzling U.S. Funds," *Los Angeles Times,* October 24, 1985, 1.

73. "Terrigno Sentenced to 60 Days in Halfway House," *The News,* May 16, 1986.

CHAPTER 10

1. LF interview with Rita Gonzales, 53, October 2, 2004.

2. See chap. 4.

3. ST interview with Bruce Reifel, 63, September 29, 2005.

4. Alycee J. Lane, "Pride at Home: Celebrating Being Lesbian and Gay in Our Own Neighborhoods," *BLK,* July 1990, 13. *BLK* was started in Los Angeles by Alan Bell in 1988 as a free publication for distribution in L.A.'s black gay bars. It soon became a national publication. Bell's

company also published *Black Lace*, a quarterly erotic magazine for black lesbians, and *Black-fire*, an erotic bimonthly for gay men.

5. ST interview with Francisco Ico del Rio, April 6, 2004.

6. Ibid.

7. ST interview with Rudy Ruano, 60, September 16, 2004.

8. Ibid.

9. ST interview with "Andreas" (pseud.), 53, December 20, 2004.

10. LF interview with Marcia Kawahara, 65, September 6, 2004.

11. The phrase "the down low" is used by African Americans to describe such covert relations.

12. ST interview with Jolino Beserra, 48, November 6, 2005.

13. ST interview with Jef Huereque, 52, December 11, 2005.

14. Few Asians went to gay bars in those years. As Eric Wat points out, the gay Asian American population grew, along with the larger Asian American population, when the Japanese and Chinese were joined by immigrants from the Philippines, Korea, and Southeast Asia: *The Making of a Gay Asian Community: An Oral History of Pre-AIDS Los Angeles* (Lanham, MD: Rowman and Littlefield, 2002).

15. LF interview with K.C. (pseud.), 61, April 22, 2004.

16. E-mail correspondence to LF from Jeanne Cordova, January 23, 2006.

17. LF interview with JJ (Jay) Vega, 50, September 18, 2004.

18. ST interview with Joey Terrill, 49, July 31, 2005.

19. Hilary E. MacGregor, "In Montebello, Producer Puts Down Roots at New Breed of Gay Bar," *Los Angeles Times*, May 23, 2001, E-1.

20. ST interview with Rick St. Dennis, 56, August 27, 2005.

21. ST interview with Gene La Pietra, 57, October 21, 2005.

22. ST interviews with Tom Gibbon, 82, June 21, 2004, and Bill Stephens, 64, August 27, 2004.

23. See Wat, *The Making of a Gay Asian Community*.

24. Erin Aubry Kaplan, "Crown Jewel: The Catch One Turns 30 This Year," *LA Weekly*, September 12–18, 2003; LF interviews with Mary Margaret Smith, 55, April 7, 2004, and Karen Ocamb, 54, August 20, 2004; *GBF*, April 2004, 30; "Major Events in Black Gay History," *BLK*, June 1989, 12.

25. Interview with Jewel Williams in "Lesbian Pride: One Day at a Time," *LA Weekly*, June 23, 1989; and ST interview with Mark Haile, 49, December 13, 2005.

26. Other gay Latino clubs that permitted dancing included La Plaza, in Hollywood (only after their lip sync drag shows in Spanish), Tabasco's, and El Barcito, both in Silver Lake. The dance floors at these clubs, however, could accommodate from a few dozen to perhaps one hundred people—never the numbers that flocked to the warehouse-like Circus.

27. Terrill interview.

28. Andreas interview.

29. Ibid.

30. Ibid.

31. Deborah Johnson and Bobreta Franklin, "Debreta's Then and Now," *Southern California Women for Understanding Newsletter*, May 1981, 13–14; also LF interview with Bobretta Franklin, 59, August 21, 2004.

32. ST interview with Horacio Roque Ramierez, 36, December 14, 2005. Some historians have suggested that working-class bars were indeed the site of community building. See, for example, Elizabeth Lapovsky Kennedy and Madeline D. Davis, *Boots of Leather, Slippers of Gold: A History of a Lesbian Community* (New York: Routledge, 1993), and Helen Branson, *Gay Bar* (San Francisco: Pan Graphic Press, 1957).

33. ST interview with Terry Gock, 52, December 2, 2005.

34. "Mexican-American Gays to Have Own Organization," *The Advocate*, August 19–September 1, 1970, 3. Steve Jordan, an L.A. Latino, called the initial meetings at MCC.

35. Interview with Estilita Grimaldo Smith in *Sister,* April 1974; and "Latin American Lesbians," *The Tide,* July 1974, 15.

36. Franklin interview.

37. Johnson and Franklin, "Debreta's Then and Now," 13–14.

38. LF interview with Ayofemi (Stowe) Folayan, 54, July 27, 2004. Folayan's observation about the "whiteness" of terms such as "gay" or "homosexual" was confirmed in the 1980s for health workers as they tried to stem the spread of AIDS in black and Latino communities. They learned to use instead terms such as "men who have sex with men."

39. LF interview with Gayle, 57, April 5, 2004.

40. LF interview with Lisa Powell, 46, August 20, 2004.

41. See, for example, "GLCSC Happenings," *The Center News,* July–August 1988, 8.

42. LF interview with Lucia Chappelle, 52, August 27, 2005.

43. LF interview with Robin Podolsky, 48, April 6, 2004.

44. ST interview with Jim McDaniels, 43, November 14, 2005.

45. Powell interview.

46. Haile interview.

47. Gonzales interview.

48. ST interview with Mario Perez Ceballos, 29, December 12, 2005.

49. ST interview with Horacio Roque Ramirez, 36, December 14, 2005.

50. Aside from gender conflicts—which were by no means limited to communities of color—gay ethnic groups could find themselves attacked from within as being too bourgeois, too influenced by the "white agenda," or too radical: See Karen Ocamb, "Phill Wilson: L.A.'s New AIDS Coordinator Talks," *BLK,* October 1990, 7.

51. LF interview with Saundra Tignor, 67, August 20, 2004.

52. Powell interview.

53. Ibid.

54. LF interview with Betty Smith, 66, December 14, 2004.

55. Haile interview.

56. LF interview with Kim Swindle-Bautista, 36, December 15, 2004. LAAPIS functions primarily as an e-mail list now. Kim Swindle-Bautista (a Korean woman who was adopted as a child and raised in the United States) explains that the organization essentially dissolved in 1998, after hosting a successful national conference at UCLA (sponsored by the Pacific Bell Telephone Company) of the Asian and Pacific-Islander Lesbian and Bisexual Women's Network. "We just burned out," she says.

57. Gina Masequesmay, "Negotiating Multiple Identities in a Queer Vietnamese Support Group," *Journal of Homosexuality* 45, no. 2 (Fall 2003): 193–215.

58. Latino artists who died of AIDS at this time include Ludar Feldenstein, Mundo Meza, Teddy Sandoval, Corey Roberts Auli, Gil Cuardros, and Jack Vargas.

59. Luis Alfaro, "Out of the Shadows: A Testimonio Against Loneliness," *Anthology of Angels,* ed. Luiz Sampaio (Los Angeles: VIVA, 1999), 3.

60. ST interview with Miguel Angel Reyes, 41, December 5, 2005.

61. Gay filmmakers as early as Mack Sennett were headquartered in Silver Lake, earning the area the nickname "the Swish Alps" (an appellation also applied to the Hollywood Hills): George Ramos, "Silver Lake: Residents of All Stripes Are Drawn to an Evolving Community," *Los Angeles Times,* November 18, 1984, C1.

62. Sam Kaplan, "Gay Street Fair: Out of the Closet and Into the Community," *Los Angeles Times,* August 26, 1980, F1.

63. Ramos, "Evolving Community."

64. Conor Dougherty, "Influx of Newcomers Changing Sunset Junction Neighborhood: Spotlight on Silver Lake," *Los Angeles Business Journal,* December 9, 2002.

65. ST interview with Michael McKinley, 47, December 30, 2005.

66. Ibid.

67. Ibid.

68. LF interview with Lori Ball, 40, and Lisa Ginsburg, 42, July 23, 2004.

CHAPTER 11

1. ST interview with Gene La Pietra, 57, October 21, 2005.

2. Michael Gottlieb et al., "Pneumocystis Pneumonia—Los Angeles," *Morbidity and Mortality Weekly Report* 30 (1981): 250–252.

3. E-mail correspondence from Michael Kearns to ST, October 31, 2005.

4. Mary McNamara, "Life Is Forever Altered as an Epidemic Turns 20," *Los Angeles Times,* June 2, 2001, B1. Voeller argued that the original name, Gay Related Immune Disorder, was inflammatory and unscientific.

5. "Blood Emergency Declared," *Los Angeles Times,* September 12, 1983, A2.

6. Mary Murphy, "The AIDS Scare: What It's Done to Hollywood," *TV Guide,* October 22, 1988, 4–9.

7. ST interview with Gene La Pietra, 57, October 21, 2005.

8. Alan Citron, "AIDS Haunts Gay Sex Life," *Los Angeles Times,* July 17, 1983, WS1.

9. Larry Kramer, "1,183 and Counting," *Frontiers* 1, no. 24 (March 30–April 13, 1983): 1+.

10. Ibid.

11. LF interview with Ivy Bottini, 78, August 19, 2004.

12. Several of the early members of MECLA had by now quit that organization and founded the Book Study Group, a secret society whose main purpose was to raise money among wealthy gays primarily to support political candidates who would help in the fight against AIDS: LF interview with Jean O'Leary, February 18, 2004, and Diane Abbitt, 62, October 17, 2005.

13. Abbitt interview.

14. LF interview with Roberta Bennett, 63, December 18, 2004.

15. LF interview with Sue Talbot, 57, and Liebe Gray, 58, October 4, 2004.

16. LF interview with Rita Gonzales, 53, October 2, 2004.

17. ST interview with Roland Palencia, 48, November 8, 2005.

18. Marylouise Oates, "Show Biz Shows Its Stuff at AIDS Benefit," *Los Angeles Times,* September 21, 1985, 5, 1. Because President Reagan had not acknowledged the AIDS epidemic until this date, some at the event booed his message.

19. Dudley Clendinen and Adam Nagourney, *Out for Good: The Struggle to Build a Gay Rights Movement in America* (New York: Simon and Schuster, 1999), 515.

20. Bill Higgins, "Gala AIDS Fundraiser Is Sedate but Still Starry," *Los Angeles Times,* February 16, 1998.

21. "3,000 Marchers Seek More AIDS Research," *Los Angeles Times,* May 27, 1983, A18.

22. ST interview with Bruce Mirken, 49, September 23, 2005.

23. ST interview with John Morgan Wilson, 60, July 18, 2005.

24. Mirken interview.

25. Clendinen and Nagourney suggest (*Out for Good,* 541) that "class frictions in California's gay community were put aside" in the campaign against Proposition 64; but as Mirken observes, frictions were rife.

26. "Dannemeyer Backs AIDS Quarantine," *Los Angeles Times,* July 3, 1986, 1+.

27. LF interview with Torie Osborn, April 30, 2004.

28. "Prop. 64 Feud Between Gays, LaRouche Backers Grows," *Los Angeles Times,* September 17, 1986, 1+.

29. Larry Day, "County Clinics in Crisis," *ACT UP/LA* (newsletter), February–March 1990, 4.

30. ST interview with Michael Weinstein, 53, September 20, 2005.

31. ST interview with John Fall, 42, October 30, 2005.

32. "Bring the Spirit of Washington Home!" flier, ACT UP/LA Collection, ONE National Gay and Lesbian Archives, University of Southern California, Los Angeles.

33. Richard Labonte, "200 Form ACT UP Group for Los Angeles," *San Diego Update*, undated clipping, ACT UP/LA Collection, ONE National Gay and Lesbian Archives.

34. David Lee Perkins, "ACT UP/LA," outreach letter, p. 3, ACT UP/LA Collection, ONE National Gay and Lesbian Archives.

35. Labonte, "200 form ACT UP Group."

36. "Bring the Spirit" flier.

37. Mirken interview. ACT UP's prime years in L.A. lasted from 1988 to 1991, though activity continued well into the 1990s.

38. ST interview with Craig Collins, 53, October 25, 2005.

39. Murphy, "The AIDS Scare."

40. Fall interview.

41. ST interview with Gunther Freehill, 52, October 27, 2005.

42. Connie Norman, "Tribal Rights," *San Diego Update*, October 6, 1993.

43. Collins interview.

44. Ibid. ACT UP was able to secure a legitimate place in the parade in subsequent years. The 1990 theme spun the right-wing panic about flag burning into an AIDS statement. Dressed in red, white, and blue jerseys made by volunteer Hollywood costumers, AIDS activists bore signs that demanded "STOP DESECRATION OF FAGS."

45. Russell Chandler, "Bishops Oppose Condoms . . . ," *Los Angeles Times*, November 10, 1989, A1. Rebelling against conservative proposals of "abstinence only" for HIV protection, these activists insisted that HIV positive men could have sex and still be responsible. They advocated condom distribution and safe-sex awareness when it was still a new concept.

46. Collins interview.

47. Hector Tobar, "Silent Activists' March Disrupts Mahony Mass," *Los Angeles Times*, December 26, 1989, B3. The group was parodying Mahony's statement in an official church paper titled *Called to Compassion and Responsibility* that safe sex was "a lie and a fraud."

48. Peter Cashman, John Fall, and Enric Morello, "Fumbling on AIDS Causes Waste, Suffering," *Los Angeles Times*, February 13, 1989, 2+.

49. In August 1988 the L.A. supervisors ordered a twenty-bed ward to open within one month. It took more than one year. David Lacaillade, Draft History of L.A. County AIDS Issues (undated), collection of Cyndy Crogan.

50. Mirken interview.

51. Ibid.

52. ST interview with Peter Cashman, 56, October 18, 2005. Other members of ACT UP confirm that MECLA distanced itself, although the MECLA co-chair, Diane Himes, expressed support for the "righteous anger" of emerging political groups to Timothy Stirton in his article, "The New Gay Activism," *Frontiers* 7, no. 7 (July 27–August 10, 1988): 22.

53. "80 Arrested as AIDS Protest Is Broken Up," *Los Angeles Times*, November 7, 1989, 1.

54. Sandy Dwyer, "Activists Confront Feds," *The News*, October 13, 1989, 1.

55. LF interview with Cyndy Crogan, 49, April 7, 2004.

56. Scott Harris, "Announcement Hailed as a Way to Teach Public Taboos," *Los Angeles Times*, November 8, 1991, A32.

57. Lucille Renwick, "A Different Front in the AIDS War," *Los Angeles Times*, October 4, 1992, 21.

58. Benita Roth, "Feminist Boundaries in the Feminist-friendly Organization: The Women's Caucus of ACT UP/LA," *Gender and Society* 12, no. 2 (April 1998): 129–145. Other estimates

have been higher. An ACT UP member, Judy Sisneros, says lesbians composed 15 percent: LF interview with Judy Sisneros, 49, April 6, 2004.

59. Osborn interview.

60. LF interview with Robin Podolsky, 48, April 6, 2004.

61. Osborn interview.

62. Podolsky interview.

63. ST interview with Mary Lucey, 49, October 17, 2005.

64. With an army of Christian fundamentalists culled from a vast base of Orange County churches, Operation Rescue had been blocking the doors of women's health clinics, intimidating women into giving up their plans to abort. Feminist Majority Foundation, an organization concerned with a woman's right to choose abortion, wanted male "muscle" to protect L.A. family planning clinics from the antichoice group. Katherine Spillar of the Feminist Majority's Clinic Defense Alliance campaign recalls, "At that time, ACT UP/LA was huge. They could mobilize tremendous numbers of people": ST interview with Katherine Spillar, 50, November 14, 2005.

65. Crogan interview.

66. Sisneros interview.

67. ST interview with Helene Schpak, 53, October 14, 2005.

68. Mary McNamara, "Life Is Forever Altered as an Epidemic Turns 20," *Los Angeles Times,* June 3, 2001.

69. Written communication to ST from Gunther Freehill, October 24, 2005.

CHAPTER 12

1. Quoted in Bettina Boxall, "L.A.'s New Gay Muscle," *Los Angeles Times Magazine,* March 28, 1993, 32.

2. Sandy Harrison, "Hail of Protests Greets Veto," *Los Angeles Daily News,* October 1, 1991, N1.

3. See Boxall, "L.A.'s New Gay Muscle," 28.

4. Torie Osborn, *Coming Home to America: A Roadmap to Gay and Lesbian Empowerment* (New York: St. Martin's Press, 1996), 140.

5. LF interview with Torie Osborn, April 30, 2004. See also Bruce Mirken and Stuart Timmons, "This Is War: A Broken Promise, a Week in the Streets, a City Transformed," *Los Angeles Reader,* October 11, 1991, 6.

6. LF interview with Robin Podolsky, 48, April 6, 2004.

7. ST interview with Michael du Plessis, 44, January 12, 2006.

8. LF interview with Cyndy Crogan, 49, April 4, 2004.

9. Ibid.

10. LF interview with Jehan Agrama, August 19, 2004.

11. Osborn, *Coming Home to America,* 144–145.

12. Crogan interview.

13. E-mail correspondence to LF from Jehan Agrama, January 14, 2006.

14. In Boxall, "L.A.'s New Gay Muscle."

15. Ibid.

16. Agrama interview.

17. "Portrayals of Homosexuals Honored," *Los Angeles Times,* September 19, 1984, E7.

18. ST interview with Chris Uszler, 54, January 19, 2006. Though AGLA dissolved after a few years, Uszler says that the group had considerable success in "making gays more visible in the movies and raising the gay profile."

19. Geffen did not come out until 1992, but prior to that time he contributed millions of dollars to gay and AIDS charities such as AIDS Project Los Angeles and GLAAD, and he was the producer of the lesbian film *Personal Best,* in 1982: See "David Geffen," *Pink,* Fall 2004, 28.

20. GLAAD had started in New York in 1985 for the purpose of countering the misinformation that was being spread about gays and AIDS. It was modeled after the Jewish Anti-Defamation League.

21. Agrama interview.

22. "Media Watch: GLAAD/LA," *Lesbian News,* June 1991, 34.

23. Ibid.

24. E-mail correspondence to ST from Judy Sisneros, January 19, 2006.

25. Du Plessis interview. In 1991, in addition to *Basic Instinct, JFK* included a baroque gay orgy scene among suspects in the president's assassination, and *Silence of the Lambs* portrayed a serial killer who donned "drag" by flaying his female victims and draping himself in their skins.

26. Queer National Kathleen Chapman remembers, "It was being heavily rumored that QN was going to release a list of queer Hollywood celebrities on the day of the Oscars, and the media got absolutely obsessed with that, in some ways more than they were about a possible disruption of the awards ceremony. QN was allegedly going to be handing out maps of the queer stars' homes, and the press really wanted to get its hands on that. As a way of throwing the whole outing issue back in the faces of the media, on the day of the Oscars, some in QN had a press conference . . . at which we released a list of celebrities who we *refused* to claim as queer." E-mail correspondence to ST January 19, 2006.

27. Jane Galbraith, "Part of Campaign Protesting Negative Stereotypes in Films: Gay Groups Plan an Oscar 'Outing.'" *New York Newsday,* March 26, 1992, 58.

28. Cathy Dunphy, "Angry Gay and Lesbian Activists Plan to Upstage Oscar Tonight," *Toronto Star,* March 30, 1992, A1.

29. "Ten Arrested at Ceremony Protest," *Los Angeles Daily News,* March 31, 1992, N1.

30. LF interview with Sylvia Rhue, 56, October 7, 2004. Los Angeles GLAAD and friends were also responsible for derailing a planned Paramount television talk show of another homophobic radio star, Dr. Laura Schlesinger. "Stop Dr. Laura" campaign member Robin Tyler called for a protest march on Paramount Studios. Their demonstration got worldwide coverage, and GLAAD was bequeathed $1 million by a donor who was impressed with the action: LF interview with Robin Tyler, 62, August 22, 2004.

31. LF interview with Judy Sisneros, 49, April 6, 2004.

32. LF interview with Sandy (pseud.), 49, April 7, 2004.

33. Agrama interview.

34. LF interview with Terry DeCrescenzo, April 4, 2004.

35. LF interview with Sheila Kuehl, 63, July 24, 2004.

36. The name was changed to the Los Angeles Gay and Lesbian Center in 1996. A longtime board member, LuAnn Boylan, observes, "We dropped Community Services' because we thought the Center was a lot broader than what those words came to mean. We still offer services to those in need, and that will always be our first priority, but we also celebrate the *wellness* of the community." LF interview with LuAnn Boylan, 57, April 7, 2004.

37. According to http://www.gaydemographics.org, Los Angeles has approximately three times the number of same-sex households as New York City. The statistic is based on the federal U.S. 2000 census: "2000 Census Information on Same-Sex Couples."

38. LF interview with Renee Cowhig, 56, July 26, 2004.

39. LF interview with Judy Abdo, 60, July 23, 2004.

40. LF interview with Rita Baird, 58, July 25, 2004.

41. Kuehl interview.

42. Ibid.

43. LF interview with Jackie Goldberg, 60, and Sharon Stricker, 61, August 20, 2004.

44. Ibid.

45. Ibid. Goldberg's ties with labor and progressives go back to her involvement with the free speech movement at U.C. Berkeley.

46. T. A. Gilmartin, "Jackie Goldberg Doesn't Care What You Call It: AB 205 Is (Almost) Marriage," *Lesbian News,* December 2004, 26–27.

47. Two more out L.A. gays were elected to the superior court in 2004: Zeke Zeidler and Donna Groman. Elsewhere in the United States, openly gay people were elected to state legislatures for the first time in 2004 in North Carolina, Idaho, and Missouri. Vermont elected its first openly gay state senator. Oregon elected Rives Kistler to its supreme court—the first openly gay person to be elected to statewide office there. Portland elected its first openly gay city council member. At the federal level, three openly gay people won reelection to Congress: Barney Frank (Massachusetts), Tammy Baldwin (Wisconsin), and Jim Kolbe (Arizona), http://www.victoryfund.org.

48. Robert Arthur, president of the Society for Senior Gay and Lesbian Citizens, fund-raising brochure. We are grateful to Carol Nottley, a member of the SSGLC board of directors, for bringing this brochure to our attention.

49. SAGE, a center for the elderly, had opened in New York City earlier, but it focused "more narrowly on home visits and self-protection," according to Vito Bruno, director of services for Project Rainbow: Lois Timnick, "Antidote to Loneliness: L.A. Opens Seniors' Gay, Lesbian Center," *Los Angeles Times,* July 18, 1982, 1+.

50. Ibid.

51. Ibid.

52. On the scarcity of money in the 1980s for all community needs outside of AIDS, see "Lesbians vs. Gays: War Over Money in the Age of AIDS," *Lesbian News,* October 1989, 1+.

53. LF interview with Ivy Bottini, 78, August 19, 2004. Bobreta Franklin, a board member on the project, points out that there are gay and lesbian elder communities elsewhere, such as The Palms in Manosota, Florida, which is connected to Leisure World, but none of these communities feature low-cost housing for the needy: LF interview with Bobreta Franklin, 59, August 21, 2004. See also Bobreta Franklin, "Sunset of Our Lives: Retirement Communities for Lesbians" (about African American lesbian senior citizens. Franklin's interview subjects were all members of United Lesbians of African Heritage's seniors' group). (Master's thesis, Pacific Oaks College, Pasadena, California, 2004).

54. In the 1990s, there were other plans to establish residential facilities for L.A. gay and lesbian elders, such as those drawn up by Pat Parks, a leader in the Coalition of Older Lesbians (COOL), but none came to fruition at that time: COOL member Laura Sherman (pseud.), 77, July 26, 2004. There have also been a variety of organizations in gay L.A. that focus specifically on the elderly. Prime Plus, for example, is a group for African American lesbian seniors under the auspices of United Lesbians of African Heritage (ULOAH). ULOAH's executive director, Lisa Powell, says that Prime Plus offers help and security for older black lesbians, who would otherwise have to return to the closet in order to get such assistance from the broader and less tolerant African American community: LF interview with Lisa Powell, 46, August 20, 2004.

55. Bottini interview.

56. "Low-Income GLBT [Gay, Lesbian, Bisexual, Transgendered] Seniors Get Housing," *Update,* July 20, 2005, 4.

57. Ibid.

58. LF interview with Lorri Jean, 47, April 30, 2004.

59. Jean and Boylan interviews.

60. E-mail correspondence to LF from LuAnn Boylan, April 13, 2004.

61. Boylan interview.

62. The Harvey Milk School in New York, which is an alternative school exclusively for LGBT youth, had started shortly before Project 10; but, Uribe says, she wanted "no dumping ground for gay kids." Her aim was to reduce discrimination in mainstream institutions rather than to segregate young people in gay institutions: LF interview with Virginia Uribe, 70, July 26, 2004. Since

the late 1980s, there have been alternative schools, such as Oasis, a continuation school for LGBT youth in Los Angeles.

63. Ibid.

64. Jackie Goldberg, who was on the Los Angeles School Board during these years, says that "once the board members met Virginia, who looks like a grandmother, they were very comfortable with her and the project. For kids who were gay to have a place to go didn't seem to them like a bad idea at all." Goldberg interview.

65. DeCrescenzo interview.

66. LF interview with Michael Marchand, December 3, 2005. We are grateful to Michael Marchand and Terry DeCrescenzo for arranging interviews for us with GLASS adolescents.

67. LF interview with "Lucy," (pseud.) 16, December 3, 2005.

68. LF interviews with "Jessica," (pseud.) 16, December 3, 2005.

69. LF interview with "Mary," (pseud.) 17, December 3, 2005.

70. LF interview with "Junior," (pseud.) 17, December 3, 2005.

71. LF interview with "Leticia," (pseud.) 17, December 3, 2005.

72. DeCrescenzo interview.

EPILOGUE

1. Pico Iyer, "Where Worlds Collide," *Harper's Magazine*, August 1995.

2. Karen Ocamb, "Villaraigosa Names Lesbian to Police Commission," *IN Magazine* (Los Angeles), February 14, 2006.

3. LF interview with Kim Swindle-Bautista, 36, December 15, 2004.

4. LF interview with Ewa (pseud.), 47, August 16, 2004. See also Diana Fisher, "Immigrant Closets: Tactical Micro-Practices-in-the-Hyphen," *Journal of Homosexuality* 45, no. 2 (Fall 2003): 185, about L.A.'s gay immigrant Russian community.

5. For a discussion of the complex diversity in the Southern California Vietnamese lesbian community, see Gina Masequesmay, "Negotiating Multiple Identities in a Queer Vietnamese Support Group," *Journal of Homosexuality* 45, no. 2 (Fall 2003): 193–215.

6. Jason Cianciotto, *Hispanic and Latino Same-Sex Couple Households in the United States: A Report from the 2000 Census* (Washington, D.C.: National Gay & Lesbian Task Force Policy Institute and the Latino/a Coalition for Justice, 2005), 45.

7. List gleaned from "Community Access" pages of *Lesbian News*, May 2004.

8. ST interview with Luis Lopez, 32, December 29, 2005.

9. Honor PAC fact sheet, 2005 (ST collection).

10. Most of these bars and clubs advertise regularly in *Divas* and *Revista Adelante*, bilingual magazines for Southern Californian lesbian, gay, and transgender people.

11. LF interview with Julia Salazar, 47, August 19, 2004.

12. LF interview with Monserrat Fontes, 64, July 24, 2004.

13. LF interview with Davi Cheng, 48, December 5, 2005.

14. Tamar Lewin, "Openly Gay Student's Lawsuit Over Privacy Will Proceed," *New York Times*, December 2, 2005.

15. With the support of several funding agencies, these ads, featuring photographs of gay, bisexual, lesbian, and transgender Asians of various backgrounds, have appeared over several years in nearly a dozen languages, including Tagolog, Vietnamese, and Hindi.

16. Lambda Legal Defense Fund news release, January 10, 2006.

17. See Lynette Clemetson, "Both Sides Court Black Churches in the Battle Over Gay Marriage," *New York Times*, March 1, 2004, A1, for a discussion of the rift in the black community over this issue.

18. Professor Robert Dawidoff, quoted in Mary McNamara, "Era of the Gender Crosser," *Los Angeles Times*, February 27, 2001, A1.

19. "Man Turned Woman Deluged by Show Offers: Fabulous Contracts Held Out for Appearances," *Los Angeles Times*, December 7, 1952, 43.

20. See V. Prince, "Charles to Virginia: Sex Research as a Personal Experience," in *The Frontiers of Sex Research*, ed. Vern Bullough (Buffalo, N.Y.: Prometheus Books, 1979), 167–175, and Vern Bullough, "Virginia Prince," in *Before Stonewall: Activists for Gay and Lesbian Rights in Historical Context*, ed. Vern L. Bullough (Binghamton, N.Y.: Harrington Park Press, 2002), 372. Magnus Hirschfeld coined the term "transsexual" in 1925.

21. See chap. 4.

22. In 1979, the City of Los Angeles also enacted Municipal Code 49.72a: "It shall be an unlawful employment practice for an employer to fail or refuse to hire, or to discharge any individual . . . on the basis (in whole or in part) of such individual's sexual orientation. . . . As used in this ordinance, the term 'sexual orientation' shall mean an individual having . . . or projecting a self-image not associated with one's biological maleness or one's biological femaleness." Despite City of Los Angeles policy, however, there continue to be allegations of police abuse against transsexuals. For example, an Amnesty International newsletter quotes a Native American transgender woman in Los Angeles: "The police are not here to serve; they are here to get served. . . . Every night I'm taken into an alley and given the choice between having sex or going to jail"; http://www.amnestyusa.org/outfront/stonewalled/abuse.

23. Odenthal is quoted in McNamara, "Era of the Cross Gender."

24. Susan Forrest, "TransUnity: Gender Explosion," http://la.indymedia.org/news/2005/06/128166.php.

25. McNamara, "Era of the Cross Gender."

26. Jeff, an FTM transsexual, was the convener, and his early work inspired the founding of FTM International in San Francisco, though little was done to establish a public group in Los Angeles for the next twenty years: ST interview with Jeff, 49, November 9, 2005.

27. ST interview with Bamby Salcedo, 37, January 11, 2005.

28. Salcedo quotes L.A. County estimates that in Los Angeles, 75 percent of transwomen are working-class Latinas.

29. ST interview with Masen Davis, 34, and Daniel Gould, 37, November 1, 2005.

30. Virginia Prince, "Homosexuality, Transvestism, and Transsexualism," *American Journal of Psychotherapy* 11 (1957): 80–85.

31. Mary Mcnamara, "Fitting into Their Own Skins," *Los Angeles Times*, February 28, 2001, E1. This is part 2 of a series that began in the February 27 issue.

32. LF interview with Raquel Gutierrez, 29, December 7, 2005.

33. LF and ST interview with David Taylor, 35, October 17, 2005.

34. "Broke-ing the Bank," *The Advocate*, February 28, 2006, 40.

35. Adam B. Vary, "The Brokeback Mountain Effect," *The Advocate*, February 28, 2006, 37.

36. *Daily Variety*, March 10, 2006.

37. Gay films triumphed at the 2005 Golden Globes. *Brokeback Mountain* won four awards, including one for "best dramatic film." The other top awards were given to *Transamerica*, about a transsexual, and *Capote*, about the gay writer.

38. The failure of the Academy of Motion Picture Arts and Sciences to name *Brokeback Mountain* "best picture" created in gay circles all over America a huge chorus of accusations of homophobia, but some gay critics point out that more complex reasons may explain why the award went to a film about racism, *Crash*, rather than to *Brokeback Mountain*: See, for example, Charles Karel Bouley, "Homophobia? Hogwash!" http://www.advocate.com, March 9, 2006.

39. Larry Gross, "Out of the Mainstream: Sexual Minorities and the Mass Media," in *Gay People, Sex, and the Media*, ed. Michella A. Wolf and Alfred P. Kielwasser (New York: Harrington Park Press, 1991), 22. See also Larry Gross, *Up from Invisibility: Lesbians, Gay Men, and the Media in America* (New York: Columbia University Press, 2001).

40. Cultural critics such as Suzanna Danuta Walters have warned against assuming that increased homosexual visibility in the media will lead to an increase in tolerance. Walters points out that the decade in which *Ellen* and *Will & Grace* came to television was also the decade in which the Defense of Marriage Act was passed and the electorate all over America voted in favor of antigay referenda. Nevertheless, she concedes, the 1990s also brought revolutionary gay images into the American living room, such as the much-noted lesbian-kiss scene with Mariel Hemingway on *Roseanne*: in Suzanna Danuta Walters, *All the Rage: The Story of Gay Visibility in America* (Chicago: University of Chicago Press, 2001).

41. In 2005, ABC offered *Crumbs, Emily's Reasons Why Not,* and *Hot Properties*; NBC offered *Inconceivable, My Name Is Earl,* and *The Book of Daniel*; CBS offered *Out of Practice.*

42. Greg Hernandez, "All in the Family," *The Advocate,* September 27, 2005, 60.

43. LF interview with Meredith Kadlec, 37, October 18, 2005.

44. Mike Goodridge, "The WB's New VIP," *The Advocate,* September 28, 2004, 53.

45. Ibid.

46. Taylor interview.

47. LF interview with Ashley Kaplan, 24, October 17, 2005.

48. Kadlec interview.

49. ST interview with Joe Libonati, 30, October 17, 2005.

50. LF interview with Stacy Codikow, 42, August 18, 2004.

51. Michele Kort, "Welcome Back to the L Word," *The Advocate,* February 1, 2005, 43.

52. Ibid.

53. Shana Naomi Krochmal, "'L Word' Tour of West Hollywood," *Planet Out Entertainment,* April 4, 2005, http://www.planetout.com.

54. See chap. 2.

55. David Colman, "Fashion Goes West," *New York Times,* March 9, 2006, E1.

56. Frank Rich, "Brokeback Mountain: A Landmark in the Troubled History of America's Relationship to Homosexuality," *New York Times,* December 18, 2005.

57. ST interview with Michael Weinstein, 53, September 20, 2005.

58. LF interview with Terry Wolverton, 50, August 19, 2004.

INDEX